THE INSIDERS'® GUIDE TO
Charlotte

BPG
BECKLYN
PUBLISHING GROUP

THE INSIDERS'® GUIDE TO

Charlotte

by
Mary C. Hopper
and
Carol Timblin

Becklyn Publishing Group, Inc.

Publishing Group, Inc.

Published and distributed by:

Becklyn Publishing Group, Inc.
P.O. Box 14154
Research Triangle Park, NC 27709
(919) 467-4035

•

SEVENTH EDITION
Summer 1998

•

Copyright © 1998
by Becklyn Publishing Group, Inc.

•

This publication is available from
Becklyn Publishing at special discounts
for bulk purchases by human resource
and relocation departments, REALTORS®,
schools, libraries and companies.
Special editions, including
personalized covers, can be created
for large quantity orders.

This book is produced under a
license granted by:

The Insiders' Publishing, Inc.
P.O. Box 2057
Manteo, NC 27954
(919) 473-6100

•

ISBN 1-887717-01-3

Becklyn Publishing Group, Inc.

President
Barbara King

V.P. & General Manager
Tim Johnson

Editor
Janice Therese Mancuso

Associate Editor
Rich Weidman

Copy Editor
David McNally

Administrative Assistants
Pam Freeth
Julie Pender
Gerry Pollard

Cover Design Assistance
Deborah Fay
Angela Miller

Editorial Assistance
Dan Leigh
Jan Cockrell Mitchell
Greg Reidinger
Alston Russell
Robin Smith

Maps
Fraser Van Asch
Crash Gregg

Art Director
Evelyn Ward

Production Assistance
Richard Ashley
Deborah Fay
Joanie Pace
Raymundo Padilla

Staff Photographers
Tim Johnson
Paula Siwek
Robert Thomason

Cover Photos:
The Billy Graham Evangelistic Association,
The Charlotte Hornets and
The Charlotte Convention & Visitors Bureau

Preface

Welcome to the 7th edition of The Insiders' Guide to Charlotte. Since this book's first edition in 1987, *The Insiders' Guide To Charlotte* has provided a one-stop source of information about this dynamic area for newcomers, visitors and locals alike.

Although the look of The Insiders' Guide series has been streamlined, readers will still enjoy the comprehensiveness that has always made this *the* guide to Charlotte. The guide has been **painstakingly researched, completely revised in format and totally updated in content**; however, things do change. By the time this edition is printed, some information will need updating. Readers comments are always appreciated, so please drop us a note if you have any suggestions or find any factual discrepancies.

This latest edition would not have been possible without the assistance of many people and organizations. They offered encouragement, as well as their thoughts and ideas about the Charlotte area, especially the Charlotte Chamber of Commerce and the Charlotte Convention & Visitors Bureau.

Charlotte is North Carolina's largest metropolitan area. The country's second largest banking center has a very supportive business environment and provides Charlotteans with a superb quality of life.

As a city on the move, the central business district, known as Uptown, is seeing a resurgence of growth. This growth is due, in part, to NationsBank and First Union being headquartered here. Both Fortune 500 companies have invested heavily in Charlotte's future by constructing new office buildings and providing over 13,000 jobs in Uptown.

Charlotte's love of professional sports, beginning with NASCAR racing, then the NBA Charlotte Hornets, the NFL Carolina Panthers and now the WNBA's Charlotte Sting, has contributed to the growth as restaurants and retail establishments open around town to accommodate sports fans. Ericsson Stadium, the convention center, a performing arts center and renovations to the airport have also contributed to Charlotte's growth. With steady population growth and annual increases in the labor force, Charlotte is definitely on the move, and according to those who work and live in Charlotte, it's moving in the right direction.

The guide is intended to give our readers an Insider's view of this dynamic area. Our *Area Overviews* chapter reviews Charlotte and takes you behind the scenes of Uptown. The chapter also includes highlights of the towns residing inside Mecklenburg County and neighboring communities.

Visitors will appreciate the chapters on *Accommodations; Bed and Breakfasts; Annual Events; The Arts; Attractions; Getting Around; Night Life; Restaurants;* and *Shopping.* Our *Spectator Sports* chapter gives you an "insider's view" of the Carolina Panthers, the Hornets, the Knights, the Checkers and NASCAR racing. Back by popular demand is our *Employment Opportunities* chapter for those individuals considering relocating to the Queen City. If you're considering relocating your business, you might be interested in the chapters on *Banking and Commerce;* and *Government, Utilities and Services.*

Newcomers will certainly find the chapter on the *History of Charlotte* insightful. In making decisions associated with moving to the area, the chapters on *Apartments and Temporary Housing; Colleges and Universities; Daytrips and Weekends; Golf in the Carolinas; Government, Services and Utilities; Healthcare; Media; Real Estate and Neighborhoods; Retirement;* and *Worship* will prove especially helpful. Parents will appreciate the chapters on *Kidstuff; Parks and Recreation; and Schools* and *Child Care.*

Please note that the area code for the Charlotte area is 704 and South Carolina is 803.

About the Authors

Mary Hopper is president of Hopper Communications, a public relations firm. She has lived in Charlotte since 1967, during which time she's been involved in many of the changes covered in this Guide, from airport expansions and the growth in the travel and tourism industry, to Uptown development and community planning. With a Ph.D. in Romance Languages from the University of Missouri, she's been a professor of Spanish at Queens College, created an award-winning public relations department for the Public Library of Charlotte & Mecklenburg County and served as Director of Communications for the Charlotte Convention & Visitors Bureau. Mary lives in historic Dilworth with two very pampered cats.

Carol Timblin, a member of the Society of American Travel Writers, has traveled and written extensively about faraway places, but her favorite topics are Charlotte, where she has lived for over 25 years, and North Carolina, her home state. She is the author of *Best Places to Stay in the South* (1992, 1994 and 1996) and *CPCC: The First Thirty Years* (1995) and the co-author of several books. She is also a contributor to several guidebooks, including the *Insight Guide to the Old South*. Carol, who earned a bachelor's degree in English from Guilford College and a master's degree from the University of North Carolina at Charlotte, has worked in the fields of business, education and journalism and has received two national awards and one state award for excellence in reporting.

Robin Smith was the President of Robin A. Smith Communications, a Charlotte-based corporate communications, public relations and marketing firm in Charlotte. A graduate of Appalachian State University, she received an M.A. in English from the University of North Carolina at Charlotte. Smith co-authored the 4th, 5th, and 6th editions of *The Insiders' Guide To Charlotte*. She contributed a great deal to the updating of the current edition prior to accepting a position in Tampa, Florida. We wish her well in her new endeavors and will miss her contributions to the Queen City.

Since we use only local authors, Smith's departure required a replacement. We were pleased to add Mary Hopper and her insights and additions to this 7th edition and welcome back Carol Timblin, the original co-author of this guide.

Your Comments

Please take a few moments to share your comments and suggestions on our "More Information" reply card and we will be happy to forward your requests for information.

Welcome Home!
to Charlotte

We just keep getting better!

Photo courtesy of Charlotte Panthers

Photo courtesy of Trotter Builders

Check us out!

Charlotte Area

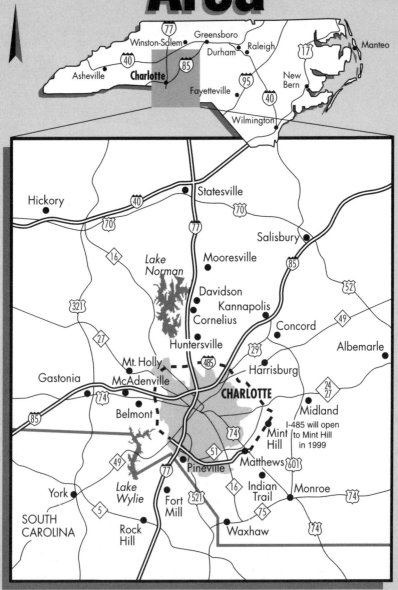

Winston-Salem · Greensboro
Durham · Raleigh
Asheville · **Charlotte** · Manteo
Fayetteville · New Bern
Wilmington

Hickory · Statesville
Salisbury
Lake Norman · Mooresville
Davidson
Kannapolis
Cornelius · Concord
Huntersville · Albemarle
Mt. Holly · Harrisburg
Gastonia · McAdenville · **CHARLOTTE**
Belmont · Midland
Mint Hill
I-485 will open to Mint Hill in 1999
Pineville · Matthews
York · Lake Wylie · Indian Trail · Monroe
SOUTH CAROLINA · Fort Mill
Rock Hill · Waxhaw

Charlotte

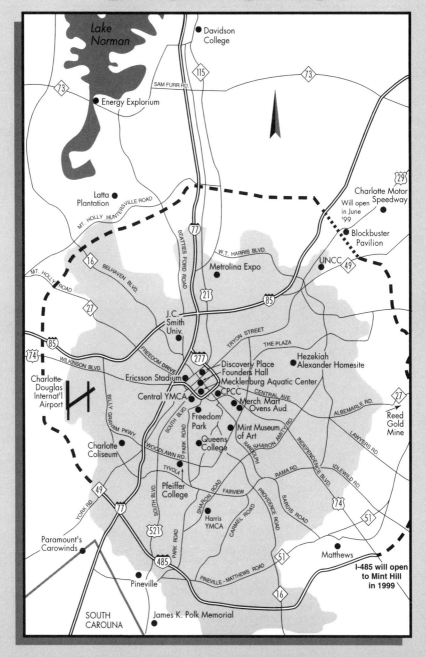

Lake Norman

Davidson College

115

73

73

SAM FURR RD.

Energy Explorium

29

Charlotte Motor Speedway

Will open in June '99

Blockbuster Pavilion

Latta Plantation

MT. HOLLY HUNTERSVILLE ROAD

16

BELHAVEN BLVD.

BEATTIES FORD ROAD

W.T. HARRIS BLVD.

UNCC

49

MT. HOLLY ROAD

Metrolina Expo

21

85

77

27

J.C. Smith Univ.

TRYON STREET

THE PLAZA

Hezekiah Alexander Homesite

FREEDOM DRIVE

WILKINSON BLVD.

85

74

277

Discovery Place
Founders Hall
Mecklenburg Aquatic Center

CENTRAL AVE.

ALBEMARLE RD.

27

Charlotte-Douglas Internat'l Airport

Ericsson Stadium

Central YMCA

CPCC

Merch. Mart
Ovens Aud.

Reed Gold Mine

BILLY GRAHAM PKWY.

SOUTH BLVD.

PARK ROAD

Freedom Park

Mint Museum of Art

SHARON AMITY RD.

RANDOLPH

INDEPENDENCE BLVD.

LAWYERS RD.

WOODLAWN RD.

Queens College

Charlotte Coliseum

TYVOLA

IDLEWILD RD.

49

77

SHARON ROAD

Pfeiffer College

FAIRVIEW

RAMA RD.

CARMEL ROAD

PROVIDENCE ROAD

SARDIS ROAD

74

SOUTH BLVD.

PARK ROAD

521

Harris YMCA

51

YORK RD.

Paramount's Carowinds

485

51

Matthews

16

I-485 will open to Mint Hill in 1999

Pineville

PINEVILLE – MATTHEWS ROAD

SOUTH CAROLINA

James K. Polk Memorial

Uptown Charlotte

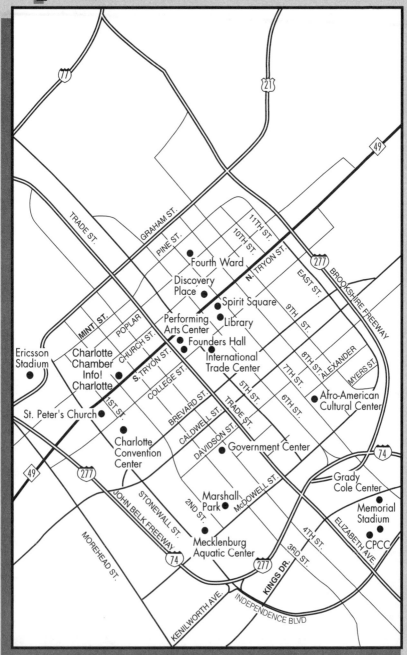

Table of Contents

Directory of Maps

STATE OF NORTH CAROLINA
OFFICE OF THE GOVERNOR
RALEIGH 27603-8001

JAMES B. HUNT JR.
GOVERNOR

Dear Friends:

As Governor of the State of North Carolina, it is indeed my pleasure to welcome you to Charlotte, our state's largest city.

Nearly 250 years ago, a Scotch-Irish settler named Thomas Polk built a cabin on a spot along a ridge at the crossing of two old Indian trading paths. Where he once lived is now the Trade and Tryon intersection, the historic heart of the city. This busy intersection is home today to the 60-story NationsBank Corporate Center!

Charlotteans do not call their central business district downtown, as in most cities. Rather, they refer to it as "Uptown" because the center city is on a ridge and you must travel "up" from surrounding areas to get there. And getting there is certainly worthwhile as you explore the Performing Arts Center, Spirit Square Center for the Arts, Discovery Place, and the Omnimax Theatre, just to name a few exciting attractions.

If you are a sports enthusiast, Charlotte is the place to be. Its natives are very proud of their Charlotte Hornets NBA team, and are thrilled to host the Coca-Cola 600, a major NASCAR race. The city is also very excited about its NFL expansion team – the Carolina Panthers – and their outstanding new football facility, Ericsson Stadium.

A large city, yes, but also a city that knows no strangers. Southern Hospitality is a way of life in Charlotte. On behalf of all our citizens, I again welcome you and invite you to enjoy all that the Charlotte area has to offer.

My warmest personal regards.

Sincerely,

James B. Hunt Jr.

The History of North Carolina

(Excerpted from an article by Dr. Jerry C. Cashion,
Research Branch, Division of Archives and History,
North Carolina Department of Cultural Resources)

Before the coming of European explorers, Native Americans inhabited the territory that is now North Carolina. Major tribes included the Tuscaroras, the Catawbas and the Cherokees. Beginning with Verrazzano in 1524, various French, Spanish and English explorers visited the area. In 1585 and 1587, English colonies were sponsored by Sir Walter Raleigh. These attempts at settlement failed. In 1629, Charles I of England declared all lands south of Virginia to be part of the British Empire. The first permanent settlement started in the 1660s when farmers settled the area around Albemarle Sound.

In 1677, economic and religious quarrels with the provisional governor in Virginia led to restrictions on shipping from North Carolina. These restrictions added to ill feelings in the state and hampered the growth of the state's significant tobacco crop. The settlers continued to resist the colonial rulings from England and Virginia and, in an attempt to restore order, the British formed the separate state of North Carolina in 1729 and sent a deputy governor to the area.

Meanwhile, the first town had been settled in 1700 and it was called Bath. After this, the population rose rapidly and settlements spread across the eastern and central (or Piedmont) part of the state.

Royal oppression mounted and American patriots talked, preached and fought for independence. Moores Creek, Halifax, Hillsborough and Fayetteville drew gatherings of North Carolinians who would be free to make their own laws and unite with the other American colonies to form the United States of America. With the famous Halifax Resolves, April 12, 1776, North Carolina became the first colony to instruct its delegates to the Continental Congress to vote for independence. General Cornwallis invaded the state in 1780 and was defeated soundly at the Battle of Guilford Courthouse. The weakened British army later surrendered in neighboring Virginia.

Conservative politicians, North Carolina representatives declined to ratify the new United States Constitution until a Bill of Rights was to be added.

Development in the state after the American Revolution was very slow. The state's economy was unable to grow due to poor transportation and communication systems. A reawakening occurred after 1835 when constitutional revisions gave more power to the western half of the state. Plank roads, canals and railroads helped solve the problem of transportation. Improved access to markets stimulated agricultural and industrial growth. Education proved to be the major key to the development of the state. The University of North Carolina, which opened in 1795, became one of the leading institutions in the nation. The state was the first in the South to establish a tax-supported system of public schools.

When the Civil War started, North Carolina was somewhat reluctant to leave the Union, but the state fought on the side of the Confederacy. The state supplied more troops and suffered more losses than any other in the Confederacy. The state's ports drew much Union fire and the Port of Wilmington remained open until the fall of Fort Fisher in January 1865. Confederate General Joseph E. Johnston surrendered to the Federal army under General William T. Sherman at the Bennett House, near the present city of Durham.

Reconstruction saw much internal upheaval. Partisan discord marked much of the remainder of the century. Industrial development outpaced a resurgence of agriculture at this time.

During the early twentieth century the foundation was laid for the state's rapid progress. Dedication to public education and highway construction became hallmarks of generations of legislators.

North Carolina devoted its human, industrial and agricultural resources to engage in two World Wars. Gearing up for wartime production, the state became more educated, urban and internationally connected. Developments in agriculture made it possible for highly efficient farms to produce an abundance of food and fiber that found its way to the national and global markets.

The Research Triangle Park was established in 1958 to boost growth in research-related fields. Located in close proximity to The University of North Carolina at Chapel Hill, Duke University in Durham and North Carolina State University in Raleigh, the Triangle contains the South's greatest concentrations of scientists, research sources, laboratory facilities and cultural resources. Industrial growth has followed the growth in research.

North Carolina is now divided into 100 counties. The state has three distinct regions: Coastal, Piedmont and Mountains. The Coastal region comprises about 45 percent of the state's area. A long chain of islands called the Outer Banks is located off the upper half of the coast. These islands average about 20 feet above sea level. Kitty Hawk, located near Roanoke Island, is where the Wright brothers ushered in the age of flight in 1903. Other islands extend as far south as South Carolina.

The Piedmont, or central part of the state, is approximately 38 percent of the area of the state. It is the prime symbol of the "New South" in which modern industry and technology have replaced agriculture as the main source of income. These industries are prevalent in Raleigh, Chapel Hill, Durham, Greensboro and Charlotte.

The Mountain region of North Carolina is bounded by two ranges of the southern Appalachians, The Blue Ridge Mountains and the Great Smoky Mountains. The mountains are renowned for a variety of crafts including pottery, wood carving, basketry, needlework, handmade rugs and bedspreads. Today the mountains have become a well-known year-round destination and Asheville is the center.

The Democratic party dominated state government for the first half of the 20th century, but in 1972 both a Republican senator and governor were elected. Democrat James B. Hunt served as governor from 1977-1985. Republican James G. Martin then served two terms. In 1992, Governor Hunt was elected to serve a third term and in 1996 was reelected to a record fourth term.

State Symbols for "The Old North State" or "The Tar Heel State"

Flowering
Dogwood

State Flag

Northern
Cardinal

Channel Bass

Plott Hound

Honey
Bee

Granite

Gray
Squirrel

State Seal

Emerald

Scotch Bonnet

Sweet Potato

Milk

Eastern Box Turtle

Shad Boat

Pine Tree

A sculpture of Queen Charlotte, crafted by artist Raymond Kaskey, greets newcomers at the Charlotte/Douglas International Airport.

Getting Around

It's been said by many business and civic leaders of Charlotte that the region has grown to national prominence due, in large part, to the Charlotte/Douglas International Airport. In truth, Charlotte is easily accessible by air and land. In town, Charlotte's transit service makes getting around convenient and easy.

Air Transportation

Charlotte/Douglas International

Eighth busiest in the country and 33rd worldwide, Charlotte/Douglas International offers nearly 500 daily flights to 190 cities with nonstop service to all 50 states, Canada, Mexico and the Caribbean via connecting flights. More than half the population of the United States lives within a 2-hour flight of the city. In addition, the airport offers non-stop international flights to and from London, England and Nassau, Bahamas.

Seven major carriers serve the airport: American, British Airways, Delta, Northwest, TWA, United and US Airways, which calls Charlotte its super hub. USAir Express serves a fast growing commuter and regional base, shuttling passengers to Charlotte for jet service to all points of the United States and abroad.

With 64 gates and plans for more, the airport is one of the area's largest employers with ranks upwards of 10,000. Boarding 18 million passengers each year, Charlotte/Douglas International is served by three major runways and a 1-million-square-foot terminal. Plans are under way to construct a fourth runway, parallel to the existing runways.

Charlotte/Douglas International is about more than just moving people, it also gives many visitors their first impression of the Queen City. As Charlotte's "front door," the airport goes to great lengths to welcome visitors to the region. Expertly landscaped, the airport greets travelers with green grass, colorful flowers and Southern camellias. A sculpture of Queen Charlotte, crafted by artist Raymond Kaskey, greets newcomers to Charlotte. Given to the city by the Queens Table, a group of anonymous benefactors, the sculpture rises nearly three stories and is situated at the main entrance of the terminal.

The terminal was expanded in 1994. Travelers pass through three central security checkpoints along a shopping mall as they make their way to the departure gates. Duty free shopping and a wide variety of concessions, including TCBY Yogurt, Cinnabon, Burger King, Pizza Hut Express, Manchu Wok, Mrs. Fields Cookies, Starbuck's Gourmet Coffee and Cheers Restaurant and Bar are available.

For the business traveler, a carpeted public lounge behind the 195,000-square-foot terminal atrium called Queen's Court gives the feel of a quiet hotel lobby. The lounge is attended by food and beverage wait staff. Desks, phones and other business amenities make the lounge convenient and functional. In addition, US Airways Club areas are located on each of the four main concourses.

There's a new twist at Charlotte/Douglas International for arriving international passengers and returning U.S. citizens. Her name is Charlie — a U.S. Department of Agriculture inspector and she has a nose for her business. If it's fresh fruit or salami, she'll smell it out. Charlie is one of three canines nationwide special enough to be

Staff Photo

The Charlotte/Douglas International Airport provides
a beautiful gateway to the Queen City.

a part of "Agricultural Beagle Brigade" and she's good at what she does. To date, Charlie's biggest haul has been 33 pounds of meat confiscated from a single passenger!

Although growing, Charlotte/Douglas International is still compact enough that getting to and from the boarding gates is not a journey in itself. The airport is a mere 15 minutes from the center of the city. Billy Graham Parkway and Wilkinson Boulevard offer easy access to the airport's 5,000-acre complex with direct access from I-85 and I-77.

Cargo traffic is quickly expanding at Charlotte/Douglas International. Currently ranked 32nd in the U.S., the airport enplanes 103,162 tons of cargo each year. During the next few years, the airport is set to spend about $21 million to build additional aircraft parking ramps and warehouse space adjacent to its runways. Facilities for U.S. Customs, cold storage cargo and a livestock area are also in the expansion plans.

Nearby, off Morris Field Drive, is a fixed-base operator, offering charter service and private flight service through Signature Flight Support (359-8415). Many of the region's corporate jets and planes are stationed at this facility.

Through able and visionary leadership, the region will continue to grow and be serviced by a state-of-the-art airport and corresponding facilities. The FAA has installed an advanced Doppler Radar system 8 miles from the airport, one of only a handful across the country. It alerts traffic control officials and pilots of weather cells, dangerous wind sheer conditions and other microburst weather conditions.

Passengers appear to be pleased with the $26 million airport expansion that features an illuminated glass-enclosed atrium with a moving sidewalk, shops and restaurants (including Cheers!, patterned after the popular television show).

Frequently Called Numbers

If you need information, here are a few of the most frequently called numbers for Charlotte/Douglas International Airport.

Aviation Department • 359-4000
Advisory Committee • 359-4848
Emergency Medical • 359-4012
Lost and Found • 359-4012
Paging Service • 359-4027
Public Parking • 359-4055
Taxi Dispatch • 359-4085
Welcome Center/Visitor Information • 359-4027

Major Carriers

American • (800) 433-7300
British Airways • (800) 247-9297
Delta • (800) 221-1212
Northwest Domestic • (800) 225-2525
Northwest Intl. • (800) 447-4747
TWA • (800) 221-2000
US Airways • (800) 428-4322
US Airways Express • (800) 428-4322
United Airlines • (800) 241-6522

Ticketing

Most of the airlines operate ticketing offices throughout Charlotte with many in the Uptown and SouthPark areas. US Airways, whose hub is in Charlotte, maintains five ticket offices throughout the city. Check with the airline to find the most convenient location for you.

Airport Transportation Services

The airport provides several options for parking. The remote and satellite lots cost $2.75 for each 24-hour period. Closer to the terminal, the daily lots cost $4.00 for each 24-hour period. Both are serviced by shuttles to the main terminal. Covered parking, adjacent to the terminal, is $12.00 for each 24-hour period.

Bus service is available between the airport and Uptown from Monday through Friday. There are a number of taxis and limousines that service the airport. Limousine service is charged according to the number of people in your party. Nine major car rental companies with more than

Photo by Robert Thomason

Queen Charlotte welcomes airline passengers to her namesake city.

Photo by Robert Thomason

Commuters can shop, bank and catch a bus at the Transportation Center.

1,400 cars are located near the airport. There are also a number of car rental agencies available throughout the city. More than 7,000 parking spaces serve the facility with more being added.

Airport Shuttle

Carolina Transportation Co., Inc. • **359-8687**
Airport Express • **359-9600**

Wilgrove Airport

Located east of Charlotte off Albemarle Road at 10525 Parkton Road, (545-1875), Wilgrove Airport has served private and commercial flights since the early 1970s. The facility has two runways totalling 3,200 feet, compared to Charlotte/Douglas' 26,345 feet. It offers hangers and tie-down services, maintenance, fuel, flying lessons and airplane charters and leasing. The Metrolina Flying Club, based there, has a staff of professional instructors and offers qualifying for all pilot ratings, from private through ATP.

Ground Transportation

Highway

Charlotte is easily accessible from the north or south by Interstate 85 and Interstate 77. I-85 passes through north of Charlotte and has several well-defined exits to bring you to the Uptown area or other points south. I-77 is slightly west of Uptown, intersecting with I-85 northwest of Uptown. From the southeast, you can enter Charlotte via U.S. Highway 74. The Outer Belt Highway, I-485, will eventually form a loop completely around the entire Charlotte area. Some sections are currently open and construction of the remaining sections is proceeding at an accelerated pace.

It is easy to get around Charlotte due to the number of major intersecting highways. Uptown Charlotte is in a grid format and the surrounding areas offer a choice of direct routes or scenic roads.

Car Rental Agencies

Alamo • 359-4360
Avis • 359-4586
Budget • 359-5000
Dollar • 359-4700
Enterprise • 391-0061
Hertz • 359-0114
National • 359-0125
Payless • 729-5377
Thrifty • 344-6076
Triangle • 359-0541

Bus Service

Carolina Trailways
601 W. Trade St. • 342-2506

Charlotte Transit
901 N. Davidson St. • 336-3366
The Transportation Center is the main depot for city public transit service. The 120 buses travel 40 routes throughout Charlotte. Service between the airport and Uptown is available Monday through Friday.

Greyhound Bus Lines
601 W. Trade St. • 372-0456

Uptown Circuit
Information • 336-8888
A free Uptown shuttle service of three electric buses runs Monday through Friday from 7:30 AM to 6 PM.

Trains

Amtrak
1914 N. Tryon St. • 376-4416
Amtrak offers passenger service north and south from its station near Uptown. Two trains of special interest to Charlotte business people are the Carolinian and the Piedmont, which offer daily service to Raleigh. The Carolinian proceeds north to New York with intermediate stops. The Crescent also provides daily service from New Orleans to New York and back via Charlotte.

 *All Aboard!*

What better way to travel than by train. The *Piedmont* and the *Carolinian* provide daily round-trip service throughout the heart of North Carolina with connections to Florida and the Northeast. Enjoy comfortable seats, panoramic views and a friendly staff. Visit the dining car for your favorite food and beverages.

The Charlotte Amtrak station is located at 1914 N. Tryon Street.

Franklin Adams

For tickets, schedules and more information call your local Amtrak station or 1-800-USA-RAIL.

www.amtrak.com   www.bytrain.org

To understand
Charlotte today,
it's important to
understand how
past events
shaped the area.

History of Charlotte

To understand Charlotte's personality today, it's important to understand how past events shaped the area. In his description of the South, University of North Carolina at Charlotte professor and historian David Goldfield said, "Soil, rivers and climate determined whether counties would flourish or decline, whether railroads and manufacturing would arrive, whether people would come or leave." Therefore, luck and location may be given credit for Charlotte's beginnings.

The Scots-Irish Presbyterians, a devout religious group, began to settle here in the 1730s. A century and a half earlier, these settlers had immigrated from Scotland and England to Ulster in Ireland, then to the Piedmont of North Carolina from Pennsylvania. Since they differed in background and religion from the Irish, there had been little blending. Set in their ways, they were "strongly Presbyterian in their determination to have both freedom of religion and government, along with freedom of the one from the other."

No one was more acutely aware of their determination than General Earl Cornwallis, who invaded Charlotte/Mecklenburg on September 26, 1780. After staying a mere 18 days, the general had racked up humiliating losses. Owing this to the "obstinate integrity" of those cantankerous early Mecklenburgers, he unwittingly coined the phrase, ". . . this rebellious country, the hornet's nest of America." You can find the term "hornets" or "hornet's nest" on our county seal as well as part of the name of an elementary school, a park and Charlotte's NBA team.

Long before Cornwallis marched in, Mecklenburgers were at odds with British rule. The settlers had been extremely loyal. They named the county Mecklenburg after the new Queen of England's German birthplace and their town Charlotte after the Queen. (This is why you'll hear Charlotte called the "Queen City" and why the top of the NationsBank wears a crown.) Still, the colonists, who already had serious financial problems, felt the continuing sting of escalating British taxes in an increasingly corrupt government.

The Crown steadfastly refused to listen to the colonists' economic plight. This provoked Commander of the County Militia, Thomas Polk, to call citizens to elect two representatives from each militia district to meet in the Charlotte Town Courthouse on May 19, 1775. The story goes that these men framed the first document "declaring the citizens of Mecklenburg free and independent of the Crown of Great Britain." They read the Mecklenburg Declaration of Independence to the assembled town at noon the following day. Unfortunately, they didn't have time to present it to the congress, and worse still, the document burned in a fire. Although historians are skeptical, Charlotteans believe that the declaration existed. They celebrate that first demand for freedom each May 20th at the Hezekiah Alexander house, the oldest standing house in Charlotte. Several years ago the kickoff speaker for the event was none other than Hezekiah Alexander's sister Elizabeth's descendant, Elizabeth Dole, who is a Salisbury native.

Unlike the Scots-Irish, the Germans wanted freedom to establish independent

Photo by Robert Thomason

The statue of Queen Charlotte stands at the intersection of Trade and Tryon streets, once a main trail for Native Americans bartering between tribes.

made Mecklenburg the mining capital of the United States and the discovery became the first building block in constructing the city as a financial center.

In 1837, city fathers built a United States Mint on West Trade Street to process gold instead of sending it to Rutherfordton for private coinage. Then a clever public relations person wrote that our streets were "paved with gold," borrowing liberally from the network of old gold mining shafts lying "beneath midtown streets." In fact, people do believe that low-value gold ore from the gold mines was used as part of the mixture to pave the main streets of Uptown.

The 1800s blossomed into a prosperous era for Charlotte with gold and iron ore operations, but the invention of the cotton gin soon overtook the difficult-to-mine gold. "King Cotton" transformed Mecklenburg into a textile leader, but nothing changed the way Charlotte did business as much as the arrival of the railroad. Its ideal location, connected by rail between Columbia and Greensboro, eventually turned Charlotte into a distribution hub. Today, Charlotte is at the center of the largest consolidated rail system in the nation, offering two major rail systems — Norfolk Southern Railway and CSX Transportation — that link 27,000 miles of rail systems between Charlotte and 22 states in the eastern United States. To Amtrak officials, trains aren't passenger transportation of the past. The Carolinian, which runs between Charlotte and Raleigh, has been so successful that a second train, The Piedmont, now also offers service between the two cities. The Crescent is still running from New Orleans to New York and back via Charlotte.

Charlotte had begun to take off economically in the 1800s, but the Civil War curtailed steady development. Although the city never saw military action, Charlotte families suffered huge casualties and the city hospitalized many wounded soldiers.

An interesting local legend from this time period dealt with the mysterious disappearance of the Confederate Treasury during a fateful wagon caravan trip through North Carolina. As the story (documented by

communities on a religious basis (such as the Moravians in Winston-Salem). The Germans also wanted to do missionary work among the Native Americans. The German sects, predominantly Lutheran and German Reformed (now part of the United Church of Christ), moved into the eastern section of Mecklenburg County. This section of Mecklenburg split in 1792 to become Cabarrus and Rowan counties. Since the predominant spoken language was English, the German minority struggled with the new language and customs and many chose to anglicize their names. In the 1800s, French Huguenots, Swiss, Highland Scotch and a large migration of Germans left Europe for many of the same reasons as the Scots-Irish, and traveled from Pennsylvania along the same route. Although Charlotte has a rich diversification of religious denominations, a strong Scots-Irish Presbyterian influence still remains.

With the discovery of gold in 1799, Charlotte grew from a village into a city. Gold

historian Burke Davis and others) goes, the treasury, accompanied by Jefferson Davis, Confederate Cabinet members and naval cadets, arrived in Charlotte where it picked up additional protection from Confederate cavalry and naval yard workers. As the caravan traveled along, some of the money was used to pay disillusioned and mutinous soldiers who demanded and received their share of back wages. When a Union attack on the caravan appeared imminent, some of the money was secretly buried or hidden on Southern plantations. Some of it was placed in a bank. Large sums were entrusted to two Confederate officers (to take out of the country) to use for continuing the war when reinforcements were received from the west and some of it was confiscated by Union soldiers. A sizable sum has never been accounted for. Don't go digging up your backyard though because historians believe the treasury was intact when the caravan left Charlotte.

When you pass by the southwest corner of Tryon and Fourth streets, note the plaque that reads, "Jefferson Davis was standing here when informed of Lincoln's death April 18, 1865." The horrified Davis knew that without Lincoln, Reconstruction of the United States was going to be an uphill battle. Charlotte was spared the worst of Reconstruction nightmares and eventually recovered to become a major production center in the 1900s. The city advanced economically in the early part of the century, although some historians feel that the Mecklenburg area did not regain its earlier momentum until after World War II.

Charlotte's way of doing business changed when visionary Daniel Augustus Tompkins came on the scene in 1883. This aristocratic South Carolinian duly noted that Charlotte was "an extremely dull place . . . but a town disposed to improve." He did a great deal to promote Charlotte's improvement with his Southern Cotton Oil Manufacturing Company, which made cooking oil and other products from cotton seeds and stimulated growth for the entire Southern textile region. Tompkins outlined a way for communities to build their textile mills in his book *A Plan To Raise Capital*. Tompkins spawned the idea of stock subscription to

Photo by Gary McCullough

Tours of the Hezekiah Alexander homesite offer an
insight to the region's colonial history.

ATHERTON
COTTON MILL

New South entrepreneur Daniel Augustus
Tompkins (1851-1914) built the Atherton
Cotton Mill on this site. Finished in 1893
the mill utilized the latest textile-making
technology. The textile mill provided a
critical boost to the early growth of the
adjoining Dilworth neighborhood.
Tompkins also built nearby housing for the
mill workers and a school for the workers'
children. A thriving mill village soon
developed in the surrounding area. Today,
the Atherton Mill building is serving a
new role in the South End community.

Charlotte's role in the Industrial Revolution is preserved in the renovated Atherton Mill.

guarantee local ownership instead of English and Northern industrialist ownership. Some of the history of this important era is preserved in the renovated Atherton Mill on South Boulevard.

Tompkins saw textiles as the engine that would drive the New South. It did, bringing men, women and children out of the fields and into the mills. The mills breathed spirit and independence into an impoverished economy, giving families a mill home and a somewhat better economic life with regular pay and easier work. Textile manufacturing hummed along, then cranked to full throttle

when tobacco giant James B. "Buck" Duke had the Catawba River dammed to build his hydroelectric plant in the early 1900s. With the advantage of good roads, the railroad, electricity and stable government, Charlotte began to prosper.

The early pioneers had only private education, usually taught by ministers or teachers who traveled from home to home. Instruction involved strictly practical ideas about learning. Schooling in religion, rudimentary skills and the learning of a trade constituted the curriculum. Something akin to public education didn't begin until 1839 when $750,000 was appropriated for North Carolina schools. Charlotte's educational direction in the 1990s has focused on creating a series of magnet schools, with each magnet school concentrated in a specific learning discipline.

In our higher education system, you'll find a number of excellent old colleges such as Queens, Johnson C. Smith and Davidson. Newer academic options, the University of North Carolina at Charlotte, which dates to 1946, and the Central Piedmont Community College, established in 1963, draw students from across the United States and from around the world.

Banking began in the Mecklenburg area with the early settlers but stayed a private business until 1865 when it became nationalized. During the Civil War, a branch of the Bank of Charlotte transported 3,000 pounds of gold bullion 18 miles to Grasshopper Springs where it remained buried until the war's end.

It was not until 1927 that a branch of the Federal Reserve Bank of Richmond was established in Charlotte, another step toward making Charlotte an important financial center. After the Second World War, two Charlotte banks, American Trust Company and Commercial National Bank, merged. The result of this merger eventually became NCNB. A few years ago, NCNB merged with C & S Sovran in Atlanta to become NationsBank. In April 1998, NationsBank merged with BankAmerica through a $66 billion stock swap to create the country's largest bank, based on deposits. No matter what vantage point you view the city from today, NationsBank's glistening crown acts as a beacon. Charlotte's second-largest bank is First Union, followed by Winston-Salem-based Wachovia, 14 smaller banks and the Federal Reserve Branch, which combine to make Charlotte the second-largest financial center in the nation.

It was during the late 1970s and early 1980s that Uptown's Fourth Ward, an area of quaint and charming Victorian homes, was rehabilitated. This brought people back to city living at a time when many people were moving to the suburbs. Lake Norman emerged from weekend cabin status to a community of year-round luxury homes and condominiums. The downside to this rapid growth is that some of these multi-complexes cause severe traffic problems. The upside is that the city is widening some congested roads and cutting new roads through residential areas to give relief to the traffic flow.

Charlotte did not begin to grow in earnest until the 1980s, following IBM's 1978 arrival, which insiders say caused the city to perk up and residential property prices to edge upward. Charlotte became an international city in the late '80s when USAirways won the London route. The 1990's international connection widened when Charlotte's NBC News channel WCNC began to broadcast headline news to viewers from Mexico to Argentina, designating it as the first United States-based Spanish language news network to cover the entire region. In addition, in 1991, WCNC became home to an overnight newscast for U.S. night owls, which added a new service for another untapped audience. The station, which changed its name to NBC 6 in 1996, is known for its cutting-edge technological innovations and was the first local affiliate to establish its own Internet website.

The arts community is strong in Charlotte due to enthusiastic arts supporters and a strong Charlotte Arts and Science Council. The Council recently received the largest Challenge grant in the nation ($1 million) from the National Endowment for the Arts, and the endowment campaign raised $26.16 million ($1 million above its goal).

Charlotte's "Cultural District" includes the N.C. Blumenthal Performing Arts Center, Discovery Place, the Afro-American Cultural

Photo by Gary McCullough

The James K. Polk state historic site in Pineville recalls the origins of the nation's eleventh President.

Photo courtesy of Charlotte Convention and Visitors Bureau

Charlotte continues to grow, in the spirit of its pioneering founders,
in finance, health care, professional sports and the arts.

Center and in the neighborhoods, Ovens Auditorium, Johnson C. Smith University, Queens College's Dana Auditorium and other varied entertainment options. Several years ago Discovery Place, a hands-on science museum, was named the top tourist attraction in the southeast by the Southeast Tourism Society. The museum continues to provide exciting programs and films in its OMNIMAX Theatre.

Charlotte may be poised to become the arts center of North Carolina, but sports is in undisputed first place. We have the Charlotte Coliseum where the NBA Hornets consistently sell out all 24,000 seats, the Knights Castle baseball field with its AAA Florida Marlins baseball farm team and the improved Charlotte Motor Speedway. Another glittering stone in Charlotte's crown is Ericsson Stadium, home of Charlotte's NFL team — the Carolina Panthers. For many, this enthusiasm for sports makes Charlotte synonymous with spectator sports, but a temperate climate also encourages year-round participation in a variety of outdoor sports.

Charlotte's mild weather and healthy business climate (low tax base) continue to attract desirable companies. In the past 10 years, Charlotte has become home or second home to industries such as microelectronics, metal working and vehicle assembly, research and development, high-tech and service-oriented international and domestic firms. Around 325 foreign-owned companies now have Charlotte facilities and aggressive planning promises that this trend will continue.

When you drive through this beautiful city designated "the city of trees," think of those early ancestors who, throughout the centuries, refused to knuckle under to failure. Their character built a foundation that was able to change — change not only for the sake of prosperity, but change for a better quality of life. You'll find that flexibility in Charlotte. It's a great place to live and raise a family.

In the past few years, Charlotte has been blessed with a great deal of positive publicity. It has been featured in publications such as *Southern Living*, *Sports Illustrated*, *Financial World*, *Newsweek*, *The Wall Street*

Journal, *The New York Times* and *National Geographic*, to name a few.

The $141 million Convention Center covers four city blocks (850,000 square feet) and is among the top centers in the nation in terms of exhibit space. The 72,500-seat Ericsson Stadium has the latest sound and video technology, 8,000 club seats and 135 luxury suites. On the east side of Uptown, the Law Enforcement Center includes fresco master Ben Long's latest work. CityFair has restaurants and shops, plus classrooms for a branch of UNC Charlotte.

NationsBank recently completed two major developments for North Tryon Street — a 30-story office tower and 20-story condominium, estimated to cost $170 million, and an office/residential complex called Transamerica Square, which cost $100 million.

Things are not only booming Uptown but all over the city. The long-awaited widening of Independence Boulevard, the main east-west corridor through the city and a heavy carrier of beach traffic, is complete from the City Center to Independence Arena. As construction on the new outerbelt (I-485) progresses, developers have positioned themselves at strategic interchanges — N.C. 49 and Arrowood Road, the new interchange at N.C. 16 S. and Providence Road W., and other locations. South of Pineville, off U.S. 521 near the outerbelt, an 1,800-acre office/retail/multifamily and single-family residence/golf community called Ballantyne is being developed. The Bissell Company and the Harris Group are developing the office/retail component while Crescent Resources is developing the golf course and residential community. The extensively developed SouthPark area has almost become a second city in recent years and now boasts the third-largest office space in the state, next to Uptown and Raleigh.

You can get a quick overview of Charlotte's character at the Museum of the New South on College Street. The touch-video obelisk, called a museum without walls, is an innovative concept that delivers Charlotte's history. In the words of First Union CEO Ed Crutchfield, "A new person coming to town or the presentation of a new idea (such as a museum without walls) has a very good chance of being accepted in Charlotte." This is the distinctive type of character trait that sets Charlotte apart from many Southern cities. Vision, character and risk are the essential catalysts guiding Charlotte into the 21st Century.

Photo by Robert Thomason

You can get a quick overview of Charlotte's character at the Museum of the New South on College Street.

The Charlotte area is divided into Uptown Charlotte, Mecklenburg towns and neighboring towns.

Area Overviews

North Carolina's Charlotte area is often discussed in terms of Uptown, Mecklenburg County and adjacent neighboring towns. Therefore, we have divided this chapter into sections that give a brief overview of each.

For More Information Contact:
INFO! Charlotte
Charlotte's Visitor Information Center
is a joint venture of the
Charlotte Convention & Visitors Bureau and
the Chamber of Commerce

330 S. Tryon St. • 331-2700, (800) 231-4636

Uptown Charlotte

Uptown is a unique place — post-modern glass towers, concrete, trees, parks and heavenly spires all point to a city on the move. To all sides of Uptown are a series of neighborhoods and districts, historically known as Wards. The hub of government, the core of business, residential neighborhoods, night life, entertainment, food and accommodations — it's all Uptown, and Uptown is growing.

Just as its headquarters dominates the Charlotte skyline, NationsBank continues to play a pivotal role in the changing face of Uptown. A joint venture with Transamerica has produced a $70 million, 10-story complex called Transamerica Square. A 30-story multi-tenant office and a 15-story office building, condo and underground parking garage were also constructed on North Tryon Street. NationsBank also has plans to turn a vacant, burned-out church into an artists' colony that will give visitors an opportunity to watch artists at work. Several of its new projects will include townhouses and penthouses and a shopping center with major department stores is also under discussion.

First Union National Bank completed an addition adjacent to One First Union Center, giving the bank additional office space and multiple levels of parking — an increasingly rare commodity as businesses swell and the city attracts newcomers. The bank also has started construction on a 27-story office tower, Three First Union Center, adjacent to its headquarters on South Tryon Street. The facility, scheduled to open in the fall of 1999, will house First Union employees and also provide restaurant and retail space.

Ericsson Stadium, a state-of-the-art facility, is home to the NFL Carolina Panthers.

Photo by Tim Johnson

The Wachovia Bank building is just one of the many banks that grace Charlotte's skyline.

Photo by Robert Thomason

Urban architecture and well-planned parks, such as Marshall Park, combine to make Uptown Charlotte an inviting area for visitors, residents and Uptown workers alike.

Read more about the stadium and the Panthers in the Spectator Sports chapter.

The Charlotte Convention Center's sprawling convention and display area allows the city to compete for all but the very largest trade shows, conventions and conferences. The Center covers 850,000 square feet and is expected to generate $275 million annually into the Charlotte-Mecklenburg economy.

To help you get your bearings Uptown, the intersection of Trade and Tryon streets is commonly referred to as Independence Square or "The Square" for short. It is at this historic intersection where two ancient Indian trading paths met. It was also where the Queen City's first settlers centered their activities and businesses. The Square was also home to Tom Polk's log structure, which residents called "the courthouse" in a successful effort to make Charlotte the county seat.

By now you're probably asking yourself, "Why do Charlotteans call their downtown area Uptown?" The answer is a simple one. Geographically, no matter where you are in the city, you have to travel uphill to get to Uptown. In 1974 a group of city leaders, led by Mayor John Belk, decided to rename the downtown jurisdiction Uptown and the name stuck.

Today more than 58,000 people work in Uptown. The city plans to increase that number to upwards of 67,000 by the year 2005 and it has put into action an Urban Design Plan to accomplish that goal by retaining existing Uptown corporate tenants and attracting new ones. The plan also calls for strengthening Uptown as a cultural center and building its residential base. The merged Charlotte Uptown Development Corporation and the Chamber's Central Charlotte Division are the driving force for implementation.

In the last decade, Charlotte has witnessed many new additions to its skyline. During the late 1980s, First Union National Bank built its 42-story corporate headquarters, bringing almost one million square feet onto the market with the tower's opening. The 12-story Charlotte-Mecklenburg Government Center followed. The Gateway Center, located down Trade Street at the traditional gateway to the Queen City offered an Uptown advantage as it came on line in the mid-80s. The Interstate Tower, a 31-story multi-tenant office tower on The Square, opened in the latter part of the 1980s. The $32 million Charlotte Apparel Center, which was purchased by NationsBank for use as corporate office space and the $10 million expansion and renovation of the main branch of the Public Library of Charlotte and Mecklenburg County have contributed to the Queen City's construction boom.

Many Uptown leaders had envisioned and spoken of the creation of an entertainment zone in Uptown. Designed as an innovative center city mall, CityFair boasts a food court, retail shops, Fat Tuesday and World Mardi Gras, a multifaceted entertainment zone. Each weekend the atrium is transformed from a mere food court into an entertainment facility of bands, costumed employees, Mardi Gras theme food and beverages and theatrical lighting.

For more sedate entertainment and fun, Bistro 100, located in Founders Hall adjacent to NationsBank Corporate Center, is a great place to dine or to meet people at its upscale wine bar. A grand, six-story glass atrium of retail stores, casual dining and The Crown Athletic Club, an upscale workout facility, Founders Hall is a fabulous place for parties, dances and charity functions.

The N.C. Blumenthal Performing Arts Center opened in 1992. A world-class performing arts center, it hosts Broadway plays, ballet, opera and symphonic performances.

A $55-million facility, the Performing Arts Center features 2,100 seats in its performance hall. It also contains a 450-seat theater and numerous rehearsal halls. It is home to many of Charlotte's arts groups such as the Carolina Opera, the Charlotte Symphony Orchestra and Charlotte Repertory Theatre.

Connected to the Blumenthal Center is the mighty NationsBank Corporate Center, also completed in 1992. Designed by world-renowned architect Caesar Pelli, it rises 60 stories and dominates Charlotte's skyline. With 1,203,177 square feet, it holds the distinction of being the largest office building in the Southeast.

The decade of the '90s has already seen much change in Uptown. Besides the Performing Arts Center, Plaza Park at The Square was completed and the Carillon office tower opened on Trade Street in 1991. Completely leased, it houses a lobby art gallery and is home to another first for Charlotte — Morton's of Chicago restaurant.

In 1991, Charlotte became one of the few American cities to house and operate an OMNIMAX Theatre, now a part of the Discovery Place Science Museum (see Attractions chapter). It offers a 180-degree viewing screen for planetarium discussions, special OMNIMAX science films, University planetary studies and is a great place to see the Rolling Stones and Pink Floyd — larger than life.

Special events are commonplace throughout Uptown. Concerts, exhibits, parades and road races — you'll see it all. The Charlotte Observer Marathon begins and ends here. Whether it's the 600 Festival Race Parade or noon concerts, Uptown is the place to be.

In the mid-1800s, the city of Charlotte was divided into four voting districts, known as wards. Today, Third and Fourth Wards offer homes, condominiums, townhouses and apartment opportunities for upwards of 5,700 people. With an increasing interest in Uptown living, several developers are heeding the call. One is Jim Gross, local architect and developer. His company, the Metropolitan Group, has renovated the old Ivey's retail store at Tryon and Fifth streets. Offering spectacular views of the city, secure living space and convenience par excellence, Ivey's Townhomes are a welcome addition to the fabric of Uptown.

Fourth Ward features numerous turn-of-the-century homes, many of which have been meticulously restored. It's a real treat to walk the quaint streets or stop by Alexander Michael's for a favorite brew, all in the shadow of the office towers. Another historic preservation effort that has been successful is the Afro-American Cultural Center, which

Photo by Robert Thomason

The 850,000-square-foot Charlotte Convention Center hosts a variety of events throughout the year.

The N.C. Blumenthal Center for the Performing Arts includes
the dramatic 2,100-seat Belk Theatre.

Photo courtesy of Charlotte Convention and Visitors Bureau

is a result of the preservation of what was Little Rock AME Zion Church, built in 1911.

The Dunhill Hotel, now on the Historic Landmarks Register, offers European accommodations for travelers to Uptown. The Cadillac Building and Crosland Retail's Latta Arcade are all testaments to successful redevelopment and historic preservation.

The bustling South End Historic District, located just a few minutes from the Convention Center, contains a cluster of former textile mills that has been converted into shops, galleries and restaurants.

For more information about historic Uptown, pick up a free guide entitled *Historic Guide to Uptown Charlotte, North Carolina,* at Info Charlotte on South Tryon Street, 331-2700. This visitors information center also has brochures on self-guided tours of Uptown and can supply you with a calendar of monthly events.

Mecklenburg Towns

While for economic reasons many Charlotte natives or newcomers may decide to work or locate their business in Charlotte, they often choose to live in one of the surrounding smaller towns within reasonable commuting distance. For those who yearn for a less complicated way of living, small-town life is very appealing.

A strong religious structure cements the foundation of all the towns, setting the tone for their quality of life. Social life centers around school activities, various clubs, sports, festivals and bazaars that include barbecues with brunswick stew or fish fries near the lake communities.

Each town has its own government and volunteer fire department. Some have their own police force while others rely on the Charlotte-Mecklenburg Police Department. Satellite offices of some Charlotte-based medical groups give Pineville, Matthews and Mint Hill a good supply of doctors and dentists. Neighbors to the north are close to the University Memorial Hospital via Harris Boulevard off I-77. Charlotte-Mecklenburg Schools provide public education. Each town has a branch of the public library. Some of the towns get water and sewer service from Charlotte while others rely primarily on wells and septic systems.

As you might have guessed, residents of the neighboring towns pay both county and town taxes, but the total amounts are less than those paid by Charlotteans (another small-town perk). The touches of modern-ization such as fast food, discount grocery chains and, yes, even condos have branched into these once unsullied hamlets.

Of course the downside of living in a small town but working in Charlotte is the commute. Still, when asked, most commut-ers feel that the quality and substance of their small-town life outweighs the traffic problems, giving them the best of both worlds. Likewise, many of the neighboring towns offer attractions and shopping that Charlotteans find worthy of a short drive.

Charlotte's rampant growth in recent years has spilled over into the six small incorporated Mecklenburg towns that surround the city. While Pineville has been engulfed almost entirely by development, Mint Hill, Matthews, Davidson, Cornelius and Huntersville are clinging to their identities, having pledged not to let the same thing happen to them. Each town has staked its claim to adjoining territory, having worked out a "sphere of influence" agreement with Charlotte on possible limits.

North Mecklenburg Chamber of Commerce & Visitors Center
Shops on the Green, Cornelius • 892-1922
Represents Cornelius, Davidson, Huntersville and Lake Norman.

Cornelius

In the period 1883 through 1888, known as the "cotton battle" time, so much cotton was shipped to Liverpool, England, from here that this area was nicknamed "Liverpool." It was not until 1893 that the town came into existence when J.R. Stough relocated part of his Davidson cotton business outside the Davidson town limit where he could do his own cotton weighing unhampered by Davidson's newly hired town weigher. Local farmers, rather than trudge up a muddy hill to Davidson, came to Stough in such abun-dance that he and associate, C.J. Johnson, conceived the idea of having a mill nearby so that cotton could be converted into cloth right there. They didn't have the money to spare but knew a man who did, Joseph Benjamin Cornelius of Davidson. Soon the cotton mill opened and the town took its name from the principal stockholder. The town was incorporated in 1905.

Cornelius remains a strong manufactur-ing and retail center, retaining its original cotton mill, now named Foamex. The town has a population of 8,000 and is governed by a mayor and a five-member council. The Cornelius Planning Department and

Photo by Tim Johnson

Cornelius offers homeowners lakefront communities.

Charlotte/Mecklenburg planners have developed a growth plan. Growth, by the way, is welcome in this small town. Cornelius has a paid police department, but fire protection is provided by volunteer firemen. The town owns a part of the Catawba Nuclear Plant, but since the summer of 1997, ElectraCities has managed power in the town. Water and sewer service are furnished by the Charlotte-Mecklenburg Utility Department.

In addition to the fast-food eateries and steak houses, Cornelius offers some really outstanding restaurants such as The Stock Car Cafe, which sports a large collection of race memorabilia; Kobe Japanese House of Steak & Seafood, featuring authentic Teppan-Yaki and a sushi bar; and Mama Mia Italian restaurant.

Nearby Davidson College provides many opportunities for educational and cultural enrichment. The Lake Norman Family Branch of the YMCA is located in Cornelius. From June through mid-October the North Mecklenburg Farmers Market is held every Saturday at Cornelius Elementary School. Students attend Alexander Jr. High in Huntersville and North Mecklenburg High School. Although many residents live in the surrounding countryside or on the lake, Cornelius offers a variety of housing options for residents. Shops on The Green, Lakeshore Marketplace, Southlake and Norman Crossing provide plenty of shopping opportunities. Movies at the Lake provides local entertainment. Cornelius continues to show expansion in its retail and real estate markets.

Davidson

Davidson promises the best of two worlds: living in a small college town that looks as if it came off the cover of an old *Saturday Evening Post* magazine and living on the lake (Lake Norman — straight across I-77 from the town). Whoever coined the phrase "southern hospitality" copied it from the townspeople of this quaint village. Davidson seems to cast a spell on those who come to visit, sometimes causing them to put down permanent roots. It's a cerebral atmosphere of friendly attitudes.

Davidson College, which dates to 1837 and is affiliated with the Presbyterian church, contributes heavily to the town's charm. In 1994, the college put the finishing touch on its $9.1-million Visual Art Center at the corner of Main and Griffith streets. Make a point of visiting the art gallery, which is open to the public free of charge. A magnificent

Photo courtesy of Davidson College

Davidson College is located 20 miles north of Charlotte.

Auguste Rodin sculpture, commissioned by the town of Calais, France, in 1884, presides over the atrium.

The first thing you'll notice as you walk down Davidson's Main Street and through the campus is an arboretum of gigantic old trees. The idea for this horticultural effort formed in 1869 when the faculty recommended that the campus reflect ". . . the forest growth of the State . . . and the general botany of the region." Over the years a variety of trees and shrubs were planted. Today, you can take a self-guided tree tour and identify 40 different varieties from their metal tags.

It should come as no surprise to find Dr. Tom Clark's sculptures of wood spirits and gnomes among Davidson's quaint shops. This former religion and art professor became a sculptor of whimsical characters and displays hundreds of his forest-dweller figures at his Main Street museum. The top floor houses Clark's personal collection of "retired" statues (now commanding a hefty sum in the secondary collectors market), but you may purchase Clark's and the works of other sculptors on the first floor. Over a million people now collect and trade Clark's imp-like creatures crafted from their creator's puckish sense of humor.

If you're hungry, you might try traditional French cuisine at Les Trois Faisans at 101 Depot Street, right around the corner from the museum. Other restaurant options are

Jaspers, 127 Depot Street; Ben & Jerry's Ice Cream & Frozen Yogurt, 202 S. Main Street; or North Harbor Cafe, 181 Harbor Drive. If you want to spend the night or are looking for a place for out-of-town guests, a good choice is the Davidson Village Inn at 117 Depot Street, which offers rooms with breakfast.

It isn't uncommon for Charlotteans and other neighbors to drive to Davidson to enjoy its many cultural amenities and sporting events. The Davidson Wildcats have had their share of basketball victories led by some outstanding coaches. The Village Green across from the downtown shopping area is the site of numerous community events, including Town Day, which is held in May.

Residents have a choice of in-town housing which includes Victorian houses, countryside living or homes on Lake Norman. River Run is based around a golf and country club. McConnell Place is a community developed by Davidson College for faculty and staff, but also has opportunities for non-college employees to build beautiful homes. In recent years a number of luxury condos have also been built on the lake, such as Davidson Landing.

Davidson, which adjoins Cornelius, is about 20 miles north of Charlotte via I-77. Incorporated in 1879, the town has a population of 4,911 not including the 1,600 students. Residents usually go to Cornelius for additional restaurants, shopping and entertainment opportunities. Davidson is governed by a mayor and five commissioners and citizens serve on a number of committees. The town has its own police force and fire protection is provided by volunteers. Residents get their water from the Charlotte-Mecklenburg Utility Department.

Huntersville

Huntersville is one of Mecklenburg's oldest towns. Originally called Craighead after a fiery Presbyterian minister, the town was renamed for Robert B. Hunter when it incorporated in 1873. The Hugh Torrance House and Store has been sitting on Gilead Road since the once itinerant peddler, Hugh Torrance, took ownership in 1779. Now a museum, the original log house and store is where neighbors once gathered to buy necessities while they no doubt exchanged dissenting talk of British rule. They had settled here near Long Creek where they farmed the rich bottom lands along river and creek banks. Sitting about 100 yards from the store you'll see Cedar Grove, the beautifully restored 1831 brick plantation home built by Torrance's son, James.

Much history has occurred in the Huntersville area. One of its most famous residents — historian and novelist LeGette Blythe — wrote about surrounding historic sites such as Latta Plantation, Alexandriana, the McIntire Place and Hopewell Presbyterian Church. Midas Spring (Mecklenburg's oldest manufacturer) and the Silas Davis General Store have changed very little since the turn of the century. Midas still pumps and sells spring water and the general store sells everything from farm implements to overalls to brogans.

Huntersville has maintained its country charm. If you overlook the utility poles, driving down Gilead Road in the springtime is like taking a step back into the past. There are rambling old homes, beautiful magnolias and stands of ancient hardwoods. The community is changing, however, as the building boom, so prevalent in other parts of the county for several years, is also taking off here.

The Central Piedmont Community College North Area Learning Center offers a variety of academic and recreational opportunities.

Huntersville is governed by a mayor and five commissioners. It has its own police department and electrical department; water and sewer service is provided by Charlotte-Mecklenburg Utility Department. Fire protection is provided by volunteers. The population is approximately 8,000.

Lake Norman

It's difficult to put into words just what it is that draws people to Lake Norman. It's more a state of mind than anything else. It's the kind of place where you can do business in casual attire. Even with its overabundance of condos, new shopping centers and growing resident base, Lake Norman is a beautiful place to live.

Lake Norman is a "working" lake, created when Duke Power Company began construction in 1959 of the Cowan Ford Dam for the generation of hydroelectric power. Completed in 1963, it was named Lake Norman after Duke Power President, Norman Atwater Cocke. The lake is claimed by the towns of Cornelius, Huntersville, Davidson, Mooresville, Troutman and Denver and located in Mecklenburg, Iredell, Lincoln and Catawba counties.

Slicing through the lake area, I-77 separates Cornelius, Davidson and Mooresville to the east, Troutman to the north and Denver to the west. Lake dwellers in each area are supplied with such services as volunteer fire departments, police departments and separate governing bodies.

As you might imagine, lakeside restaurants and shopping areas with a good representation of real estate firms are scattered about central areas of the lake, but it isn't uncommon to see corn fields sandwiched between expensive homes in this original farming community. Since Duke Power gave its employees first option on lake lots, you'll see many summertime mobile homes sitting compatibly beside luxury condos and developments.

Sailing is a favorite pastime
on Lake Norman.

The *Lake Norman Magazine*, a free monthly publication, informs residents and neighbors of upcoming events. Lake Norman's largest festival, LakeFest, is held annually the second weekend in September at Jetton Park. The festival attracts more than 15,000 people with live entertainment, art, food, activities for children and a dog show.

The North Mecklenburg Chamber of Commerce operates a Visitors Center at Exit 28 (I-77). The center is open seven days a week except on major holidays and provides maps, brochures, real estate and recreational information and exhibits on the towns in the area.

Matthews

Matthews Chamber of Commerce
250 N. Trade Street, Suite 204 • 847-3649

If a movie company was searching for a quaint, 18th-century country village look, it would need search no farther than Matthews. The town looks and feels laid-back. The antique and craft shops in turn-of-the-century buildings have made it something of a tourist town and a fast-developing antique center.

Matthews was known as Stumptown when it was first settled in the early 1800s because of the stumps left from the forests that covered the section. It was said that a wagon couldn't make a U-turn without running into a stump. The town later became Fullwood to honor John M. Fullwood, who operated Stagecoach Inn and became the area's first postmaster in 1825. When incorporated in 1879, the townspeople renamed it Matthews for Watson Matthews, principal stockholder of the railroad. Eventually 13 trains came through Matthews every day and the Matthews Train Depot, built in 1874, became the center of activity.

When gold was discovered in the area in the early 1800s, Matthews shared in the bounty. The Rea Gold Mine was established where Sardis Road North is today and the Tredenic Mine was located near McAlpine Creek in the present Stonehaven area. Unfortunately, the gold found at these mines was of such fine texture that it finally became too expensive to process.

In the center of downtown on North Trade Street, you'll find Renfrow Hardware where on any given morning in the past, the town elders gathered around the black potbellied stove to discuss politics. You can still buy seed and garden supplies, hardware items, clothing, hoop cheese, soft drinks and pickles at this store, which has served the community since the early 1900s. Another important historic structure is the Reid House one block from downtown. Built in the early 1900s, it is on the National Register of Historic Places and is used for Victorian teas, weddings, family gatherings and socials.

Today Matthews is home to some very prominent companies including Family Dollar, Inc., Pic 'n Pay, PCA International, Conbraco Industries, ALLTEL Service Corporation, Harris-Teeter, Rexham, A.E.P. Industries and many others. Windsor Square Shopping Center, Matthews Festival and many other shopping centers offer shopping, hotel, office and business spaces, plus a variety of fast-food, ethnic, seafood and steak restaurants. The Matthews Community Farmers Market offers fresh fruits, vegetables, organic flowers, fresh baked goods, herbs and more. The market, located on North Trade Street, is open every Saturday from May to November.

Matthews hosts a number of events throughout the year that offer a variety of entertainment and family fun for everyone. Matthews ALIVE!, the town's annual Labor Day celebration, attracts visitors by the thousands. The Matthews Auto Reunion, held the second Saturday in June, is a delight to auto enthusiasts of all ages. Matthews Music in the Park features outdoor concerts in Stumptown Park beginning in May and running through August. ArtFest of Matthews, a two-day open-air fine arts celebration, showcases juried artists. Merry Magical Christmas begins with the annual tree lighting and Santa making a personal appearance. Breakfast with Santa is a very popular event.

The Matthews Athletic and Recreation Association involves over 1,000 children annually in sports programs. A few years back, as the Matthews Little League All Stars prepared to defend their state championship title at Arthur Goodman Memorial Park, two skydivers dropped from 3,500 feet to deliver the game ball to the pitchers' mound at the close of the national anthem.

Central Piedmont Community College is building a brand new satellite campus near U.S. 74 and I-485. The Matthews Playhouse of Performing Arts is designed to create a performing and entertainment environment for area young people and produces four plays a year. The Matthews Community HELP Center offers food, clothing and shelter to those in need.

The opening of Presbyterian Hospital Matthews in August 1994 added a great deal to Matthews' quality of life. The 102-bed private hospital located at 1500 Matthews Township Parkway offers a full range of medical services.

The town, about 12 miles east of Charlotte, offers a variety of housing options beginning at $100,000. The population has grown from 91 residents in the town's first census in 1880 to 18,362 today. Citizens are governed by a mayor and six council members. The town has its own police force and is served by two volunteer fire departments,

Matthews-Morningstar and Idlewild. Water and sewer service is provided by the Charlotte-Mecklenburg Utility Department.

Mint Hill

Mint Hill Town Hall
7151 Matthews-Mint Hill Rd. • 545-9726

What really makes Mint Hill unique is the superior overall quality of life it offers. It has wide open spaces, neat homes in all price ranges and a lack of strip development that sets it apart from all the other Mecklenburg towns. Through the years Mint Hill has had perhaps the most stringent zoning laws in the county and in 1986 adopted a land-use plan to steer and guide growth through the year 2000. It also has one of the lowest tax rates of municipalities in Mecklenburg County.

Settled in the mid-1700s by Scots-Irish Presbyterians, Mint Hill has a rich heritage. Philadelphia Presbyterian Church, established in 1770 in one of Mecklenburg's eight original communities, is one of the area's oldest churches. Its chapel, built of handmade bricks made on the spot in 1826, may be the oldest church building in continuous use in the county. Its history and that of the once-agrarian community are chronicled in the Historical Room. The Mint Hill Historical Society has renovated a turn-of-the-century doctor's office into The Mint Hill Country Doctor's Museum off N.C. 51. It is open for guided tours the second Sunday of every month from 2 PM to 5 PM, during special community events and for groups by appointment. Call 573-0726 or 888-2271 for information. Nearby Bain Academy was

Photo by Robert Thomason

This turn-of-the-century doctor's office is now a museum.

established in 1889 as a prestigious boarding school and still serves as a public elementary school.

Mint Hill was an early military muster ground and has had several industries including gold mining. There are a few manufacturers in the area today, but Mint Hill is primarily a residential community with several stores. A number of fine developments have been built, including Farmwood, known for its large lots and houses.

Mint Hill is currently the third-largest town in Mecklenburg County with a population of over 15,000. It was incorporated for the second time in its history in 1971. The town has a number of very active civic clubs. Mint Hill Athletic Association provides opportunities for youth sports year round and all residents enjoy the town's two parks, Mint Hill Park on Wilgrove and the town's most recently developed 54-acre passive/active recreational facility, Mint Hill Park on Fairview. Both parks offer a variety of recreational opportunities, including soccer and softball fields, tennis courts, volleyball courts, nature trails, a nine-hole disc golf course, children's playgrounds and an in-line skate path. Mint Hill Madness, an arts and crafts fall festival, is a popular annual event.

Few small towns anywhere have a white-columned brick hardware store as their focus. Mint Hill does. If you want to find out what's going on in town, stop in at McEwen Hardware Store on the square. You can also run into neighbors and friends at the post office and various shopping centers around town. The Marketplace at Mint Hill has two floors of 70 specialty and antique shops that offer merchandise from stationery to furniture. Penny's Place and Shomar's in the Mint Hill Festival and Happy's Restaurant in Lawyers Square offer camaraderie and good food. Carolina Creamery in McEwen Square is a favorite for ice cream lovers during the summer months.

Residents are governed by a mayor and four commissioners. Day-to-day operations of the town are carried out in an ultra-contemporary town hall. Mint Hill uses the services of the Charlotte-Mecklenburg Police Department, but provides its own fire and emergency protection through a volunteer fire department. At this time, most residents rely on wells and septic tanks, but some developments have their own water and treatment systems. Water and sewer bonds were approved by voters in late 1994 and the Charlotte-Mecklenburg Utility Department is currently extending water and sewer lines.

Pineville

Pineville Town Hall
118 College St. • 889-2291

Incorporated in 1873, Pineville still has the look of yesteryear. Hanging baskets of flowers now adorn the old-fashioned black metal light posts along Pineville's four-lane Main Street. Crepe myrtle trees add a soft look to this town of 18 antique shops where you'll feel comfortable strolling down the street. If you want to pass the time of day with the local folks, Blankenship's Feed and Seed Store is the place to do it. This nostalgic-looking little village lies in sharp contrast to Carolina Place Mall and its many surrounding enterprises located, as the natives say, "down the road a piece" on Hwy. 51. This former cotton patch is located about 12 miles from Uptown Charlotte and today it is lined with shopping centers, office complexes, a branch of Mercy Hospital and various restaurants. Insiders like Joe's Crab Shack at 10405 Centrum Parkway and Trio, a contemporary restaurant offering a varied menu, at 10709 McMullen Creek Parkway.

The town's recreation department offers many activities for all ages at Lake Park, including Camp Pineville, a summer camp for children. Team sports are supervised by the Greater Pineville Athletic Association.

Pineville's most famous native son was James Knox Polk (1795-1849), 11th President of the United States. The James K. Polk Memorial, south of town on U.S. 521, consists of several home and barn structures of the period. Each year Polk's birthday is celebrated on the site with demonstrations in weaving and cooking food of his era.

Pineville has a population of over 3,000 residents. It is governed by a mayor and four council members and operates its own

Photo courtesy of N.C. Travel & Tourism

Although named the Charlotte Motor Speedway, this popular attraction is located in western Concord.

electrical distribution system and telephone company. Water and sewer service is furnished by the Charlotte-Mecklenburg Utility Department. The town's police department operates its own dispatching and 911 systems. The Pineville Volunteer Fire Department, originally the Fire Brigade that was organized in the 1850s, provides fire protection.

Neighboring Towns

Belmont

A few years back the spring festival in Belmont was renamed Garibaldi for the man who pioneered the town's beginnings. John Garibaldi built a railroad water tank 1 mile west of the Catawba River in the early 1870s that resulted in a station stop. Garibaldi's tank serviced trains on the Atlanta and Charlotte Railroad, which in turn opened the path for this area to become heavily industrialized with textiles.

The Cathedral at Belmont Abbey College is the only abbey cathedral in the country. The Abbot has jurisdiction over eight western North Carolina counties. The painted glass windows in the cathedral are worth a visit. They came from Myers Brothers Studios in Bavaria and received four gold medals at the Chicago World's Fair in 1892. The college is also the site of a massive block of granite that was once an Indian altar and later used to exhibit and auction slaves. The 3-foot by 4.5-foot stone is now used as a baptismal font. An equally enticing draw is the 480-acre Daniel Stowe Botanical Garden, which is an all-season attraction in the area.

Worth a visit is the Piedmont Carolina Railroad Museum. In addition to antique boxcars, the museum has a Western Union display that demonstrates the old method of sending telegrams. The museum is open only on the weekends, (704) 825-4403.

Although the Sisters of Mercy closed Sacred Heart College in the late '80s, they remain a major presence in the area. Members of the order direct Saint Joseph's Hospital in Asheville and Holy Angels Nursery in Belmont. They live in the Mother house, a huge stone building at Sacred Heart.

Concord

In 1887, after the economic hardships of Reconstruction, James W. Cannon started his cotton mill in order to take advantage of this strong cotton-farming region. That plant was the beginning of the textile manufacturing giant, Fieldcrest-Cannon. Mr. Cannon built a palatial white Victorian home on Union Street and was later followed by his top managers who also built grand homes there. The street is in the historic district of the town and is part of a walking tour that includes almost 30 houses, churches and other structures.

Cannon's influence is still seen in the Cannon Memorial Library and the up-to-date Northeast Memorial Hospital. Like Belmont, much of Concord's industry is traditionally related to textiles, but with the major presence of Philip Morris USA, Concord is trying to shuck its mill town image. The Philip Morris plant has one of the largest collections of North Carolina arts and crafts, including the world's largest quilted tapestry, which can be seen during free tours of the plant. Another change has been brought about with Perdue Farms, the single-largest duck hatchery and the second-largest duck processor in the world.

As the county seat of Cabarrus, Concord's city limits are adjacent to Charlotte's boundaries and the Charlotte Motor Speedway is located here. The superspeedway, which also features NASCAR short-track racing, has become very important to the economy of Concord. Another major attraction in the area is the Reed Gold Mine. Many cultural events are staged by the Cabarrus Arts Council, the Cabarrus Art Guild and the Old Courthouse Theatre. The best known restaurant in Concord is Troutman's, which specializes in barbecue.

The Rocky River Golf Course, designed by Don Maples, is located near the Concord Regional Airport.

Fort Mill, S.C.

Like so many small towns that emerged because the railroad made a stop there or someone put in a cotton gin, Fort Mill was so named for two separate occurrences — a fort and a mill. The fort was built in the late 1750s by South Carolina's governor to protect the friendly Catawba Indians in the area from attacks by the Shawnee and Cherokee tribes. In 1775, a gristmill was erected on Steele Creek.

In addition to its Native American heritage, Fort Mill has an interesting colonial past that can be traced through its remaining historic sites. These include the Spratt family graveyard, Spratt's Spring where General Cornwallis camped during the American Revolution, Confederate Park, Springfield Plantation and White Homestead.

The town remains fairly untouched by development. A crescent of land to the north of town was purchased by textile manufacturer Elliott Springs during Revolutionary times. It remains with the Close family (Springs' descendants) who have placed 2,200 acres in a land trust, creating the Anne S. Close Greenway, and have planned for careful development of the remaining property.

Fort Mill has approximately 5,600 residents and is close to the major population centers of Rock Hill and Charlotte. Residents enjoy the amenities of the Leroy Springs Recreation Complex, which includes an indoor-outdoor swimming pool, tennis courts, handball courts, ball fields, billiard room, exercise rooms, saunas, whirlpool, hiking/jogging trails, picnic areas and arts and crafts instruction. Paramount's Carowinds and the Museum of York County are also nearby.

Fort Mill is the home of the Charlotte Knights, the AAA home team of the Florida Marlins' baseball team. Knights Stadium is a $15-million facility, which opened in 1990. It seats 10,000 and is located on I-77 S. and Gold Hill Road, just 1 mile past Carowinds Boulevard.

Gastonia

When the railroad came to Gastonia, textile mills and other manufacturing companies followed. The town blossomed into a city with a current population of almost 62,000 residents. Today Gaston County has 488 manufacturing firms and is one of the foremost counties in the country in the number of cotton bales and man-made fibers consumed in textile mills as well as in the number of operational textile spindles.

Home decorators throughout North and South Carolina have purchased upholstery and drapery fabric at either Luxury Fabrics or Mary Jo's Fabric Store. That's how good the prices and selection are at these two Gastonia stores. But fabric isn't Gastonia or Gaston County's only draw. The Schiele Museum, one of the most visited museums in the Carolinas, houses the largest collection of land mammal specimens in the Southeast. It has a reconstructed Catawba Indian village and an 18th-century farm. The museum also features a 360-degree planetarium.

Men especially will enjoy the C. Grier Beam Truck Museum located between Gastonia and Kings Mountain in the town of Cherryville. It has a good display of the original trucks (some from 1927) that transported foods and merchandise over our highways. The history of trucking is well chronicled, explaining its growth and development from 1931 through the '90s. Cherryville is also the site of the only four extant paintings of the American Tobacco Company's famous bull that advertised the Bull Durham brand. The bull was painted in 1910 and covered with plaster for 80 years before being restored.

Take a day to visit Cleveland County's Kings Mountain National Military Park (about 10 miles southwest in South Carolina). This marks the spot where our countrymen broke apart Britain's southern campaign, capturing 1,100 Tories. Midway between Gastonia and Kings Mountain is Crowders Mountain State Park. You can get in a little rock climbing here and wander through its beautiful hiking trails. The mountain has been designated as a N.C. Scenic Byway.

Military buffs will want to take a Sunday afternoon to visit the American Military Museum of Gastonia. Here you'll find uniforms and artifacts from every war from the Civil War to Desert Storm, plus a diorama of Pearl Harbor under Japanese attack. A

Photo by Robert Thomason

The County Courthouse is a well-known landmark in Gastonia.

few miles away in Dallas, be sure to take in the Gaston County Museum of Art & History. This museum gives you a great insight into what life was like in the agricultural, then textile environment of the 19th century. It features the largest public collection of horse-drawn vehicles in North Carolina.

There's also wide emphasis on the arts in Gaston County. Theater groups include the Gastonia Little Theatre, Belmont Playmakers, Gaston Children's Theatre and Cherryville Little ·Theatre. Gastonia has a small symphony as well as a choral society. The Starving Artists Festival in September and Serendipity in the Park and the Phoenix Air Show in October draw thousands of visitors to the area. If you've ever wondered why many seafood restaurants are called "fish camps," take in the annual Fish Camp Jam in downtown Gastonia in October and you'll understand why.

Indian Trail

Indian Trail was so named for the Native American Indian path that ran straight through it from Petersburg, Virginia, to Waxhaw in the 1800s. It's east of Charlotte about 1 mile off N.C. 74 (Independence Boulevard) on Indian Trail Road. When the town incorporated in 1907, it was designed as a circle extending a half-mile in all directions from a point in the center of the railroad tracks at the intersection of the main street. Today the town stretches for miles. Like so many tiny towns, Indian Trail was just a place to stop along the road until the railroad came through in 1874 connecting it with Charlotte and Monroe. Cotton bales lined the railway platforms for many years and the town had a fine gin. Stores, churches, a sawmill and a brickyard made this a thriving community until the Great Depression of 1929. Then times were lean until World War II.

Indian Trail still retains its rural beauty and many dedicated citizens are the third and fourth generation in the community. Although Indian Trail is considered a Charlotte bedroom community, it's actually located in Union County. The town has a mayor and a five-member city council.

Kannapolis

Kannapolis was restored to a New England-style village in the early '80s, adding charm to this southern mill town. Like its neighbor Concord, Kannapolis was settled by the same wholesome Dutch, Irish, German and Scots stock. These basically agrarian people were "tickled pink" when James Cannon bought a 600-acre former cotton plantation 7 miles north of his first plant in Concord to build another textile plant. Cannon laid out an entire village which he called Kannapolis, a combination of two Greek words meaning "City of Looms." It also meant steady employment for hundreds of families.

As in Concord, the mill-town influence is becoming a thing of the past, but evidence is still around. For a glimpse of the past, visit the Fieldcrest Cannon Museum and Exhibition at the Cannon Village Visitor Center. This exhibit includes the world's largest towel, an antique hand loom, samples of textiles that are more than 1,200 years old, a hands-on demonstration of sheet fabric printing, an interactive touch-screen monitor that details textile manufacturing processes and a pictorial description that explains how a towel is made. The exhibit also includes a 20-minute multi-image show conducted in a 100-seat theater.

People used to go to Kannapolis to buy towels by the pound. Today they make a day of shopping for everything imaginable in Cannon Village with its national outlets, boutiques, specialty shops and restaurants. There are 44 different stores anchored by the Fieldcrest-Cannon Bed and Bath Outlet, the first outlet store. As might be expected, Fieldcrest-Cannon, purchased by Pillowtex Corporation in September 1997, is the city's largest employer, providing jobs for 9,000 area residents.

In 1995, a state-of-the-art baseball stadium was constructed in Kannapolis as the new home of the Piedmont Boll Weevils, the class A affiliate of the Philadelphia Phillies.

The population of the city is approximately 35,000. Kannapolis is within 15 to 35 minutes of six colleges and universities, including Rowan Community College, Catawba College and Davidson College. The Rowan-Cabarrus Community College South Campus is near Kannapolis.

Lake Wylie, S.C.

When Native American Siouan tribes separated from their parent tribes to move southward, they settled in the fertile valley of the Catawba river that lies between the North and South Carolina borders. These Native Americans called themselves Kawahcatawbas, which translates to "The People of the River." Today the new settlers who make their homes on that river, now called Lake Wylie, are also "The People of the River." They don't draw their livelihood from the river as the Catawba Indians did, but they are drawn to the river for the sense of renewal and completeness that it gives their lives.

Lake Wylie is named for Dr. W. Gill Wylie, the doctor who convinced Ben and Buck Duke to invest in a hydroelectric power operation on the Catawba River. In 1904, Wylie brought in his engineer, William S. Lee, to design the $8 million project that would convert water power into energy from the proposed 12,455-acre lake. The lake's waters were mud red in those early days when lots were leased to power company employees for $45 a year.

There are restaurants, marinas and two shopping centers near the lake. You can sail or motor up to the lake entrance of the Daniel Stowe Botanical Garden.

Lake Wylie really began to develop residentially in the '70s when two major developments were built, giving area residents the option of living at the lake and working in Charlotte or Rock Hill. Many new neighborhoods have sprung up, but the first developments, River Hills Plantation and Tega Cay, continue to be sought after by "river people" who add golf and tennis to water recreation.

Neighbors and visitors use Lake Wylie's beautiful 325 miles of shoreline to sail, water ski, swim, fish and participate in boat races and sailing regattas. You'll find that marinas are a good source of information on activities in the area and offer a full range of services and storage facilities for your boat. There is a public access boat ramp at McDowell Park. You can drop anchor in a quiet cove and enjoy a picnic lunch.

McAdenville

Nearly two million people come to see the lights at McAdenville every Christmas. This tradition began over 35 years ago when the Men's Club of McAdenville asked for a meeting with the owners of Stowe-Pharr Mill.

The Town of McAdenville is also known as "Christmastown USA."

The members asked the mill owners what they thought about the idea of generating Christmas spirit by decorating a few trees around town. Both Mr. Stowe and Mr. Pharr not only supported the idea but offered to pay for the decorations and electricity. Those nine decorated trees have grown every year to now include almost every tree in town, making this tiny town of 830 people "Christmastown USA." During the holidays the town is transformed by thousands of lights — a sight you shouldn't miss. You'll find the reflection of red, blue, green and white lights upon the little pond near the town's center especially beautiful.

This is a classic mill town located on the South Fork River only about 15 minutes away from Charlotte and it has changed very little since it was built in the 1800s. The entire town, complete with shops, churches, schools and houses, is owned by Pharr Yarns.

Monroe

The 1886 Union County Courthouse, which dominates the town square and the 1847 Monroe City Hall are part of the National Register District of downtown Monroe. Whenever filmmakers need authentic small-town courthouses of yesteryear, they head for Monroe. The town has several other historic structures of note, including a Seaboard Railroad Station and many residential structures. The earliest inhabitants of the area were the Waxhaw Native Americans. They were followed by German, English and Scots-Irish settlers in the 1800s. Union County was carved out of Anson and Mecklenburg counties in 1842 and the city of Monroe was incorporated in 1844.

The area has many diverse industries — manufacturing facilities for heat-treated metal alloys, door closers, automobile and aircraft parts and textiles. The area is also known for its production of poultry, soybeans, corn, beef, swine, cotton and other products. Wingate University, a four-year institution with a unique approach to education, is located in nearby Wingate. Theater, music and the visual arts flourish in Monroe.

Mooresville

In Iredell County, before 1857, twenty-five residents of a dusty little wide place in the road, known as Shepherd's Crossroads, met with officials from the Atlantic, Tennessee and Ohio Railroad who wanted to build a railroad depot in the center of their community. John Moore, a wealthy farmer and merchant, was the only one willing to donate land for the depot and a cotton-weighing platform. Consequently, the crossroads was renamed Moore's Siding (later changed to Mooresville). The North Carolina General Assembly appointed commissioners to lay out the town "with town limits one mile as the crow flies in every direction from said depot," which split the town evenly down the middle on either side of the railroad tracks. Moore insisted that the proposed 60-foot-wide streets be changed to 40-foot widths so they wouldn't cut into his cotton fields and also insisted that Main Street curve away from the railroad tracks in order for him to sit on his front porch after lunch and see if passing wagons were stopping at his store across from the depot.

Except for the absence of wagons and the addition of utility poles, nothing much has changed the architecture or the atmosphere of downtown Mooresville since those early days. The same color awnings and glass front have remained at D.E. Turner Hardware since it moved to its "new location" across from the depot on Main Street in 1902. Inside, the original, now sagging wood floor, same wooden counters and a rolling 20-foot wood ladder make you feel like time has stood still — and that's the way people like it. A frozen treat from Mooresville Ice Cream Company completes this tradition.

The depot has been recycled into an arts center and the town recently dedicated its new Citizen Center, which has an auditorium, exercise pool and banquet facilities for around 500. The North Carolina Auto Racing Hall of Fame, featuring 30 race cars and racing memorabilia, is also here. Mooresville, also officially known as Race City, USA™, is home to close to 50 of NASCAR's top racing teams and related racing businesses. Some of Winston Cup's highest-caliber teams are based in Mooresville, such as Penske Racing South, SABCO, Rudd Performance Motorsports, Rousch Racing and many more, making it a racing fan's top choice to visit.

The town's growth area is a few miles north on N.C. 150 where shopping malls, fast-food establishments and motels have sprung up in the last few years. The influx of such Japanese industries as Matsushita and NGK have added a cultural resource to the community's growing industrial sector.

Mount Holly

The town derives its name from the mill established there by the Rhyne family. This is where Gaston County's textile empire began. Today textiles continue to dominate the town. It now boasts several textile manufacturers and supports companies that make textile dyes and chemicals. As is true in many textile towns, loyalty to church and civic clubs is a reaffirmation of the residents' fine work-ethic values.

Rock Hill, S.C.

Just 20 minutes south of Charlotte is Rock Hill, South Carolina, a growing community with an active business climate and educational opportunities. Rock Hill has four industrial parks and the busiest general aviation airport in the area. The city has over 200 manufacturing businesses, producing everything from pneumatic hand tools to egg rolls to textiles. York Technical College provides training for many area industries. The city is also home to Winthrop University, a four-year institution with undergraduate and graduate programs.

Settled in the 1800s and now a part of South Carolina's Olde English District (see Daytrips and Weekends chapter), Rock Hill is rich in history. Two sites that Charlotteans enjoy visiting are Glencairn Garden and the Museum of York County. Once the private garden of Dr. and Mrs. David A. Bigger, Glencairn Garden was opened to the public in 1960. It is also a popular site during the annual Come-See-Me Festival, an 11-day spring event that features exhibits, concerts, gourmet gardens, crafts, road and bicycle

Photo by Tim Johnson

Many Charlotteans attend Winthrop University located in nearby Rock Hill.

races, children's events, a parade and fireworks. Vernon Grant, the creator of Kellogg's Rice Krispies' Snap, Crackle and Pop, designed the frog that serves as the festival's emblem.

The Museum of York County's wild animal collection is one of the most comprehensive anywhere. Featured are animals from Africa, North America and South America. The museum also devotes space to exhibits on York County, Indian tribes of the area, photography and traveling shows. The Settlemyre Planetarium and the Rock Hill Telephone Company Museum are also popular with visitors. The Rock Hill Transportation Exhibit, located downtown, features an Anderson 640 touring car made by the Anderson Motor Company in 1915.

Salisbury

Two-and-a-half centuries ago, Salisbury was the jumping-off point for pioneers, visionaries and even a few scoundrels and fugitives who were on their way to the American frontier. When General Nathanael Greene rode into Salisbury in 1781, he stopped off at Mrs. Elizabeth Maxwell Steele's tavern. After Mrs. Steele heard of the pitiful conditions of Greene's troops, she gave him two small sacks of money for provisions. As he accepted the gift, the General saw the portraits of King George III and Queen Charlotte on the tavern wall. He turned the picture of the king to the

wall and wrote on the back with a piece of chalk: "O George! Hide thy face and mourne." Today you can find those portraits, with the inscription still legible, hanging at the Thyatira Presbyterian Church. In the church cemetery, a monument marks the grave of Mrs. Steele.

A century ago Salisbury and nearby Spencer were important stops on Southern Railway's line. Salisbury's Spanish mission-style train station designed by Frank Pierce Milburn in 1907 has been beautifully restored and now serves as the home of the Historic Salisbury Foundation, Inc.

Trains are also the focus of the N.C. Transportation Museum, once the largest steam locomotive repair facility between Washington, D.C., and Atlanta. Also worth a visit is O.O. Rufty's General Store, located on E. Innes Street. You'll have fun in this store. It still carries everything from horseshoes to hunting caps. Take note of the nails in the floor that are still used to measure the lengths of cord. If you visit on a Saturday or Sunday afternoon, take a tour of Dr. Josephus Hall's Home. He was the doctor for the nearby Confederate prison. The home was requisitioned by General Stoneman during the Civil War. Mrs. Hall, who etched her name in a window glass to prove ownership of this lovely mansion, instructed Stoneman to keep his soldiers' horses off her boxwood path borders. The boxwoods, as well as the home's interior, remain intact.

The courthouse in Salisbury reflects the character of the historic district.

Twenty-three blocks comprise the National Register Historic District , whose character has been saved by the Historic Salisbury Foundation, Inc. Several historic buildings are open to the public any time of the year, but you can get into private homes only during the annual Historic Salisbury October Tour. Crafts are also demonstrated at this time. Another good time to visit the city is during the Christmas season when some of the historic buildings are decorated for the holidays.

This active community always has something going on such as the Autumn Jubilee. There is also the National Sportscasters & Sportswriters Hall of Fame Awards and a full season of concerts with a full-scale symphony orchestra. You'll find an art gallery, a sensory garden for the visually impaired, choral groups, a community theater and three outstanding colleges: Catawba, Livingstone and Rowan Cabarrus Community College. You'll also find historic buildings such as the 1819 Rowan Museum, the CLDL Stone House built in 1766 and the 1839 Salisbury Female Academy. Rowan County has some fine parks and recreational areas. One worth the drive from Charlotte is Dan Nicholas Park.

The Visitors Center, 132 E. Innes St., is open Monday through Friday from 9 AM until 5 PM, Saturday from 10 AM until 4 PM, and Sunday from 1 until 4 PM. Here you'll find brochures on the Salisbury Heritage Tour (a self-guided tour of 95 historic buildings and sites), audio tape guided tours and information on Volkswalk, a historic 10K walk that is sponsored by the Tar Heel State Walkers Volkssport Association of the American Volkssport Association. While in town, plan to see the 127' x 48.5' mural painted on the side of Wachovia Bank & Trust, the largest mural in the state, which depicts Salisbury's heritage at the turn of the century.

There's a lot of old money in Salisbury. Residents have made their fortunes in textiles and chemicals. Salisbury is also where Food Lion, Inc., the nationally known supermarket chain, began and is headquartered.

Statesville

Pioneer John Edwards purchased a land grant from the Earl of Granville in 1751 for this land. At first the settlers described their new community as Fourth Creek, meaning the fourth creek west of Salisbury. The name is still retained in the Fourth Creek Presbyterian Church and Burying Ground. Four years later, Governor Arthur Dobbs chose the area for a fort to safeguard settlers from French and Indian attacks. The fort, named after Dobbs, successfully repelled a Cherokee attack but was later abandoned and fell into ruin. You can see artifacts on display at the fort's Visitors Center.

In 1789, the town was incorporated as Statesville. There are two theories on the origin of the new name: one says the early pioneers desired to honor the original 13 states and the other says it was named for the stopover for travelers on the then famous States Road.

The town prides itself on three historic districts and the historic downtown, which is centered at the square. The only original building still standing downtown is the Statesville Drug Company with its signature clock on top. The clock, costing $500 in 1890, was renovated in 1990 and its chime can be heard on the hour and half hour. Statesville has many homes and buildings listed in the National Register of Historic Places and is undergoing a Main Street transformation that has already made great progress in returning much of the city's original design. Mitchell Community College is located in the heart of one historic district that features 170 buildings.

The Zebulon Vance Home, where Governor Vance lived and practiced law, is here. This 1832 house, which is open to the public, served as his headquarters during his exile from the state Capitol in Raleigh during the last months of the Civil War.

Although Statesville is historic, it doesn't live in the past. The old textile plants have been replaced by German machinery manufacturers, Japanese engine manufacturers, a plastic recycling plant and a movie production company. Statesville's Balloon Works is the largest manufacturer of hot air balloons. What started out as a small pig pickin' for eight balloonists and 300 spectators in 1973 has become the nationally recognized Hot Air Balloon Rally that draws 50 balloonists and a crowd of over 30,000 every year. It's an event you don't want to miss.

In 1997, Statesville, out of 120 cities that had applied, was named the All-American City by the National Civic League. Three community projects helped Statesville receive the honor: Save the Depot, a restoration project; CommuniCare, an after-school tutoring program for minority children; and the Open Door Clinic, a clinic built and paid for by volunteers and located at the shelter that provides free medical care to the homeless. On top of all that, Statesville is a nice place to live and educate children.

Tega Cay, S.C.

With excellent schools and strong community spirit, Tega Cay is a wonderful place to raise a family or even retire. It is located on the east side of Lake Wylie just 15 miles south of Charlotte. The name "Tega Cay" means "beautiful peninsula" in Polynesian, and the South Seas theme was carried out in the street names and in the architecture of this picturesque area. Incorporated on July 4, 1982, the city has 16 miles of shoreline, a rugged topography and is densely wooded with tall pines and hardwoods. Each Fourth of July, the city celebrates its birthday with ceremonies, parades, fireworks and the cutting of a birthday cake made in honor of our country's birthday.

Waxhaw

Most people come to this quaint area of south Union County near the South Carolina border for the antiques. More than 18 antique

shops are open just about every day year round and more are open on weekends. If you tire of looking for treasures, consider some of the other sites. Six miles to the east is the Mexico-Cardenas Museum at JAARS (Jungle Aviation and Radio Service). The museum honors Lázaro Cardenas, Mexico's former president, who was a close associate of JAARS founder Cameron Townsend. The museum offers a glimpse into the work of this unique world organization that has about 250 specialists translating the Bible into languages all over the world. Or you might head to Cane Creek Park, a 1,000-acre recreation facility surrounding a large lake. It offers camping, boating, fishing and picnicking. The Andrew Jackson Museum has a large display of historic artifacts. An annual military reenactment is staged with the museum's assistance.

Some folks take regular trips to Waxhaw to eat at the Bridge and Rail Restaurant. If you like country food, this is the place to visit. The helpings are large and the atmosphere in this historic setting is ideal. The walls are filled with photographs of Waxhaw's past.

A number of special events are also worth a visit: the Waxhaw Woman's Club Antique Show, the last full weekend in February; *Listen and Remember,* an outdoor drama that tells the story of President Andrew Jackson and the Waxhaw Native Americans, performed each weekend in June; the Old Hickory Classic Festival in the spring and late summer; and the Scottish Fair in October featuring bagpipes and traditional Scottish game competitions. Be sure to wear your plaid!

York, S.C.

State brochures proclaim York the "Charleston of the Upcountry" and rightly so. York, the county seat, is a part of South Carolina's Olde English District (see Daytrips and Weekends chapter) and boasts 46 historic sites dating from 1790 to the early 1900s. The U.S. Department of the Interior has designated York as one of the largest historic districts in the country. Near York are Kings Mountain National Military Park and Historic Brattonsville, known for its early American architecture.

From budget motels to luxury hotels, Charlotte offers business and leisure travelers numerous choices.

Accommodations

Charlotte's popularity as a travel destination is evident in the steady increase in hotel rooms provided in the county. From budget motels to luxury hotels, Charlotte offers business and leisure travelers numerous choices.

If you are a first-time visitor and want to bring your pet, you need to be aware that under North Carolina law pets are not allowed in hotels and motels although some places make provisions or allowances for them. Keep in mind that during special events, home games or large conventions the availability of rooms in certain areas may be limited or in some cases nonexistent. So plan ahead and make your reservations as soon as you know when you'll be visiting this top travel destination.

Price Code

For the purposes of comparing prices, we have categorized accommodations with one to four dollar signs ($) based on the typical daily rates charged for a standard room with two double beds — weekend rates are usually less and some hotels offer attractive weekend packages. Keep in mind that these rates are subject to change; however, to give you a rough idea of what to expect, we offer the following guide:

$	$31 to $50
$$	$51 to $75
$$$	$76 to $100
$$$$	More than $100

Since Bed and Breakfasts have become so popular, they have been given their own chapter (see Bed and Breakfasts chapter). If you are intending to stay more than a week, you may enjoy residing at an extended-stay facility (see Apartments and Temporary Housing chapter).

Hotels and Motels

Adam's Mark Hotel
$$$ • 555 S. McDowell St. • 372-4100

Overlooking Marshall Park and the Mecklenburg Aquatic Center, this large convention hotel is within short commuting distance of the Uptown financial district. It's very spacious with 598 rooms, 37 suites and large meeting spaces. It also has the best view of the Charlotte skyline anywhere in town. The hotel has added a $6-million, 16,000-square-foot ballroom, doubling its meeting space and allowing it to handle an increased number of convention bookings. Bravo! and Appleby's are well-known restaurants located in the hotel and its high-energy nightclub, CJ's, is one of the city's most popular late-night spots. Guests may enjoy the Nautilus-equipped health club, indoor pool, whirlpools, saunas and convenient parking.

Arena Inn
$ • 3000 E. Independence Blvd. • 377-1501

This 176-room hotel is conveniently located next to the Merchandise Mart and Ovens Auditorium. It has reasonably priced rooms with parking by your door. Guests can eat at Valentino's Restaurant and enjoy swimming in the large hotel pool. The hotel offers its guests lounge as well as health and fitness club privileges.

Best Western Airport Hotel
$$-$$$ • 2707 Little Rock Rd. • 394-4301

This 215-room hotel near the airport caters to corporate clients. It houses a lively lounge called Razzles and an attractive dining room, The Greenery, which features piano music. There is an indoor spa, heated outdoor pool and meeting space for up to 200. All guests receive free airport shuttle service.

Best Western Luxbury Inns
$$-$$$ • 4904 N. I-85 • 596-9229
9701 E. Independence Blvd. • 845-5911

Especially popular with corporate clients, these 98-room/suite inns offer luxury accommodations at economy prices. Guests enjoy a complimentary breakfast in the pink marble lobby, cable TV, free *USA Today* newspaper, a swimming pool and small meeting rooms. The East Independence location offers free local calls.

Charlotte Hilton at University Place
$$$-$$$$ • University Place • 547-7444

This modern property is located in the center of University Place, a European-style village of shops, theaters and restaurants. It offers 243 rooms, meeting rooms, lakeside lounges, an exercise room, outdoor pool and continental breakfast on weekends. It is also convenient to the Blockbuster Pavilion.

Charlotte Hilton Executive Park
$$$$ • 5624 Westpark Dr. • 527-8000

Located at Tyvola Road Exit 5 off I-77, this is a full-service hotel with 178 spacious guest rooms, including 34 one-bedroom suites. The Cafe on the Veranda serves breakfast, lunch and dinner and the Gershwin Lobby Bar is available for cocktails and piano music. This Hilton offers 10,000 square feet of meeting space with a beautiful courtyard area for outdoor functions. An exercise facility is available as well as a heated outdoor pool and Jacuzzi. Located only 6 miles from the airport, the hotel provides complimentary airport transportation.

Charlotte Marriott City Center
$$$$ • 100 W. Trade St. • 333-9000

The Marriott City Center sits on the corner of Trade and Tryon streets in the heart of the city on the spot once occupied by North Carolina's first skyscraper. It features an atrium that links shops and offices in Independence Center. The hotel has 431 guest rooms and suites, a health club, indoor pool and Champions sports bar. The hotel's restaurant, J.W.'s Steakhouse, has recently added a cigar bar.

Charlotte Marriott at Executive Park
$$$$ • I-77 and Tyvola Rd. • 527-9650

Designed with both large and small meetings in mind, the Charlotte Marriott at Executive Park has 297 rooms, 8 parlors plus the Presidential suite, an indoor/outdoor pool, an exercise room and tennis courts. Locals and out-of-towners mix at Gratzi Bar and Grille. Nonrefundable, reduced rates are available with 14-day advance bookings.

Comfort Inn Lake Norman
$$-$$$ • 20740 Torrence Chapel Rd., Cornelius • 892-3500, (800) 228-5150

This Comfort Inn and its sister inns in Monroe, Matthews and Concord/Kannapolis are all owned and operated by Inn Development and Management. All offer good service and quite a few amenities that you won't find elsewhere, such as in-room coffee makers, refrigerators and safes, some in-room Jacuzzis, an exercise facility and a free deluxe continental breakfast. The inns also offer free popcorn, apples, newspapers and more. The Lake Norman Inn is only 3 miles from the lake. Other Comfort Inns are located at the airport and Westpark Drive.

Photo by Tim Johnson

The Charlotte Hilton at University Place offers relaxing lakeside lounges.

Courtyard by Marriott

$$$-$$$$ • 800 E. Arrowood Rd. • 527-5055
SouthPark • 552-7333
University City • 549-4888

These economy to mid-priced motels were built with the business traveler in mind. Each Courtyard features an attractive small lobby and lounge, Courtyard Cafe restaurant (serving breakfast daily), a swimming pool, whirlpool and exercise room.

Days Inn

$-$$ • (800) DAYS INN
Airport, I-85 & Billy Graham Pkwy. • 394-3381
Carowinds, 3482 Carowinds Blvd. • 332-9354
Downtown, 601 N. Tryon St. • 333-4733
Sugar Creek, 1408 Sugar Creek Rd. • 597-8110
Sunset, I-77 N. & Sunset Rd. • 598-7712
Woodlawn, 118 E. Woodlawn Rd. • 525-5500

Although all of these locations are Days Inns, they are not all owned by the same companies and amenities vary.

Doubletree Club Hotel

$$$$ • 895 W. Trade St. • 347-0070

Located just west of Uptown, the Doubletree has 187 rooms. This modern hotel offers a full-service health club, outdoor pool and meeting rooms. Casual dining is available in Orchards Restaurant. All guests receive free Doubletree chocolate chip cookies. A free shuttle to Uptown and shopping is available weekdays.

Dunhill Hotel

$$$$ • 237 N. Tryon St. • 332-4141

The 1929 Dunhill Hotel is one of Charlotte's few remaining landmark hotels. Its 60 guest rooms are elegantly furnished in 18th-century decor. Some rooms have a Jacuzzi and a sitting area. Room service is available from its Monticello Restaurant. Computer-compatible phones and fax facilities are also available.

Econo Lodge

$-$$ • I-85 at Sugar Creek Rd. • 597-0470

This is an economy motel — one of four in the city and one of 400 in the nation, for which Charlotte serves as headquarters. Other properties are located on Clanton Road, on Westpark Drive and I-85 at Little Rock Road.

Embassy Suites

$$$$ • 4800 S. Tryon St. • 527-8400

Embassy Suites has 274 two-room suites and 10,000 square feet of meeting space. The hotel features P.J. McKenzie's restaurant and lounge, indoor pool, whirlpool, sauna and exercise facility. Guest suites have two TVs, two telephones, a coffee maker with coffee, a microwave and a mini refrigerator. Guests receive a complimentary cooked-to-order breakfast, manager's reception each evening and complimentary airport shuttle service.

Fairfield Inn by Marriott

$-$$ • I-85 and Sugar Creek Rd. • 596-2999

This is Marriott's version of an economy motel, but with some special touches such as large, well-lit work areas in the rooms. Guests receive complimentary coffee and tea each morning, free local calls and cable TV. There's also an outdoor pool for relaxation. Frequent travelers often join the INNsiders Club, which gives them special privileges. Another Fairfield Inn is located near the airport, 392-0600.

Staff photo

The Hyatt Hotel at Southpark offers luxurious accommodations and special amenities in a convenient location.

The Four Points Hotel

$$$$ • 201 S. McDowell St. • 372-7550

Formerly the Government House Hotel, this full-service hotel offers 195 rooms and meeting space and is convenient to Uptown Charlotte and McDowell Park. The hotel has Wellington's Restaurant and the Hunt Club and Tavern.

Hampton Inn

$$-$$$ • I-77 Executive Park • 525-0747
I-85 and Billy Graham Pkwy. • 392-1600
8419 U.S. 29, University Place • 548-0905
Statesville Rd., Cornelius • 892-9900
9615 Independence Pt. Pkwy. • 841-1155

These five economy inns offer quality accommodations, value pricing, free extras and a 100% Satisfaction Guarantee. Free extras include an outstanding continental breakfast, local telephone calls and airport transportation. The I-77 Executive Park location has an exercise facility and an outdoor pool.

Hilton Charlotte

$$$$ • 222 E. Third St. • 377-1500

Charlotte's fourth-largest hotel is also one of the most striking and boasts the city's largest ballroom. Located directly across from the Convention Center, the Hilton caters to a mostly business clientele, providing complimentary coffee and newspaper for its club members. The 410 rooms, plus privileges at the YMCA Health Club, meeting facilities and Alfiere's Restaurant, make this hotel a good Uptown choice.

Holiday Inn Center City

$$$$ • 230 N. College St. • 335-5400

This inn, adjoining the Charlotte International Trade Center, has 300 guest rooms, 28 suites, a complimentary fitness room and jogging track, indoor parking, a rooftop pool and spa. Complete dining facilities are available at the Starlight Cafe and guests can relax at the newly renovated Matthews Pub. You can pick up something special in the hotel gift shop and make travel arrangements through the inn's travel agency.

Holiday Inn Independence
$$ • 3501 E. Independence Blvd. • 537-1010

Newly renovated, with 176 rooms and three meeting rooms, this hotel near the old Coliseum and the Charlotte Merchandise Mart is making a quick comeback. The Library serves three meals a day. Marilyn's Lounge memorializes the famous Hollywood actress, Marilyn Monroe.

Holiday Inn University Executive Park
$$$$ • 8520 University Executive Park Dr. • 547-0999

Located across from University Place in northeast Charlotte, this hotel is convenient to the University Research Park, UNC Charlotte, Charlotte Motor Speedway and Blockbuster Pavilion. Business professionals love this seven-story hotel, as each of its 177 rooms has a work desk, direct-dial telephone, computer/fax hookup, complimentary newspapers and other extras. Each of its two suites also has a coffee maker and refrigerator. Guests staying on the Crown Executive floor get even more amenities, including express check-in and check-out. Meeting/banquet facilities and equipment are available.

Dining is offered in Mr. P's Restaurant and Lounge and a number of good restaurants are located in the area. The hotel also offers an outdoor lap pool, whirlpool, sauna and exercise facilities.

Holiday Inn Woodlawn
$$$ • 212 Woodlawn Rd. • 525-8350

With 425 guest rooms and over 17,000 square feet of meeting and banquet facilities, this hotel is Charlotte's third largest. One of the most outstanding features of the hotel is its atrium. Characterized by tranquil gardens and reflection pools, it houses both a casual restaurant and a lovely pre-function area. O'Hara's, one of Charlotte's liveliest nightspots, features live entertainment and complimentary hors d'oeuvres. Other amenities include a state-of-the-art exercise facility, swimming pool, airline ticket office and complimentary limousine service to and from the airport.

Homewood Suites
$$$-$$$$ • 8340 N. Tryon St. • 549-8800

This spacious, apartment-style suite hotel is comfortably furnished with all the features and amenities you expect and some that may surprise you. Separate sleeping and living areas, two remote-controlled color TVs and a videocassette player are standard. A complimentary deluxe breakfast buffet is served daily with an

The Radisson Plaza Hotel is connected to an indoor mall of shops and restaurants.

evening social hour that includes a light meal. You can work off stress at the exercise center, sports/activity court, swimming pool or whirlpool.

Hyatt Hotel
$$$$ • 5501 Carnegie Blvd. • 554-1234

All 262 rooms of this SouthPark area Hyatt are beautifully appointed. The hotel has an indoor pool, sauna and fitness club. Each room comes with a hairdryer and a coffee maker. The Hyatt also boasts one of the best Italian restaurants in town, Scalini, and offers 24-hour room service. You will like the hotel's free valet parking and complimentary airport shuttle service. This is an elegant place to stay and you'll appreciate the helpful and friendly staff.

La Quinta Inn-Airport
$$ • 3100 S. I-85 Service Rd. • 393-5306

This economy motel on the west side of town is close to restaurants and the airport and is within easy distance of major Charlotte attractions. Guests receive free, unlimited local calls, satellite TV, continental breakfast, 24-hour coffee in the lobby, a courtesy van to and from the airport and other specials. There is an outdoor pool and restaurant nearby. Another La Quinta is located on Nations Ford Road near I-77, 522-7110.

The Park Hotel
$$$$ • 2200 Rexford Rd. • 364-8220

The Park Hotel's extraordinary staff, dedicated to personal service and attention to detail, makes every stay memorable. Located in the heart of SouthPark, this hotel exemplifies gracious living. Although the hotel has 194 rooms and space for small meetings, there's an intimacy here you don't find in a regular hotel. Oversized guest rooms are decorated in 18 different combinations of color and fabric with 18th-century pieces and original lithography commissioned by the hotel. Guests dine in Morrocrofts, an authentic New York-style restaurant, and lunch is served on the patio. The hotel features a full-service fitness center, an outdoor swimming pool, complimentary daily newspapers, airport limousine service and turndown service with chocolates left on the down pillows.

Quality Inn & Suites CrownPoint
$$-$$$ • 2501 Sardis Rd. N. • 845-2810

Located on Charlotte's east side near shops and restaurants, this hotel offers 100 rooms and suites and meeting space. Guests receive free local calls and a complimentary deluxe continental breakfast.

Radisson Plaza Hotel
$$$$ • 101 S. Tryon St. • 377-0400

Completely remodeled, this 365-room Uptown hotel offers many outstanding features. Guests enjoy the luxury of the Lobby Court Lounge featuring TV sets, a pool table and board games. The hotel offers a complete breakfast and a light evening meal, plus drinks and bedtime cookies and milk. The same amenities are offered on the 14th floor. The most expensive room in the house is named for comedian Bob Hope. Located on the lobby level, Azaleas serves breakfast, lunch and dinner, plus a luncheon buffet. A short walk from the escalator is the entrance to the Overstreet Mall, an indoor mall featuring over 100 shops and six restaurants. Radisson Plaza guests may use the hotel's exercise facility and the adjoining Tower Athletic Club at no additional charge.

Ramada Inn Carowinds
$$ • 225 Carowinds Blvd., Ft. Mill, S.C.
• 334-4450

This 210-room Ramada Inn sits directly across the street from Paramount's Carowinds theme park and Outlet Marketplace shopping center. Complimentary shuttle service is offered to Paramount's Carowinds and the airport. Amenities include a swimming pool, fitness center, Jacuzzi, sauna and game room. Children under 18 stay free and the hotel welcomes small pets. Mini-suites are available. Madeline's is a full-service restaurant and serves a free breakfast to guests on weekdays. The hotel also has a lounge, plus banquet and meeting rooms.

Red Roof Inn
$-$$ • I-85 at Billy Graham Pkwy. • 392-2316
I-77 at Nations Ford Rd. • 529-1020
1-85 and Sugar Creek Rd. • 596-8222

At the Red Roof Inn, you get a few extras that most economy motels don't offer — free morning coffee and a weekday newspaper, free ESPN, CNN and first-run movies and unlimited local calls. The 85-room inn at Billy Graham Parkway is located near the airport.

Residence Inn by Marriott
$$$-$$$$ • 5800 Westpark Dr. • 527-8110

This 80-suite hotel near Tyvola Road and I-77 doesn't look like a hotel, but it's a great place to hang your hat for a few days. Each one- and two-bedroom suite comes with a fully equipped kitchen, living room, wood-burning fireplace, one or two baths and a private entrance. Guests can also enjoy access to an outdoor heated pool, a spa and a

sports court. Continental breakfast, satellite television, grocery shopping service and morning newspaper are all complimentary at this Marriott-franchise hotel. Another Marriott property by the same name is located near University Place, 547-1122.

Sheraton Airport Plaza Hotel
$$$$ • I-85 at Billy Graham Pkwy. • 392-1200

This bright, well-appointed luxury hotel is close to the airport and the Coliseum. It offers 222 rooms, executive suites and a Presidential suite, a number of meeting rooms, complimentary airport shuttle, fitness center and indoor/outdoor pool. A daily copy of *USA Today* and a fruit bar are complimentary from 6:30 to 9:30 AM Monday through Friday. You can dine at Oscar's Restaurant.

SouthPark Suite Hotel
$$$$ • 6300 Morrison Blvd. • 364-2400

The 208 one- or two-bedroom luxury suites come with a living room, dining area and fully equipped kitchen. Guests can dine in or buy grocery items in the Market Cafe. The hotel has a health center, outdoor pool and meeting rooms. Airport limousine service is available. Special weekend packages are offered.

Sterling Inn
$$ • 242 E. Woodlawn Rd. • 525-5454

This upscale economy motel may well be one of Charlotte's best-kept secrets. In lieu of meeting rooms and restaurants, the inn focuses on large, comfortable rooms that are tastefully decorated. Guests receive *USA Today* free on weekdays. You'll enjoy a complimentary full continental breakfast in the elegant sunken parlor. A conference room is available upon request. The inn, just off I-77, is near a number of nice restaurants and offers a free shuttle service to the airport.

StudioPLUS
$$-$$$ • 123 E. McCullough Dr. • 510-0108
5830 Westpark Dr. • 527-1960

Each of these 71 efficiency-type suites provides all the comforts of home: fully equipped kitchen featuring a full-sized refrigerator/freezer, microwave, conventional oven and stove, pots and pans, plates, silverware

and appliances. The smallest unit works well for the individual business traveller. For a relocating family, the Studio Deluxe offers a living room area that includes a sleeper sofa. Swimming pool and workout facilities are also available for guests.

Summerfield Suites Hotel
$$$$ • 4920 S. Tryon St. • 525-2600

Only 6 miles from the Charlotte/Douglas International Airport, this 135-room hotel offers a complimentary breakfast buffet and has a complimentary airport shuttle.

Woodlawn Suites Hotel
$$$-$$$$ • 315 East Woodlawn Road • (800) 522-1994

This hotel is conveniently located off I-77 South near the Charlotte Coliseum and the airport. It offers 97 suites for those who may desire more than one room. The hotel provides a complimentary full-service breakfast buffet. An airport shuttle is available to hotel guests at no additional charge. This hotel is particularly attractive to extended-stay travelers.

Wyndham Garden Hotel
$$$-$$$$ • 2600 Yorkmont Rd. • 357-9100

On the south side of town near the Charlotte Coliseum and York Road Renaissance Park, this 173-room hotel caters to individual, corporate and motor coach travelers. Guests may take advantage of the in-room movies, coffee maker and a complimentary copy of *USA Today*. The hotel has a heated lap pool, whirlpool and exercise room. The Garden Cafe provides meals.

CHARLOTTE ACCOMMODATIONS

HOTEL/MOTEL	ADDRESS	AIRPORT	SHUTTLE	PHONE
Adam's Mark	555 S. McDowell St.	$$$	Y	372-4100
AmeriSuites Charlotte	7900 Forest Point Blvd.	$$	Y	522-8400
Arena Inn	3000 E. Independence Blvd.	$	N	377-1501
Best Western Luxury Inn	9701 E. Independence Blvd.	$$-$$$	N	845-5911
Best Western Luxury Inn	4904 N. I-85 Service Rd.	$$-$$$	N	596-9229
Best Western Airport Hotel	2707 Little Rock Rd.	$$-$$$	Y	394-4301
Brookwood Inn	1200 W. Sugar Creek Rd.	$-$$	N	597-8500
Comfort Inn	5822 Westpark Dr.	$$-$$$	N	525-2626
Comfort Inn Airport	4040 S. I-85	$$-$$$	Y	394-4111
Comfort Inn Lk. Norman	20740 Torrence Chapel Rd.	$$-$$$	N	892-3500
Courtyard by Marriott	800 E. Arrowood Rd.	$$$-$$$$	N	527-5055
Days Inn	118 E. Woodlawn Rd.	$-$$	N	525-5500
Doubletree Club Hotel	895 W. Trade St.	$$$$	N	347-0070
Dunhill Hotel	237 N. Tryon St.	$$$$	Y	332-4141
Econo Lodge	I-85 at Sugar Creek Rd.	$-$$	N	597-0470
Embassy Suites	4800 S. Tryon St.	$$$$	Y	527-8400
Fairfield Inn	5415 N. I-85 Service Rd.	$-$$	N	596-2999
Four Points Hotel	201 S. McDowell St.	$$$$	N	372-7550
Hampton Inn	I-77 Executive Park	$$-$$$	Y	525-0747
Hilton at University Place	University Place	$$$-$$$$	N	547-7444
Hilton Charlotte	222 E. Third St.	$$$$	Y	377-1500
Hilton Executive Park	5624 Westpark Dr.	$$$$	Y	527-8000
Holiday Inn Center City	230 N. College St.	$$$$	N	335-5400
Holiday Inn Independence	3501 E. Independence Blvd.	$$	N	537-1010
Holiday Inn University Park	8520 Univ. Exec. Pk. Dr.	$$$$	N	547-0999
Holiday Inn Woodlawn	212 Woodlawn Rd.	$$$	Y	525-8350
Homewood Suites	8340 N. Tryon St.	$$$-$$$$	N	549-8800
Hyatt Hotel	5501 Carnegie Blvd.	$$$$	Y	554-1234
La Quinta Inn-Airport	3100 S. I-85 Service Rd.	$$	Y	393-5306
Marriott City Center	100 W. Trade St.	$$$$	N	333-9000
Marriott Executive Park	5700 Westpark Dr.	$$$$	Y	527-9650
The Park Hotel	2200 Rexford Rd.	$$$$	Y	364-8220
Quality Inn & Suites	2501 Sardis Rd. N.	$$-$$$	N	845-2810
Radisson Plaza Hotel	101 S. Tryon St.	$$$-$$$$	Y	377-0400
Ramada Inn Airport	I-77 at Clanton Rd.	$$	Y	527-3000
Red Roof Inn	I-85 at Billy Graham Pkwy.	$	N	392-2316
Residence Inn	5800 Westpark Dr.	$$$-$$$$	N	527-8110
Sheraton Airport Plaza	I-85 at Billy Graham Pkwy.	$$$$	Y	392-1200
SouthPark Suite Hotel	6300 Morrison Blvd.	$$$$	Y	364-2400
Sterling Inn	242 E. Woodlawn Rd.	$$	Y	525-5454
StudioPLUS-Tyvola	5830 Westpark Dr.	$$-$$$	N	527-1960
StudioPLUS-University	123 E. McCullough Dr.	$$-$$$	N	510-0108
Summerfield Suites Hotel	4920 S. Tryon St.	$$$$	N	525-2600
Woodlawn Suites Hotel	315 E. Woodlawn Rd.	$$$-$$$$	Y	522-0852
Wyndham Garden Hotel	2600 Yorkmont Rd.	$$$-$$$$	Y	357-9100

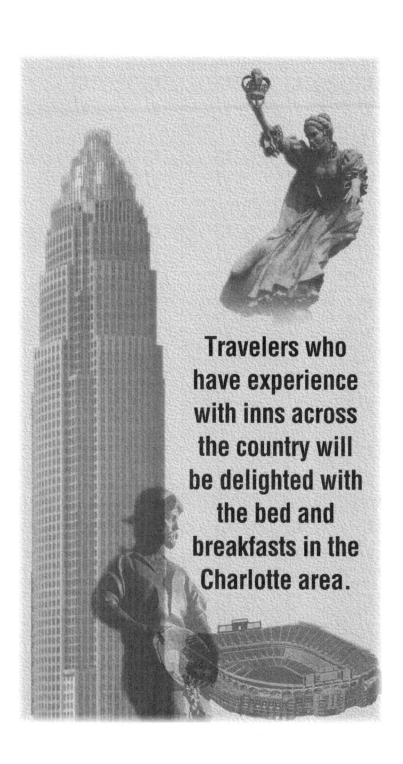

Travelers who have experience with inns across the country will be delighted with the bed and breakfasts in the Charlotte area.

Bed and Breakfasts

Bed and breakfast inns are so popular that they deserve their own chapter. Travelers who have experience with inns across the country will be delighted with the bed and breakfasts in the Charlotte area. If you have yet to stay at a bed and breakfast, a special treat awaits you.

Price Code

For the purposes of comparing prices, we have categorized accommodations with two to four dollar signs ($), based on the typical daily rates charged for a standard room with two double beds. Keep in mind that these rates are subject to change; however, to give you a rough idea of what to expect, we offer the following guide:

$$	$51 to $75
$$$	$76 to $100
$$$$	More than $100

Charlotte

The Elizabeth Bed & Breakfast
$$-$$$ • 2145 E. 5th St. • 358-1368

Since 1990, Joan Mastny has been welcoming guests with old-style Southern hospitality to this 1927 lavender "lady" in the historic Elizabeth area. The location is convenient to shops, restaurants and Uptown. This bed and breakfast offers three European-style rooms and one cottage with antiques and decorator linens. All rooms are air-conditioned and have private baths. Telephones and televisions are available upon request. A full Southern breakfast is served daily.

The Homeplace Bed & Breakfast
$$$-$$$$ • 5901 Sardis Rd. • 365-1936

You can take a real trip down memory lane during a visit to The Homeplace at the corner of Sardis and Rama roads. Sleep under a comfy quilt in a four-poster bed surrounded by family heirlooms, including paintings by John Gentry, owner Peggy Dearien's father. Then wake up to the sounds of birds just as the first owner, the Reverend R.G. Miller, did at the turn of the century in what was rural countryside. Enjoy one of Peggy's full breakfasts and discuss the morning news with her husband Frank. The Homeplace has two guest rooms with private baths, plus one suite with bath. It's the perfect place for your wedding night!

The Inn Uptown
$$$$ • 129 N. Poplar St.
• 342-2800, (800) 959-1990

Hornet's Nest Liniment, concocted in 1897 by one of the original owners, Walter Mullen, is no longer available at this beautifully restored bed and breakfast conveniently located in Uptown within walking distance of Discovery Place, Founders Hall, Spirit Square and numerous other attractions. The whirlpool bath at the top of a spiral iron staircase in the Tower Suite, however, is bound to soothe your aching muscles. A groom once delivered a half bushel of rose petals that were spread over this room's queen-size bed. Less romantic souls will appreciate the Inn's showers (with three body sprays). Four of the

Photo courtesy of The Inn Uptown

The Inn Uptown is located in the heart of Uptown Charlotte.

handsomely appointed rooms have fireplaces and all six have writing desks and phones with modem capabilities. Fax and copier machines are available along with a dry-cleaning service, a morning newspaper and a meeting room. Guests are served a complimentary full breakfast in the dining room of this three-story brick home, historically known as the Bagley-Mullen house.

The Morehead Inn
$$$$ • 1122 E. Morehead St.
• 376-3357, (888) MOREHEAD

Just minutes from Uptown Charlotte and Ericsson Stadium, The Morehead Inn is an elegant Southern estate endowed with quiet elegance and fine antiques. This historic Dilworth home features spacious public areas with intimate fireplaces, luxurious private rooms and a lovely two-bedroom carriage house. Built in 1917 and renovated in 1995, the Inn has earned a first-class reputation as one of the finest inns in the South with numerous awards for renovation, cuisine and service. In addition to overnight accommodations, the Inn provides a gracious setting for seminars, business luncheons, executive meetings and some of the city's

grandest weddings and social events. Features include 12 elegantly appointed guest rooms, all with private baths, five indoor meeting areas, a complete business center and a secluded outdoor courtyard. Corporate and special package rates are available.

Roswell Inn
$$-$$$ • 2320 Roswell Ave. • 332-4915

You can wake up to the appetizing smell of homemade biscuits and rolls or maybe coffee cake being prepared by effervescent innkeeper Lea Harrison from her own special (passed down from generations) recipes. During the warmer season you can dine on the terrace in one of Charlotte's loveliest gardens, then walk beneath towering trees through Myers Park, one of the city's oldest neighborhoods. This beautifully decorated, family heirloom-filled home is an inviting place to relax over afternoon Russian tea or old-fashioned lemonade with warm-from-the-oven cookies. It's a short drive to Uptown and the airport.

Davidson

Davidson Village Inn
$$$-$$$$ • 117 Depot St. • 892-8044

Located close to Davidson College, this inn was built in 1993 on the same site as the original Maxwell Chambers Hotel. Four of the 18 rooms are suites and all rooms provide guests with a private bath. A full continental breakfast and an afternoon tea are served daily. Business travelers may use the conference room, photocopier, fax and other services. Business functions and corporate meetings are well suited for this inn located in the heart of Davidson. The inn has designated smoking rooms.

Lake Wylie

Still Waters Bed & Breakfast
$$-$$$ • 6221 Amos Smith Rd. • 399-6299

Located on Lake Wylie, Still Waters is 15 minutes from Uptown and 10 minutes from the airport. With a little notice, innkeepers Janet and Rob Dyer will pick up out-of-town guests at the airport. Since a boat ramp and boat slips are part of the Still Waters property,

you can even bring a boat if you have one. If you don't, The Dyers have a paddle boat, rowboat and a motorboat that guests can use to tour the lake. If you'd rather relax, just sit on the dock and fish. For the more active, tennis, volleyball or basketball can be played on the Sport Court. This rustic, log-sided 1930's home provides the perfect escape for world-weary travelers. The home has two bedrooms, a bedroom suite and a guest cottage that includes a fireplace and a whirlpool bath. A full breakfast is served daily. If you would like a private phone or television in your room, please make your request at the time of reservation. Fax and modem capabilities for business travelers are available.

Victorian Villa On Lake Wylie
$$$-$$$$ • 10925 Windy Grove Rd. • 394-5545

This home, built in the 1920s, has been painstakingly restored and renovated since it was moved onto lakefront property. Innkeepers Chan and Nancy Thompson, along with daughter Amy, welcomed their first guest in the fall of 1997. They serve a full breakfast to guests in the sun room that overlooks the lake. Guests may relax and fish off the dock or perhaps take a tour of the lake on their boat. The villa has over 2,500 feet of deck to enjoy the views of the lake. All suites are furnished with antiques and some even come with wet bars and sitting areas. The villa is located close to the airport and the Coliseum and is only a short ride to Uptown attractions.

Rock Hill

The Book & The Spindle
$$ • 626 Oakland Ave. • (803) 328-1913

Close to Winthrop University, a selection of restaurants, art galleries and performance centers, this historic brick Georgian home has four guest rooms. Each is decorated in a different South Carolina theme and has a private bath, cable TV and coffee maker.

East Main Guest House
$$-$$$ • 600 E. Main St. • (803) 366-1161

Conveniently located in the Historic District, the East Main Guest House has three guest rooms with private baths and cable TV. A fax machine is available for corporate travelers.

Park Avenue Inn
$$ • 347 Park Ave. • (803) 325-1764

A large front porch with rocking chairs and twin parlors add charm to this inn, built in 1916. Three guest rooms are furnished with antiques and all have private baths.

In Charlotte, food
is now known as
cuisine and
it is savored in
sophisticated
settings.

Restaurants

Pasta places, bistros and bakery cafes, coffeehouses and ritzy delis. Doesn't anyone stay home and cook anymore?

For years we've been taking home Chinese and barbecue, but now the variety is diversified. Baby back ribs, a dozen or more different types of fresh pastas with homemade sauces (ready to pop into the microwave), fresh homemade sausages, chicken to die for, roasted vegetables, spicy Thai wonders and fresh baked bread are just a small sample of what's available.

Of course, chains and "fast-food" places dot the landscape, but Charlotte supports numerous fine restaurants. Chefs trained in Europe and culinary institutes throughout the United States perform their wizardry with both rare and common ingredients. Food is now known as cuisine and it's savored in sophisticated settings.

Price Code

We have included a price code that gives you a general idea of how much a dinner for two, excluding appetizers, desserts or alcoholic beverages, will cost. Daily specials are offered at many restaurants. Some restaurants offer senior citizen discounts, children's menus and early evening dining discounts. Prices do not reflect sales tax or gratuities, which should be 15 to 20 percent for good service.

Although menu suggestions and days open are included, keep in mind that these, as well as restaurant ownership and food prices, may change. Call ahead for more specific information.

$	Under $20
$$	$21 to $35
$$$	$36 to $50
$$$$	$51 and up

American Cuisine

Bistro 100
$$-$$$ • 100 N. Tryon St., Founders Hall • 344-0515

You can feel comfortable in jeans or a tuxedo in this upscale-but-relaxed French and American restaurant. Although the Bistro seats 300, the floor plan wraps from one dining area to the next, providing a cozy atmosphere.

You'll love the complimentary roasted elephant garlic served with hot-from-the-oven sourdough bread. The chef has taken the best from both American and French culinary techniques by cooking with fresh herbs and roasting rather than frying. The result is wholesome and delicious with the possible exception of homemade desserts, which may be more delicious than wholesome. Insiders like the Chocolate Paradise, but the Bistro also offers fresh berries and sorbets. Bistro 100 serves lunch and dinner seven days a week. Reservations are recommended.

Cafe Verde
$-$$ • 1408 East Blvd., Inside Talley's Green Grocery, Dilworth Gardens Shopping Ctr. • 334-9200

Cafe Verde features food that is often hard to find in other Charlotte restaurants. You'll get a full bouquet of natural, vegetarian and ethnic foods. The menu includes hot entrees such as vegetarian lasagna and Mexican dishes with black and red beans.

The cafe offers homemade soups, sandwiches on whole-grain breads and a fresh salad bar. Baked goods and desserts are made daily. The cafe also caters to people with special dietary needs, including low fat, low cholesterol, low sugar, low salt and dairy free. Cafe Verde offers lunch and dinner Monday through Sunday.

Fifth Street Cafe is a great Uptown getaway for lunch or dinner.

Fenwick's On Providence
$$ • 511 Providence Rd. • 333-2750

Fenwick's offers fine dining in a casual, intimate atmosphere. Fresh seafood and salads, grilled chicken and steaks are popular menu items, but the fabulous breads, muffins and desserts are worth the price of the meal. No reservations are accepted. Fenwick's is open for lunch and dinner Monday through Saturday.

Fifth Street Cafe
$$ • 118 W. 5th St. • 358-8334

This is a great Uptown getaway for lunch, dinner or a drink after work. It serves excellent pasta, pork, stuffed chicken, filet mignon and fresh seafood. There is a room upstairs for private parties. Lunch is served Monday through Friday; dinner Monday through Saturday.

Hotel Charlotte Danny's Speakeasy
$$ • 705 S. Sharon Amity Rd. • 364-8755

The furnishings and decor of the original Hotel Charlotte located Uptown were transported to the suburbs and serve as a backdrop for this old Charlotte tradition.

For lunch, try burgers or po' boys with "add-ons" of your choice. For dinner, try the Shrimp Creole, Steak Diane, Crawfish Etouffee or Jumbo Gumbo. The restaurant's wine and beer clubs are just the thing for sampling a wide variety of beverages (it boasts of more than 100 varieties of beer). Live Maine lobster with New England clam chowder is featured the first full weekend of each month and two weekends later.

Closed on Sunday, Hotel Charlotte serves lunch Monday through Friday and dinner Monday through Saturday. At the other end of the parking lot, look for Danny's Too. It serves breakfast, lunch and dinner seven days a week. The menu features even more of a New Orleans' flavor.

Morrocrofts Restaurant
$$-$$$ • 2200 Rexford Rd., The Park Hotel • 364-8220

Located in the luxurious Park Hotel, this superb restaurant offers three meals a day, each wonderfully prepared and presented. In addition, a special menu is provided from 3 to 5:30 PM. On Sundays there is a truly spectacular brunch.

The Quad
Central Piedmont Community College
Elizabeth Avenue at Kings Drive • 330-4173

In addition to offering courses from food preparation to ice sculpting, the school features a teaching dining room. This semi-circular building with floor to ceiling glass windows allows diners a view of the city while they are served ambitious preparations. Since the chefs and waitpersons are students and the building is their lab, you only pay for the food and tips, making this the tastiest secret in Charlotte. While lunch and dinner are generally served Tuesday through Thursday during school sessions, reservations are taken by telephone only on Fridays from 9 AM until noon. A word of caution: call early, the Quad can become booked in 45 minutes.

Townhouse Restaurant
$$$$ • 1011 Providence Rd. • 335-1546

This restaurant has been a landmark at the intersection of Queens and Providence roads for over 50 years. Today it is a warm, casually elegant restaurant where regional American cuisine is expertly prepared and served. In addition to the extensive list of fine wines, the wine bar offers a choice of 12 to 15 different wines, including champagne and port, by the glass. The Townhouse is open for dinner every night.

Barbecue

The barbecue debate will live forever. Some like Eastern-style barbecue (vinegar-based), some like Lexington style (hickory-smoked), or Memphis and Texas-styles (tomato-based). Then comes the discussion of whether barbecue should be sliced or chopped. We feel you should try them all to be a real insider.

Bubba's Barbecue
$$ • 4400 Sunset Rd., (Exit 16-B from I-77 N.) • 393-2000

Bubba's cooks the whole pig, using peppers and spices in a vinegar base. You can also order shrimp, barbecue chicken, barbecue beans, barbecue french fries, brunswick stew and, of course — hush puppies. In true Southern tradition, Bubba's offers sweet potato pie and key lime pie.

If you choose take-out, remember to purchase a bottle of Bubba's sauce — it's not included with a regular take-home order. Bubba's is open for lunch and dinner daily.

Carolina Country Barbecue
$$ • 838 Tyvola Rd. • 525-0337
2522 N. Sardis Rd. • 847-4520

Come hungry. This restaurant has fine Southern-style barbecue, pit cooked and hickory smoked. Expect big portions and good service. Both locations are open for lunch and dinner seven days a week.

Hog Heaven Barbecue

$$ • 1600 Purser Dr. • 535-0154

You'll get delicious Lexington-style barbecue that features pork, chicken, ribs and homemade brunswick stew in a great atmosphere. Hog Heaven is open Monday and Tuesday for lunch and Wednesday through Saturday for lunch and dinner.

Old Hickory House

$$ • 6538 N. Tryon St. • 596-8014

The Old Hickory House serves terrific pit-cooked barbecue — pork, beef, ribs and chicken — and brunswick stew, too. It has take-out and catering is available. Open for lunch and dinner Monday through Saturday.

Ole Smokehouse #1

$$ • 1513 Montford Dr. • 523-7222

This landmark serves great barbecue — ribs, chicken, beef and pork — but it also has steaks and fresh seafood for the nonbarbecue lovers in your crowd. Be sure to inquire about the daily specials. It's open for lunch and dinner Tuesday through Sunday.

Red, Hot & Blue

$$ • 2530 N. Sardis Rd. • 814-9940

Red, Hot & Blue is the local home of Memphis barbecue, whether it's ribs, a tasty barbecue sandwich or the delicious chili. It offers authentic hickory smoked chicken, ribs, pulled pork and beef brisket. It's worth a trip just to try the delicious homemade desserts, especially the peanut butter pie. Blues memorabilia covers almost every inch of wall space and there is nonstop background blues music that ranges from upbeat and sassy to downright moody. Red, Hot & Blue is open daily for lunch and dinner.

Rogers Barbecue

$$ • 901 N. Wendover Rd. • 364-2939

In addition to great barbecue for lunch or dinner, you can get a good old-fashioned breakfast here. On Monday it is open for breakfast and lunch; Tuesday through Saturday, breakfast, lunch and dinner; and on Sunday it serves breakfast only.

Photo by Tim Johnson

Champps Americana offers a wide variety of sandwich and entree items in addition to daily drink specials.

Bistros, Bars & Grills

Photo Courtesy of Frank Manzetti's

Alexander Michael's

$$ • 401 W. 9th St. • 332-6789

This is one of Fourth Ward's favorite spots. Drop by for lunch or for a drink and dinner after work and enjoy the friendly neighborhood atmosphere. It's open for lunch and dinner Monday through Saturday with a brunch on Sunday and open for dinner on Sundays during football season.

Champps Americana

1601 E. Woodlawn Rd. • 523-1443

On Charlotte's south side, Champps Americana offers a wide variety of sandwich and entree items in addition to daily drink specials. Nightly events such as Bingo, Name That Tune and Karaoke begin around 9 PM. These activities combined with the sports atmosphere make this restaurant a unique dining experience. It's open seven days a week for lunch and dinner. Brunch is served on Sunday.

Charley's Restaurant

$$ • Sharon Rd., SouthPark Mall • 364-7475

Charley's serves tasty soups, salads and sandwiches. Its most popular items include the "great chicken sandwich" and the grilled chicken salad. A pleasant atmosphere makes this a good place to unwind after shopping at the mall. The restaurant is open for lunch and dinner Monday through Sunday.

East Boulevard Bar & Grill

$-$$ • 1601 East Blvd. • 332-2414

This is a place to sit back and just enjoy the food and your friends. It was "in" before sports bars hit the scene. Famous for its "poppers," menu items run the gamut from burgers and chicken wings to soups and salads. Open for lunch and dinner seven days a week.

Five Steps Down Pub & Grill

$-$$ • 116 Middleton Dr. • 372-1846

Nestled in Myers Park, this pub is a local favorite. If you want a great burger or chef salad, this is the place. Bar none, Five Steps has the best grilled cheese sandwich in town. Open for lunch and dinner daily.

Frank Manzetti's features garlic butter croissants & a 38-ounce Porterhouse.

Frank Manzetti's Bar & Grill

$$-$$$ • 6401 Morrison Blvd. • 364-9334

This steakhouse features Pittsburgh-style chargrilled steaks, ribs, chicken and specialities such as International Nachos with a variety of toppings, Gumbo, Oven-Roasted Salmon and a 38-ounce Porterhouse for Two. Fabulous garlic butter croissants are served with meals. Call for phone-ahead seating, reservations and food to go. It's open for lunch and dinner seven days a week.

French Quarter

$ • 321 S. Church St. • 377-7415

This restaurant began as a little lunch place in the heart of Uptown serving good food at a reasonable price. The salads (taco, chef's and Greek) are delicious or you might want to try a chicken sandwich. It's open for dinner with a light menu of burgers and pastas. Lunch and dinner are served Monday through Friday.

Glorious Cuisine

$$$-$$$$ • 9315 Monroe Rd. • 847-8331

This casual American bistro serves both European and American cuisine. The European bakery specializes in buttercream cakes and extraordinary wedding cakes.

Sunday brunch features a variety of tasty dishes, including Eggs Benedict plus a complete omelette and pancake bar, chef-carved ham and roast beef and other delicious surprises. Leave room for dessert — the baked goods, made on the premises, are out of this world. The restaurant is open for lunch Monday through Friday and for Sunday brunch.

Grady's American Grill
$$-$$$ • 5546 Albemarle Rd. • 537-4663

This is a favorite gathering spot for east side residents and suburbanites. You'll find friends gathered around the Cheers-like bar or on the patio in nice weather. The menu includes just about everything from soup and salad to steaks and chicken. No reservations are accepted, but call-ahead seating is available for lunches and dinners Sunday through Saturday.

Jack Straw's
$-$$ • 1936 E. 7th St. • 347-8960

Jack Straw's is a great place to get anything from a burger to a steak in a very casual atmosphere. The kitchen serves up homemade soups, salads, specialty sandwiches and a wide range of entrees, including pastas, fresh seafood, ribs and steaks. Live music is featured Wednesday through Saturday nights. Private parties are welcome and all menu items are available for take-out. The restaurant is open for lunch and dinner from Monday through Saturday.

Loafers Restaurant & Bar
$$ • 4715 E. Independence Blvd. • 568-9209

Loafers is "Charlotte's Own Cheers" serving American cuisine with a Tex-Mex flair and an array of frozen drinks. The restaurant is open every day from lunch until late night. There is live music Tuesday through Saturday and Karaoke on Wednesday.

McGuffey's
$$ • 9709 E. Independence Blvd., Windsor Square • 845-2522

The regular menu includes honey-mustard chicken, pasta, seafood and stir fry and is served from lunch through dinner daily. It also has a late-night menu seven nights a week. The restaurant's low-calorie and low-fat entrees are approved by the American Heart Association. Brunch is offered on Sunday.

Photo by Tim Johnson

The French Quarter serves a variety of specialty salads.

Photo by Tim Johnson

Providence Bistro is the sister restaurant to the popular Providence Cafe.

Newmarket Grille
$$-$$$ • 8136 Providence Rd.,
The Arboretum • 543-4656

Newmarket's specialty is cooking on the grill — particularly seafood. Pasta and chicken entrees are also available. Newmarket serves lunch and dinner every day and is especially popular with the Sunday lunch crowd.

PJ McKenzie's
$$-$$$ • 4800 S. Tryon St. • 529-1922

This restaurant serves seafood and steaks along with a salad bar in a fun-filled atmosphere. It also has delicious desserts and specialty drinks. Don't miss the nightly specials. Lunch and dinner are served every day.

Price's Chicken Coop
$ • 1614 Camden Rd. • 333-9866

This family-owned take-out food establishment, founded in 1962, is a "legend in its own time." Its principal product is fried chicken, but it has expanded its menu to include fried fish, sandwiches, Eastern North Carolina barbecue with all the trimmings of hush puppies, potato salad, slaw and even pies. This is the best place around for instant parties or plan-ahead events. Lunch and early dinners are served from Monday through Saturday.

Providence Cafe
$$-$$$ • 110 Perrin Pl. • 376-2008

Though the accent here is primarily Mediterranean, it's sufficiently eclectic to include Gumbo and Blackened Filet of Tenderloin. Healthy, diet conscious dishes include Black Bean Cake on fresh greens with goat cheese dressing and hickory grilled brochette of seasonal vegetables.

When the temperature begins to climb, Insiders head for the patio or dine inside in the open ceiling, two-story Artichoke Room. Providence Cafe is open for lunch and dinner seven days a week and also offers brunch on Sunday.

Providence Bistro & Bakery
$-$$ • 8708-I J.W. Clay Blvd. • 549-0050

A sister restaurant to Providence Cafe, Providence Bistro features fresh baked focaccia and other breads baked daily. All chicken, steak and fish entrees are grilled over hickory wood and an eclectic variety of daily specials are offered. Fresh brewed cappuccino and specialty coffees can be enjoyed on the patio overlooking a lake side setting. It is open for lunch and dinner daily and for brunch on Sunday.

Photo by Tim Johnson

300 East offers a variety of pizzas and grinders.

Providence Road Sundries
$$ • 1522 Providence Rd. • 366-4467

Known simply as "Sundries," this is the place to go for great burgers and sandwiches. It's also the place to go to see or be seen by the local Yuppie crowd. Sundries is open seven days a week for lunch and dinner.

Red Rocks Cafe & Bakery
$$ • 4223-8 Providence Rd. • 364-0402

This trendy, upscale restaurant offers everything from deli to dinner to take-out. The cuisine is health conscious without sacrificing taste. Roasting, grilling, steaming, as well as low-fat and low-salt, are cooking options. The bakery has fresh daily offerings that you can take home.

The menu is varied with rib-eye steak, pasta dishes, chicken, chili, burgers and stick-to-the-ribs salads topped with either chicken or fish. An extensive wine list, imported beers and iced and herbal tea are available. Desserts are a rich European affair, especially when accompanied with a specialty coffee. Red Rocks serves lunch every day and dinner Monday through Saturday. On Sundays a brunch is provided.

Roasting Company
$ • 1601 Montford Dr. • 521-8188

From fresh vegetables (hot and cold) to appetizers, salads or tacos, you won't be disappointed in the quality of the food, which is served in a casual, pleasant atmosphere. Roasting Company is open seven days a week for lunch and dinner.

Sonoma on Providence
$$ • 801 Providence Rd. • 377-1333

Sonoma on Providence features the hottest trends in American Cuisine. This local favorite also has an award winning wine selection. It's open Monday through Friday for lunch and dinner and Saturday and Sunday for dinner.

Spratt's Kitchen & Market
$ • 100 N. Tryon St., Founders Hall • 344-0864

When you're Uptown shopping or on your lunch hour and don't have much time or money, Spratt's cafeteria-type deli is the place to go for a scrumptious quick meal. You can build your own sandwich or salad, charged by the pound, from a vast array of deli selections on homemade breads or select from the hot vegetables, pasta bar or cold salad bar. For dessert, try something from the Bistro 100 bakery or a nonfat frozen yogurt.

There is a wide assortment of imported beers and good selection of wines, plus tea and soft drinks. Espresso, cappuccino and gourmet coffee are also available. If it's one of those busy days Uptown, delivery service is also available. Spratt's is open Monday through Saturday morning to mid-afternoon.

300 East
$$ • 300 East Blvd. • 332-6507
This place has it all — from pizzas to grinders — including a good chunky chicken salad. It's a great place to start Sunday morning off with a relaxed brunch in informal surroundings. The restaurant is open seven days a week for lunch and dinner.

Village Tavern
$$ • 4201 Congress St. • 552-9983
The Tavern's huge outdoor patio is a great place to meet with friends for a drink when the weather is nice. The Sunday brunch menu offers several different omelettes and a variety of Eggs Benedict. For a change of pace, try the Crab Cake Benedict or the Belgian Waffles. Nice crunchy salads and good sandwiches are available for lunch. The restaurant is open seven days a week for lunch and dinner.

Caribbean Cuisine

Anntony's Caribbean Cafe
$$ • 2001 E. 7th St. • 342-0749
145 Brevard Ct. • 339-0303
Anntony's offers a variety of Caribbean cuisine, the most popular being the rotisserie-style Caribbean chicken served with your choice of greens, rice or potato salad. Take-out is available. At the E. 7th Street location, lunch is served Monday through Friday and dinner Monday through Saturday. Live entertainment is featured on Friday and Saturday nights. The Brevard Court location is open only for lunch Monday through Friday.

Cajun & Creole Cuisine

The Bayou Kitchen Restaurant & Bar
$$-$$$ • 1958 E. 7th St. • 332-2256
What's important here is the food — some of the best Cajun-Texas cuisine in town. Several varieties of Etouffee (crawfish, shrimp and catfish), Gumbo and Creole dishes (shrimp, crawfish and chicken), Po' Boys, Texas-style barbecue and daily specials such as Red Beans & Rice, Blackened Chicken Creole and Smoked Sausage, often served with mashed potatoes and cream gravy and many choices of vegetables. Want dessert? Don't pass up the New Orleans-style bread pudding.

A good selection of beers, including Dixie, Lone Star and Abita are available. The restaurant is also the home of ever popular Cajun Cowboy Catering. The Bayou Kitchen is open seven days a week for lunch and dinner.

Photo by Tim Johnson

Anntony's Caribbean Cafe has two convenient locations.

Photo by Tim Johnson

Fat Tuesday is famous for its frozen drinks.

Cajun Queen

$$-$$$ • 1800 E. 7th St. • 377-9017

Cajun Queen's Bayou-inspired kitchen turns out authentic Cajun food. It specializes in blackened fish and steaks, but also offers crawfish, shrimp, Etouffee and its own homemade Oreo cheesecake and Bourbon Bread Pudding. Nightly, live Dixieland jazz entertainment adds spice to your dining enjoyment in this attractive restaurant located in a charming old home. Dinner is served every day.

Fat Tuesday

$-$$ • 211 N. College St., CityFair • 375-3288

Frozen daiquiris at their finest! Located in the center of Uptown Charlotte, Fat Tuesday serves up over 20 different flavors of specialty frozen drinks. Delicious appetizers and sandwiches are created from recipes direct from New Orleans. Fat Tuesday is open seven days a week for lunch and dinner and it serves free daiquiri samples all the time.

Bourbon Street Station

$$$ • 6101 Old Pineville Rd. • 522-0231

Look for the old train car and you've found the right place. Specializing in grilled and blackened steaks, prime rib, seafood, chicken and great Cajun cuisine. Lunch and dinner are served Monday through Saturday.

Continental Cuisine

Carpe Diem

$$-$$$ • 431 S. Tryon St. • 377-7976

The quiet surroundings make this fabulous little restaurant a comfortable place to

Photo by Tim Johnson

The Cajun Queen offers authentic New Orleans cooking.

Photo by Tim Johnson

The Lamplighter is the place to celebrate a special event.

enjoy a superb meal of American food with ethnic influences. Lunch is served Tuesday through Friday; dinner Tuesday through Saturday.

The Lamplighter
$$$$ • 1065 E. Morehead St. • 372-5343

A popular spot, The Lamplighter offers the best in Continental and American cuisine. It's the perfect place to impress, whether it's a business associate or the favorite person in your life. Dinner is served seven days a week. Reservations are recommended and jackets are requested. The restaurant can accommodate large parties for lunch; call ahead to make arrangements.

The Melting Pot
$$$ • 901 S. Kings Dr., Kings Court Plaza • 334-4400

The Melting Pot features a relaxed atmosphere and offers a variety of fondue. Choose from beef, chicken or seafood or select cheddar or Swiss cheese fondue served with fruit and fresh breads. For dessert — chocolate fondue, of course. The Melting Pot is open for dinner seven days a week. Reservations are recommended, especially on weekends.

Metropolitan Cafe
7822 Fairview Rd. • 362-1666

The Metropolitan Cafe is tucked away in a little shopping center on Fairview Road between Sharon and Carmel roads. For lunch, choose from a wide selection of sandwiches or pastas. The dinner menu features a variety of chicken, beef, pork, lamb, fish and pasta dishes — all equally well prepared and presented. Try the antipasto dish as an appetizer. The chef creates many dishes with chicken, but the Mediterranean lamb dish and the sauteed veal are delicious. There are daily specials for lunch and dinner and the menu changes every two months. Lunch and dinner are served Monday through Saturday.

Pewter Rose Bistro
1820 South Blvd. • 332-8149

This bistro offers a quiet, expertly prepared lunch or dinner that exemplifies creative cuisine at its best. Try the Grilled Portobello Mushroom, brushed with herb-infused oil, or the Almond Baked Brie with bourbon and brown sugar. The restaurant occupies a renovated textile mill and is decorated in an eclectic style with treasures from attics and flea markets. Sometimes there's music. Late night appetizers and desserts

Pewter Rose Bistro offers indoor and outdoor dining.

are served in the bar on weekends. Lunch and dinner are served seven days a week.

Deli

Dikadee's Deli
$ • Twin Oaks Shopping Ctr. • 333-3354

This deli offers fabulous soups, salads, sandwiches and incredible desserts. It's open from Monday to Saturday.

Pasta & Provisions
$ • 1528 Providence Rd. • 364-2622
8016-100 Providence Rd. & Rt. 51 • 543-7595
127 N. Tryon St. • 342-2200

Technically speaking, Pasta & Provisions is not a restaurant. It's more of a take-out place, but we put it in this section so you wouldn't miss it. When you're too tired or busy to cook, this is an excellent place to pick up dinner. Pasta and sauces are made fresh daily — with over 20 different types of pasta available.

You can also purchase fresh baked bread and Italian specialty items such as olive oil and wine. Hours and days open vary at each location.

Rusty's Deli & Grille
$ • Quail Corners Shopping Ctr. • 554-9012
5445 77 Center Dr. • 527-2650
Providence Commons • 845-8505

Each Rusty's provides a good place to grab a quick bite with great sandwiches and salads and an extensive selection of wines. Hours and days open vary at each location. Fax orders are accepted; call for fax number.

Family-Style Dining

Anderson's Restaurant
$ • 1617 Elizabeth Ave. • 333-3491

Family-owned and operated, Anderson's is an institution in Charlotte. The home fries are the best in town and the restaurant is famous for its pecan pie. Breakfast, lunch and dinner are served Monday through Friday. Breakfast and lunch are served on Saturday.

Charlotte Cafe
$ • Park Road Shopping Ctr. • 523-0431

This is one of the best moderately priced places to go for breakfast. The extensive menu includes everything from deli items to steaks, seafood, a variety of Italian dishes and 25 different home-cooked vegetables daily. The Cafe is open for breakfast, lunch and dinner Monday through Saturday.

Cupboard Restaurant
$ • 3005 South Blvd. • 523-9934

Another Charlotte institution, the Cupboard offers no frills, family dining. It is famous for its wonderful homemade rolls, delicious banana cream and coconut cream pies. It's open Monday through Friday, serving breakfast, lunch and dinner.

Gus' Sir Beef Restaurant
$ • 4101 Monroe Rd. • 377-3210

It's not unusual to see a line of people all the way to the parking lot of this family-style restaurant. It's been serving vegetables fresh from the garden for over 30 years. No fats are used to cook the delicious squash, greens and other vegetables. You'll also appreciate the lean roast beef. Lunch and dinner are served Monday through Saturday.

Lupie's Cafe
$ • 2718 Monroe Rd. • 374-1232

The hot, super hot and too hot chili are this cafe's drawing card. The meatloaf tastes as good as Mom's homemade. This folksy place, which grows on you, is where you'll rub elbows with politicians and mill workers. Lunch and dinner are served Monday through Saturday.

Fish Camps

An old Charlotte area tradition, fish camps have passed out of vogue but not out of business. Informal and inexpensive eateries, they built their reputation for years on generous portions of fresh fried fish, served piping hot, with French fries, cole slaw and hush puppies. Fish camps have broadened their menus to include broiled and baked fish, baked potatoes and garden salads in order to offer health-conscious eaters more choices.

These indigenous restaurants are found in out-of-the-way places — down country roads, beside riverbanks and in small communities nearby. A few Charlotte establishments have weathered stiff competition from other restaurants and continue to pack in crowds of hungry diners. The greatest concentration of the old-fashioned fish camps (and the most authentic) is found near the Catawba River in neighboring Gaston County. We recommend the following fish camp restaurants:

Photo by Tim Johnson

The chili, served hot, super hot or too hot, is the Lupie's Cafe drawing card.

Charlotte

Fish Farm Seafood Restaurant
1200 Sam Newell Rd. • 847-8578
Closed Mondays

The Hide-A-Way Inn
8517 Monroe Rd. • 537-4418
Closed Mondays

Mayflower Seafood Restaurant
East Town Market Shopping Ctr. • 566-0940
Open seven days a week

The Seafarer Seafood Restaurant
9306 Albemarle Rd. • 536-7540
Closed Mondays and Tuesdays

Gaston County

Lineberger's Fish Fry
4253 S. New Hope Rd. • 824-1587
Closed Sundays

Stowe's Fish Camp
281 Union/New Hope Rd. • 864-2114
Closed Sundays and Mondays

Twin Tops Fish Camp
4574 S. New Hope Rd., Belmont • 825-2490
Closed Sundays and Mondays

French Cuisine

La Bibliotheque
$$$-$$$$ • 1901 Roxborough Rd. • 365-5000
    La Bibliotheque means library in French and the cuisine is mastered using traditional French techniques. Bookcases line most of the walls, making you feel like you're dining in a friend's lavish walnut library. You'll find this elegant restaurant inside the Roxborough Building across from Specialty Shops on the Park. The food is excellent and sure to impress the most sophisticated connoisseur in both quality and presentation. Choose from an extensive international wine list to complement your meal. Lunch is served Monday through Friday and dinner is served every night except Sunday.

The Silver Cricket
$$$$ • 4705 South Blvd. • 525-0061
    Unpretentious from the outside, this quiet, intimate restaurant serves outstanding New Orleans Creole and French country cooking in an authentic French Quarter decor. The atmosphere is romantic and the service is great. Dinner is served seven nights a week.

German Cuisine

Rheinland Haus
$$ • 2418 Park Rd. • 376-3836
    From the moment customers come through the door, owner James Emmanuel goes way out of his way to make them feel comfortable. Naturally, the primary accent is on German food, but you'll also find plenty of American-style choices as well. The atmosphere is robust and there's entertainment Friday and Saturday nights. On the first Monday of each month, a German Sauerkraut Band will get you into the spirit of a *Hof Brau Haus* in Europe. Lunch and dinner are served Monday through Saturday.

Indian Cuisine

India Palace
$$ • 6140 E. Independence Blvd. • 568-7176
    India Palace is the place for authentic Indian cuisine. Chicken tandori is prepared in a traditional tandori oven. Try the shrimp marsala and daily luncheon specials. Don't miss this international treat. It's open for lunch and dinner seven nights a week. There is also a buffet luncheon Sunday through Thursday.

Italian Cuisine

Bravo Ristorante and Lounge
$$$ • 555 S. McDowell St. • 372-5440
    Every meal makes an entrance with the restaurant's singing waiters. This is the

perfect spot to entertain business clients or out-of-town guests or to celebrate a special occasion with family and friends. Dinner is served seven days a week. Brunch is served on Sunday.

Caffe 521
$-$$ • 521 N. College St. • 377-9100

This Uptown restaurant straddles the line between Spain and Italy. With its rose/brown cinder-block walls, tiled floor and ladder-back chairs, Caffe 521 has a comfortable atmosphere.

You can order seafood, veal, chicken and pasta with a variety of sauces. Garlic chicken or shrimp is a winner, especially with a good imported wine or European beer. Try the pizza made with sun-dried tomatoes. The restaurant gives special attention to vegetarian dishes. Flan is a good choice for dessert. Lunch is served Monday through Friday; dinner is served seven days a week.

Carlo's of South Boulevard
$-$$ • 6625 South Blvd. • 554-0994

Great Italian food is served throughout the day and into the evening at Carlo's.

Check out the early-bird special for dinner. It's open for lunch Monday through Friday. Dinner is available seven days a week.

Castaldi's Italian Bistro
$-$$ • 311 East Blvd. • 333-6999

Located in the historic home where Carson McCullers wrote *The Heart Is A Lonely Hunter*, Castaldi's offers gourmet-Italian fare using the freshest ingredients and latest cooking techniques. Choose from a variety of pastas and pizzas. Castaldi's is known for its fish entrees and you can have yours baked, broiled, grilled or sauteed. Lunch is served Monday through Friday; dinner seven days a week.

Chelsea's Italian Ristorante
3113 N. Sharon Amity Rd. • 536-2333

The rich fabrics and soft lighting create an intimate and cozy atmosphere that's perfect for romance and an unforgettable dining experience for patrons. The service is attentive and professional. The classic Northern Italian dishes are prepared just so, with an emphasis on freshness and presentation. The wine list includes many good selections.

Photo by Tim Johnson

Frankie's Italian Grille has a 1940's New York restaurant flair with Frank Sinatra's music creating the atmosphere.

Chelsea's is open for dinner Tuesday through Saturday. Reservations are advised because of the limited seating capacity.

Frankie's Italian Grille
$$-$$$ • 800 E. Morehead St. • 358-8004

Frankie's Italian Grille, a 1940's New York Italian restaurant, features a variety of Italian specialties, pastas and pizzas baked in a wood-burning oven. Photographs of New York and piped-in music create the feeling of that era. Entrees and desserts are so huge you should plan to share them. Lunch is served Monday through Friday (try the homemade potato chips). Dinner is served every night.

Little Italy Restaurant
$ • 2221 Central Ave. • 375-1625

Serving favorite Italian dishes since 1959, this restaurant offers daily specials. Take-out is also available. Lunch and dinner are served Monday through Saturday.

FYI
Unless otherwise noted, the area code for all phone numbers in this chapter is 704.

Luisa's Brick Oven Pizzeria
$-$$ • 1730 Abbey Pl. • 522-8782

Determined to capture the distinctive taste of Italian pizza remembered from her childhood, Luisa imported a wood-burning oven from Italy. She combines the freshest vegetables, the finest meats, unique herbs and the best of cheeses to create her pizzas. The same attention to detail goes into the preparation of other menu items. Luisa's is open for lunch Monday through Friday and for dinner seven days a week.

Mama Ricotta's
$$$ • 8418 Park Rd., Quail Corners Shopping Ctr. • 556-0914
901 S. Kings Dr. • 343-0148

Want international flair coupled with dynamite Italian food and wine? This is a great place for Italian cuisine in the Southeast Charlotte area. Dinner begins with fresh baked Italian bread served with olive oil for dipping. The pasta dishes are all delicious — the pasta with prosciutto is beyond imagination. Dinner is served seven days a week.

Mangione's Ristorante
$$ • 1524 East Blvd. • 334-4417

This wonderful restaurant has become a tradition in the Charlotte area. Enjoy all of your favorite Italian dishes in a warm, friendly atmosphere. Mangione's is open for lunch Monday through Friday and dinner Monday through Saturday.

The Open Kitchen
$$ • 1318 W. Morehead St. • 375-7449

In business since 1952, this is the kind of place to bring the kids and let them feast on spaghetti while Mom and Dad savor the finer subtleties of Italian cooking. Italian specialties include scaloppine, parmigiana, cacciatore and gourmet pasta dishes. Pizza is also available. It's open for lunch Monday through Friday and for dinner seven days a week.

Scalini
$$$$ • 5501 Carnegie Blvd., Hyatt Charlotte • 554-1234

Scalini serves Mediterranean cuisine in the evening and oversized salads and sandwiches for lunch. Try the whole roasted Red Snapper. Breakfast and lunch and dinner is served seven days a week.

Spaghetti Warehouse
$-$$ • 101 W. Worthington Ave. • 376-8686

This is a large but very reasonably priced and efficient restaurant. Great spaghetti dishes with combinations are available and served in an atmosphere surrounded by antique memorabilia. The Minestrone and Italian Wedding soups are a real treat. The restaurant is open for lunch Monday through Saturday and for dinner seven days a week.

Villa Antonio Italian Restaurant
$$-$$$ • 4707 South Blvd. • 523-1594

The restaurant's authentically prepared Italian cuisine is simply delicious and the quiet, romantic atmosphere will create a very special evening. Lunch is served Monday through Friday and dinner every night.

Photo by Tim Johnson

Since opening in trendy South End, Zarrelli's has become not only a friendly neighborhood restaurant but one that also attracts local celebrities.

Zarrelli Italian Restaurant
$-$$ • 1801 South Blvd. • 335-7200

Neal Zarrelli, known for his powerful renditions of "The Star Spangled Banner" at Charlotte Hornets' and Carolina Panthers' games, has been setting restaurant standards since he first hit the Charlotte scene a few years ago. He even brought in Italian brick masons to build the first wood-burning brick oven in the Carolinas — essential for baking their delicious mouth-watering pizzas. The full-service restaurant offers more than pizza, of course. The menu features a variety of fish, veal and chicken dishes, plus fresh pasta — all beautifully prepared and presented. Patrons are delighted with traditional favorites such as lasagna and manicotti, as well as some not-so-easy-to find dishes such as Pasta Putenesca.

Since opening at this location in trendy South End, Zarrelli's has become not only a friendly neighborhood restaurant but one that also attracts local celebrities. Most evenings you'll find Neal and his wife Lois greeting guests. Neal's impromptu singing and musician Gabriel Kucko's renditions on the piano are an added attraction.

Low Country Cuisine

The Blue Marlin
$$-$$$ • 1511 East Blvd. • 334-3838
Crowne Point/Matthews • 847-1212

Bill Dukes, creator of the popular Long Horn Steakhouse on East Morehead, has introduced a new type of restaurant to Charlotte featuring Low Country cuisine. The atmosphere is eclectic, suggestive of the beach or the Low Country around Charleston or Beaufort, South Carolina. Menu selections include Low Country favorites such as Shrimp and Grits, Carolina Crab Cakes, Oyster Skillet Bienville and Cajun Chicken Breast, as well as pasta, steaks, chops and fish. For dessert, you might want to try the Homemade Cobbler or Key Lime Pie.

The bar is a favorite gathering place for locals. Both locations are open for dinner every day.

Mexican/Spanish

El Cancun Mexican Restaurant
$-$$ • 5234 South Blvd. • 525-5075
3001 E. Independence Blvd. • 376-9424
5661 Farm Pond La. • 536-7757
1401 E. Morehead St. • 347-2626

El Cancun serves authentic Mexican food prepared fresh daily. Outdoor dining is available at the Farm Pond Lane location. Take-out is also available. Lunch is served Monday through Friday. Dinner is served every night.

La Paz Restaurante
$$ • 523 Fenton Pl. • 372-4169

Located just off Providence Road, this is probably Charlotte's most popular Mexican restaurant serving traditional Mexican and regional southwestern cuisine. The food is excellent and there is a great upstairs bar that also serves dinner. It serves a dynamite margarita. Take-out is available and the restaurant has preferred seating for parties of eight or more. La Paz is open for dinner seven days a week.

Monterrey Restaurante Mexicano
$$ • 10707 Park Rd. at N.C. 51,
Park 51 Shopping Center, Pineville • 541-6664
Windsor Square Shopping Ctr. • 841-8068

Each is a casual, fun restaurant featuring fantastic Mexican cuisine. If you like large margaritas, order the extra-large one, which is five times their normal size. The restaurant is open for lunch and dinner seven days a week.

Olé Olé
$$$ • 709 S. Kings Dr. • 358-1102
19708 N.C. 73 W. (on Lake Norman in Cornelius) • 892-7150

The original restaurant on South Kings Drive has quite a following and it's usually crowded at lunch and dinner. Colorful Spanish dishes are served amid Spanish-style decor. Entrees featuring chicken, seafood, pork and beef dishes are usually served with saffron rice, vegetables and/or a generous house salad. The menu also includes a variety of appetizers, soups, salads and vegetarian plates, plus several international and traditional Mexican choices. You can get imported and domestic beer, liquors and

Photo by Tim Johnson

Olé Olé serves colorful Spanish dishes amid Spanish-style decor.

special coffees such as Cafe Mexicano (coffee with tequila and kahlua).

The South Kings Drive location serves lunch Monday through Friday. Both locations serve dinner seven days a week.

Pancho & Lefty's Tex-Mex Cantina
$$ • 601 S. Kings Dr., Kings Point Shopping Ctr. • 375-2334

Nachos, quesadillas, fajitas, mesquite grilled burgers, Tex-Mex chili and much more are featured on the appetizer menu. For dessert, how about a frozen margarita pie? Try the exceptional chicken fajitas or shrimp fajitas for something different and delicious. It's open for lunch and dinner Monday through Saturday and for dinner only on Sunday.

Tio Montero
$$-$$$ • 207 Johnston Dr., Pineville • 889-2258

This location serves authentic Spanish dishes such as: Figlo — eggplant smothered in Spanish cheese; Zarzuela — seafood in tomato sauce; Mero en Sal — cod baked in salt; and a great paella. Tex-Mex dishes are also on the menu. Dinner is served Tuesday through Saturday.

Oriental Cuisine

Baoding
$$$ • 4722 Sharon Rd., Sharon Corners Shopping Ctr. • 552-8899
227 W. Trade St., Carillon Bldg. • 370-6699

The Sharon Road restaurant's design looks more like an upscale New York eatery than the typical Oriental restaurant. The North Chinese food is chic, matching the decor. You'll know it's Oriental, but modern preparation techniques make dining here exceptional. Both restaurants are open for lunch and dinner seven days a week. Take-out is available.

Chef Chen
$$ • 8200 Providence Rd., The Arboretum • 541-1678

The wonderfully spicy Sezchuan cuisine is a real pleaser. Try the restaurant's fried

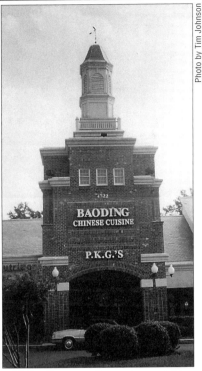

Photo by Tim Johnson

At Baoding you will experience some of the best Chinese cuisine in Charlotte.

dumplings. Chef Chen is open for lunch Monday through Saturday and dinner seven days a week. A buffet lunch is offered on Sunday.

Kabuto Japanese Steak House
$$ • 446 Tyvola Rd. • 529-0659
1001-K. E. W.T. Harris Blvd. • 548-1219

This Japanese steak house and sushi bar has chefs that prepare your meal at your table as you watch. Lunch is served Monday through Friday and dinner is served seven days a week.

Nakato Japanese Restaurant
$$$ • 8500 Pineville-Matthews Hwy. • 543-8899

Steak, chicken and seafood are cooked right before your eyes by skillful chefs. The restaurant has a tatami room, where patrons

Nakato Japanese Restaurant has a tatami room where patrons sit on cushions.

Photo by Tim Johnson

sit on cushions and a floating sushi bar. Reservations are suggested. Nakato is open for dinner seven days a week.

Restaurant Tokyo
$$$ • 4603 South Blvd. • 527-8787

Savor Japanese food at its finest at this wonderful restaurant. Sushi is served at your table or from the spacious sushi bar. You can't go wrong with the sukiyaki or the outstanding Tokyo Tempura. Tokyo Restaurant is open for lunch from Monday through Friday and for dinner seven days a week.

Shun Lee Palace
$-$$ • 4340 Colwick Rd. • 366-2025

This is a favorite Chinese restaurant for many Charlotteans. It offers a wide variety of entrees to choose from serving Mandarin, Szechuan, Hunan and Cantonese cuisine. Lunch is served Monday through Friday; dinner is served seven days a week.

Thai House
$$ • 3210 N. Sharon Amity Rd. • 532-6868

Offering classic Thai cuisine, this small, intimate restaurant on Charlotte's east side is a quiet respite from the hustle-bustle of the city. The menu features more than 70 traditional recipes — seafood, chicken, duck, pork and beef, served with hot rice and spicy sauces (mild, medium or hot). Try the "King and I" prepared with grilled Thai whole shrimp seasoned with fresh garlic, tomatoes, chili pepper, onion and carrots garnished with broccoli or the "Gulf of Siam" featuring a choice of shrimp, baby clams, squid or seafood combination cooked in a clay pot and served with vegetables and spices. The Thai House has a second location in McMullen Creek Shopping Center and is open seven days a week for lunch and dinner.

Thai Taste
$$ • 324 East Blvd. • 332-0001

The curry dishes at Thai Taste are excellent — just let the waitperson know how "hot and spicy" you'd like it to be. Lunch is served Monday through Friday and dinner is served every night.

Wan-Fu
$$-$$$ • 10719 Kettering Dr. • 541-1688

Some of the finest Chinese food in the city is served here with entrees expertly prepared and beautifully presented. Wan-Fu is open for lunch and dinner seven days a week.

Seafood

The Fishmarket
$$$-$$$$ • 6631 Morrison Blvd. • 365-0883

The Fishmarket has been providing "fine dining" to Charlotteans since 1981. It's open for lunch Monday through Friday and dinner nightly.

Key Wester Bar & Grill
$$-$$$ • 4544 South Blvd. at Sterling Dr. • 522-6100

With homage to Hemingway — Ernest, of course — this popular restaurant offers great seafood served in casual, fun surroundings. The soups are dynamite and so is the seafood. The outdoor patio and the fresh seafood market make this place a real find. This bar and grill is open for lunch and dinner seven days a week.

Shark Finns
$$ • 6051 Old Pineville Rd. • 525-3738

This "gulf coast crab shack" serves an incredible and unusual variety of fresh seafood in a fun, casual atmosphere. It also offers sandwiches, salads, spicy jambalaya and gumbo. Specials on shrimp and oysters are served every night.

Live music on Friday and Karaoke on Saturday nights provide additional entertainment. It's open for dinner seven days a week.

Sports Bars & Grills

Coach's Sports Bar & Grill, Inc.
$$ • 10403 Park Rd. Ext. • 544-0607
Recorded Information • 561-3730

Open continuously from lunch till late night every day, this recent addition to the Charlotte Sports Bar scene is the home of Dom Capers' Coach's Show. It offers a full menu, champion size pool tables, darts, 20 TVs and a variety of video games.

Jocks & Jills Sports Grill
$$ • 4109 South Stream Blvd. • 423-0001

With four distinct menus, 96 TVs and 15 satellite channels, Jocks & Jills has your sports event covered. The casual Bar & Grill dining side offers burgers and sandwiches, while the more upscale Bistro side provides a variety of chef's specials. You may even see one of your favorite athletes dining or dancing beside you. Located directly across from the Charlotte Coliseum, a shuttle service is offered for premiere sporting events.

Photo by Tim Johnson

The Thai House features classic Thai cuisine in an intimate setting.

Photo by Tim Johnson

Your family can still enjoy the convenience of a drive-in restaurant at Town & Country or South 21 Curb Service.

The Press Box
$$ • 1627 Montford Dr. • 523-4981

One of the first sports bars in the city, The Press Box has six regular TVs, a widescreen TV and terrific food. Favorites include the Matheny Burger, the Pita Kabob and the Honey Delight, all served with those famous cottage fries. Don't miss the Hot Fudge Cake for dessert. The Press Box is open every day for lunch and dinner.

Sandwich Construction Co.
$$ • 7801 University City Blvd. • 597-0008

Soups, sandwiches, burgers, salads and a variety of daily specials are served alongside NASCAR memorabilia. This casual dining spot is located near UNC Charlotte and is open 7 days a week for lunch and dinner.

Scoreboard Restaurant
$$ • 2500 Crown Point Executive Dr. • 847-7678

Opened in 1987 by father and son team Bob and Jamie Jerles, Scoreboard Restaurant has ribs, chicken, sandwiches and the best wings in town. With seating for 300, the four widescreen and four smaller TVs and video games provide plenty of entertainment. It is open for lunch Friday through Sunday and for dinner seven days a week.

Steak Houses

Beef 'N Bottle
$$-$$$ • 4538 South Blvd. • 523-9977

If you're looking for an old-time Charlotte steak house with a romantic touch, try this one. Famous for its superb steaks, it also offers excellent seafood dishes and has an extensive wine list. The restaurant is open for dinner Monday through Saturday.

H. Dundee's Steak House
$$ • 8128 Providence Rd., The Arboretum 543-6299

H. Dundee's serves food in a casual, Australian atmosphere. The prime rib comes in three sizes and the homemade desserts are a real delight. If you aren't too hungry, you might make a meal out of the Blooming Onion, from the list of appetizers. Both locations serve dinner seven nights a week.

Hereford Barn Steak House
4320 N. I-85 at Graham St. • 596-0854

One of Charlotte's oldest steak houses, the Hereford Barn is the real McCoy, offering thick steaks served with potatoes and a large salad. Dinner is served Tuesday through Saturday.

Meadowview Steak House & Piano Bar
$$-$$$ • 9727 E. Independence Blvd., Matthews • 847-3238

A cut above the usual steak house, this upscale restaurant features an elegant dining room and piano bar, plus private dining rooms. Prime rib, steaks and seafood are the specialties of the house. All entrees are served with French onion dip and chips, a house salad with homemade dressing, potatoes or rice, a vegetable and homemade onion rings and bread. Dinner is served Monday through Saturday.

The Palm
$$$ • 6705 Phillips Place Ct. • 552-7256

The Palm is a classic American steak house that has served huge cuts of prime beef and jumbo lobsters since 1926. Dinner is served seven days a week and lunch is served Monday through Friday.

Ranch House of Charlotte
$$-$$$ • 5614 Wilkinson Blvd. • 399-5411

Serving Charlotte since 1951, the Ranch House offers the finest cuts of aged USDA charbroiled steaks and fresh fish nightly. Private dining is available. This restaurant is open Monday through Saturday for dinner.

Charlotte is also home to several national and regional steakhouse chains. Some of the more popular include:

Lone Star Steak House & Saloon
$-$$$ • 3101 N. Sharon Amity Rd. • 568-2388
5033 South Blvd. • 523-2388
10610-A Centrum Pkwy., Pineville • 543-1922
20609 Torrence Chapel • 896-5600

Longhorn Steakhouse
$-$$$ • 700 E. Morehead St. • 332-2300

Morton's of Chicago, The Steakhouse
$$$$ • 227 W. Trade St. • 333-2602

Outback Steakhouse
$$ • 1412-A East Blvd. • 333-0505
1015 Chancellor Park Dr. • 598-7727
501 N. New Hope Rd., Gastonia • 864-9889
16400 N. Cross Dr., Lake Norman • 895-1888
Windsor Square, Matthews • 845-2222
1319 River Run, Rock Hill, S.C. • (803) 329-6283

No matter what your musical taste, lifestyle or entertainment preferences are, Charlotte has something for you.

Night Life

No matter what your musical taste, life-style or entertainment preferences, Charlotte has something for you. Keep in mind, however, that Wednesday night is party night for the singles crowd — the night to see and be seen — and Saturday night is always popular. So plan accordingly and don't be surprised if you have a 45-minute wait at your favorite restaurant or bar.

The law requires that all public facilities serving mixed drinks also serve food and are able to prove that at least half of their income is derived from food sales. Private clubs aren't bound by this law, but don't be misled by the term "private." Most clubs will allow entrance if you pay a nominal membership fee, usually about $10. If they restrict entrance to members only, hang around outside. You can usually convince a member to take you in as a guest for a couple dollars and you can settle up with your "host" once you're inside.

Alexander Michael's
401 W. 9th St. • 332-6789
Tucked away in historic Fourth Ward in the Uptown area, Alexander Michael's is known for its long wooden bar. A great lunch or dinner spot, it's well-loved by residents and neighbors.

Atlantic Beer & Ice
Corner of 7th & Tryon Sts. • 339-0566
Atlantic Beer & Ice is hopping, thanks to landlord NationsBank and the folks who run Dilworth Brewing. Good food, live entertainment each Thursday, Friday and Saturday, a cigar bar with pool tables upstairs and Charlotte's young professionals have created another new "in-spot" Uptown.

The Baha
4369 South Tryon St. • 525-3343
The Baha offers a variety of music from Retro '80s to live Reggae in a 10,000-square-foot two-level building. It's Charlotte's newest and largest dance club. Beer, wine and mixed drinks are served. Cover charges vary.

Bar Charlotte
300 N. College St. • 342-2557
Open each Thursday, Friday and Saturday, this Uptown Charlotte club offers a variety of entertainment that will appeal to almost every taste.

Bopper's Bar and Boogie
5237 Albemarle Rd. • 537-3323
On Tuesdays and Sundays, Bopper's plays beach music. Wednesday is ladies' night. The private club features music from the '50s to the present and crowds tend to be from the mid-thirties to mid-forties.

CJ's at The Adam's Mark
555 S. McDowell St. • 372-4100
This hotel bar is a great place for after hours entertainment. CJ's offers music, dancing and entertainment.

Cajun Queen
1800 East 7th St. • 377-9017
Fabulous New Orleans-style food mixes with great conversation and music to create a Cajun experience in Charlotte. If you're looking for Dixieland jazz at its best, plan on a visit to Cajun Queen.

Coach's Sports Bar & Grill
10403 Park Rd. • 544-0607
With 18 TVs, Coach's offers the ultimate in its coverage of sporting events. There's a nice selection of sandwiches and beer specials and a game room featuring three pool tables and the only virtual reality golf game in the Carolinas.

Comedy Zone
5317 E. Independence Blvd. • 568-4242

Want to see the famous Carrot Top or any number of the other hot comedians on the national circuit? You'll find them at the Comedy Zone. Call for reservations; it's often sold out.

Coyote Joe's
4621 Wilkinson Blvd. • 399-4946

A country night club, Coyote Joe's sports a large dance floor that's usually full of fun-loving people doing the Texas two-step. Not sure of the steps? No problem. On Wednesday and Friday, you can take dance lessons. Sunday is family day.

Double Door Inn
218 E. Independence Blvd • 376-1446

Many a name band started here and great music is always guaranteed. This is definitely a jeans place — nothing fancy. You can catch jazz on the first Sunday night of the month when the Charlotte Blues Society meets here. Monday night features a house band. A second nightclub, Double Door Inn at the Lake, is located on N.C. 73 in Cornelius, 892-6766.

The Excelsior Club
921 Beatties Ford Rd. • 334-5709

The historic Excelsior is almost 50 years old, making it the oldest nightclub in the Carolinas. Patrons must be over 26 and show ID. The club features disco and a cover is charged.

Fat Tuesday
211 N. College St. • 375-3288

Located at World Mardi Gras, Fat Tuesday offers live rock and top 40 music with a cover on weekends. Fat Tuesday is known for its frozen daiquiris that are offered in 20 different flavors.

Frank Manzetti's Bar & Grill
6401 Morrison Blvd. • 364-9334

Located at Specialty Shops on the Park, Frank Manzetti's is a SouthPark hot spot after work and on the weekends. The bar attracts a wide variety of folks, but it tends to be a professional group. Manzetti's is also known for its great food —

especially its ribs and its chicken breast salad with honey mustard.

Jack Straw's
1936 E. 7th St. • 347-8960

"A Tavern of Taste" — that's how Jack Straw's bills itself. And so it is. A great place for conversation and to meet and greet, Jack Straw's is located in the Elizabeth neighborhood, drawing residents from all over for great food, beverages and music.

Milestone Club
3400 Tuckaseegee Rd. • 398-0472

The Milestone is a real dive and proud of it too. It features fabulous up-and-coming bands you won't hear anywhere else in the city. The walls are covered with graffiti, but it has an eclectic charm that attracts punks, yuppies, matrons and mainstream — throwing them all together for a great time. With a nightly cover, you'll only find beer and colas in cans.

The Moon Room
433 S. Tryon St. • 342-2003

Located Uptown not far from Ericsson Stadium, this club is open Thursday, Friday and Saturday nights and offers appetizers and desserts with live jazz or acoustic music on the weekends. There is a cover charge.

Mythos
300 N. College St. • 375-8765

Mythos has taken Charlotte's alternative and progressive dance fans by storm. Award-winning for its progressive, techno and European dance music, Mythos offers a killer sound and laser light show with different themes—from Rave night to Rock Lobster night. Free parking is available across the street in the Holiday Inn parking lot. It's open Tuesday through Thursday from 10 PM until 3 AM, but remains open until 4 AM on Friday and Saturday. On Tuesdays, 18 and up are admitted.

PJ McKenzie's
4800 S. Tryon St. • 529-1922

This bar is located in the lobby area of Embassy Suites Hotel and it's a popular spot for travelers and locals alike. Sunday is singles night. It's open seven days a week.

The Palomino Club
9607 Albemarle Rd. • 568-6104

Primarily a private country and western music club, this club often features big name talent. On Wednesday, Friday and Saturday, you can Texas two-step to the tunes of a live band. An adjacent bar — The Roxy — plays Top 40, beach and rock, and features a DJ on Friday and Saturday evenings. Club membership is inexpensive and available at the door.

Pewter Rose Bistro
1820 South Blvd. • 332-8149

Situated on the second floor of a renovated warehouse in Dilworth, the Pewter Rose Bistro is a favorite of Charlotteans. Not only does it have one of the most complete wine lists in the city, it offers live music in the bar and patio area on weekends.

The Press Box
1627 Montford Dr. • 523-4981

The Press Box was a sports bar back before anyone knew what a sports bar was. It has seven televisions (one widescreen) and serves great sandwiches, dinners and munchies with a wide selection of favorite beverages.

Providence Cafe
110 Perrin Place • 376-2008

Owned by a prominent business leader in the area, Providence Cafe is a delightful place for lunch or dinner, but it has also become a local hangout for the Myers Park and professional crowd. The beautiful people can be seen regularly in the bar area and on warm days the patio is filled. Weekends and after-hours are the best times to go.

Rainbow Deli Cafe
The Arboretum
8200 Providence Road • 541-1811

Easy listening entertainment and Karaoke is offered on Wednesday nights. Mixed drinks, beer and wine are available.

Razzle's Lounge
2707 Little Rock Rd. • 394-4301

Located in the Best Western Airport Hotel, Razzle's offers live top 40 sounds and beach music, Tuesday, Wednesday, Friday and Saturday. Cover varies and there is a dress code.

Photo by Robert Thomason

Mythos offers entertainment until the early morning hours.

A popular shrimp buffet is offered Thursday night prior to an evening of comedy entertainment followed by a D.J.

Ri Ra's
208 N. Tryon St. • 333-5554

Ri Ra's offers an authentic Irish pub with an atmosphere to match.

Selwyn Avenue Pub
2801 Selwyn Ave. • 333-3443

One of Charlotte's great neighborhood hangouts, Selwyn Pub is usually packed on Wednesday evenings and after Hornets games.

SouthEnd Brewery & Smokehouse
2100 South Blvd. • 358-4677

This microbrewery offers at least six different custom brews made on the premises. Live nightly entertainment and a menu featuring smoked and grilled foods and pizza are offered in an elegant atmosphere. A cover fee is charged.

The Village Tavern
Rotunda Building, SouthPark • 552-9983

Terrific food and a fabulous patio make this a popular after-work hangout for young

An evening of fun awaits you at
World Mardi Gras.

professionals. The tavern offers live music
on Thursday evenings during the summer.

World Mardi Gras
211 N. College St., City Fair • 333-2263

Certainly one of the more innovative
night spots around opened in the autumn
of 1994. CityFair's first- and second-story
atriums have been transformed into an entertainment extravaganza, complete with
live music, great food and beverages and
theatrical lighting, all centered around a
Mardi Gras theme.

Concerts

For big-name concert performances,
there are three main venues in Charlotte:
The Paladium Amphitheatre at Paramount's
Carowinds, 588-2606, seats 13,000; Blockbuster Pavilion, 549-1292, seats 19,000;
and the Charlotte Coliseum, 357-4700,
seats 24,000.

Special Events

On Friday afternoons, there are several
outdoor after-work parties during the spring
and summer. Alive After Five, held Uptown
on Friday afternoons in the late spring and
early fall, entertains several thousand
Uptown workers in an after-work concert
series. It's a respectable "meet market."

June Jam is an outdoor concert around
the lake at University Place. This series lasts
from 5:30 to 9:30 PM for a 10-week season,
May through July.

Cinemas

Arboretum Stadiums
8008 Providence Rd. • 556-6843

Carolina Pavilion 22
Carolina Pavilion Shopping Center • 643-4262

Cinemark Movies 10
Independence Blvd. at Windsor Sq.,
Matthews • 847-2006

Delta Road 6 Cinema
8800 East W.T. Harris Blvd. • 532-9117

Manor Theater
607 Providence Rd. • 334-2727

Matthews Festival Theatres
10404 Independence Blvd. • 847-7469

Movies at Sardis
9630 Monroe Rd. • 847-2024

Movies at The Lake 8
20310 Chartwell Ctr. Dr., Cornelius • 892-3841

Park 51 Cinema
10621 Park Rd. • 542-5551

Park Terrace
Park Road Shopping Center • 556-6843

Phillips Place Stadiums
Fairview Rd. near SouthPark • 556-6843

SouthPark Mall Cinemas
Sharon & Fairview Rds. • 364-6622

Tower Place Festival 8
N.C. 51 & Park Rd. • 541-9010

Town Cinema 6
8640 University City Blvd. • 549-1629

LATE NIGHT COFFEE SHOPS

Coffee Shop	Address	Telephone
Barnes & Noble Cafe	3327 Pineville-Matthews Rd.	341-9365
Barnes & Noble Cafe	4700 Sharon Rd.	554-7906
Borders Books & Music	3900 Colony Rd.	365-6261
Coffeeworks	Arboretum Shopping Ctr.	542-9975
Caribou Coffee	1531 E. Blvd.	334-3570
Caribou Coffee	731 Providence Rd.	332-9948
Caribou Coffee	20619 Torrence Chapel Rd.	895-0116
Caribou Coffee	1909 Matthews Twnshp Blvd.	814-0538
Caribou Coffee	4327 Park Rd.	523-6822
Dilworth Coffee House	1235-B East Blvd.	358-8003
Jackson's Java	8544 University City Blvd.	548-1133
La-Dee-Da's	1942 E. 7th St.	372-9599
Peabody's Coffee Co.	4732 Sharon Rd.	556-1700
Queen City Coffee Roasters	8502 Park Rd.	556-9771
Starbucks Coffee Co.	1961 E. 7th St.	333-5880
Starbucks Coffee Co.	9211 N. Tryon St.	547-1787
Starbucks Coffee Co.	545 Providence Rd.	372-1591
Starbucks Coffee Co.	210 S. Sharon Amity Rd.	442-0333
Starbucks Coffee Co.	6701 Morrison Blvd.	365-5194
Starbucks Coffee Co.	1811 Matthews Twnshp Blvd.	844-0848
Zach's Coffee House	Sardis Crossing Shopping Ctr.	844-0233

University Place 6 Cinemas
8925 J.M. Keynes Dr. • 547-1187

Second Run Cinemas

Queen Park Cinemas
3700 South Blvd. • 523-6600

Regency Theaters
6434 Albemarle Rd. • 536-5378

Specialty Theaters

OMNIMAX Theatre
Discovery Place • 372-6261
    This state-of-the-art theater features a five-story, 79-foot-diameter tilted dome theater. Surround yourself with sight, sound and motion!

Silver Screen Cafe
4120 E. Independence Blvd. • 535-8333
    This unique theater allows you to be served with food, beer and wine while you enjoy a movie. The menu has a wide variety of items, including pizza, burgers and wings. Domestic and imported beer as well as a selection of wines are available.

Belmont Drive-In Theater
314 McAdenville Rd. • 825-6044
    Take a trip back to the '50s at this drive-in. Located in nearby Belmont, this theater offers first-run movies as well as some second-run movies.

Shoppers will discover an abundance of choices awaiting them in the Queen City.

CharlotteShopping

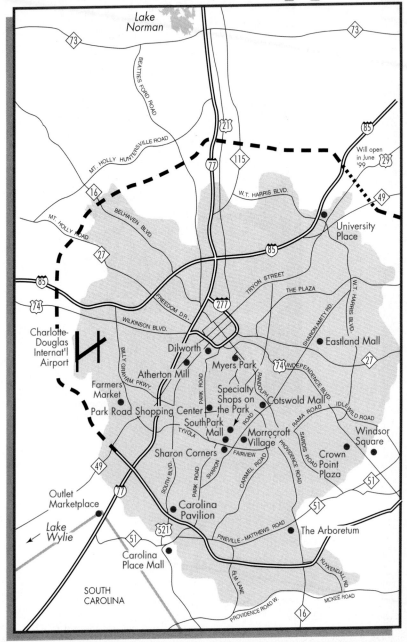

Lake Norman

73 — 73

BEATTIES FORD ROAD

MT. HOLLY HUNTERSVILLE ROAD

21

77 115

85

Will open in June '99

29 US

49

16

BELHAVEN BLVD.

W.T. HARRIS BLVD.

University Place

MT. HOLLY ROAD

27

85

University Place

85

74 US

27

TRYON STREET

THE PLAZA

W.T. HARRIS BLVD.

FREEDOM DR.

277

SHARON AMITY RD.

WILKINSON BLVD.

Charlotte-Douglas Internat'l Airport

Dilworth

Eastland Mall

BILLY GRAHAM PKWY.

Atherton Mill

Myers Park

74 INDEPENDENCE BLVD.

27

Farmers Market

PARK ROAD

Specialty Shops on the Park

RANDOLPH

Cotswold Mall

IDLEWILD ROAD

Park Road Shopping Center

SouthPark Mall

ROAD

Morrocroft Village

RAMA ROAD

Windsor Square

TYVOLA

Sharon Corners

FAIRVIEW

SARDIS ROAD

PROVIDENCE ROAD

Crown Point Plaza

51

49

77

SOUTH BLVD.

PARK ROAD

SHARON

CARMEL ROAD

51

Outlet Marketplace

Carolina Pavilion

51

Lake Wylie

51

521

PINEVILLE - MATTHEWS ROAD

The Arboretum

Carolina Place Mall

ELM LANE

KUYKENDALL RD.

SOUTH CAROLINA

MCKEE ROAD

PROVIDENCE ROAD W.

16

Uptown Shopping

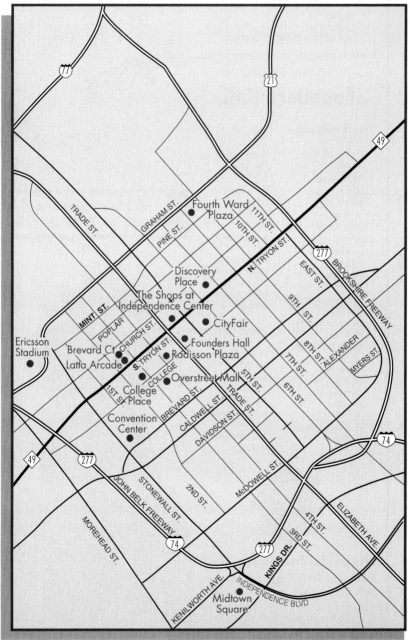

77

21

49

277

BROOKSHIRE FREEWAY

TRADE ST.

GRAHAM ST.

PINE ST.

11TH ST.

10TH ST.

N. TRYON ST.

EAST ST.

Fourth Ward Plaza

Discovery Place

9TH ST.

The Shops at Independence Center

MINT ST.

POPLAR

CHURCH ST.

CityFair

8TH ST.

ALEXANDER

MYERS ST.

Ericsson Stadium

Brevard Ct.

Latta Arcade

S. TRYON ST.

Founders Hall

Radisson Plaza

7TH ST.

College Place

1ST ST.

COLLEGE

Overstreet Mall

BREVARD ST.

5TH ST.

6TH ST.

TRADE ST.

Convention Center

CALDWELL ST.

DAVIDSON ST.

74

49

277

STONEWALL ST.

2ND ST.

McDOWELL ST.

74

MOREHEAD ST.

JOHN BELK FREEWAY

KENILWORTH AVE.

Midtown Square

INDEPENDENCE BLVD

KINGS DR.

277

3RD ST.

4TH ST.

ELIZABETH AVE.

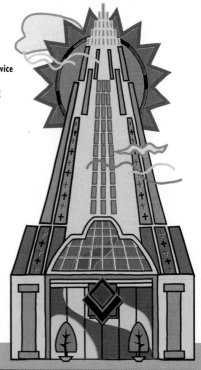

Shopping

Shoppers will discover an abundance of choices awaiting them in the Queen City. Visit outlet centers for name-brand clothing and shoes at discount prices. Browse specialty shops, upscale boutiques and galleries for that one-of-a-kind item. Enjoy the best national retail stores at regional megamalls. Choose fresh fruits and vegetables at Charlotte Regional Farmers Market. Explore small towns for great buys on a variety of antiques. Experience the bustling South End District, a cluster of former textile mills that has been converted into shops, galleries and restaurants. Shopping is truly an adventure in Charlotte!

Shopping Malls

Something new is happening in Charlotte shopping malls. For years shopping malls have displayed children's art and crafts to bring out the crowds. This may not have totally disappeared, but innovative marketing ideas are making their mark. SouthPark Mall, for example, brought in museum-quality sculpture to decorate its corridors during a month-long event entitled "Hot Art — Cool Jazz."

Carolina Place Mall
11025 Carolina Place Pkwy., Pineville • 543-9300

Carolina Place must be praised for its architecture. The entrances have a roundish, inviting look and the mall itself curves. Abundant natural light floods the common areas. The developers, from Atlanta, managed to attract some big names — Belk, Dillard's, Hecht's, Sears and JCPenney — as anchors. There are a few locally owned specialty stores, such as Fancy Crafts and Lamb Christian Books, and if you are interested in model trains, check out the Great Train Store. The Rose Garden Food Court, a variety of specialty stores and restaurants, is also in the mall. Parking is plentiful and

the mall is conveniently located near the Beltline.

CityFair
211 N. College St. • 375-2980

Located in the heart of Uptown, CityFair offers a variety of specialty shops, a food court and entertainment. At CityFair you'll find Casual Effects Apparel, Global Galleries Jewelry, Mary M. Bernot Le Salon, Carpinelli's Color Copies and Work or Play. The food court provides a tempting array of international delights, local fare, sandwiches and specialty coffee.

In the evening, listen to live music while you enjoy the food at Fat Tuesday.

Cotswold Mall
224 S. Sharon Amity Rd. • 364-5840

Cotswold Mall, one of Charlotte's early malls, has undergone a complete transformation in the past few years. The mall houses Marshalls and Stein Mart. Carmen Carmen Salon E'Spa, originally an upscale hair salon that expanded into a full-fledged daytime spa, is also located here. You can find unusual gifts at several unique mall shops, including Dreams and Dragonflies and Skillbeck Gallery featuring handmade pottery and other art objects.

For a meal or a snack try Spoon's, known for its homemade ice cream and sandwiches (try the hot dogs!), Wolfman Pizza or Hickory Hams.

Eastland Mall
5471 Central Ave. • 537-2626

Located at the corner of Central Avenue and Sharon Amity, about 15 minutes from Uptown, Eastland Mall serves the retail needs of East Charlotte. The mall is anchored by Belk, Dillard's, Sears and JCPenney. Eastland offers a wide variety of merchandise with 125 stores, including a few interesting and locally owned variations on the standard theme. By far the most remarkable feature of this mall is its ice-skating rink, which rests gracefully in the lowest level. The rink adds a special touch to shopping during the Christmas holidays.

Founders Hall
100 N. Tryon St. • 331-0075

In the lobby of the NationsBank Corporate Center are three large frescoes by North Carolina artist Ben Long: *Making/Building, Chaos/Creativity* and *Planning/Knowledge*. Visitors can enjoy these dynamic depictions before shopping at Founders Hall. Express World Brand offers dresses and accessories and Julie's Too has great buys for business as well as casual ensembles. Men will appreciate Jos. A. Bank Clothiers for its fashionable selection of men's clothing. Stop at Eastern Lobby Shops for some of the nation's top newspapers and magazines, The Bookmark for the latest new edition and The Blossom Shop for exotic flowers flown in from around the world, plus lovely plants and gifts. Sunrise Cleaners, First Impression Auto Care, Sir Speedy Printing, Package Plus II and Simpson Photo provide a wide range of services.

The Performing Arts Center Box Office is convenient for making reservations or picking up event tickets and you can work off the stress of the day on state-of-the-art equipment at Crown Athletic Club.

You can have an inexpensive deli-cafeteria lunch or do some grocery shopping at Spratt's Kitchen & Market. Go downstairs and you have a choice of lunch, or later on, dinner or drinks after work at Bistro 100.

Rock Hill Galleria
2301 David Lyle Blvd.
Rock Hill, S.C. • (803) 324-1711

Just over the South Carolina border, about 15 miles south of downtown Charlotte, Rock Hill Galleria's blend of contemporary and traditional architecture provides a showcase for its merchants. Belk, JCPenney, Sears and Wal-Mart are surrounded by a fine assortment of specialty shops and eating establishments.

SouthPark Mall
4400 Sharon Rd. • 364-4411

SouthPark is located at the corner of Sharon and Fairview roads and is probably the best known and most frequented mall in the area. Anchors at SouthPark are Belk,

Photo by Robert Thomason

Founders Hall is an elegant part of the NationsBank Corporate Center.

Dillard's, Hecht's and Sears. The mall is single-story with 115 stores and it is the only place in the 13-county metropolitan area where you can find such upscale retail leaders as Ann Taylor, Benetton, Nature Company, The Disney Store, Eddie Bauer, Caswell Massey, Laura Ashley and many others. Locally owned Perry's at SouthPark, a well-known jewelry store, is also located here.

The food court offers fast food and remains a busy gathering spot and Arthur's, located in Belk's, provides great food and gourmet selections to go.

Shopping Centers

The Arboretum

The Arboretum at the corner of Providence Road and N.C. 51 is one of the busiest suburban shopping centers in Charlotte. Wal-Mart, Michael's Crafts, Bed, Bath & Beyond and Zany Brainy blend with some very special boutiques such as Sidestreet where wives of the Charlotte Hornets find the beautiful casual outfits they wear to the games.

It has become something of an entertainment center as well with a branch library, several movie theaters and restaurants,

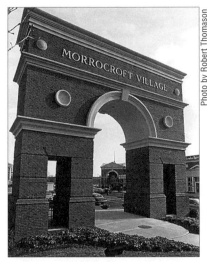

Morrocroft Village

including the New Market Grille (offering indoor and outdoor dining), H. Dundee's Steak House, CoffeeWorks, Rainbow Deli & Cafe, The Akropolis and many fast-food eateries.

Atherton Mill

Located at the corner of Tremont Avenue and S. Tryon Street, Atherton Mill, circa 1893, has been reclaimed for an entirely new concept in shopping. At Interiors Marketplace at Dilworth, more than 80 interior designers, antique and architectural dealers have subleased space and decorated it with imports from around the world. Also housed at Atherton Mill are Art Vivant, Gallery W.D.O., Busbin Lamps, Dilworth's Little Secret and Pastis Restaurant.

Carolina Pavilion

Carolina Pavilion is a strip shopping center that opened in 1997 on South Boulevard at I-485. Tenants include such discount giants as Target, Office Max, Marshall's, Best, Sports Authority, Baby Superstore, Circuit City, Rhodes Furniture and Kids 'R Us. Also located at Carolina Pavilion are Waccamaw pottery, Goody's, M.J. Designs, Homeplace, Kohl's, Media Play and several fast-food restaurants.

CrownPoint Plaza

CrownPoint, at the corner of E. Independence Boulevard and Sardis Road N., offers such super stores as Lowes Building Supplies, Babies R Us, Value City Furniture and Off Broadway Shoes. You'll find The Blue Marlin, Carolina Country Barbecue and the Scoreboard Restaurant here. On the west side of Sardis Road N., which splits the center, are a Super Kmart Center and Chili's.

Midtown Square

Midtown Square is best known for its outlet-type stores such as Burlington Coat Factory, Hit or Miss, Dress Barn, Famous Footwear and Publishers' Warehouse. It also houses the original Dreams and Dragonflies, featuring unusual gift items, apparel and jewelry. A variety of service-oriented stores and fast-food outlets are also located here.

Morrocroft Village

Morrocroft Village has style and Harris Teeter, the shopping center's drawing card, certainly has a style worth noting. This grocery has it all, including a florist and a self-serve luncheon restaurant. The village is full of fancy and clever boutiques and specialty stores such as Papitre, which has stationery and gifts, Jos. A. Banks Clothiers and Paul Simon's for men's clothing, Lynda Reid, for women's clothing and Paula Gould for jewelry.

One of Charlotte's better art galleries, Jerald Melberg Gallery is here and if you need something both traditional and unique for your home, then swing by De La Maison Furnishings. Borders Books & Music provides a wonderful collection of books and music and a gourmet coffee bar and Ruby Tuesday Restaurant is known for its wonderful salad bar.

Park Road

Charlotte's oldest shopping center houses a variety of food, service and specialty shops. Harris Teeter, Eckerd drugstore, Great Outdoor Provision Company, Reading China, GNC and a branch of the post office are located here. Julie's, Catherine's and Dress Barn offer women's clothing; Rack Room Shoes and Brownlee Jewelers may help complete the outfit. Elfrieda's Flowers, Time & Place Clocks and Corners Framing are a few of the other shops at Park Road.

Little Professor Book Center is an excellent source for books on a variety of subjects. Blackhawk Hardware carries a good line of tools and gardening supplies, as well as household items. Thrifty shoppers will appreciate the Junior League's Thrift Shop (530-2 Brandywine Avenue) that is tucked into the Park Road Back Court, along with several restaurants. The shopping center is also home to Park Terrace Theaters, the Charlotte Cafe that serves breakfast, lunch and dinner and Sir Edmond Halley's, which offers English and Australian pub food.

Sharon Corners

Opposite SouthPark Mall, this shopping center has been redesigned into a two-story architectural blend of Georgian and Colonial Williamsburg with open walkways, plantation moldings and cupolas. The upscale Our Place boutique for women, Men's Wearhouse and Chocolate Soup, which has some original designs for children, make this a clothing center for the entire family.

A Barnes & Nobles Bookstore that has a coffee bar and offers a small luncheon menu is very popular. For those who love the out-of-doors, you'll find a great selection at Jesse Brown's Outdoors. The shopping center has Lions Ltd. Fine Jewelry, American Tuxedo, Fast Frame, Bell Atlantic Mobile, P.K.G.'s Packaging Store and Kinko's.

At Sharon Corners, you'll also find the Original Pancake House; Harper's Restaurant; Baoding, a high-tech-designed Oriental restaurant; Peabody's Coffee; and Manhatten Bagels.

Specialty Shops On The Park

Located on Morrison Boulevard, across from SouthPark Mall, this unique shopping plaza offers an unusual blend of national and locally owned specialty shops. Here you'll find The Carriage, Talbot's, Talbot's Kids and Taylor, Richards & Conger for the latest in fashion apparel. Elizabeth Bruns offers exquisite jewelry and china, Williams-Sonoma has a wonderful gourmet kitchenware selection and The Mole Hole features unique gifts and home accessories.

Frank Manzetti's, a classic American grill; Caffe Milan offering northern Italian food; Cino Grille, featuring southwestern food; and Morrocroft's, in the Park Hotel on Rexford Road, offer a variety of fine dining establishments.

University Place

University Place near UNC Charlotte has been the catalyst for retail and commercial development in the northeast area. Patterned after European villages, even down to the red tile roofs on the buildings, the shopping center is built around a small man-made lake. Various retail stores, doctors' offices, movie theaters and restaurants are all within walking distance via connecting pathways of residential areas and the university. Choices of restaurants include Ciro's Italian Restaurant, House of Taipei and Providence Bistro & Bakery.

Windsor Square

Windsor Square North and Windsor Square South are located on Independence Boulevard in Matthews. Between the two you'll find Waccamaw Pottery, Sam's Wholesale Club, Burlington Coat Factory, Hamrick's and Media Play. There is a variety of retail and service stores in the area.

Windsor Square has about a dozen fast-food eateries and many popular restaurants including Meadowview Steakhouse, Outback Steakhouse, McGuffey's Steakhouse and Monterrey Mexican Restaurant.

Neighborhood Retail Centers

With small and medium-sized shopping centers springing up all over the place, many people do most of their shopping close to home or work. Smaller than shopping centers, neighborhood retail centers are primarily an attraction due to their supermarkets, drug stores, dry cleaners and other service-related establishments. Many are often home to some fascinating retail options. Here are a few of the special ones.

Dilworth

From the intersection of South Boulevard to Queens Road, a drive down East Boulevard in the Dilworth neighborhood offers a varied shopping experience. Browse through one-of-a-kind shops, some free standing or clustered together in centers.

Near South Boulevard you'll find a cluster of antique and consignments shops and some restaurants. At Kenilworth Commons, you can take a break at Dilworth Coffeehouse, visit Honeychile Gifts and browse through Dayna Shoes and Personally Yours.

At the intersection of Scott Avenue and East Boulevard is Dilworth Gardens with a variety of specialty shops, Cafe Verde in Talley's Green Grocery and Outback Steakhouse. Across East Boulevard The Shops at Twin Oaks has I.C. London for lingerie, Cotswold Photographers and Dikadee's Deli. Along this stretch of East Boulevard are a variety of shops and restaurants and service facilities.

Myers Park

Myers Park offers a veritable mecca of specialty shopping. Dotted along Providence Road from Morehead Street to Dartmouth Place are a number of specialty shops, services and restaurants. Colony, Reid's Fine Foods, which makes home deliveries, Grodzicki & Co., Queen Charlotte's Antiques Ltd., Mecklenburg Design Center and Golden Goose Maternity & Children's Apparel are just a few.

Outlet Malls and Shopping

Cannon Village
200 West Ave., Kannapolis • 938-3200

Cannon Village features off-price linens, housewares, books, rugs and apparel. More than 250,000 square feet of furniture, an Antique Mall, a free textile museum and a multi-image theatre are also located here.

Luxury Fabrics & Interiors
U.S. 321, N. Gastonia • 825-3696

Just outside of Gastonia, this outlet offers a large selection of drapery, upholstery and slipcover fabrics and trim.

Mary Jo's Cloth Store, Inc.
401 Cox Rd., Gastonia • 861-9100

Located in the Gaston Mall, Mary Jo's has fabric for all your sewing needs, bridal, calico, drapery and upholstery, and trims and notions.

The Resale Shop
Consignment Since 1952

Clothing and *much, much* more!
Be sure to see our great
selection of accessories
and household items.

Mon. - Fri. 10-5 Sat. 10-4
1920 E. 7th Street
376-1312

Outlet Marketplace
3700 Ave. of the Carolinas
Fort Mill, S.C. • (803) 548-5888

Bass, Carolina Pottery, Corning-Revere, Country Seat Outlet, Dress Barn, Hamricks and Van Heusen Direct are a sample of what this outlet mall offers. Stop at the Farmers Market to check out the local produce or have a snack or meal at the food court.

Woonsocket Spinning Factory Outlet
1400 Chippendale Rd. • 563-5489
4701 Monroe Rd. • 537-7015

Periodically, you'll find terrific buys on cashmere coats and jackets, as well as camel hair and cashmere cloth.

Consignment Shopping

Currently, more than 80 consignment shops dot the Charlotte area. Fashionable styles for women, children and men and just about everything else can be found at these shops throughout the city, as well as in Matthews, Mint Hill and Pineville. The Consignment & Resale Association of the Carolinas publishes a brochure listing approximately 40 consignment shops in the Charlotte area. You'll find the brochure in many of the shops.

The Classy Closet
1605 East Blvd. • 372-6249

Opened in 1980, The Classy Closet offers new and still tagged items, along with used women's clothing. A large selection of petite sizes are available.

Consignment World
533 N. Polk St., Pineville • 889-8966
10916 E. Independence Blvd., Matthews
• 847-2620

Two locations offer clothing for the entire family, baby equipment, furniture and household items.

Dilworth Consignment Shop
310 East Blvd. • 332-0668

Carefully selected women's clothing, vintage hats and jewelry, cards and unique gifts are offered at this shop.

Encore
1721 Kenilworth Ave. • 332-3365

Behind Dilworth Brewing you'll find Encore, offering designer and name-brand fashions.

Finders' Keepers
1201 Matthews Township Pkwy., Matthews
• 847-1672

Here you will find top quality, designer labels clothing for ladies, including jeans, sportswear, career dresses and suits as well as manufacturers' samples and below-wholesale jewelry. You can also find a good selection of cocktail/evening wear and maternity clothes.

In a Nutshell, Inc.
6138-A E. Independence Blvd. • 536-5418
This consignment shop carries a good selection of infant's and children's clothing.

JB's Consignment Warehouse
3813 South Blvd. • 522-7505
The Consignment Warehouse, Antique Corral and Gigantic Tent Sale cover 2 1/2 acres and offer antiques, general household goods, art, furniture and jewelry.

Kidsense
The Centrum, N.C. 51 • 543-4435
This shop offers a little bit of everything for girls and boys from infant to size 14.

The Resale Shop
1920 E. Seventh St. • 376-1312
A particular favorite, now well past its fourth decade, The Resale Shop not only carries clothing, but also lots of accessories as well as household items.

Sweet Repeats
300 East Blvd. • 372-0002
This consignment shop features expensive designer clothing.

Recommendations

Many specialty retail stores are hidden away, so they take some scouting out. There are just too many great stores to list, but we have mentioned some of the most popular in the area. For additional selections, check out the various Charlotte publications, as specialty stores advertise frequently. Or ask the locals about some of their favorite stores. Here are a few of ours.

Antiques

Antiques abound in Charlotte and in the surrounding areas. Check the Yellow Pages and pick up a copy of the *Antique and Gift Guide For North Carolina,* (336) 292-5870, available at most antique shops.

Antique Shops of Pineville
Main St., Pineville
South of Charlotte, a variety of antique shops offer Early American, English and Continental furniture, old books, antique linens, Persian rugs and much more.

Blacklion
10605 Park Rd. • 541-1148
Blacklion features a variety of antiques, artwork, lamps, rugs, furniture and gifts located in individually decorated show spaces.

Brem House
211 East Blvd. • 375-7800
Direct importers from Europe, this shop specializes in 18th- and 19th-century mahogany and pine, ironwork, porcelain and reproductions.

By-Gone Days Antiques, Inc.
3100 South Blvd. • 527-8717
If you are considering remodeling, this shop specializes in architectural antiques.

Churchill Galleries, Inc.
Phillips Place • 552-8088
This established dealer of fine antiques specializes in European furniture, porcelain, decorative objects and custom lamps.

The Crescent Collection
2318-C Crescent Ave. • 333-7922
This shop specializes in fine 18th- and 19th-century English antiques.

Interiors Marketplace
2000 South Blvd. • 377-6226
Located in Atherton Mill, a beautifully restored textile mill, more than 85 shops offer art, antiques, furnishing and accessories from around the world.

Metrolina Expo
7100 N. Statesville Rd. • 596-4643
One of the largest collections of furniture, home accessories, estate jewelry, vintage clothing and other collectibles are

for sale the first and third weekends of each month at the Metrolina Expo. Special shows are held at various times throughout the year. Call for show dates.

Market Place at Mint Hill
11237 Lawyers Rd. • 545-3117

The center of town provides a charming setting for 70 vendors to display their antiques and specialty items.

Queen Charlotte Antiques
603 Providence Rd. • 333-0472

This well-established store specializes in unusual English and French antiques.

Queen City Antiques & Collectibles
3892 E. Independence Blvd. • 531-6002

Over 50 dealers feature furniture from the late 1800s to 1950s, china, glassware and jewelry.

Waxhaw Antique Village
Providence Rd., Hwy. 16

This turn-of-the-century town is an antique lover's paradise with numerous shops filled with antiques and collectibles.

Book Stores

Barnes & Noble
3327 Pineville/Matthews Rd., The Arboretum • 341-9365
10701 Centrum Park, Pineville • 541-1425
5837 E. Independence Blvd. • 535-9810
4720 Sharon Rd., Sharon Corners • 554-7906

This national chain has a large selection. The Arboretum and Sharon Corners locations also have Starbucks Cafes.

The Bookmark
Uptown in Founders Hall • 377-2565

The Bookmark offers bestsellers, hardbacks, paperbacks, audiotapes and rentals. Special orders and gift certificates are available.

Borders Books & Music
Morrocroft Shopping Center • 365-6261

Located near SouthPark, Borders Books has redefined the bookstore experience, thus encouraging patrons to stay and linger. A special events coordinator arranges book signings and special events to draw crowds and the store offers wonderful magazine, newspapers, music and audio book sections. You'll also find a coffee bar offering exotic coffee blends and scrumptious desserts.

Gray's College Bookstores
9430 University City Blvd. • 548-8100

Gray's specializes in college, medical, nursing and allied health publications.

The Little Professor Book Center
Park Road Shopping Center • 525-9239

Owned by John Barringer, this shop has been a favorite among local bookworms for more than a decade.

MediaPlay
10011 E. Independence Blvd., Matthews • 847-4103
4716 South Blvd., • 525-2416
8600 University City Blvd., • 595-9956

These national mega-size bookstores also carry music, software and videos.

Poplar Street Books
226 W. 10th Street • 372-9146

With new, used and rare books and sheet music Poplar Street Books looks like something out of a Dickens' novel. Local literati and writers' groups hang out here and poetry readings are often held on Sunday afternoons.

Publishers Warehouse
401 S. Independence Blvd. • 373-0070

This shop inside the Midtown Square Mall features book liquidations, remainders and blank journals. The easiest access is from South King's Drive.

Waldenbooks
Carolina Place Mall • 544-2810
Eastland Mall • 568-5782

A national chain that offers the latest bestsellers plus thousands of other titles. It also carries newspapers and magazines.

Children's Books

Black Forest Books & Toys
115 Cherokee Rd. • 332-4838
Personalized attention and a good selection of both books and toys for children are hallmarks of these shops.

Bedford Falls Toy Shop
625 S. Sharon Amity Rd. • 365-8697
4217 Park Rd. • 527-1921
Children and young adults enjoy shopping the wide selection of books, games and many unusual toys found here.

Specialized Book Stores

Carolina Bookshop, 2440 Park Road., 375-7305, and Dilworth Books, 2035 South Boulevard, 372-8154, are located in Dilworth, have knowledgeable owners and are a good source for used and antique books.

The Baptist Book Store, 5412 South Boulevard, 523-5980, and Byrum's Christian Book Shop at 2329 The Plaza, 331-9717, offer a wide assortment of Christian books and music.

For those with a metaphysical turn of mind, check out Central Sun Storehouse, 1825 E. Seventh Street, 333-9200, or Unity Bookstore at 1000 E. Woodlawn Road, 523-0062.

Horizon Books, 10811 Pineville Road, Suite 1, Pineville, 643-7307, fax 643-7309, is a discount book locating and ordering service operated by Charles J. DiPerna for businesses, schools and individuals.

Clothing and Shoes

We can hardly scratch the surface of great specialty shops and boutiques around town, so we will have to settle for mentioning those that are either institutions in Charlotte or special places we are admittedly subjective about.

Benetton
SouthPark Mall • 364-1660
Benetton interprets the hottest fashion trends in a combination of colors, style and fabrics. Its mix-and-match concept offers the flexibility of coordinating classic separates into an exciting new look or blending them into your existing wardrobe.

The Carriage
6401 Morrison Blvd. • 364-0474
For classic Charlottean high fashion, you can't go wrong. This shop offers everything the well-dressed woman needs.

Dayna Shoes
1235-A East Blvd. • 343-2962
A great place to buy designer and name-brand shoes at discounted prices.

Designer Shoe Warehouse
3531 Tryclan Dr. • 525-4090
Shop Thursday through Sunday for a wide selection of shoes at incredible prices.

Fairclough & Co. Inc.
102 Middleton Dr. • 331-0001
One of the finest men's clothing stores in the city, this store offers tailored classics and exquisite styles and fabrics, from formal to casual. Service is its special strength, from helpful advice to coordinating an entire wardrobe.

Paul Simon for Women
1033 Providence Rd. • 333-6139
For classic women's clothing and fabulous accessories, from casual day wear to professional, this shop has it all — and in lots of sizes.

Lebo's
4118 E. Independence Blvd. • 535-5000
2901 Freedom Dr. • 394-4151
Lebo's offers all types of dancewear, aerobicwear, English and Western ridingwear and footwear in hard to find sizes.

Off Broadway Shoe Warehouse
2412 Sardis Road N. • 845-9028
201 W. Morehead St. • 347-1296
Open from Thursday through Sunday, each store has over 25,000 pairs of women's and men's designer shoes at discount prices.

Our Place

Sharon Corners • 554-7748

While the salespeople put together a stunning outfit, including accessories and jewelry, you can have a cup of coffee or a glass of wine and a snack. You'll feel pampered and have fun with the experience.

Perris Boutique

2907 Selwyn Ave. • 338-9011

With one-of-a-kind fashions and accessories, this great little boutique offers a high fashion alternative to the classical look.

Petite Panache

1041 Providence Rd. • 334-5833

This shop caters to women 5'4" or under who are looking for better-priced clothes and terrific accessories. It also offers wardrobe planning.

Taylor Richards and Conger

6401 Morrison Blvd. • 366-9092

This store offers elegant lines and classic European cuts for men. From jackets and fun wear to heavenly ties, formal wear and suits, this store is a treat.

Paul Simon Co.

1027 Providence Rd. • 372-6842
Morrocroft Village • 366-4523

Both shops offer a wonderful selection of men's clothing in a quiet and comfortable setting. Paul and his staff are always available to offer advice and assistance on everything from ties to shirts, suits to sports coats.

Carl Walker

715 Providence Rd. • 334-1003

Carl and his staff cater to women of discriminating taste and carry designer fashions for women of all ages.

Children's Clothing

For a fresh splash of unique clothes and furnishings for the itsy bitsy to the toddler-four crowd, stop by Bellini in the Kings Court Shopping Center at 901 S. Kings Drive, 377-6888. Bellini manufactures its own whimsically styled furniture, offering handpainted tables, chairs and toy chests. By selecting from the beautiful Posies christening gowns to the Trucfuchi, Sweet Potato and Itsy Bitsy fun fashions, junior can sport the haute couture look.

Baby Town, 3701 Monroe Road, 377-4111, and Babies R Us at Carolina Pavilion, 643-2229, and at 2408 Sardis Road N., 841-2229, also offer wonderful selections of furniture, toys and clothing. Kids Place at the Arboretum, 544-2311, and London Britches, Specialty Shops on the Park, 366-6111, have great selections.

Food

Arthur's
SouthPark Mall • 366-8610

This bakery, gourmet food, gift, coffee, tea, basket, chocolate and candy shop is also an award-winning wine shop and a great restaurant. The shop is neatly tucked away on the first level of Belk's and features a complete selection of California and imported wines, along with Charlotte's largest wine bar. Arthur's also has shops at Belk Eastland and Carolina Place Mall.

Charlotte Regional Farmers Market
1715 Yorkmont Rd. • 357-1269

Operated by the N.C. Department of Agriculture, this is the largest farmers market in the county and most Saturdays it takes on the atmosphere of a friendly country fair. In the past few years, some savvy farmers have branched out to include many items you'd find in the grocery store, such as bananas and pineapples, and the bouquets of farm-grown flowers have almost been nosed out by local area nurseries that bring truckloads of plants and shrubs. On the whole, shopping at farmers markets is a bit less expensive and a lot more fun. You'll get to know regular craftspeople,

plus find a revolving number of new ones each time you visit. This market is open during the blooming season from Tuesday through Saturday.

Fresh Market
4215 Providence Rd. • 365-6659
7623 Pineville-Matthews Rd. • 541-1882

Each store is filled with the sights and aromas of fresh vegetables, freshly ground coffee, cheeses, an old-fashioned butcher's shop, fresh seafood, a bakery, wine and all sorts of unusual items for the gourmet.

The Home Economist
5410 E. Independence Blvd. • 536-4663

This store has literally hundreds of foods that you can buy by the ounce or by the pound. It also sells natural foods, natural personal care products, vitamins, wines, herb teas, gourmet coffee, baking supplies and more. The store offers a full-service deli featuring homemade soups, sandwiches and salads.

Mecklenburg County Market
1515 Harding Place

One of the oldest in Charlotte, this farmers markets is open from 7 AM to 12 PM, Saturdays and Wednesdays. It's best to get there early to purchase home-baked goods, fresh vegetables and canned jams and jellies. The brick building is small, but you'll be surprised at the diversity. Bonsai trees, homemade crafts and flowers round out the offerings.

Morehead Seafood
919 S. McDowell St. • 375-4408

This shop offers a wide variety of fresh fish and shellfish six days a week.

Talley's Green Grocery
1408 East Blvd. • 334-9200

Charlotte's first whole foods supermarket, Talley's, features locally and organically grown produce, antibiotic- and hormone-free meats, free range poultry, milk in glass bottles, the freshest seafood — cleaned and cut into fillets in the store, wines, beers, coffee and cheeses from around the world. It has a tremendous selection of bulk items and gourmet and natural packaged items.

Nonfood items include a complete line of nutritional supplements, cruelty-free body care products and environmentally safe household products. All this, plus the in-house Cafe Verde (see Restaurant chapter), which features fresh and wholesome meals, makes Talley's a popular stop for today's health-conscious shoppers.

International specialty food stores have become very popular. Check out Parthenon Gift and Gourmet Shop at 4328 Central Avenue, 568-5262; Oriental Foods at 4816-B Central Avenue, 537-4281; Caribbean Foods at 1403 Eastway Drive, 563-5208; Jasrone Tropicana Mart at 2315 Central Avenue, 342-2098; and Middle East Deli at 4508 E. Independence Boulevard, 536-9847. Along South Boulevard, look for Las Dos Rosas Mexican Food Market at 7015, 554-9902, or Park-N-Shop at 4750, 521-8255. Other stores with an international flavor include Vietnam Oriental & Seafood Market at 2417 N. Tryon Street, 347-1747, and Payal Indian Groceries & Spices at 6400 Old Pineville Road, 521-9680.

Gifts, Stationery and Paper Products

With letter writing becoming fashionable again, stationery and paper goods stores have sprung up all over Charlotte. Visit any of the ones listed below for a wide selection. You may also want to check out some discount paper and party supply stores, such as If It's Paper at 5102 South Boulevard, 529-1236, and Papertown, 4420 Monroe Road, 342-5815.

The Buttercup
343 Providence Rd. • 332-5329
This shop offers a wonderful selection of all types of paper goods and distinctive gifts. You'll find unique items for entertaining, birthday, baby, anniversary or graduation gifts and for those little touches that make a house a home. The entire upstairs is devoted to stationery supplies with hundreds of invitations and announcements for all occasions.

Bush Stationers & Gifts
117 Middleton Dr. • 333-4438

Located in the middle of Myers Park in a unique 1920's house, this shop maintains an extensive variety of stationery and invitations, collectibles and giftware and toiletries by Crabtree & Evelyn and Cassell Massey.

M. Grodzicki & Co.
611 Providence Rd. • 334-7300

This shop features sophisticated items such as china, silver and home accessories and casual, fun items for parties, as well as cards, stationery, balloons and baskets, plus its own spicy peanuts and Belgian chocolates.

Papitre at Morrocroft Village
3908 Colony Rd. • 364-4567

This south Charlotte stationery store carries a wide variety of in-stock invitations and can even perform the miracle of 24-hour turnaround when needed.

Home Furnishing

North Carolina is home to just about every major furniture manufacturer in the country. Here are just a few of the large variety of home furnishings and accessories and numerous professionals to help you put it all together.

Accessible Environments, Inc.
1125 E. Morehead St. • 376-6641

For stylish, barrier-free interiors, owner Calvin Hefner, A.S.I.D., offers designs for the disabled and aging population.

Boyles Furniture
I-77 & Nations Ford Rd. • 522-8081

Boyles offers discounts of 40-50 percent below retail on famous-name manufacturers.

Colony Furniture Shops
811 Providence Rd. • 333-8871

The area's oldest complete interior design showroom features distinctive furnishings, period antiques and handmade rugs.

The Design Place
820 South Blvd. • 333-5208

Specializing in custom accessories for the home since 1979, this shop also offers a large selection of wallpaper and fabric that can be viewed by appointment only. The staff is knowledgeable, friendly and experienced in residential and commercial interior design.

Drexel Heritage
11410 Carolina Place Pkwy. • 542-4770

This shop offers both low prices and an extensive assortment of home accessories.

Becky Gill Interiors
4007 Meadowridge Dr. • 542-5583

This shop has been specializing in traditional and transitional interiors for over 10 years.

Lee Lighting
9600 Monroe St. • 847-8765

Ideal Lighting offers a wide selection of lighting fixtures and other related products. Trained consultants are available to assist in the showroom or at your home.

Interiors Marketplace
2000 South Blvd., Suite 200 • 377-6226

Located in a beautifully restored textile mill adjacent to restaurants and Charlotte's famed trolley, Interiors Marketplace features over 85 shops offering art, antiques, furnishings and accessories from around the world.

Marcella Davis Interiors
Pineville • 889-2492

Available by appointment only, Marcella Davis Interiors specializes in space planning, color and lighting coordination, and selecting and blending furniture styles, fabrics and accessories. Custom window treatments and special finishes for walls and furniture are also available. A booth showcasing decorative items is at Blacklion on Park Road.

Mecklenburg Furniture
520 Providence Rd. • 376-8401

A unique source for home furnishings, from traditional to contemporary, this store also offers accessories, fabrics, wall coverings and specialty items and it has experienced designers on staff.

Metro-Designs For Modern Living
911 E. Morehead St. • 375-4563

Here you'll find contemporary and unusual home furnishings and accessories.

Persian Rug House
312 Main St., Pineville • 889-2454

The Persian Rug House has the largest selection of Persian rugs in the area. In business since 1986, it buys and trades old rugs and provides professional cleaning, repair, appraisal, pick up and delivery.

Robbie A. Warren Interiors
316 Main St., Pineville • 889-4426

Established in 1989, this firm offers custom interiors from single-room projects to full-scale home design by appointment only.

Edward H. Springs Interiors, Inc.
1236 E. Morehead St. • 376-6461

Serving the Charlotte area since 1970, this shop deals in residential and commercial design by appointment only.

Carol Troy Interiors, Inc.
2318 Crescent Ave. • 554-5600

In business for over 10 years, this firm specializes in residential and small commercial projects, blending the owners' special treasures with a mix of contemporary and traditional styles.

Jewelry

Donald Haack Diamonds
4611 Sharon Rd. • 365-4400

This store maintains one of the largest diamond inventories in the Southeast and has an international reputation for dealing in quality gems. When looking for that perfect stone, this is the place to go.

Perry's At SouthPark
SouthPark Mall • 364-1391

Perry's is one of Charlotte's finest and most unusual jewelry stores. Perry's can buy, sell on consignment, trade or repair your family treasures.

Special Places

Every city has a few places that defy being put into a category, and Charlotte has its share.

The Celtic Trader
645-G Pressley Rd. • 527-3800

Far more than a specialty music store, it's the only store in Charlotte that holds weekly jam sessions. Owner, Rege Malady happens to be a big folk music enthusiast and can help you find about anything you're looking for in folk music. You'll find musical instruments hanging from the walls and ceiling, sheet music, tapes, CDs and even jewelry from the British Isles. Each Thursday around 8 PM you'll hear musicians, some from as far away as West Virginia, sit in with the regulars for the weekly session. If you haven't been to this free event, by all means treat yourself.

Central Sun Storehouse
1825 E. Seventh St. • 333-9200

A variety of products and services for the mind, body and spirit can be found here. Health foods, herbs, an extensive book department with an emphasis on spiritual self-development and metaphysical topics, tapes to meditate or relax by, New Age music, natural cosmetics, crystals, and precious and semiprecious stones are available. A spiritual astrologer and massage therapist are on staff, and classes on such topics as meditation and astrology are offered.

Jesse Brown's Outdoors
4732 Sharon Rd. • 556-0020

Since 1970, this store has been offering the best in flyfishing, backpacking, climbing, camping, and outdoor equipment and clothing. It has the area's largest selection of Fly Fishing, The North Face, Barbour and Filson merchandise. Flyfishing clinics and camping rentals are available.

Renfrow's General Store
188 N. Trade St., Matthews • 847-4088

It's worth a special trip to Matthews to visit Renfrow's General Store because it provides a step back in time to what a dry goods store was like at the turn of the century. Where else could you find such items as bib overalls and animal feed, as well as garden supplies, kitchen products, hardware and housewares?

Science Hobbies
901 North Wendover Rd. • 367-2215

In business over 30 years, Science Hobbies is not a traditional hobby shop. It has evolved into an eclectic shop where you can find just about anything from lab wares to wooden ship models to beads. The shop specializes in material for science projects. If you want it, you'll find it at Science Hobbies. And if you don't, the sales staff will go that extra mile to find it for you.

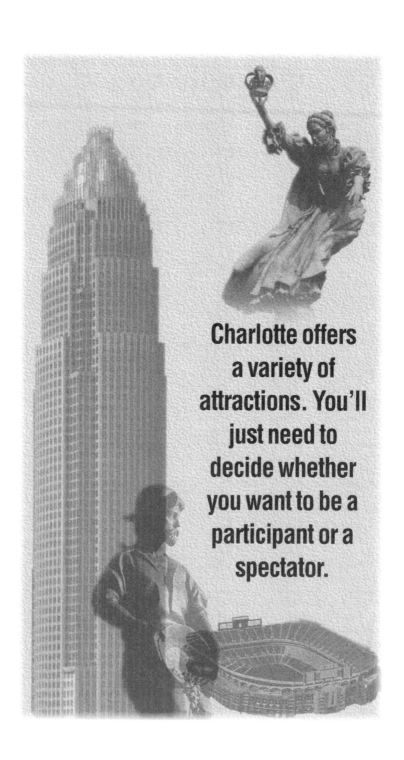

Charlotte offers a variety of attractions. You'll just need to decide whether you want to be a participant or a spectator.

Attractions

Charlotte offers a variety of year-round and seasonal attractions. You'll just need to decide whether you want to be a participant or a spectator. Additional suggestions on things to do and places to visit in the Metrolina area are given in our chapters on Annual Events, Mecklenburg Towns, Neighboring Towns, and Daytrips and Weekend Vacations.

Afro-American Cultural Center
401 N. Myers St. • 374-1565

Saved from demolition and beautifully restored, this former Little Rock AME Zion Church in the heart of First Ward promotes, presents and preserves Afro-American cultural history. The Center includes an art gallery and theater and offers educational classes. It is open from 10 AM until 6 PM Tuesday through Saturday and from 1 until 5 PM on Sunday. No admission is charged.

Blockbuster Pavilion
707 Blockbuster Blvd. • 549-5555

Blockbuster Pavilion, located 11 miles from Uptown on U.S. 29 North, promotes spectacular, state-of-the-art, star-studded entertainment. Performances run from April through October at this outdoor amphitheater. Since it opened, the Pavilion has showcased world-class concerts, Broadway shows, opera and ballet and the most popular rock, country and pop stars.

Guests can bring a blanket and relax outside with refreshments from the concessions (guests aren't allowed to bring their own food). Lawn chairs are available for rent with the proceeds going to a local charity. The $14.5 million, 19,000-capacity facility offers great acoustics and good sight lines. For business needs, the Pavilion offers private boxes, club seating, hospitality tents and VIP parking.

Carolina's Aviation Museum
Charlotte/Douglas International Airport
4108 Airport Dr. • 359-8442

Dedicated to preserving the aviation history of the Carolinas, the Carolinas Historic Aviation Commission's Air Museum offers visitors an opportunity to view aircraft on display. The museum is open Monday through Thursday and Saturday from 10 AM to 5 PM and Sunday from 1 to 4 PM. There is no charge.

Charlotte Coliseum
100 Paul Buck Blvd. • 357-4700
• Ticketmaster: 522-6500

This 24,000-seat facility is the home of the National Basketball Association Charlotte Hornets and the Women's National Basketball Association Charlotte Sting. Atlantic Coast Conference basketball, the circus and the Ice Capades are big crowd pleasers here each year, as well as other sporting events, pageants, concerts, rodeos, horse shows and big-name entertainment.

Charlotte Motor Speedway
Concord • 455-3200

America's premier NASCAR facility is home to the Coca-Cola 600, the Red Dog 300 and The Winston each May. The All Pro Bumper to Bumper 300 and the UAW-GM Quality 500 are held in October. Every April and September, the speedway hosts an "Automobilia" event featuring major auto shows. Throughout the year, group and individual tours are available and a gift shop is open. For more information on the Charlotte Motor Speedway and speedway events, see "Racing" in the Sports chapter. The mailing address for the Charlotte Motor Speedway is P.O. Box 600, Concord, NC 28026.

Charlotte Museum of History & Hezekiah Alexander Homesite
3500 Shamrock Dr. • 568-1774

Charlotte's oldest home, built in 1774, served as the home of Hezekiah and Mary Alexander and their 10 children. Alexander was a blacksmith and planter by trade and assumed a leadership role in the new community called Charlotte. He eventually became a signer of the Mecklenburg Declaration of Independence.

Today his homesite, plus a replicated kitchen and reconstructed spring house, is the site of two special annual events: Colonial Christmas with weekends devoted to music, crafts and food and Rites of Spring, featuring the way colonists celebrated, with sheep shearing, music and other activities.

Changing exhibits in the adjacent Museum of History focus on local, regional and state history as well as on special collections. Guided tours are given by the active docents who serve the homesite. Groups are encouraged to make arrangements for morning tours.

The house and museum are open from 10 AM until 5 PM Tuesday through Friday and from 2 until 5 PM on weekends. Tours of the homesite are given at 1:15 and 3:15 PM Tuesday through Friday; 2:15 and 3:15 PM Saturday and Sunday. The museum is free, but admission is charged for the hour-long guided tour of the homesite. The fees are $4 for adults, $3 for seniors 65 and older and $2 for children ages 6-16.

Charlotte Trolley and Museum
2104 South Blvd. • 375-0850

The museum provides a glimpse into Charlotte's past before buses and automobiles were a common sight. Refurbished Trolley Number 85, the last working trolley in Charlotte, is available for rides from Dilworth's South End to the Convention Center. The museum and trolley are also available to rent for parties or other special occasions. The museum and trolley operate on Friday, Saturday and Sunday from 10 AM to 6 PM. Museum admission is free; trolley fare is $2.00 per person.

Discovery Place
301 N. Tryon St. • 372-6261, (800) 935-0553

Discovery Place is one of America's top science museums. This hands-on science

Photo Courtesy of Charlotte Convention & Visitors Bureau

Charlotte's oldest home is the Hezekiah Alexander House built in 1774.

Photo Courtesy of Charlotte Convention & Visitors Bureau

The OMNIMAX Theatre and Planetarium at Discovery Place provide hours of fun.

and technology museum in Uptown Charlotte welcomes over 400,000 visitors annually and is open every day of the year except Thanksgiving and Christmas. The museum offers an OMNIMAX Theatre and Planetarium combination that is unique to the United States. With a 79-foot dome, the planetarium is the largest in the nation.

Among the permanent exhibits are the Collections Gallery, the Aquarium and the Knight Rain Forest. "Hands-on" exhibits are also featured with a collection of experiments designed to teach the basic principles of science through color, motion and perception. The Challenger Learning Center presents a simulation of earth's rendezvous with Halley's Comet in 2061. Kid's Place, an early childhood learning area, features the Puppet Place stage with shows that delight visitors of all ages. The museum has hosted outstanding traveling exhibits such as Dinosaurs, The Magic School Bus, Bionics and Transplants, Science in Toyland and 1492: Two Worlds of Science.

The Exhibit Hall hours are from 9 AM to 5 PM Monday through Friday, Saturday from 9 AM to 6 PM and Sunday from 1 to 6 PM. Reservations for regularly scheduled

OMNIMAX and planetarium shows can be made by telephone. Call for current admission rates and discounts. The first Wednesday of each month is "Wonderful Wednesday" and admission is free for everyone after 2 PM. Annual family memberships entitle holders to unlimited visits and special benefits. The museum also sponsors regular workshops, field trips, camps and learning vacations.

EnergyQuest
4850 Concord Rd., York, S.C.
• **(803) 831-3612, (800) 777-0006**
Located at the Catawba Nuclear Station, self-guided tours are designed to provide information about nuclear power. EnergyQuest is open Monday through Saturday from 9 AM to 5 PM. Picnic areas and group tours are available.

Energy Explorium
At Lake Norman
13339 Hagers Ferry Rd., Huntersville
• **875-5600**
Operated by Duke Power Company and located near the McGuire Nuclear Station, this energy information center offers

hands-on exhibits of model nuclear and coal-fired power plants and a film entitled, *Lake Norman — the Great Inland Sea*. You can walk through the wildflower garden, travel the one-mile nature trail or enjoy a picnic lunch. The Energy Explorium is accessible via boat and car and is open every day of the year except Thanksgiving, Christmas Eve, Christmas and New Year's Day. Hours are 9 AM until 5 PM Monday through Saturday and noon until 5 PM Sunday. Inquire about tours for McGuire's Control Room Simulator. No admission is charged.

Fourth Ward
Uptown Charlotte

In the mid-1800s, Charlotte was divided into four political wards. The northwest quadrant, called Fourth Ward, was a prosperous area containing the homes of merchants, ministers, physicians and others. In the early 1900s, the trolley expanded travel throughout Charlotte, and Dilworth and Myers Park became the prestigious places to live. By the '50s, Fourth Ward was becoming an undesirable area with abandoned or substandard housing, scattered businesses and crime.

By 1970, when many homes had been destroyed by fire, vandals and neglect, the Junior League, UNC Charlotte and a few other civic-minded people had a dream. It was of interest to the city, banks and, most importantly, the residents to save Fourth Ward and make it a desirable area once again. By 1978, most of the homes had been bought by adventurous, modern-day pioneers. The restoration was strictly governed by the homeowners association and this is now a beautiful, active community that has increased the tax revenue to the city tenfold. This turn-of-the-century Victorian neighborhood, in the heart of Uptown, is a nice spot for strolling during the day or for taking the tour of homes at Christmastime.

Fresco at St. Peter's Catholic Church
507 S. Tryon St. • 332-2901

The ancient art form of fresco, which means fresh, can be seen in the magnificent work of North Carolina native Ben Long in this beautiful 1893 Charlotte church. The fresco is a triptych depicting The Agony, The Resurrection and Pentecost. Long apprenticed with Pietro Annigoni of Florence, Italy, for seven years. Besides this one, the artist has two fresco works in Italy, several in West Jefferson and Glendale Springs, North Carolina (one of the largest tourist attractions in North Carolina) and one in the NationsBank Corporate Center in Uptown Charlotte. In addition, he recently completed a fresco for the new Law Enforcement Center at 601 East Trade Street. The church is open to visitors from 10 AM until noon and from 1 until 4 PM Sunday through Friday and from 10 AM until 4 PM on Saturday. Visitors are requested to be sensitive to parish activities such as masses and weddings. No admission is charged.

Gaston County Museum of Art & History
131 W. Main St., Dallas • 922-7681

Located in the historic Dallas court square in the restored 1852 Hoffman Hotel, this museum features Victorian Period rooms with changing exhibits on American art and history. The largest public collection of carriages and sleighs in the state is displayed in the Stowe Carriage House.

Historic Rosedale
3247 N. Tryon St. • 335-0325

In the early 1800s, builders of finer homes fully utilized their artistic abilities producing elegant results. Not always able to find or afford exotic woods such as rosewood and mahogany, the builders became skilled at painting substituted wood to look like the expensive original materials. These faux (fake) finishes, as they were called, grace many of America's most famous homes. At Rosedale, the 1815 private home of Archibald Frew, you'll need to stand within 8 inches of the mahogany paneling before discovering that the wood has been painted.

Frew's diverse occupations as merchant, postmaster and tax collector took him through many coastal areas where he became enamored of classic architectural styles with plantation overtones. When you visit the restored home,

you'll see Frew's taste in carved Adams mantels, elaborate cornices, detailed moldings, a classic porch and dormers.

Unfortunately, Frew lost his home in 1819 in a federal bankruptcy case. His brother-in-law, William Davidson, purchased the stately home and it remained in the same family for 170 years. In 1986, Rosedale was sold to the Historic Preservation Foundation of North Carolina. After an extensive restoration, the home opened to the public in November 1993 in conjunction with the Mint Museum's exhibit, "Classical Taste In America." Today you can take the docent-led, one-hour tour through the home that is largely unfurnished to showcase the decorative elements.

You can also tour the restored boxwood garden where you'll see seven "treasure trees," some thought to have been planted by Archibald Frew and three of which are considered to be the largest known of their species in this area. Rosedale is open each Thursday and Sunday from 1 until 4 PM February through November and during the week by appointment. Tours during the week must include a minimum of 10 people. Admission is $3 per person. Children younger than 12 and members of Historic Rosedale are admitted free. Group rates are $2 per person (15 or more). For more information write to Historic Rosedale, P.O. Box 6212, Charlotte, NC 28207.

Info Charlotte
330 South Tryon St.
331-2700, (800) 231-4636

Operated jointly by the Charlotte Convention & Visitors Bureau and the Charlotte Chamber, Info Charlotte is a colorful and unique marketing center. This 5,000-square-foot building includes a variety of displays such as The Wonder Wall with three CD-interactive informational kiosks that allow you to explore the area and obtain information at the touch of the screen, a 50-seat theater showing tourism videos narrated by the late Charles Kuralt and an 8' x 8' model of Charlotte that spotlights areas of interest at the push of a button. Wrapped around Info Charlotte's 17-foot ceiling is a photographic time-line tracing the history of Charlotte from the 1700s to today. Racks of free brochures and a wide variety of Charlotte and North Carolina souvenirs are available. Open Monday through Friday from 8:30 AM to 5 PM, Saturday from 10 AM to 4 PM and Sunday from 1 to 4 PM.

Latta Place
5225 Sample Rd., Huntersville
- **House: 875-2312**
- **Visitors Center: 875-1391**

This early 1800 river plantation was owned by James Latta, a prosperous traveling

Latta Place offers a glimpse of life in the early 1800s.

merchant who bought wares in Charleston and Philadelphia and peddled them to his Carolina Piedmont neighbors. Costumed guides give tours of the two-story house, which is on the National Register of Historic Places. The plantation comes complete with farm animals and a unique equestrian center.

Tours are given by appointment Tuesday through Friday and at 1:30, 2:30 and 3:30 PM on Saturday and Sunday. Admission for the tour is $4 for adults, $3 for students and seniors and $2 for ages 6 through 12. Children under five are admitted at no charge. For details on Latta Plantation Park, check our chapter on Parks and Recreation.

McIntyre Historic Site
Off Beatties Ford Rd. • 875-1391

This northern Mecklenburg historic area marks the place where the famous Battle of the Bees occurred in 1780 when 14 farmer/ soldiers drove off a regiment of General Cornwallis' army with the help of an overturned bee's nest that targeted the Tories. A self-guided trail interprets the battle. Information on this attraction is available from the Latta Plantation Visitors Center.

Mecklenburg Aquatic Center
800 E. Second St. • 336-3483

The Aquatic Center, located in Uptown Charlotte, is owned and operated by the Mecklenburg County Park and Recreation Department. This state-of-the-art swimming complex seats approximately 1,300 spectators. The facility includes a 50-meter swimming pool, two 3-meter diving boards and two 1-meter diving boards. The main pool includes a hydraulic floor that allows the depth of the water to be adjusted for various activities and instruction. This handicap-accessible facility also includes a 25-yard hydrotherapy pool, a 16-foot in-ground spa and an exercise/fitness room.

The Aquatic Center is the site of Charlotte UltraSwim, an amateur swimming competition that has featured Olympians, world record holders and teams from around the world, the 1995 YWCA Nationals and numerous local and regional events.

Metrolina Expo Center
7100 Statesville Rd. • 596-4643

In 1971, a small number of vendors set up their tables and sold their wares at the Charlotte Fairgrounds. As "flea markets" became the rage of the times, the Fairground Flea Market grew rapidly. Savvy entrepreneurs use the market as a place to bring in a little extra cash or unload overruns from local factories.

On the first and third weekend of every month, the country's largest monthly antiques and collectibles flea market is held here. Antique dealers converge from Maine, Iowa, California, Texas, Florida and many states in between. They bring with them some of the finest antique furniture available as well as old farm implements and rare tools. Every conceivable type of old glassware, crystal and china passes through the gates, along with all kinds of memorabilia. For the shopper, Metrolina Expo is filled with old-fashioned nostalgia amidst a happy carnival-like atmosphere. The first weekends of April and November feature an Antique Spectacular.

In addition to the incredible first and third weekends of each month, a special Summer Craft Show and a Christmas Country Show draw thousands of shoppers. General admission is charged; however, senior citizens are admitted for half-price and children younger than 12 are admitted free. Hours are from 8 AM to 5 PM on Saturday and from 9 AM to 5 PM on Sunday. Plentiful free parking makes this a fun place to explore and discover hidden treasures.

Mint Museum of Art
2730 Randolph Rd. • 337-2000
• Taped Highlights: 333-MINT

The Mint served the region as the first branch of the Philadelphia Mint, coining $5 million in gold from 1836 until the outbreak of the Civil War. A grassroots effort during the Depression saved the original Strickland building from demolition and moved it to its present Randolph Road site where, in 1936, it opened as the state's first art museum. The Mint has since grown and is now one of the Southeast's leading art museums.

The collections include important American and European paintings and sculpture, Pre-Colombian, African and Spanish Colonial art, historic costumes, regional crafts and one of America's premiere collections of pottery and porcelain. The permanent collection is enhanced by special changing exhibitions, including major exhibitions on national tour. In early 1999, the Mint Museum of Craft and Design will open on North Tryon Street, featuring collections of ceramics, glass, wood and fibers.

Photo Courtesy of Charlotte Convention & Visitors Bureau

The Mint Museum of Art is one of the Southeast's leading art museums.

Throughout the year, lectures, seminars, teaching programs for children and adults, films, festivals and other activities that supplement the exhibitions are available. The Mint is open 10 AM until 10 PM on Tuesdays, 10 AM until 5 PM Wednesday through Saturday and 12 until 5 PM on Sunday. Admission is $4 for adults — members and children younger than 12 are admitted free. Admission is free on Tuesday evenings from 5 until 10 PM and the second Sunday of each month. For current program information, call the taped highlights number.

The Museum of the Alphabet
Davis Road at JAARS Ctr., Waxhaw • 843-6066

Reading and writing seem very basic to most of us, but few of us realize that approximately half the world's 6,000 plus languages are still without a written form. The Museum of the Alphabet focuses on the written language, where it began and how it developed, by tracing the history of alphabets

This Totem Pole, made by third graders from used telephone equipment, is found at the Museum of York County.

and other writing systems from the beginning to the present. Both ancient and modern alphabet makers are highlighted in the picturesque settings of the museum displays. You'll see the Chinese alphabet (oldest system, unchanged in 4,000 years) as well as Hebrew, Greek, Aramaic, Arabic and English. Because of the scholarly presentation of the displays, children younger than 12 should be accompanied by an adult. The museum is open from 9 AM until noon and 1 until 3:30 PM Monday through Saturday. No admission is charged, but donations are appreciated.

Museum of the New South
324 N. College St. • 333-1887

Located Uptown, this is Charlotte's only regional museum that features the history of the New South from post-Reconstruction to the present. A unique aspect of the museum is the "hear, touch and see" exhibits of artifacts and stories of the Piedmont region. The museum sponsors exhibits, lectures, tours and programs for all ages. The museum is open Tuesday through Saturday from 11 AM to 5 PM. Admission is $2 for adults, $1 for students and seniors or $5 for families. On the second Saturday of each month admission is free.

Museum of the Waxhaws
Hghwy. 75, Waxhaw • 843-1832

Through an audio/visual program you'll discover the backcountry and pioneering life-style of the Scots-Irish who settled in this area. This memorial features exhibits and other educational programming. The museum is open Wednesday through Saturday from 10 AM to 5 PM and on Sunday from 1 to 5 PM. Admission is $1 for adults and children over 12.

Museum of York County
4621 Mount Gallant Rd., Rock Hill, S.C.
• (803) 329-2121, (800) 968-2762

This museum is a true find for children and adults as well. The museum's phenomenal animal exhibits are reminiscent, though on a smaller scale, of New York's Natural History Museum. The museum also features a planetarium, art and astronomy exhibits and curriculum-based school programs. It offers an excellent gift shop and is open from 10 AM until 5 PM Monday through Saturday and from 1 until 5 PM on Sunday. From Charlotte take I-77 South to S.C. 161 (exit 82A), turn right onto Celanese Road and right on Mount Gallant. Admission is $4 for adults and $3 for students and seniors. Children younger than 5 are admitted at no charge and every third Sunday of the month admission is free.

North Carolina Transportation Museum at Spencer Shops
411 S. Salisbury Ave., Spencer
• **636-2889**

This former repair shop for Southern Railway Company features transportation displays and train rides on specified days. You'll see N.C.'s first Highway Patrol car, railway cars and engines and antique cars. The site has a terrific gift shop with railroad items not found elsewhere. This intriguing museum for railroad buffs is open from 9 AM until 5 PM Tuesday through Saturday and from 1 until 5 PM on Sunday from April through October. From November through March, the hours are 10 AM until 4 PM and 1 until 4 PM on Sunday. Admission is $3.50 for adults and $2.50 for children. To get to Spencer Shops from Charlotte, take I-85 N. to exit 70.

Paramount's Carowinds
Exit 90 off I-77 S.
(800) 888-4386

Paramount's Carowinds, a world-class 100-acre theme park, features more than 40 rides, shows and movie-theme experiences for all ages as well as numerous shops and restaurants. The 1996 addition to the rides was the DROP ZONE Stunt Tower, which offers the awesome thrill of a high altitude free-fall. It's located in WAYNE'S WORLD, an 8-acre area based on the movie. A recent $7 million expansion added five new attractions and doubled the size of the Water Works water entertainment complex.

In 1999, Top Gun will join the existing rollercoasters, Hurler, Vortex, Thunder Road, Carolinas Cyclone, Carolina Goldrusher, Taxi Jam and Scooby-Doo's Ghoster Coaster,

Photo Courtesy of Paramount's Carowinds

The DROP ZONE Stunt Tower, at Paramount's Carowinds, treats daring riders to a 174-foot, 56 m.p.h. free-fall.

which are located throughout the park. Other popular attractions include Animation Station, a colorful cartoon fantasyland; WaterWorks, a miniature water park for young children; all-family water attractions such as Rip Roarin' Rapids and WhiteWater Falls; The Carousel, a 1923 antique featuring 68 hand-carved wooden horses; and Carolina Sternwheeler, a three-deck riverboat that navigates a quarter-mile lagoon.

Some restaurants are Casey's Grill, which offers a variety of hot dogs; WINGS, where you are surrounded by authentic antiques and bi-plane era props; and Stan Mikita's Diner, featuring some of Wayne's and Garth's favorite foods.

The 13,000-seat Paladium Amphitheatre hosts big-name concerts and special events each season. The shows run from mid-April to mid-September and tickets must be purchased in addition to Park admission.

Open weekends spring and fall, daily during summer, Paramount's Carowinds popular one-price ticket covers all rides and park shows. 1998 general admission for ages 7 to 54 is $29.99 and $17.99 for children ages 4 to 6 and seniors 55 and older. Children 3 and younger are admitted free. A special "after 5 PM" admission price of $15 for all ages is also available. Family and individual season passes are valid for unlimited visits to any Paramount theme park. Paramount's Carowinds Campground is open year round. When planning a trip to Paramount's Carowinds, try to choose a date that falls outside the park's busiest times. Lines are usually shorter on Sundays than Saturdays. Weekdays from June 1 to August 18 are even better. Hours and operating dates vary, so before planning a visit it is a good idea to call the Information Center.

Philip Morris
U.S. 29 S., Concord • 788-5699

This manufacturing center and museum in Cabarrus County is set in an area of pastures, woods and lakes. You'll find an extensive collection of North Carolina folk art with good representations of pottery, earthenware, baskets, paintings and the world's largest hanging quilted tapestry, which was hand-stitched in Franklin, North Carolina. Another interesting exhibit is its collection of over 1,500 postcards depicting every region of the state from the beaches to the mountains.

James K. Polk Memorial
U.S. 521, Pineville • 889-7145

James K. Polk was born in a log cabin in Pineville in 1795. His homestead has been reconstructed and is now a state historic site.

Photo courtesy of Paramount's Carowinds

Paramount's Carowinds WaterWorks offers 12 acres of wet and cool fun.

Photo by Robert Thomason

James K. Polk, 11th President of the United States, is memorialized at the Polk Memorial. The flavor of those times is captured in several period buildings.

Polk's 200th birthday was celebrated on September 4, 1995, with a number of special events, including the issue of 1,000 bicentennial stamps that were cancelled on postcards at the Polk Memorial.

Guided tours of the buildings are available anytime but are especially beautiful when the candles are lit at the annual Christmas celebration. The Polk Memorial is open from 9 AM until 5 PM Monday through Saturday, April through October; and from 10 AM until 4 PM Tuesday through Saturday, November through March. Sunday hours are 1 until 5 PM April through October and 1 until 4 PM November through March. Admission is free. For more information, write to James K. Polk Memorial, P.O. Box 475, Pineville, NC 28134.

Reed Gold Mine
Stanfield • 786-8337

Reed Gold Mine is the site of the first authenticated gold find in the United States. Residents of the area know the story of young Conrad Reed, who discovered a 17-pound gold nugget in 1799, and how his family used it for a doorstop for three years before selling it at the ridiculous price of $3.50 to a Fayetteville jeweler.

Today visitors flock to this remote Cabarrus County spot where they can tour the underground mine, walk the nature trails,

enjoy a picnic or learn more about gold mining in the museum. There is a 20-minute film that serves as a great introduction. April through October you can pan for gold ($2 per pan of dirt or $1 per pan for groups of 10 or more). Hours are from 9 AM until 5 PM Monday through Saturday from April through October and 10 AM until 4 PM Tuesday through Saturday from November through March. Sunday hours are 1 to 5 PM during the summer season, but are one hour shorter during the winter. No admission is required at this wonderful historic site.

Schiele Museum
1500 E. Garrison Blvd., Gastonia
• 866-6900

This museum is one of the most visited museums in North Carolina. It features an outstanding exhibit of the state's natural history, an extensive collection of North American land mammals, plus a planetarium. It is a museum that will excite both children and adults, especially those who visit the pioneer site where living history demonstrations are staged throughout the year. The museum is open 9 AM to 5 PM Monday through Saturday and 1 to 5 PM on Sunday. From Charlotte, take I-85 S. to Gastonia's New Hope Road exit. Follow New Hope Road to Garrison Boulevard. No admission is charged.

Daniel Stowe Botanical Garden
6500 S. New Hope Rd., Belmont
• 825-4490

Located on a 450-acre site on Lake Wylie, just outside of Belmont, the Daniel Stowe Botanical Garden is being developed over the next 40 years to become one of the leading botanical gardens in the United States. The master plan began to unfold in 1995 with the construction of the 110-acre Phase I major gardens and a permanent Visitors Pavilion due to open in May 1999. The garden is expected to attract upwards of 1,000,000 visitors annually.

There are over 10 acres of perennials, daylilies, annuals and herbs surrounded by rolling meadows. There is also a Visitors Center and a gift shop. The gardens are open from 9 AM to 5 PM Monday through Saturday and Sunday from 12 to 5 PM. The gardens are closed Thanksgiving, Christmas and New Year's Day.

UNC Charlotte Botanical Gardens
N.C. 49 N • 547-2364, 547-4286

A beautiful way to escape any time, but especially on rainy days, the tropical atmosphere of the McMillan Greenhouse will revitalize your sagging spirits. The UNC Charlotte Botanical Gardens are located in the northeast area of the university campus at the corner of Mary Alexander and Craver roads. Park at the greenhouse. Stroll through the Van Landingham Glen amidst the profusion of rhododendron and enjoy the plants in the Susie Harwood Garden. The gardens are open every day; the greenhouse is open from 9 AM until 4 PM

Photo courtesy of DSBG; photo by Mike Bush

The Daniel Stowe Botanical Garden is located in Belmont, N.C.

The beautiful gardens at Wing Haven offer a sanctuary for all.

weekdays and 10 AM until 3 PM Saturday. Special tours can be arranged.

Wing Haven Gardens & Bird Sanctuary
248 Ridgewood Ave. • 331-0664

Wing Haven was only a bare 3-acre patch of land in 1927 when Edwin and Elizabeth Clarkson built their home and began working on their garden in this quiet pocket of Myers Park. Now, almost 70 years later, the fruits of their labors are enjoyed by more than 9,000 visitors each year.

The gardens are now the responsibility of the Wing Haven Foundation, a nonprofit corporation. Membership is open to anyone. The gardens are open 3 until 5 PM Tuesday, 10 AM to 12 PM Wednesday and 2 until 5 PM Sunday. Guided tours may be arranged Tuesdays through Fridays. Admission is free.

The wealth
of places,
events
and activities
in the metropolitan
Charlotte area
appeal to the
kid in all of us.

Kidstuff

Community leaders have been known to boast that "Our city has no limits!" When you explore the wealth of places, events and activities in the metropolitan Charlotte area that appeal to the kid in all of us, it's easy to agree. The possibilities here are indeed almost limitless. Here's a smattering of what Insiders in the Queen City recommend to newcomers and visitors with kids in tow. For more ideas, check out our Attractions, Daytrips and Weekends, and Parks and Recreation chapters. Local newspaper dailies and free specialty publications (see *Charlotte Parent: Our Kids & Teens Magazine*) are good sources for information on upcoming family events and activities.

Museums and Historic Sites

Afro-American Cultural Center
401 N. Myers St. • 374-1565

The Afro-American Cultural Center is located in an old restored AME Zion church. It offers an art gallery with changing exhibits, theatre and musical productions and classes and programs for adults and children. Call for information on upcoming exhibits and programs.

Charlotte Museum of History & Hezekiah Alexander Homesite
3500 Shamrock Dr. • 568-1774

The Charlotte Museum of History gives you a "slice of life" of the North Carolina Piedmont region with a special focus on the history of Charlotte and Mecklenburg County. The museum offers exhibits, classes, arts and crafts demonstrations and occasional special events. Admission to the museum is free.

The Hezekiah Alexander homesite, home to a signer of the 1775 Mecklenburg Declaration of Independence, was built in 1774 of stone quarried nearby. It is the oldest original dwelling still standing in Mecklenburg County and is listed in the National Register of Historic Places. A reconstructed barn, a kitchen and a spring house are also on the property. The house has been restored and furnished with North Carolina antiques.

Guided tours ($4 for adults, $3 for seniors 65 and older and $2 for children ages 6 to 16) are given Tuesday through Sunday afternoons. The homesite hosts several events of interest to children throughout the year, including the Rites of Spring (where sheep shearing is a popular spectator sport), a Summer Sampler and a Colonial Christmas program.

Charlotte Trolley and Museum
2104 S. Blvd. • 375-0850

In addition to two restored trolleys, exhibits, a film depicting trolley restoration and a gift shop, this museum offers trolley rides from 10 AM to 6 PM Friday, Saturday and Sunday. The charge is $2 for a roundtrip ride and is free for children younger than 12 with an adult. You can also rent the carbarn for parties.

Discovery Place
301 N. Tryon St. • 372-6261, (800) 935-0553

Discovery Place is one of the largest and most exciting science and nature museums in the country. It contains the OMNIMAX Theatre, a planetarium, a replica of a tropical rain forest, aquariums, discovery areas for young children and much more. It's easy to spend a day or two inside the sprawling complex in Uptown Charlotte.

Annual memberships are available — you'll want to come multiple times a year — and the museum also honors memberships from other science museums throughout the country. The museum offers classes, workshops and day camp activities for children of all ages.

Latta Place
5225 Sample Rd., Huntersville • 875-2312

Latta Place encompasses over 700 acres of land surrounding the restored and furnished house (circa 1800) of James Latta, a merchant and planter in the Catawba River region. Guided tours are available of the house, which is listed in the National Register of Historic Places. There are outbuildings and gardens to explore and farm animals graze nearby.

The Carolina Raptor Center (see the Science, Nature and the Outdoors section of this chapter), the Latta Plantation Equestrian Center and a bird sanctuary are also on the park grounds by Mountain Island Lake just northwest of Charlotte. During the summer the park operates one-week day camps and offers riding instruction and classes on equestrian care.

Plan to bring a picnic and spend a sunny afternoon hiking, canoeing or riding horses through the old plantation grounds. Call for information on admission charges and activity fees.

International House
322 Hawthorne La. • 333-8099

Special programs featuring art activities, music, costumes, displays, dolls and folktales of the cultures of 19 different countries are offered by the International House staff on site and at other locations. International Camp is available to children ages 5 to 10 every summer. Recent camp participants have taken pretend trips to Guatemala, England, Russia, Thailand and The Netherlands. International House also holds several sessions of Camp Espanol and Camp Francais during the summer.

Mint Museum of Art
2730 Randolph Rd. • 337-2000

The Mint was originally built as the first branch of the United States Mint in 1836. Among other uses, the building later served as a headquarters for the Confederacy and as a hospital. The Mint building was moved to its present location in 1933 and opened as North Carolina's first art museum in 1936.

The Museum includes fine collections of Pre-Columbian art, American and European paintings, decorative arts and special collections such as North Carolina and African galleries. The Mint sponsors many programs for children and adults, including classes, workshops and family events. Exhibits change several times each year. Past favorites have included exhibits of treasures from ancient Egypt and costume displays. Recent exhibits have featured interactive computer programs geared toward children.

Children under the age of 12 are admitted free and everyone receives free admission on Tuesday evenings from 5 to 10 PM and on the second Sunday of each month.

North Carolina Transportation Museum
Historic Spencer Shops
411 S. Salisbury Ave., Spencer • 636-2889

This state transportation museum is located on the site of the former Southern Railway locomotive repair facility. Railway cars and engines, antique cars and N.C.'s first Highway Patrol car are exhibited here. Train rides are available. Admission to the museum is free.

Public Library of Charlotte and Mecklenburg County
310 N. Tryon St. • 336-2725

The main library and all its branches offer a wealth of activities for children throughout the year — storytimes, educational programs, films and videos, family day programs and special exhibitions and events. Its facilities offer traditional services and the latest in computer technology. The library was named "Library of the Year" in 1995, "Library of the Future" in 1996 and its youth coordinator won the prestigious Grolier Award in 1996. Call the main number or any of the 22 branches for details and times.

Reed Gold Mine
State Historic Site
9621 Reed Mine Rd., Stanfield • 786-8337

The Reed Gold Mine is the site of the first documented discovery of gold in the United States. There is a museum, guided tours of the old mine and — the favorite for children — panning for gold! Admission to the site is free; there is a small charge of $2 per pan for gold panning.

The Morrison Regional Library offers a wealth of activities for children.

Schiele Museum of Natural History & Planetarium
1500 E. Garrison Blvd., Gastonia • 866-6900

The Schiele Museum has a fine collection of North Carolina natural history exhibits, including native mammals and flora of the Piedmont, as well as changing exhibits that have included favorites like Native American artifacts. The museum hosts living history programs several times a year, portraying reenactments of life in North Carolina in earlier times. The planetarium shows change periodically and may give a peek at the night sky or a look at comets and meteors. The Schiele is one of North Carolina's most popular science and discovery museums. Admission is free, but there is a charge for the planetarium show.

Entertainment

Mecklenburg County Aquatic Center
800 E. Second St. • 336-3483

Swimming couldn't be more fun at this downtown aquatic center.

Celebration Station
10400 Cadillac St., Pineville • 552-7888

This is a popular spot for birthday parties, family outings and more. There is miniature golf, bumper boats, go-cart rides, batting cages, a video arcade and Harry's New Clubhouse, a huge indoor play station, featuring a monstrous two-story slide. When you're tired from all the activity, there's lots to eat and drink while you rest up for the next go 'round.

Charlotte Climbing Center
619 S. Cedar St. • 333-ROCK

This is the first and largest fully equipped indoor climbing facility in the state. The indoor climbing programs teach valuable climbing skills while allowing kids and adults to challenge themselves, stretch their limits, build self-confidence and, best of all, have a great time doing it! More advanced climbers can opt for an outdoor trip to Crowder's Mountain, Table Rock or a variety of other climbing areas. During the summer, the center offers week-long climbing camps. For a unique birthday party, check out the various packages offered by the center. Remember, it never rains indoors!

Children's Theatre of Charlotte
1017 E. Morehead St. • 376-5745
Box office: • 333-8983

The Children's Theatre of Charlotte has been producing professional performances by and for kids ages 3 to 18 since 1948. The Theatre's Mainstage productions are for the whole family. The Second Stage shows are performed by kids in grades 8 and up. The

Theatre also hosts other productions by local and touring theater groups.

The Children's Theatre also sponsors educational programs teaching drama, puppetry and creative movement to young thespians. During the summer the organization offers drama camps for ages 4 to 11 at the Theater on East Morehead Street, Matthews Community Center, the Jewish Community Center and Steps 'N Motion Dance Studio.

David B. Waymer
Aeromodeler Flying Field
15401 Holbrooks Rd., Huntersville • 875-1549

David B. Waymer District Park, a part of the county park system, provides a safe zone for flying motorized model airplanes. The park also has athletic fields, a picnic shelter, playground and recreation center.

Ice Chalet
5595 Central Ave. • 568-0772

Though ice skating has never been the South's biggest sport, it's been growing in popularity in recent years. Now anyone can enjoy skating all year long at the Ice Chalet at Eastland Mall. Adults and children can take lessons or just skate for the pure pleasure of it. It's also a great place for a birthday party. There is an admission charge and groups get special rates. You may rent skates or bring your own.

Laser Quest Charlotte
5323-A E. Independence Blvd. • 567-6707

Play a leading part in laser tag, a game for kids, ages 7 to 77. The indoor facility also stages birthday parties. Game reservations are accepted. Admission is charged.

Paramount's Carowinds
1-77 S. • (800) 888-4FUN

What better to fulfill a child's fantasy than a day in Hanna-Barbera Land with Yogi and BooBoo Bear? Paramount's Carowinds has big fun for little visitors at RipTide Reef water park, Zoom Zone where kids are in the driver's seat, the WaterWorks children's play area and the 1998 expansion to Animation Station, a playland for families with young children, which features more than 15 attractions and shows. For the older child, WAYNE'S WORLD and the Southeast's best selection of roller coasters will provide a day of fun and excitement. When it's time for a treat, drop in at the Richard Scarry Busytown Cafe. For more information on Paramount's Carowinds, see the Attractions chapter of this Guide.

Spirit Square Center for the Arts
345 N. College St. • 372-9664

There's just about everything associated with the arts here: galleries with a variety of changing exhibits, two theatres for dramatic and musical productions and classes galore for adults

Photo courtesy of Lazy 5 Ranch

More like a small zoo, Lazy 5 Ranch delights children with over 400 species of animals.

and children! Spirit Square is located in a renovated church building, creating a unique setting for artistic expression.

Science, Nature And The Outdoors

Carolina Raptor Center at Latta Place
Sample Rd., Huntersville • 875-6521

The Raptor Center is a conservation and environmental education center and is dedicated to caring for injured birds of prey and releasing them back into the wild. The raptors are in cages along a trail almost a mile long. The Edna S. Moretti Environmental Education Center is also located here. The Raptor Center is open Tuesday through Saturday from 10 AM to 5 PM and Sunday from 12 to 5 PM. The fee is $4 for adults and $2 for students. Children under 5 are admitted free. See the Museums and Historic Sites section of this chapter for more information on Latta Place and its features.

Discovery Place
301 N. Tryon St. • 372-6261, (800) 935-0553

See the Museums and Historic Sites section of this chapter.

Energy Explorium
13339 Hagers Ferry Rd., Huntersville • 875-5600

The Energy Explorium, operated by Duke Power, offers a unique look at energy and electricity with its hands-on displays about nuclear and coal-produced energy. You can explore the exhibits, play an array of interactive video games or see a film, "The Inland Sea," about the creation of Lake Norman. There are nature trails and a wildflower walk on the grounds, giving a nice blend of indoor and outdoor things to do. Admission is free.

Lazy 5 Ranch
N.C. 150 E., Mooresville
663-5100 or 278-2618

Not your typical ranch, the Lazy 5 is more like a small zoo that stretches over 180 acres of rolling farmland. Visitors can take a leisurely ride along the gravel road in their own vehicles and view the animals or opt for a horse-drawn wagon ride. There are over 400 species of animals, many of which come from different continents and have an assortment of exotic names. The animals roam freely and are not at all shy. They know the routine and will cautiously approach your vehicle — probably hoping that you stocked up on the feed available for purchase at the Welcome Center.

You and your children will be amazed by the beauty of the ranch and the peaceful nature of its inhabitants. Younger children will love the petting area where they can get close to a variety of small and large critters, from baby goats and lambs to camels. The Lazy 5 Ranch opens at 9 AM Monday through Saturday and at 1 PM on Sunday. It closes each day one hour before sunset. The charge

Photo by Tim Johnson

The natural setting of the public parks attract families and wildlife alike.

is $7.50 for adults and $4.50 for ages 2 through 12 and over 60.

McDowell Park and Nature Preserve
N.C. 49, Lake Wylie • 588-5224

This 800-plus acre park on Lake Wylie offers lots of activities. You can go boating or canoeing, fish, walk on the miles of nature trails or visit the indoor nature center. Campsites and picnic facilities are open all year long. The park sponsors special programs throughout the year: evening campfires and storytelling, moonlight hikes and nature classes for young and old. Admission is charged.

Mecklenburg County Park and Recreation's Ecology Programs
• 598-8857

A number of ecology programs geared to children and adults are offered at various parks in the county. The program lineup includes the following: Adult Naturalist Series; Bog, Pond, and Wildlife Garden Workshop; Exploring the Carolinas Series; Wildlife of Cowan's Ford; Interpretative Canoe Rides; Tots 'N Tales; Run With the "P.A.K." Ecology Club; Just for Seniors; Senior Excursions; and Primitive Technology Workshops. Call for details.

Reedy Creek Park and Environmental Center
2900 Rocky River Rd. • 598-8857

Most of this 700-acre nature preserve is in its natural wooded state. There are several lakes on the property, nature trails, picnic sites, ball fields and a playground. The Environmental Center has exhibits and hands-on activities to enjoy and explore. Admission fees are charged for the park, the Environmental Center and the nature hour. Call for details.

Wing Haven Gardens & Bird Sanctuary
248 Ridgewood Ave. • 331-0664

Wing Haven is a beautiful garden and bird sanctuary in the middle of Charlotte, the former home and grounds of Elizabeth and Edwin Clarkson. Over 4 acres are filled with woods, formal gardens and lovely walks. The home is also open. There is a garden shop, tours of the home and grounds and special children's programs throughout the year. Wing Haven is open on Sunday from 2 to 5 PM, Tuesday from 3 to 5 PM, Wednesday from 10 AM to 12 PM and at other times by appointment. Admission is free.

Camps

Mecklenburg County Park and Recreation offers extensive day camps and playground programs during the summer. Day camps with structured activities are available at 16 recreation centers, including Recreation On The Move, which is a mobile recreational unit, fully staffed and equipped to provide supervised experiences in athletics, arts and crafts, music, dance and special events. The cost varies depending on the program.

Playground programs for which there is no charge are given at seven sites and feature planned activities as well as free time. A number of city-wide special events, such as the Junior Tennis Tournament, are planned each summer at Renaissance Park.

Mecklenburg County Park and Recreation holds one-week day camps at five different sites, featuring special programs, field trips, games, athletics and arts and crafts. The David B. Waymer Complex offers a free playground program. The Harris YMCA offers coed day camps at Queens College and on site. The YWCA on Park Road holds an annual Kamp-a-Long for girls and boys. Camp Arrowhead at the Simmons YMCA is another day camp choice.

One of the finest coed boarding camps in the Southeast is YMCA-affiliated Camp Thunderbird on Lake Wylie where kids learn to water ski, sail, swim and participate in competitive sports and other activities. (The camp is also a center for the YMCA's extensive Y-Indian Guide program.) Most YMCA camps offer counselor-in-training programs for teens. Since the YMCA camps are very popular, it's a good idea to register early. Some scholarships are available.

The Jewish Community Center's day camp is Camp Maccabee, which is open to everyone, regardless of religious faith. A number of day care centers and learning/tutoring centers in the Charlotte area also offer summer programs. Call local facilities for more information.

**Charlotte
offers
a full calendar
of special events.**

Annual Events

In addition to attractions, Charlotte offers a full calendar of special events. Some of the major events are listed below. More detailed calendars are available upon request from the Charlotte Convention & Visitors Bureau Information Center, 330 S. Tryon Street, Charlotte, NC 28202, 331-2700.

The state's annual "Calendar of Events" booklet is also a handy reference. It's available at N.C. Welcome Centers or by calling or writing the N.C. Division of Travel and Tourism, (800) VISIT NC, 430 Salisbury Street, Raleigh, NC 27611. Local newspapers are always a good way to keep informed on the specific dates of these events. Events are listed in alphabetical order within each month.

January

Disney on Ice
Charlotte Coliseum, off Tyvola Rd.
• 357-4701
Disney's ice spectacular featuring well-known performers comes to Charlotte each year with a different theme. Call the box office for 1999 dates and admission prices.

Martin Luther King Day Parade
Uptown Charlotte • 377-0048
Martin Luther King Day is celebrated on the third Monday of each January. Charlotte holds an annual parade in Uptown to celebrate Martin Luther King's achievements. The parade starts about 10 AM at LaSalle Street and proceeds to Beatties Ford Road to Trade Street to Kings Drive. A program follows at the Grady Cole Center Memorial Stadium, 310 North Kings Drive.

Mid-Atlantic East Coast World Championship Rodeo
Independence Arena,
2700 E. Independence Blvd. • 882-6994
Believe it or not, you can catch a first-class rodeo here in Charlotte. The rodeo usually runs for three days in late January. Call for dates and ticket information.

February

Annual Heart Ball
Various locations • 374-0632
This black-tie gala, held the last Saturday of the month, features a silent auction, a seated dinner and dancing to live music. Proceeds benefit the American Heart Association. Reservations are required.

Ringling Brothers Circus
Charlotte Coliseum, off Tyvola Rd.
• 357-4701
The circus comes to town each year, usually in mid-February. Tickets for this popular annual extravaganza may be purchased at Ticketmaster.

Southern Spring Show
Charlotte Merchandise Mart, 2500 E. Independence Blvd. • 376-6594
(800) 849-0248
Southern Shows, founded by Robert and Joan Zimmerman in 1959, is Charlotte's home-grown producer of consumer and trade shows held throughout the Southeast. One of Charlotte's most popular events, the Spring Show draws thousands of visitors from across the state and beyond to see the latest in home, gardening and outdoor exhibits and merchandise. The Spring Show usually starts the third week in February. Admission is charged.

March

Charlotte New Plays Festival
NC Blumenthal Performing Arts Center, 130 N. Tryon St. • 372-1000

Each March, the Center produces four to five new plays by aspiring Charlotte area playwrights. See these new works before they are "discovered" by Broadway. Call the Center's box office for ticket prices.

April

Antique Spectacular
Metrolina Expo, 7100 Statesville Rd. • 596-4643

Antique dealers and shoppers from all over the country are attracted to this huge event. More than 5,000 dealers usually attend the show, which takes place the first weekend of April.

Automobilia
Charlotte Motor Speedway, Concord • 455-3200

A popular annual event, this "swap meet" features new, concept and classic cars and parts, and attracts automobile enthusiasts from all over the United States during the first week of April.

Center CityFest
Uptown Charlotte • 455-3200

The first-annual Center CityFest was held April 24-26, 1998, in an effort to fill the void left by the cancellation of SpringFest. The event offers 60 regional and national music act. Headliners for the 1998 festival included Violent Femmes, Ben Folds Five, Cravin' Melon, Jerry Lee Lewis and Joan Baez. Center CityFest also includes an artist park displaying the works of 150 regional artists; children's activities such as art classes, face-painting and clown shows; and a food tent.

Charlotte Observer Marathon & Festival
Uptown Charlotte • 358-5798

This annual 26-mile marathon, which attracts runners and spectators from all over the country, will next take place on April 10, 1999. The race starts at South Tryon Road and proceeds to Morehead Road, to Kings, to Queens, to Park, circles Hwy. 51 and back. An entry fee is charged if you want to participate, but it is free to spectators. The festival also includes a 10,000-meter race and noncompetitive bicycling and in-line skating demonstrations.

Charlotte Steeplechase
Gus Eubanks Rd., Monroe • 423-3400

Spend a day in the country enjoying friends, a grand lawn party and five thoroughbred horse races over fences. The event, which features the NationsBank Queen's Cup, traditionally takes place the last Saturday in April at the Charlotte Steeplechase race course in southern Union County. Doors open at 10 AM, with opening ceremonies at 12 and the first race at 1:30 PM. Races run rain or shine. Proceeds go to regional charities such as the Hospice of Union County.

Come-See-Me Festival
Rock Hill, S.C. • (800) 681-7635

Approximately 125,000 people converge on Rock Hill's Cherry Park during this 11-day event, which features exhibits, concerts, crafts, hot-air balloons, road and bicycle races, a soap box derby, children's events, a parade and fireworks. The festival also includes a golf tournament held at the new Waterford Golf Course. Vernon Grant, the creator of Kellogg's Rice Krispies' Snap, Crackle and Pop, designed the frog that serves as the festival's emblem. To get to Cherry Park, take exit 82B off I-77 and go a half-mile west.

Earth Day Charlotte
Uptown Charlotte • 336-3625

This outdoor family event is held in Marshall Park on the Saturday closest to April 22nd, Earth Day. The free, all-day celebration offers environmental exhibits, entertainment, children's activities and food available for purchase. For more information, write to Earth Day Charlotte, P.O. Box 33483, Charlotte, NC 28233-3483.

Loch Norman Highland Games
Near Lake Norman • 875-3113

Since 1954, Grandfather Mountain near Linville, North Carolina, has drawn throngs to the Highland Games. Mecklenburg's festival is smaller, but really brings out the crowds. There's plenty to see, do and eat at the Highland Games, so don your kilt or jeans and listen to Celtic music. The event draws bands from Georgia, the Carolinas, Kentucky and Tennessee. Competitions in piping, drumming, harp, fiddle, Highland dance, archery and more are held all day during the third weekend in April. Other activities include the caber toss and sheepdog herding demonstrations. Rural Hill Plantation is located off Beatties Ford Road, about 1 mile past Latta. Turn left onto Neck Road and follow the signs to the games. Admission is charged.

Mint Museum Home & Garden Tour
Various locations • 337-2000

Taking this tour provides an opportunity to see some of Charlotte's more beautiful homes. The tour usually takes place during the third week in April and admission is charged. Call for dates.

Southern Ideal Home Show/Spring
Charlotte Merchandise Mart, 2500 E. Independence Blvd. • 376-6594
(800) 849-0204

Held the first weekend of April, this popular Southern Shows extravaganza features new home furnishings. Admission is $5.00.

May

Davidson Town Day
Davidson, N.C. • 892-3349

Davidson celebrates its annual festival the first Saturday in May on the Village Green with varied entertainment choices, many games and demonstrations, and lots of good food. Take an old-fashioned carriage ride around town, participate in the merchant-sponsored Treasure Trek or sign up for the

45-minute stroll to raise money for Habitat for Humanity. To get there, take the Davidson exit 30 off I-77.

Denver Strawberry Festival
Denver, N.C. • 483-2281

On the Saturday of Memorial Day weekend an incredible supply of baked foods with strawberries is offered by local churches at the East Lincoln High School, 6471 Hwy. 73. Enjoy a hayride or wander among the local crafts and other planned entertainment.

GaribaldiFest
Belmont, N.C. • 825-0505

The town's former Spring Showcase was renamed GaribaldiFest after John Garibaldi, who built Garibaldi Station in the 1870s. Bluegrass bands and Gospel Singers entertain and the sidewalks are lined with arts and crafts. For a taste of the past, try a horse and buggy ride. There is also an antique car show. The festival ends with a downtown street dance. This event usually takes place on a Saturday in the middle of May. Take I-85 S. to the Belmont exit. No admission is charged.

Home Depot Invitational
Piper Glen Golf Club • 846-4699

This annual golf invitational is a seniors tournament held at Tournament Players Club. Admission is charged.

Lake Norman Festival
Mooresville • 664-3898

Held two weekends prior to Memorial Day weekend, this annual festival begins with the Beach Jam and Shag Contest in downtown Mooresville on Friday evening beginning at 6:30 PM. On Saturday, Main Street is closed to traffic to make room for arts and crafts booths, a children's fun fair and much more. Take the Mooresville exit 36 off I-77. No admission is charged.

Ole Time Fiddler's and Bluegrass Festival
Union Grove, N.C. • 539-4417

This event was started in 1924 by Harper Van Hoy's father, H.P. Van Hoy, as a community project to support the local school.

During the third weekend in May folks gather for this three-day celebration of dancing and playing authentic old-time music. You can join in at the competitions or workshops for autoharp, hammered dulcimer, bass fiddle, dobro, harmonica, banjo and guitar, or be a part of the clogging and storytelling programs. The regulars swap jokes as they eat homemade barbecue and ice cream. Spacious Fiddlers Grove Campground, 1819 W. Memorial Highway, north of Statesville, is equipped with electricity and hookups for RVs. Admission is charged. For more information, write to P.O. Box 11, Union Grove, NC 28689.

600 Festival Race Parade
Uptown Charlotte • 455-6814

This Uptown Charlotte Parade occurs on Tuesday of May race week featuring NASCAR drivers, show cars, marching bands and clowns. Fireworks follow the parade.

Speed Street
Uptown Charlotte • 455-6814

The Speed Street Festival is held Thursday, Friday and Saturday of May race week. It features live entertainment, interactive exhibits, food, show cars, racing memorabilia and more.

The Winston
Goody's Pole Night
Carquest 300
Coca-Cola 600
Charlotte Motor Speedway, Concord • 455-3200

These exciting stock car racing events occur during May race week, culminating with the Coca-Cola 600, the longest Winston Cup race on the NASCAR circuit. Admission is charged.

June

Afro-American Art Expo
Friendship Missionary Baptist Church, 3301 Beatties Ford Road • 535-3247

This expo features artwork, African artifacts, jewelry, cloth, shirts, books, cards and other items related to African culture

made by artists from throughout the Southeast. No admission is charged.

Charlotte Orchestra Pops Concerts
SouthPark Mall, 4400 Sharon Rd. • 364-4411

Throughout July, these free concerts offer residents a chance to spread a picnic and enjoy light music outdoors in the vicinity of the mall.

Juneteenth
Johnson C. Smith University • 332-0441

Juneteenth commemorates the true Independence Day for African-Americans, June 19, 1862, the first act prohibiting slavery, 1865 when Union troops arrived in Galveston, Texas, to enforce the end of slavery and 1964 when the Civil Rights Act was passed. Charlotteans celebrate with a banquet and dance and Family Day in mid-June.

Listen and Remember
Waxhaw, N.C. • 843-2300

This outdoor drama, which will celebrate its 35th season in 1999, recalls the days of Waxhaw's Indians and early pioneers, including Andrew Jackson's family. Beginning with events in 1670, the play culminates with Jackson's presidency. It is held at 8:30 p.m. each Friday and Saturday night in June. Admission is charged.

July

Family Fourth Celebration
Memorial Stadium • 353-0200

This is by far the best place in town to see fireworks and display one's patriotic feelings.

Reenactment of
the Battle of Huck's Defeat in 1780
Historic Brattonsville, S.C. • (803) 684-2327

This exciting all-day drama of the American Revolution is held on the second Saturday in July. Historic Brattonsville is near McConnells, South Carolina, 9 miles south of York off S.C. 322 on S.R. 165, Brattonsville Road. Take Exit 82B off I-77 S. This road

Photo by Ann Hawthorne, courtesy of Fiddler's Grove Inc.

The Ole Time Fiddler's and Bluegrass Festival is held on Memorial Day weekend.

becomes Brattonsville Road in 15 miles. Follow the historic markers. Admission is charged.

West Charlotte Fest
Uptown Charlotte • 377-0048

An annual day of good food, fun, games and arts and crafts. The festival is located along Tryon Street from Trade Street to Second Street. No admission is charged.

August

Bon Odori Festival
Uptown Charlotte • 336-8888

The Bon Odori Festival is a celebration of Japanese culture. Ethnic dances are performed on a ceremonial platform. You will even hear a Japanese-American drum team and be invited to join in the dance contest. There are exhibitions and demonstrations of origami paper folding and Shuji calligraphy. Children's activities include games and face-painting. This is a great opportunity to taste Japanese food, including sushi and other exotic dishes, and experience an authentic Japanese tea ceremony. A nominal admission is charged.

Charlotte 3 on 3
Uptown Charlotte • 334-3ON3

This annual popular basketball tournament allows the basketball junkie to test his or her skills against players of similar ability. The tournament is open to all ages and skill levels with all proceeds going to Habitat for Humanity. Each team, made up of four players (three at a time on the court) is categorized by age, height, basketball experience and ability, and is scheduled against similar teams in one of several divisions.

Dilworth Jubilee
Latta Park • 373-0190

Held at the 2,247-acre Latta Place on the second Saturday in August, this neighborhood get-together has grown in popularity and draws visitors from all over the city. The Dilworth Home Tour is held on both Friday and Saturday of that weekend.

WPEG Summerfest
Blockbuster Pavilion • 549-5555

Admission is charged for this annual Urban R&B Festival and Concert held at the

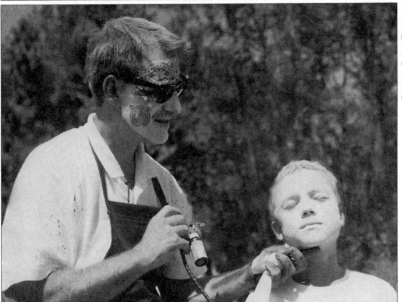

Face painting is a popular activity for kids at the annual Lakefest.

19,000-seat Blockbuster Pavilion located 11 miles from Uptown on U.S. 29 North.

September

ArtFest of Matthews
Downtown Matthews • 847-3649

This is an annual juried fine arts festival held in late September. No admission is charged.

Carolina Homecoming Festival
Paramount's Carowinds • 588-2600

This is all-day celebration of folk music features nationally known and regional performers. Call for date.

Festival in the Park
Freedom Park • 338-1060

One of the largest and longest running festivals in Charlotte, the all-volunteer-run festival features arts and crafts, food, clowns, games and performances by various organizations. No admission is charged.

LakeFest
Jetton Park at Lake Norman • 525-3784

More than 15,000 people attend this festival held at Lake Norman, which features entertainment, art, food and activities for children.

Matthews ALIVE!
Downtown Matthews • 845-1153

This outdoor family arts and crafts festival is held on Labor Day weekend.

National Balloon Rally
Iredell County Fairgrounds • 873-2892

This is a four-day event that paints the sky with colorful expressions of beauty and whimsy. The extravaganza features balloon rides, contests, arts and crafts, military displays, activities for children and food. The event is normally held the third weekend of September. Admission is charged.

Serenade to Autumn Fashion Show
Ovens Auditorium • 372-3600

Hosted by Belk Stores, Serenade to Autumn is a preview of fall fashions and attracts top designers such as Alexander Julian. Admission is charged.

Southern Women's Show
Merchandise Mart • 376-6594 or
(800) 849-0248

This event from September 17 to 20, 1998, abounds with exhibits, merchandise and information of special interest to women. Admission is $6 at the door; $5 in advance.

Symphony ASID Designer House Preview Party
ASID Designer House • 525-0522

This premiere black-tie event, held at a different location each year, takes place the evening before the Designer House opens to the public. Cocktails, a silent auction, a seated dinner, dancing to live music and a tour of the home complete this fabulous evening. This event is often a sellout, so make your reservations early. Call for date and time.

Symphony Guild of Charlotte ASID Designer House
Various locations • 525-0522

Charlotte designers show off their talents, offering the latest in decorating trends during this three-week event. There is a gift shop featuring antiques, collectibles, artwork and Christmas decorations, and a tea room is open for lunch. All proceeds go to the Charlotte Symphony Orchestra and Charlotte Youth Orchestra.

UNC Charlotte International Festival
UNC Charlotte • 547-2410

This is UNC Charlotte's salute to a variety of international cultures. The festival showcases the countries that are represented in Charlotte through arts, crafts, food and entertainment. No admission is charged.

"Yiasou!" Greek Festival
Holy Trinity Greek Orthodox Cathedral
• 334-4771

Greek food, music, dancing and arts and crafts are featured at this authentic event sponsored by Charlotte's large Greek community. A nominal admission fee is charged. No admission is charged for seniors and children younger than 12.

Photo courtesy of North Carolina Division of Travel and Tourism

The Statesville Balloon Rally is a not-to-be-missed event.

October

Carolina Renaissance Festival
Hwy. 73, North of Charlotte • 896-5555

Ten acres of beautiful woods and meadows are transformed into a 16th-century European Village and form the setting for hundreds of elaborately costumed performers that re-create the atmosphere of a European Market Faire. Artisans' exhibits of period handiwork fill the village marketplace and period food is available. The Carolina Renaissance Festival is held on seven weekends from October to November. Admission is charged.

Christmas Made in The South
Charlotte Convention Center • 847-9480

Admission is charged to this annual juried arts and crafts show highlighting over 400 artists and craftsmen.

Haunted Homesite Tour
Charlotte History Museum & Hezekiah Alexander Homesite • 568-1774

Pumpkin decorating, bobbing for apples, candlelight tours of homes and scary stories around a campfire are part of this Saturday before Halloween event. Admission is charged.

Mint Museum Antique Show and Sale
Charlotte Merchandise Mart • 337-2000

This massive show provides a good opportunity to view and buy quality antiques. Admission is charged.

Remodel Charlotte Show
Charlotte Merchandise Mart • 376-6594

This show on house remodeling features exhibits, special events and speakers. Admission is charged.

Southern Ideal Home Show
Charlotte Convention Center • 376-6594

Exhibits and merchandise of interest to homeowners and would-be homeowners are featured at this popular home show.

Waxhaw Scottish Games
Briarwood Farm, Waxhaw • 843-3288

Admission is charged to attend these traditional Scottish games, which draw upwards of 2,000 spectators.

Winston Pole Night
All-Pro Bumper to Bumper 300
UAW-GM Quality 500
Charlotte Motor Speedway • 455-3200

October is another exciting month of racing at the Charlotte Motor Speedway.

Staff Photo

The Carolina Renaissance Festival begins in October.

November

Carolinas Carousel Parade
Uptown Charlotte • 372-9411

This Thanksgiving Day event, one of North Carolina's most extravagant Christmas Parades, marks the beginning of the Christmas season.

Shrine Bowl Game
Ericsson Stadium • 358-7000

This is the annual showdown between high school all-star football players from the two Carolinas held at the 72,500-seat stadium. Admission is charged.

Southern Antique Spectacular
Metrolina Expo Center • 596-4643

This show hosts dealers and antique buffs from across the country for a three-day antique extravaganza. Admission is charged.

Southern Christmas Show
Merchandise Mart • 376-6594

A winter wonderland of crafts, gifts, food and anything remotely connected with the Christmas season, this mid-November show is a Charlotte tradition. The show includes cooking clinics, crafts demonstrations and a food pavilion.Thousands of visitors come to get a head start on their Christmas shopping. Call for ticket prices.

SouthPark Holiday Tree Lighting
SouthPark Mall • 364-4411

Tens of thousands gather after Thanksgiving dinner to hear music and watch Santa light the 60-foot tree.

SouthPark Turkey Trot
SouthPark • 554-1234

This annual 8K road race is run on Thanksgiving Morning. All proceeds go to charity. The event begins at the Hyatt Charlotte and is preceded by a Sports Expo.

December

Basketball Tournament of Champions
Charlotte Coliseum • 357-4700

The Harris Teeter/Pepsi Challenge is a playoff of four basketball teams representing neighboring states: UNC Charlotte, USC, UTN-Chattanooga and VA Tech. The tournament is held at the 24,000-seat Charlotte Coliseum.

Colonial Christmas
Charlotte History Museum and Hezekiah Alexander Homesite • 568-1774

Colonial Christmas is a unique way to get into the Christmas spirit with the singing of Christmas carols, the arrival of the minister on horseback and the serving of cider and gingerbread. The event takes place at the Hezekiah Alexander Homesite, Charlotte's oldest home. Admission is charged.

Christmastown USA
McAdenville • 824-3190

Neighboring McAdenville is the site of this spectacular Christmas light show. It has been staged by Stowe-Pharr Yarns for decades in the quaint mill village near Gastonia.

Kwanzaa
Afro-American Cultural Center • 374-1565

This annual religious and cultural celebration focuses on African heritage and the family.

The Nutcracker
Blumenthal Performing Arts Center • 333-4686

Presented annually by the North Carolina Dance Theatre, *The Nutcracker* ballet features over 100 artists and tells the time-honored story of Clara and her trip to the land of the sugar plum fairies. Admission is charged.

Singing Christmas Tree
Ovens Auditorium • 374-1564

This celebration of Christmas in song is a Charlotte tradition held at the 2,603-seat Ovens Auditorium. Admission is charged.

Victorian Christmas Celebration
Reed Gold Mine • 786-8337

Christmas music by local choirs, demonstrations of Victorian crafts, guided underground tours and complimentary punch and cookies make this family event a holiday favorite. The event is held at the Reed Gold Mine, site of the first authenticated gold find in the United States.

In Charlotte, art has a serendipitous way of showing up where you'd least expect to find it.

The Arts

In the spring of 1995, the Charlotte-Mecklenburg Arts & Science Council endowment campaign, headed by Nations-Bank Chairman and Chief Executive Officer Hugh McColl Jr., soared to a whopping $26.16 million ($1 million above its goal) with major contributions from local corporations and anonymous donors. The successful campaign involved 150 volunteers and nearly 1,500 donors and it quickly become a national model and the envy of major cities around the country.

That successful campaign followed the Arts & Science Council's receipt of the largest Challenge Grant in the nation from the National Endowment for the Arts in 1995. The bulk of the $1 million grant ($800,000) has gone to the Council; the remainder to the Mint Museum of Art.

The arts and sciences are important to Charlotteans. A few years back under the Charlotte Public Art Program, city government passed a law requiring that one percent of all new public building costs be allocated to some form of artistic expression. This is why you'll see a variety of art gracing our buildings.

In Charlotte, art has a serendipitous way of showing up where you'd least expect to find it. The Queens Table, an anonymous group, has donated art throughout the city. Most notable are the statues at Trade and Tryon streets and Queen Charlotte at the airport. Ben Long's frescoes in the Nations-Bank Corporate Center at 100 N. Tryon greet visitors as they enter the building.

You don't usually anticipate discovering an art gallery in the lobby of an office building, but in the Carillon Building you'll find the Hans and Walter Bechtler Gallery. "Our Public Image," is an exhibit with a video of regional sculptures, monuments, buildings, obelisks and landmarks. In the same gallery, hanging from the Carillon Building's three-story lobby ceiling, is Jean Tinguely's flashing light mobile. You may also be surprised to find that Steven Siegel's work in the Carillon Building Park, entitled "Bridge," is actually a biodegradable newspaper sculpture that you can walk across. As concluded in the video by painter and poet Willie Stratford Sr., "Art is not what you do with your hands. It's what you do with your heart. It represents the soul of a city."

For many summers, Uptown business people and shoppers have spent lunch outside listening to the free SummerStage lunchtime concert series featuring everything from jazz to beach music. The shows rotate among Two First Union (301 S. Tryon), Carillon Building Park (201 W. Trade) and NationsBank Plaza (101 S. Tryon) and offer yet another way to sandwich a little art into the workday.

Unquestionably, one of the most exciting things happening on the art scene today is the infusion of art into every school subject (yes, math and science, too) in the Charlotte-Mecklenburg School System. The plan was initially targeted at Charlotte's two arts magnet schools, but will spill over into the traditional school system now that funding has been received. Educators have long believed that art may provide the catalyst to help students learn difficult subjects.

Before Charlotte had an inkling that the city was being considered as "a national model for arts education," our arts organizations were already at work instilling art appreciation in the city's school-age population on two levels, observation and participation.

For example, Opera Carolina's OperaFest, a one week summer program for minority teens, encourages the development of skills essential for individual achievement and allows participants to assist in solving problems while learning the techniques involved in creating an opera or musical theater work. In addition, the Charlotte Symphony offers two separate programs — the Junior Youth Symphony for younger children and the Charlotte Youth Symphony for teenagers. Youngsters are admitted to both groups through auditions judged by symphony musicians. The 50 to 60 member groups perform throughout the community at churches, colleges and at the Symphony's Designer House. From this exposure, it is not unusual for a youth member to graduate to Symphony Orchestra status.

On a weekly basis, one of the best ways to find out what's happening in the arts is through *The Charlotte Observer's* Sunday Arts section. The E & T section, available in Friday's paper, will let you know what's going on around town and in the Carolinas. The Charlotte-Mecklenburg Arts & Science Council, 372-9667, 227 W. Trade Street in Suite 250 in the Carillon Building is the official cultural agency that raises and disburses money to affiliated groups. The Arts & Science Council is a good place to start if you are interested in becoming involved in the community's art programs and a good source of information on current events.

The following is a guide to the Charlotte arts community broken down into sections on dance, music, theater, visual arts and writing.

Dance

Charlotteans have come to respect and appreciate dance as an art form. A major reason for dance's popularity is the North Carolina Dance Theatre, 372-0101. It is one of the few professional classical and ballet dance companies in North Carolina. Touring extensively through Europe and America, NCDT has performed at Spoleto, the American Dance Festival in Durham and the Aspen Dance Festival in Colorado. It has become one of the most sought after and highly acclaimed professional dance companies performing today and is probably the state's most widely known cultural ambassador.

Under the artistic direction of the late Salvatore Aiello, the Dance Theatre developed an exciting and versatile repertoire that

Photo courtesy of N.C. Dance Theatre; photo by Charles & Mary Love

North Carolina Dance Theatre performs the ballet *La Mer.*

ranges in style from breathtaking interpretations of full-length classical ballets to bold, witty and moving contemporary pieces. Its 1994-95 production of *Carmina Burana* with the Charlotte Symphony Orchestra was a sellout. Under the internationally acclaimed leadership of current artistic director Jean-Pierre Bonnefoux, the Dance Theatre continues its tradition of excellence. Every year NCDT stages an elaborate production of *The Nutcracker* at the Blumenthal Performing Arts Center — a production involving over 100 artists, many of whom are found through open auditions. (Tickets to the performances are available through the Performing Arts Center Box Office, 372-1000, or call NCDT at 372-0101.) A couple of years ago NCDT opened DancePlace, the official school of North Carolina Dance Theatre. DancePlace offers a wide range of classes and dance-related educational activities for all ages and abilities. The school's primary focus, however, is to train aspiring young professional dancers. Its studios are located at 800 N. College Street.

There are many opportunities for young people who wish to study dance in the Queen City. Dance studios and schools for children abound. Insiders agree that some of the best training is given by Gay Porter's Charlotte School of Ballet (one of the city's oldest schools), Claudia Folts' Mercure's Ballet School and Barbara Morgan's Rhythm Dance Studio, Ltd.

Children may also take dance classes through QUILL at Queens College, Community School of the Arts and Children's Theatre. Adult classes are available at Central Piedmont Community College (CPCC), Queens College, the University of North Carolina at Charlotte, the YWCAs and Community Schools of the Arts.

CPCC's DanceCentral, under the direction of Katharyn Horne and Mary Anne Mee, does some commendable productions. Catchin' On, an adult modern dance company headed by Barbara Meadows, attracts dancers from varied backgrounds who are interested in improvisational, African and jazz dancing. UNC Charlotte productions, under the direction of faculty members Sybil Huskey, Delia Neal and Vincent Brosseau (who heads up Danceworks) are excellent.

Clogging and square dancing, as well as Cajun dancing and contra dancing, have become very popular in recent years. Clogging (indigenous to the North Carolina mountains), square dancing and the Texas Two-Step are now performed all over the Southeast. Charlotte has dozens of square dance clubs. In addition, there are gatherings for contra, Cajun, Scottish and other international dances. For more information, contact any of the schools listed below:

The Ballet School
8612 Monroe Rd. • 536-0615

Barbara Morgan's Rhythm Dance Studio, Ltd.
9506-C Monroe Rd. • 845-5260

Brousseau's Danceworks
7601 Briardale Dr. • 537-5150

CPCC
1201 Elizabeth Ave. • 330-6982

Charlotte School of Ballet
627 S. Sharon Amity Rd. • 366-9675

Community School of the Arts
Spirit Square • 377-4187

DancePlace
North Carolina Dance Theatre
800 N. College St. • 372-3900

Dance Unlimited
5606 E. Independence Blvd. • 536-2293

QUILL
Queens College, 1900 Selwyn Ave.
• 337-2537

UNC Charlotte
College of Arts and Sciences • 547-2482

YWCA
3420 Park Rd. • 525-5770

Music

Music is everywhere in Charlotte. Throughout the summer, the Charlotte Chamber of Commerce sponsors a series of 2-hour-long SummerStage Concerts. Different Uptown locations play host to everything from jazz to exotic steel guitars. The summer also brings the Symphony Orchestra's lighter musical offerings in the Summer Pops Concert series at SouthPark.

In September, the annual Carolinas Homecoming Folk Music Festival is held at Paramount's Carowinds Campground, where sing-a-longs mix well with Scottish tunes, bluegrass and spirituals. The Celtic Trader, 527-3800, the international music store at 645-G in Pressley Park off S. Tryon Street, features local folk artists such as Marilyn Price and John and Pat Trexlar on Thursday nights.

If it's musical instruction you want, check out Community School of the Arts, CPCC, UNC Charlotte, Queens College and other music clubs. A diverse collection of the city's musical groups is noted below. Call the public library or the Arts and Science Council for more detailed information.

American Harp Society, Charlotte Chapter
Contact: Lorraine Little • 568-8249

The objectives of the Charlotte Harp Society are to develop among its members and the public an appreciation of the harp as a musical instrument, to offer a variety of presentations about the harp through concerts and school programs and to support the arts in our city. Each spring, student auditions with a well-known harpist clinician are held, culminating in a student recital. Periodically, members perform in large harp ensemble concerts.

Carolina Crown Drum and Bugle Corps
Contact: Doug Madar • 347 2500

This outstanding group is comprised of 60 high school students, ages 15 to 21, who come from all over the Carolinas and Georgia. This all volunteer organization rehearses and performs with the drum corps relying solely on brass and percussion instruments. The color guard unit (descendant of the units formed by veterans' groups after World War I) is not what you'd expect and the music isn't of the John Philip Sousa variety either. You'll hear musical selections that run the gamut from jazzy show-business numbers to light classical. The Corps travels 15,000 miles a year to compete throughout the United States. Auditions are held in late November and early December.

Carolina Pro Musica
2516 E. 5th St. • (phone and fax) 334-3468

Established in 1977, this ensemble offers concerts featuring pre-1800 music with historic instruments and period dress in a concert series at St. Mary's Chapel, as well as throughout the community and the Carolinas.

Carolinas Concert Association, Inc.
P.O. Box 11356, Charlotte, NC 28220
• 527-6680

Founded in 1930, this group is Charlotte's oldest concert organization. Each year the association offers a season of classical music by outstanding orchestras, dance companies, soloists and instrumentalists from around the world. Season memberships are available.

Chamber Music of Charlotte
• 535-3024

This musical group is a nonprofit organization of approximately 85 musicians who play early and modern instruments. The group includes string quartets, Baroque ensembles, dance bands, jazz groups and other combinations of instruments — music professionals who play for weddings, parties and other private and public events for a fee. The organization also assists musicians of all levels in finding places to play in the Charlotte area.

Photo courtesy of Charlotte Children's Choir; photo by Melvin Clark

The Descant Choir is part of Charlotte Children's Choir.

Charlotte Children's Choir

P.O. Box 411072, Charlotte, NC 28241
Contact: Nancy Jo Michaud • 583-1197

Founded in 1986, the Charlotte Children's Choir is one of the area's premier arts organization for young people. The group is made up of three choirs involving over 150 children from seven counties. Participants study and perform a variety of music, sing in many languages, receive music education and Kodaly and basic rhythm training. Membership is open to children ages 8 to 15.

There are several major group concerts during the year with the December and May concerts being the most popular. The choir also participates in competitions and provides special performances. It has toured the United States, Canada and other countries. A modest tuition fee helps support the program and financial assistance is available. The organization also receives support from the Arts and Science Council Fund Drive and the Grassroots Arts Program of the North Carolina Arts Council.

Charlotte Choral Society

1900 Queens Rd. • 374-1564

This nonprofit society is made up of three choral groups: the Mainstage Choir, the producers of the nationally recognized *Singing Christmas Tree* and the Broadway and popular performance of *On the Town*; The Festival Singers, a 32-voice select choir specializing in short form classical and sacred selections; and IMPROMPTU!, a 12-voice jazz ensemble available for corporate and community entertainment. The Charlotte Choral Society choirs are open to any interested community singer who qualifies through audition.

Charlotte Flute Association

Contact: JoAnn Johnson • 563-6784

This group sponsors the Charlotte Flute Choir and brings to Charlotte some of the world's finest flutists for concert performances and master classes.

Charlotte Folk Music Society

P.O. Box 9007, Charlotte, NC 28299
• 372-FOLK

The Charlotte Folk Music Society was formed to preserve traditional mountain music, but has expanded to include other elements of mountain life. The society sponsors and/or participates in many area festivals, including the annual Carolina's Homecoming Festival held in September at

Paramount's Carowinds Campground. This celebration honors the best of Appalachian, bluegrass, Celtic, black string, minstrel, children's folk and blues musicians in a fun setting. The 500-member organization has monthly meetings and publishes a magazine for its members, listing workshops, classes and concerts sponsored by the society.

Through Central Piedmont Community College, classes are held on folk instruments such as the Appalachian dulcimer, old-time banjo, fiddle, folk music guitar, recorder and autoharp. There are even swing band classes. On Sunday evenings at 6 PM the Old-Time Music Jam class meets at Bryant Music Building on the CPCC campus to jam and play and sing the old-time music — jigs, reels and old-time Gospel are part of the fun. If you play or sing the blues (or simply just listen), drop in at the Double Door Inn, 218 E. Independence Boulevard, on the first Monday evening of the month when the Charlotte Blues Society, 455-5875, gets together.

Charlotte Jazz Society
P.O. Box 37002, Charlotte, NC 28237
• 525-9346

This 300-member group, organized in 1985, promotes awareness of America's native musical form — jazz. The society promotes local and regional jazz musicians through such events as Jazz-a-thon, which is an 8-hour event held in the spring and other well-received special programs. The society, in cooperation with UNC Charlotte, sponsors a high school and college jazz competition and scholarship fund. The society also sponsors a club crawl at varied locations.

Charlotte Music Club
P.O. Box 37181, Charlotte, NC 28231
Contact: Richard Boward • 366-2578

Affiliated with the National Federation of Music Clubs and the North Carolina Federation of Music Clubs, the 110-member Charlotte Music Club meets the third Monday of each month from September through May (except for December). For over four decades the club has sponsored the annual performance of Handel's *Messiah* at Ovens Auditorium the first Sunday in December. This performance is free to the public, but donations, which go toward musical scholarships for Mecklenburg students, are appreciated. In 1996, the club gave scholarships to eight music students. Club members also volunteer time at local hospitals, nursing and retirement homes, shelters and rehabilitation centers. Founded in 1925, the Charlotte Music Club is the parent of many musical organizations such as the Charlotte Symphony, Opera Carolina and the Oratorio Singers.

Charlotte Philharmonic Orchestra
P.O. Box 470987, Charlotte, NC 28247
• 846-2788

The 75 members of the Charlotte Philharmonic Orchestra perform under the baton of Maestro Albert E. Moehring and offer 10 to 12 concerts each season. Concerts are performed at N.C. Blumenthal Performing Arts Center, Ovens Auditorium and Oasis Shrine Temple. Reasonable ticket prices and unique programming of classics, Broadway and show tunes have made the orchestra popular. Guest artists include the 100-voice Philharmonic Chorus, solo vocalists, ballet dancers and world-class instrumentalists. In 1996 the Philharmonic released their first CD, "Timeless Moments."

The Philharmonic has performed in concert with recording artists Natalie Cole, John Tesh, Linda Ronstadt and Yanni, among others. The orchestra recently recorded a TV commercial for Time-Life Records and has contracted with the Motion Picture Company of Los Angeles to make motion picture sound tracks.

Charlotte Piano Teachers Forum
Contact: Lois Harris • 366-8473
(Teacher referrals)

This group with 170 members from the Carolinas holds monthly meetings and recitals during the school year. It also holds an annual workshop with Friends of Music at Queens College and sponsors the Charlotte Piano Teachers Forum audition each spring. The group also participates in the North

Carolina Federation of Music Clubs and the North Carolina Music Teacher Association auditions. If you're looking for a piano teacher, this is a good place to find one.

Charlotte Symphony Orchestra
211 N. College St.
• 332-0468 • Box Office: 332-6136

The Charlotte Symphony Orchestra was founded in 1932 by Guillermo S. De Roxlo and today is under the baton of internationally acclaimed Music Director Peter McCoppin. The orchestra is made up of 60 musicians and each year entertains over 250,000 people.

The 40-week season is highlighted by the orchestra's 14-concert Classical Series featuring world-renowned guest artists and conductors and a nine-concert Winter Pops season. The orchestra also performs free summertime Pops at SouthPark concerts. All regular season concerts are performed in the Belk Theater of the North Carolina Blumenthal Performing Arts Center.

Community School of the Arts
4949 W. Albemarle Rd. • 377-4187

In his work as church organist and choir director at First Presbyterian Church, Henry Bridges realized that the vacant Sunday schoolrooms and idle pianos could be put to good use. In 1969, he organized what would later become Community School of the Arts, a flourishing school that now reaches 4,000 students throughout the Charlotte-Mecklenburg area. The school — which offers courses in music (piano, strings, brass, woodwinds, guitar, voice, Suzuki violin and Orff), dance (beginning through classical ballet, jazz and tap) and visual arts (beginning to intermediate drawing, images and materials) — is currently directed by Gene C. Wenner. The outreach program is free to all participants and is

Photo courtesy of Charlotte Philharmonic Orchestra; photo by Johnell Kinsey

Charlotte Philharmonic Orchestra and chorus is conducted by music director, Albert E. Moehring.

presented through Community School of the Arts and various agencies. A number of scholarships are available.

Opera Carolina
345 N. College St., Ste. 409
• 332-7177 • Box Office: 372-1000

Opera Carolina is the oldest and largest professional opera company in the state. The company's productions feature singers and artistic personnel of national and international stature, alongside local and regional singers and technicians of exceptional ability. Opera Carolina's education division presents fully staged operas/musicals and curriculum-based activities to schools and community groups throughout the state. Opera Carolina's community programs department creates opportunities designed for and in collaboration with the region's minority communities.

Oratorio Singers of Charlotte
211 N. College St. • 332-0468

The 150-member Oratorio Singers of Charlotte has merged with the Charlotte Symphony Orchestra. Together, they present three major concerts each season — including Handel's *Messiah* — joined by nationally recognized guest soloists. Also included in the organization is the 34-member Oratorio Singers Chamber Chorus, which performs throughout the Carolinas at locations such as the Piccolo Spoleto Festival in Charleston, S.C., and the 60-member Charlotte Youth Oratorio Singers, which provides an important educational program to students from more than 15 area high schools.

Queens Community Orchestra
1019 Circlewood Dr.
Contact: Aleo Sica • 364-4917

This string orchestra of professional and amateur musicians presents two concerts a year.

Society for the Preservation and Encouragement of Barbershop Quartet Singing in America
205 Altondale Ave.
Contact: Carl deBrosse
• 334-6631, 535-7619

Chartered in 1950, the Charlotte Chapter of the Society for the Preservation and Encouragement of Barber Shop Quartet Singing in America consists of a board of directors, officers, the Gold Standard Chorus and several quartets. The chapter produces its own annual shows and the annual "Singing Valentines," which involves a quartet delivering a valentine anywhere in the Charlotte area for a nominal fee on Valentine's Day. The group participates in civic functions, performs for numerous audiences around the Metrolina region and is supportive of area charity organizations. The chorus has competed on an international level and has won many regional competitions.

Charlotte's Gold Standard Chorus is composed of men of all ages. Men who wish to share in the unique camaraderie of one of Charlotte's finest singing organizations are encouraged to join.

Sweet Adelines International – Queen Charlotte Chorus
Contact: Susan Scott • 542-1266, 847-8507

Sweet Adelines trains its members in musical harmony, barbershop style, without instrumental accompaniment. The Queen Charlotte Chorus presents an annual show at Ovens Auditorium and performs for private groups, civic and community groups and others. Call for audition information.

Theatre

Theatre is alive in Charlotte. From professional to budding stars, there are various places throughout the city that will satisfy your appetite for live performances. If you are an aspiring actor, you might want to check into the First Friday of the Month Club for Working Actors of Charlotte. Paul Kronsberg, 535-5775, is the contact for this organization.

Afro-American Children's Theatre
345 N. College St. • 372-7410, 372-5000

Children from the ages of 5 to 18 are given the opportunity to express their unique creativeness in a series of workshops that include dance, storytelling, juggling, writing and exploring Africa. Each year, the workshops work toward a central theme that culminates in a theatrical production.

Central Piedmont Community College
1201 Elizabeth Ave.
General Information • 330-2722
Box Office • 330-6534

Performances of Broadway-style shows in Pease Auditorium on campus are a treat for locals and visitors alike. Each summer a show is included for children. Its popular, professionally staged productions of summer musicals and comedies are often sold out.

Charlotte Repertory Theatre
2040 Charlotte Plaza
• Box Office: 333-8587

This collaborative Equity professional theater company was established in 1977 to provide entertainment and heighten appreciation of professional theater. As the area's only repertory company, it presents a cycle of new, contemporary and classical works. The Repertory Theatre provides a professional opportunity for area artists and provides the community with wonderfully diverse professional theater. Recent successes include a collaborative production of Shakespeare's *A Midsummer Night's Dream* with the Charlotte Symphony Orchestra and the world premiere of *Signature*, a new work by Pulitzer Prize winning playwright Beth Henley. An additional benefit is its New Play Festival of staged readings of new plays in progress. Under the same umbrella, Charlotte Repertory now offers both the PlayWorks and the Golden Circle Theatre Series with performances at the Blumenthal Center.

Children's Theatre of Charlotte
1017 E. Morehead St.
• 376-5745 • Box Office: 333-8983

With both a production and education program, The Children's Theatre is the place for burgeoning Sarah Bernhardts and Lawrence Oliviers. The production program has four components — Mainstage, productions geared for the entire family; Second Stage, a series of plays performed by and for young actors and audiences in the eighth grade and up; Tarradiddle Players, the touring component of the theater; and

Photo by Robert Thomason

The Afro-American Cultural Center chronicles Charlotte's rich diversity.

Special Events, productions not produced by the Theatre. The education program offers children aged 3 to 18 classes and workshops in theater arts, creative drama and dance. Founded in 1948 by the Junior League, the Children's Theatre became independent in 1952. Programs and performances are held in its 300-seat facility on East Morehead Street.

Davidson College Theater Department

P.O. Box 340, Davidson, NC 28036
• Information: 892-2361
• Box Office: 892-2340

The Davidson Theatre Department presents four full-length plays and several one-acts each year. Performances are held at Hodson Hall in the John Cunningham Fine Arts Building and the adjacent Studio Theatre.

Davidson Community Players

P.O. Box 76, Davidson, NC 28036
Contact: Kim Beard • Information: 892-7953

Founded in 1965, this community theater for the North Mecklenburg area presents two major summer productions, a winter children's play, "fireside" readings, dinner theater productions and receptions.

The Ensemble Company

1017 E. Morehead St.
Contact: Jill Bloede • 376-5745

This company is cosponsored by Children's Theatre and Charlotte-Mecklenburg Schools and students receive school credit for their work. The company is cast only by audition and is open to all high school students, but it is intended for the very serious drama student. Students engage in intense study and acting techniques throughout the nine-month session with professional theatre teachers and directors. Two productions are staged each year in Children's Theatre's downstairs Black Box Theatre. The Ensemble Company is Charlotte's only pre-professional training program for young actors.

Listen and Remember

Waxhaw • 843-2300

Performed annually each Friday and Saturday evening in June, the historical outdoor drama *Listen and Remember*, staged

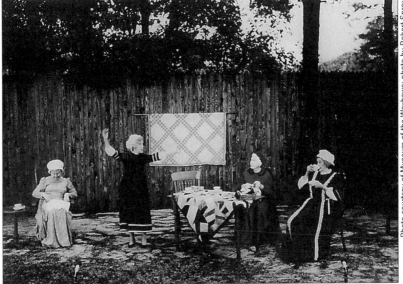

Photo courtesy of Museum of the Waxhaws; photo by Robert Sproul

The historical drama *Listen & Remember* is performed each Friday and Saturday evening in June.

The Blumenthal Performing Arts Center has become one of the finest venues for performing arts in the nation.

in an outdoor amphitheater, portrays American history lived by early pioneers of the Old Waxhaw Settlement, among them the family of young Andrew Jackson. A reenactment of the Revolutionary War depicts the thirst for freedom that motivated those early settlers.

Johnson C. Smith University
100 Beatties Ford Rd. • 378-1069

Performing in historic Biddle Hall, JCSU puts on two plays a year, plus a Christmas program. The productions are diverse, ranging from Neil Simon comedies to ancient Greek tragedies.

Matthews Community Theatre
100 McDowell St., Matthews
Contact: Chuck Haley • 847-5480

Now in its seventh year of production, the Matthews Community Theatre, organized as the result of a Matthews survey, is self-supporting and branching out in its new season. Broadway comedies are performed with a slightly different twist. Volunteers are always needed for set building, costumes and the many other tasks involved in play production.

Metrolina Theatre Association
Contact: Tom Hall • 330-6835

This is the umbrella agency for theater in the region. It supports and promotes growth of dramatic arts in the Metrolina area through CPCC. It debuted in 1984 and currently serves 50 members and maintains contact with 50 additional theater companies.

North Carolina Blumenthal Performing Arts Center
130 N. Tryon St. • 372-1000

The *creme de la creme* of art buildings — the dazzling Blumenthal Center opened in the Uptown NationsBank Complex in late 1992. Everyone got in on the act of erecting this building. Charlotteans voted $15 million in bonds for the project and the state allocated an additional $15 million. Over 67,000 children contributed a quarter each to the Performing Arts Campaign and corporate and private donations fused this dream into reality. The foundation has raised a significant general endowment fund to supplement operating expenses and subsidize lower rents for performing groups. This awesome, five-level building with its dramatic marble and mosaic tile interior includes the 2,100-seat Belk Theatre performance hall for the symphony and opera and the 440-seat smaller Booth Theatre for local and regional theatrical productions. For convenience, a glass walkway connects the center to a guarded parking garage. In the fall of 1996, Charlotte residents flocked to the center to see a stellar production of *Phantom of the Opera*.

Omimeo Mime Theatre
P.O. Box 221267, Charlotte, NC 28222
Contact: Eddie Williams • 553-0032

Founded in 1978 by Hardin Minor and Eddie Williams, this performance troupe presents eclectic, unpredictable, often hilarious vignettes that integrate mime, mask, dance and clowning into a unique movement theater experience. Omimeo Mime has created a number of original productions and collaborated with a wide variety of guest artists. The repertory includes *Mime Time, Satire and Slapstick, Close Encounters of the Invisible Mind, The Whiz Bang Circus* and other hits. Omimeo Mime also offers residencies and workshops in mime and clowning.

Ovens Auditorium
2700 E. Independence Blvd. • 372-3600

Ovens Auditorium, formerly the city's main performing arts center with 2,603 seats, books arts-oriented productions locally, but also offers touring Broadway plays as well as musical productions and other commercial events. In addition, Ovens Auditorium provides space for such community events as dance recitals and graduations.

People First Players
• 365-3454

An improvisational group whose focus is on reducing the stigma of mental illness, the players are made up of a group of individuals diagnosed with mental illness. The players rehearse through improvisational workshops, then carry their message to the community. Organized in 1991, the players have performed for civic, church and mental

health associated agencies, while touring throughout North Carolina. Each production is original, calling for the audience to suggest the characters and topic within special guidelines.

Queens College Theatre
1900 Selwyn Ave. • 337-2332

Queens College puts on two major plays each year, plus a variety of smaller productions presented around campus.

Tarradiddle Players
1017 E. Morehead St. • 342-0730

Since 1971, The Tarradiddle Players, founded by the late Connie Welch, has provided the experience of quality theatre to young people throughout the Carolinas. The troupe, now the touring arm of Children's Theatre, performs at its theater and at other Charlotte facilities, as well as at schools, community halls and festivals. It also offers children's theater workshops for groups.

Theatre Charlotte
501 Queens Rd.
• 376-3777 • Box Office: 334-9128

Theatre Charlotte, founded in 1927 as the Little Theatre of Charlotte, is the *grande dame* of theater in Charlotte — and North Carolina — as the oldest community theater in the state. Over the years, it has performed more than 350 main stage productions to more than 500,000 people. The company produces six plays a year and has a full-time staff of four, plus hundreds of volunteers. Theatre Charlotte is a nonprofessional theater company. Workshops, musicals and classic Broadway plays are given every other month, year round.

UNC Charlotte Department of Dance and Theatre
• 547-2482

The Department produces four to five major productions during the school year, as well as occasional student productions. Held at Rowe Auditorium, the productions include contemporary and classical plays and musicals, dance concerts and original theatre and dance productions.

Visual Arts

There are, as we've noted all along, a lot of free things to do in Charlotte, but probably none of the arts is as free to see or as approachable as the visual arts. You can even get in free at the Mint Museum on certain days. Around the city, but especially in Historic North Charlotte and on North Davidson Street between 34th and 36th streets, you can visit galleries on the first and third Fridays of the month from September through May in what is called The Gallery Crawl. We've outlined many of the visual arts outlets in town.

Afro-American Cultural Center
401 N. Myers St. • 374-1565

The Center is headquartered in a fully restored church near McDowell Street and Seventh in an area of the city known as First Ward. Its purpose is to preserve African-American history and culture and offer a forum for multicultural events, performances and exhibitions. It offers a gallery of changing art exhibits, dance presentations and theater.

The Annex Gallery of Coffey and Thompson
1423 E. 4th St. • 334-4332

The Annex gallery features original art by artists from around the country, from contemporary to traditional, plus it has a wide selection of signed, limited edition prints. It also features bronze sculptures and wood carvings.

Center of the Earth
3204 N. Davidson St. • 375-5756

Center of the Earth, the first art gallery in Historic North Charlotte, opened in 1989. Owner/sculptor J. Paul Sires and owner/artist Ruth Ava Lyons have the largest offering of contemporary sculpture in Charlotte. A few figurative pieces stand among abstract works of stone, steel and wood. Many narrative pieces convey simple to complex messages. This gallery differs from the usual mainstream

Photo by Tim Johnson

Art can be found in many places, including Atherton Mill.

commercial galleries in that it became an outgrowth of the owners' search for an interesting place to work, educate the community and carry the work of local, regional and national artists. The distinctive difference in their approach focuses on the work's integrity, not its marketability. Always a favorite on the gallery art crawls and a recipient of the Governor's Business Award, the Center is open 11 AM to 5 PM Tuesday through Friday, 1 to 5 PM Saturday, 1 to 4 PM Sunday and by appointment.

Farvan International Gallery
119 E. 7th St. • 375-1424

Farvan International Gallery, which opened in early 1987, features museum-quality collectibles and better gifts from East Africa, Egypt, Morocco, Afghanistan, Guatemala, Indonesia and Turkey. You'll find etched gourds, ebony sculptures,

The Mint Museum, built in 1836 to process gold, opened in 1936 as the first art museum in North Carolina.

musical instruments, masks, ceremonial pieces, jewelry, clothing and collections from private estates. The Atherton Mill Farvan Gallery on South Boulevard has a slightly different personality with architectural pieces from Morocco.

Gallery W.D.O.
2000 South Blvd. • 333-9123
The gallery's name is shorthand for "well-designed objects" and it lives up to its name. Art educator Rob Williams collects an astounding array of art from jewelry and glass to furniture and pottery. Located in Atherton Mill, this gallery participates in the first Friday Gallery Crawl.

Hodges Taylor Gallery
401 N. Tryon St. • 334-3799
Opened in 1980 by Dot Hodges and Christie Taylor, Hodges Taylor Gallery was Charlotte's first Uptown gallery and helped start The Gallery Crawl. Since its inception, the gallery has represented professional artists throughout the Southeast. An active exhibition schedule from September through May features these award-winning artists working in a variety of media.

Jerald Melberg Gallery
3900 Colony Rd., Morrocroft Village • 365-3000
The gallery's primary focus is paintings, drawings, prints and sculptures by living American artists with national and international reputations. Owner Jerald Melberg has an eclectic taste and the gallery demonstrates that he looks for works with an inner spiritual quality that take them a step beyond. The gallery opened in 1984.

The Light Factory
809 W. Hill St. • 333-9755
The Light Factory Photographic Arts Center was formed in 1972 and incorporated as a nonprofit arts organization dedicated to promoting photography as a fine art and communications medium. Since that time, The Light Factory has evolved into the foremost photographic resource facility in the Southeast. Its unique gallery has exhibited fine art and documentary photography by many outstanding artists and its website has received national acclaim. Continuing its long-term commitment to photographic education, it sponsors exhibitions, classes, lectures and workshops as well as community outreach programs.

Mint Museum of Art
2730 Randolph Rd.
- **337-2000**
- **Taped Highlights: 333-MINT**
Built in 1836 on West Trade Street, the building originally processed gold that came from 75 to 100 gold mines discovered around Charlotte in the early 1800s. In 1933, the

building was moved to its Eastover location. Reconstructed, the classic structure opened in 1936 as the first art museum in North Carolina.

The American Museum Association and the National Endowment for the Arts have each hailed Charlotte's Mint Museum as a national model for regional and mid-sized museums. Mint visitation and membership represent the city's diversity of interests and populations. Hosting major national tour exhibitions and organizing Mint exhibitions for national tour are mere hints of the museum's ever-increasing popularity. Other reasons for its popularity point to innovative educational approaches and a diversified programming schedule that serves up tantalizing artistic exhibits. The Mint's work using computers and CD-ROMs to expand arts education is a national model.

The museum offers a summer series of weekly workshops for elementary-age children to senior high students. These sessions let students explore the history and themes of the museum's collection through five studio art experiences. In addition, students are served through a year-round Student Artist Gallery. All school groups throughout the Carolinas and neighboring states are admitted free. School teachers can earn a part of their recertification through an intense summer program introducing them to current and future exhibits.

The outdoor Jazzy Ladies series during the summer entertains with live jazz blended with Hollywood film classics. The Faux Ball, in the fall, swings into more imaginative socializing and the Kentucky Derby Party is kind of the "coming out" event for spring, now attracting up to 2,000 guests. Other social focuses are family festivals, seminars led by world-renowned art figures and the most enthusiastic exhibition opening parties found anywhere in the Carolinas.

In early 1999, the Mint Museum of Craft and Design will open at the former Montaldo's building at 218 North Tryon Street, featuring collections of ceramics, glass, wood and fibers. NationsBank provided $8.2 million to donate and renovate the 82,000-square-foot building, the largest bequest in Mint Museum history.

Admission is $4 for adults, $2 for students ages 14 to 18, free for children younger than 12 and free on Tuesday evenings from 5 to 10 PM and on the second Sunday of each month. (For more information on the Mint's collections, see the listing under Attractions.)

Permacolor Division
McNeal Gallery
226 E. Tremont St. • 333-9201

Owner Mark McNeal opened this gallery in the early '70s, making it one of the oldest galleries in Charlotte. It features the largest collection in the east of reproduction prints by Andrew Wyeth and his family, many of them collectors' items, and also has original art in all media.

Photo by Tim Johnson

Gallery W.D.O. is just one of the many unique galleries in Charlotte.

Pope's Gallery
1029 Providence Rd. • 342-1774

Pope's Gallery at the Arboretum
8016 Providence Rd. • 541-3199

In business for 25 years, Pope's sells original watercolors, oils, original paintings by Carolina artists, posters, serigraphs, pottery, statuary, limited edition prints and British restrikes from old antique steel plates and botanicals. Custom framing is also offered.

Queens Gallery & Art Center
1212 The Plaza • 372-2993

The gallery features mostly local young artists, many of them students, to provide them with a springboard, but it also works with professionals. Queens doesn't have formal exhibits, but the gallery, housed in an old church, can be rented for local art exhibits and other functions such as wedding receptions and parties. It also provides framing services and sells art supplies.

Spirit Square Center for the Arts
345 N. College St. • 372-9664

Spirit Square is a multi-arts complex providing classrooms, studios, two art galleries, two performance centers and office space for small arts organizations. The center opened in 1975 in the renovated First Baptist Church and has added two adjoining buildings. Adult and children can take classes in clay, fiber arts, drawing, printmaking and theater.

Walden Gallery
4607 Parview Dr. • 333-6631

Diana Walden opened her first gallery in August 1987. There are Southwestern American native lithographs, etchings and engravings; works by local artists and photographers, including fine art reproduction posters.

Art Instruction

If you are interested in honing your artistic skills or finding instruction for your child prodigy, you'll almost find what you're looking for at either of the following schools.

Central Piedmont Community College
P.O. Box 35009, Charlotte, NC 28235
• 330-5009

Central Piedmont Community College offers classes in most of the visual arts, during the day or at night, for personal enrichment or to earn a degree. The Gallery, next to Pease Auditorium in the Richard H. Hagemeyer Learning Resources Center, offers rotating exhibits, some of which feature art by students and faculty.

Community School of the Arts
4949 W. Albemarle Rd. • 377-4187

Founded in 1969, Community School of the Arts offers classes in music, dance, visual arts, piano and violin for children aged 3 up to senior citizens. A variety of classes is held at its facility. Scholarships are available.

Writing

Charlotte Public Library's NOVELLO is a week-long festival held each year in mid-October. Pat Conroy (*The Prince of Tides*) is headliner for the 1998 festival. Past events have featured famous writers such as Kurt Vonnegut, Toni Morrison, Patricia Cornwell, Maurice Sendale, Dr. Cornel West (*Race Matters*) and John Naisbitt (*Global Paradox*). In addition to nationally renowned writers, NOVELLO also encourages local and regional writers to give workshops and speak at other functions.

Charlotte has had its share of literati through the years — the unforgettable Harry Golden, creator of *The Carolina Israelite* and author of *Only in America* and Carson McCullers, who wrote *The Heart Is a Lonely Hunter*. Charles Kuralt, who died in 1997, will always be remembered for his *On the Road* stories that aired over CBS. Former WBTV's news anchor Bob Inman, known for *Home Fires Burning*, which was later produced on the Hallmark Hall of Fame, has gained national prominence. Frye Gaillard and Ruth Moose also get national attention. Noteworthy poets include Dannye Romine Powell, Irene Honeycutt, Judy Goldman, Rebecca McClanahan and others.

Charlotte is kind to writers and has quite a colony of them who produce everything from travel stories to science fiction to romances to mainstream novels. If you want to enjoy the company of other writers, there are many opportunities for doing so through writing classes offered in local colleges and workshops sponsored by writers' groups.

Carolina Romance Writers
P.O. Box 470761, Charlotte, NC 28226

Affiliated with Romance Writers of America, Carolina Romance Writers meets the third Saturday of the month for a luncheon discussion and program. Open to published and unpublished writers, this active group sponsored a romance conference last year with professional guest speaker writers and editors. Its monthly newsletter, *A Final Draft*, offers helpful industry news, tips concerning writing problems, editors and agents. If you are interested in writing category or mainstream romance, you'll find Carolina Romance Writers a helpful organization.

Charlotte Writers' Club
Contact: Dede Wilson • 365-6846

This is Charlotte's oldest writing organization. It is open to professional and amateur

FYI

Unless otherwise noted, the area code for all phone numbers in this chapter is 704.

writers. Meetings are held the third Monday of each month at Christ Church, 1412 Providence Road, and are followed by light refreshments. The club sponsors four writing workshops per year. All activities, including regular meetings, are open to both members and nonmembers. In addition, the club holds seven contests each year, which include writing for: articles, short stories, juvenile stories, short stories by student only, children's stories, long short stories and poetry. Members can submit without cost, but nonmembers are charged a nominal fee.

North Carolina Writers' Network
P.O. Box 954, Carrboro, NC 27510
• (919) 967-9540, (919) 929-0535 fax

This nonprofit, statewide organization publishes a bimonthly newsletter, sponsors an annual conference and offers a wide variety of information and support for fiction and nonfiction writers and poets.

Women in Communications, Inc.
P.O. Box 11952, Charlotte, NC 28220

The Charlotte chapter of Women in Communications, Inc., an organization for professional communicators, holds monthly meetings, including an annual spring luncheon that features a national speaker and honors local communicators. Men interested in joining the group shouldn't let the name discourage them. Rest assured, they are welcome and can become members.

The Mecklenburg
County Park and
Recreation
Department
maintains the parks,
recreational centers,
swimming pools,
greenways,
golf courses and
historic sites.

Parks and Recreation

The Charlotte area has over 150 parks (14,000 acres) and 17 public recreational centers offering numerous programs. Two major lakes are within easy driving distance: Lake Norman to the north with over 520 miles of shoreline and Lake Wylie with 325 miles of shoreline shared between North and South Carolina.

The Mecklenburg County Park and Recreation Department maintains the parks, recreational centers, swimming pools, greenways, golf courses and historic sites and offers a wide variety of programs. You can find out about registering for team sports such as basketball and football by calling the Mecklenburg County Park and Recreation Department, 336-5800, but you should also watch for notices in your neighborhood announcing sign-ups. If you or someone in your family has a disability, you'll be pleased to know that the Mecklenburg County Park and Recreation Department offers equal access to all recreation programs for persons with special needs. To reserve county facilities, call the individual park.

Not every park in the city and county is listed in this Guide. We offer a sampling and invite you to explore the many other parks that are scattered throughout Charlotte.

Coulwood District Park
Coulwood Park Rd.

Located next to Coulwood Junior High School, this 27-acre park includes an amphitheater, 4 lighted tennis courts, 2 softball fields, a picnic shelter and a concession stand. The 18-hole Sunset Hills Public Golf Course is also located here at 800 Radio Road, 399-0980.

Freedom Park
1900 East Blvd. • 336-2663

This 107-acre park underwent massive renovations and reopened to the public in early 1995. It is one of Charlotte's most heavily used parks and has softball fields, several playgrounds, lighted tennis courts and paved walkways. Activities are centered around the lake, which serves as the official residence of the local duck population. Festival In The Park, one of the park's most popular events, is a 4-day festival held in September of each year.

Grady Cole Center
310 N. Kings Dr. • 353-0200

The Grady Cole Center hosts a number of exciting events, plus antique and craft shows, political rallies and gospel sings. Adjacent is Memorial Stadium, which offers up a number of high school and college football games.

Hornet's Nest Park
6301 Beatties Ford Rd. • 336-8096

This 110-acre park boasts the area's only motocross track and has hosted national tournaments. It also offers softball, fishing, hiking, picnic shelters, a bicycle trail, a playground and tennis courts. A petting zoo featuring farm animals is open every day except on Mondays.

Freedom Park is one of Charlotte's most heavily used parks.

Idlewild Road Park
10512 Idlewild Rd. • 568-4044

Idlewild Road Park covers 100 acres and serves residents in the Mint Hill/Matthews area. It offers a children's playground, softball field and picnic shelters and sites.

Jetton Park
1900 Jetton Rd., Huntersville • 336-3854

Lake Norman is the centerpiece of this 105-acre park, which is located on a peninsula with inviting coves on two sides and a broad stretch of water at its toe. A loop road winds through the oblong-shaped park and there are over 2 miles of asphalt bike paths, plus another mile of gravel trails that dip in and out of the shoreline. Tennis courts are scattered among gazebos and picnic tables and canoes are available for rent. No swimming is allowed and the park has no boat launching ramps. Admission is charged.

Latta Place
5225 Sample Rd., Huntersville • 875-1391

This 2,247-acre nature preserve on Mountain Island Lake is centered around the restored 1800's river plantation home of James Latta. The park contains the Carolina Raptor Center where injured wildlife are cared for, a canoe access area and a Visitors Center. The Equestrian Center features two horse arenas, 80 permanent stalls and 7 miles of bridle trails. Individuals may use the trails or school in the Equestrian Center free of charge. The park sponsors special events such as photo safaris, night fishing, sunset canoeing, summer hayrides and hunter safety courses. Annual special events include a triathalon held in June and Spooktacular Halloweek in October. At the new boat rental harbor, canoes and johnboats are available for a small fee.

Marshall Park
Third and McDowell Streets

Close to Uptown, this park is frequently used for local festivals. A gushing 50-foot fountain and beautiful flowers with the Charlotte skyline for a backdrop make this an oasis in the city. A statue of Martin Luther King Jr. is located in the park.

McAlpine Creek Park
8711 Monroe Rd. • 568-4044

The first developed greenway in the county's system, this 360-acre park stretches from Independence Boulevard to Sardis Road along McAlpine Creek. It is a wildlife sanctuary with nature trails. Park users enjoy several miles of bike paths and cross-country trails, soccer fields, picnic areas and a lake and there are special events such as creek walks and fishing clinics.

McDowell Park and Nature Preserve
15222 York Rd. • 588-5224

One of the county's largest, this park encompasses 894 acres on Lake Wylie. It offers year-round camping, hiking, fishing, picnicking and other activities. You can launch your boat free of charge or rent a paddleboat or canoe during the summer months. There are 4 miles of nature trails and a nature center with hands-on exhibits. Special programs include campfire programs and ghost stories, wildlife programs, stargazing and creek stompin'. From April through September, on weekends and holidays, a small admission fee is charged.

FYI

Unless otherwise noted, the area code for all phone numbers in this chapter is 704.

North Mecklenburg Park
16131 Old Statesville Rd., Huntersville

Facilities at this 88-acre park in North Mecklenburg include ball fields for soccer, softball and baseball, as well as a picnic shelter and concession stand.

Park Road Park
5300 Closeburn Rd.

This 124-acre park has a 12-acre fishing lake, plus ball fields, lighted tennis courts, a basketball court, playground, picnic shelters and nature trails. Located in Southeast Charlotte, the park is very popular and is enjoyed by many local residents.

Ramsey Creek Park
18441 Nantz Rd., Huntersville • 336-4200

Ramsey Creek is a 46-acre park offering a beach area, fishing pier, picnic tables, nature trails and a play area for small children. Sometimes there are special programs or live performances by musicians and jugglers. Sailboarding is taught at the park and sailing regattas are popular.

Reedy Creek Park
2900 Rocky River Rd. • 598-8857

This 699-acre park near Hickory Grove offers an Environmental Education Center, nature trail studies, ball fields, picnic areas, a playground and a short walking path.

St. Mary's Chapel
1129 E. 3rd St. and Kings Dr. • 333-1235

Near Uptown, this tiny park is the home of the Charlotte/Mecklenburg Vietnam Veterans' War Memorial. The memorial stands near the picturesque chapel, the only remaining structure on the original site of Thompson Orphanage and is an attractive setting for weddings and concerts.

Veterans Park
2136 Central Ave.

Built to honor Lt. Budd Harris Andrews, who crashed his airplane in 1945 to avoid hitting a Charlotte neighborhood, this 22-acre park serves the Plaza-Midwood area. It has ball fields, lighted tennis courts, a playground and an indoor shelter.

York Road/Renaissance Park
1525 Tyvola Rd. West

This 332-acre park in southwest Charlotte offers tennis, softball, volleyball, mountain biking and a playground area.

Fauna and Flora

Daniel Stowe Botanical Garden
6500 S. New Hope Rd., Belmont • 825-4490

After a brief orientation at the Visitors Center, you may take a self-guided tour through the Cottage Garden, the Four Seasons Garden, the Vegetable Garden and the Woodland Walk Trail. Activities include birdwatching, children's programs, nature studies and wildflower walks.

Glencairn Garden
Rock Hill, SC • (803) 329-5620

The grounds contain 6 acres of dogwoods, azaleas, lily ponds and fountains. Plants bloom throughout the year.

Photo courtesy of Wing Haven Gardens

Wing Haven Gardens and Bird Sanctuary is a local favorite.

UNC Charlotte Botanical Gardens
UNC Charlotte, Hwy. 49 • 547-2555

This collection of three gardens offers a wide variety of natural treasures. The selection ranges from vines, succulents and water plants from around the world to 50 species of wild ferns and 800 species of indigenous trees, shrubs and wildflowers.

Wing Haven
Gardens & Bird Sanctuary
248 Ridgewood Ave. • 331-0664

Designed to nurture birds, the gardens provide cover, food and nesting sites. Statues, birdbaths and plaques complement the setting. Established in 1927 by Elizabeth and Edwin Clarkson, the formal gardens and wooded areas cover three acres. Open Sunday, 2 to 5 PM; Tuesday, 3 to 5 PM; and Wednesday, 10 AM to 12 PM.

Recreation Areas

Crowders Mountain State Park
Gaston County • 853-5375

For those who love the adventures of hiking, birdwatching and rock climbing this is an accessible getaway place. There is also a 9-acre lake for fishing.

Kings Mountain
National Military Park
York Co., SC • (864) 936-7921

The scene of an important Patriot victory in 1780, the Battle of Kings Mountain, the park covers 3,945 acres. Special events around October 7 each year are held to commemorate the battle. A visitors center and self-guided tours are available.

Kings Mountain State Park
Upper Piedmont Region, SC • (803) 222-3209

Sprawling over 7,000 acres, the park offers two lakes with swimming, trails, fishing, boat rental, a bridle trail and stable, miniature golf and campgrounds.

Recreation Centers

YMCA of Greater Charlotte
Metropolitan Office, (Administrative Office)
500 E. Morehead St. • 339-0379

The YMCA operates a variety of popular programs in Charlotte, including after-school care, summer camp and a summer resident camp. Locations throughout the area offer different classes and programs including:

aerobics, aquatics, baby-sitting, baseball, basketball, canoeing, corporate wellness, dance classes from ballet to jazz, gymnastics, fitness instruction, martial arts with an emphasis on self-defense, sailing, swimming, tennis, water skiing, yoga and many more. Call for more information on a specific location's facilities and programs.

Central Branch
400 E. Morehead St. • 333-7771
Camp Thunderbird
Lake Wylie, S.C. • (803) 831-2121
Harris Branch
5900 Quail Hollow Rd. • 552-9622
Johnston Branch
3025 N. Davidson St. • 333-6206
Lake Norman Branch
21300 Davidson St., Cornelius • 892-9622
McCrorey Branch
3801 Beatties Ford Rd. • 394-2356
Mooresville Branch
664 E. Plaza Drive #4, Mooresville • 662-9622

Simmons Branch
6824 Democracy Dr. • 536-1714
Siskey Branch
3127 Weddington Rd., Matthews • 845-9622
Program Ctr., 4780 Kuykendall Rd. • 846-2477
University City Branch
8100 Mallard Creek Rd. • 547-9622
Uptown Branch
200 One First Union Center • 333-9622
YWCA Main Branch
3420 Park Rd. • 525-5770

Arts & Crafts

The popular Neighborhood Arts Program is an ongoing (September through March) cooperative arts education and enrichment program involving the Community School of The Arts and the Mecklenburg County Park & Recreation Department. These free classes are for all ages with a focus on serving those individuals who otherwise might not have the chance to discover their unique artistic talent

PARKS AND RECREATION CENTERS

Name	Address	Phone Number
Parks & Recreation Staff Office	1900 Park Dr.	336-2884
Albemarle Road Center	5027 Idlewild Rd., N.	567-1941
Boulevard Homes Center	16020 Brooksvale St.	399-8166
Marion Diehl Center	2219 Tyvola Rd.	527-0237
Double Oaks Center	1326 Woodward Ave.	336-2056
Naomi Drenan Center	950 Beal St.	365-1265
Earle Village Center	610 East 7th St.	336-2095
Enderly Park Center	1220 Clay Ave.	393-7333
Greenville Center	1330 Spring St.	336-3367
Hawthorne Center	345 Hawthorne Ln.	336-2008
Amay James Center	2425 Lester St.	336-3053
Latta Center	500 East Park Ave.	336-2533
Methodist Home Center	3200 Shamrock Dr.	568-3363
Revolution Center	1201 Remount Rd.	336-3841
Sugaw Creek Center	943 Sugaw Creek Rd.	596-0107
Tuckaseegee Center	4820 Tuckaseegee Rd.	399-4492
David B. Waymer Complex	14200 Holbrooks Rd., Huntersville	875-1549
West Charlotte Center	2400 Kendall Dr.	393-1560

or to work alongside a professional artist. The schedule includes classes in music, dance, drama, visual and media arts.

During the summer, another arts and crafts program is held on each Saturday from 10 AM to 12 PM at participating parks. The Community School of the Arts, the Mint Museum, Discovery Place, International House, the Public Library, Spirit Square, Theatre in the Park and Museum of the New South rotate to make each Saturday morning experience different. The child may be painting with watercolors, guided by an instructor from the Mint Museum, one week and finding out how bubbles form from a Discovery Place teacher the next. Children can see Shakespeare performed live or participate in various musical interests that may lead them to sign up for the Community School of the Arts enrichment classes.

At most of the recreation centers, students may choose a variety of courses: ceramics, sculpturing, woodcarving, drawing and painting, enameling, sewing and other crafts. For details about both programs, call the Parks and Recreation Department at 336-3854.

Parks and Recreation programs aren't the only game in town when it comes to arts and crafts. The Community School of the Arts, 377-4187, which specializes in music, has art classes other than the classes offered through the Neighborhood Arts Program. The county's Agricultural Extension Office sponsors classes through the 4-H Club program, 336-2082, and through Family and Consumer Education, 336-2692. You might also check Central Piedmont Community College, 330-5009, the Jewish Community Center, 366-5007, and Charlotte/Mecklenburg Schools' Summer Enrichment Programs, 343-5567, for arts and crafts classes.

Recreational Activities

Baseball

You can play baseball through a number of different avenues. Neighborhood athletic groups, the Parks and Recreation Department and the YMCAs have programs for all ages. The city offers organized league play for ages 5 through 18. Participants are placed in compatible age divisions to provide proper training and skill development through organized practices and games. T-Ball and Coach Pitch programs are geared to children ages 5 to 8 while baseball and girls' softball programs offer organized league play. For more information, call 336-2884.

Basketball

Budding Atlantic Coast Conference athletes can get a head start at any of the many basketball programs available through the city recreation centers, neighborhood athletic associations, YMCA programs or Salvation Army Boys Clubs. Sign-ups for organized City Leagues for youths ages 7 to 17 begin in October at participating recreation centers. Team registration is held during October and November with practice and exhibition games in December and regular season games in January. Qualifying teams participate in citywide, regional and state tournaments. For more information, call 336-2884.

Bryan Adrian conducts annual basketball camps for young people at UNC Charlotte. Call 372-3236 for details. The YMCA sponsors a basketball league for players 18 and older and the city offers organized league play for adult men and women as well as industrial teams. Registration for summer games (June through August) is held in May; for winter games (December through April), in October. Call 336-2884.

Boating

Boating is very popular in Charlotte-Mecklenburg due to easy access to Lake Norman, Mountain Island Lake and Lake Wylie. Lake Norman has over 520 miles of shoreline; Lake Wylie has 325 miles. Residents enjoy sailing, water skiing, fishing and other water-associated activities, including boat races and sailing regattas. To find out where and when, check with one of the numerous marinas surrounding both lakes.

Most of the marinas provide the full range of services for boat owners, including storage,

supplies and repairs. At Lake Norman, you might check out Harbortown Marina, 825-5050, or at Lake Wylie, check out Lake Club Marina, 331-9027, Carolina Crossing Marina, 588-5463, Long Cove Marina & Yacht Club, 588-1467, and Tega Cay Marina, 543-1899.

Public boat ramps are available at McDowell Park and Nature Preserve, Ramsey Creek Park, Copperhead Island and Jetton Park on Lake Norman. Call 336-2884 for more information.

Bowling

Bowlers will find plenty of competition at Brunswick Lanes' two locations on East Independence Boulevard and Freedom Drive, at Centennial Lanes, at University Lanes and at George Pappas Park Lanes. In Matthews, Carolina Lanes has a new, large facility. If you want to join a league, check with one of the above lanes.

Camping

You can't pitch a tent just anywhere in Charlotte/Mecklenburg, but it's perfectly fine to do so at McDowell Park and Nature Preserve. Camping is also permitted at Paramount's Carowinds, Duke Power State Park on Lake Norman, Morrow Mountain State Park near Albemarle and Kings Mountain State Park in South Carolina. A few of the marinas around Lake Wylie and Lake Norman also offer camping sites.

Cycling

The Charlotte area is rich in cycling opportunities for riders of all abilities. The gently rolling countryside offers pleasant routes for the recreational road rider while occasional longer climbs challenge the fitter cyclists. Although Dilworth has long hosted a criterium around Latta Park, cycling has become even more popular since the 1996 Tour Du Pont came through Charlotte.

A permanent bike route, designated by oval signs with a bike symbol, makes a 10-mile loop between southeast Charlotte and Uptown. Bike racks are stationed at most public buildings and bike lockers are located beside

Charlotte Transit shelters along Central Avenue. There is also a great biking opportunity at McAlpine Creek Park on a pit gravel trail.

Groups of colorfully clad riders are a common sight along the back roads in the Waxhaw, Monroe and Huntersville areas on weekends. Off-road riders new to the area will be pleasantly surprised to learn that trail riding is available within a short distance from Charlotte. Cane Creek Park, near Waxhaw, has many miles of highly prized "single track" trails ranging from fairly easy for the new rider to fairly challenging for the more adventurous souls. Check with local bike shops for additional information on trails and activities.

Day Camps

The Mecklenburg County Park and Recreation Department offers extensive day camps and playground programs during the summer. Day camps with structured activities are available at 16 recreation centers including Recreation On The Move, which is a mobile recreational unit, fully staffed and equipped to provide supervised experiences in athletics, arts and crafts, music, dance and special events. The cost varies, depending on the program. Free playground programs are available at seven sites and feature planned activities as well as free time. The David B. Waymer Complex is one site that offers a free playground program. A number of citywide special events, such as Junior Tennis Tournament, are planned each summer at Renaissance Park. Mecklenburg County Park and Recreation holds one-week day camps at five different sites, featuring special programs, field trips, games, athletics and arts and crafts.

The Harris YMCA offers coed day camps at Queens College and on site. The YWCA on Park Road holds an annual Kamp-a-Long for girls and boys. Camp Arrowhead at the Simmons YMCA is another choice. One of the finest coed boarding camps in the Southeast is YMCA-affiliated Camp Thunderbird on Lake Wylie where kids learn to water ski, sail, swim and participate in sports and other activities. The camp is a center for the YMCA's extensive Y-Indian Guide program.

Most YMCA camps offer counselor-in-training programs for older young people. Since the YMCA camps are very popular, it's a good idea to register early. Some

Photo by Tim Johnson

Many of the parks offer playground programs at day camps during the summer.

scholarships are available. The Jewish Community Center's day camp is Camp Maccabee and a number of day care centers and learning/tutoring centers in the Charlotte area also offer summer programs.

Fishing

There are plenty of lakes and streams in the Charlotte/Mecklenburg area. If you use live bait, you can fish for free in your home county. Using lures requires a $5.00 state license, available at any local bait and tackle shop. A number of parks — Latta Plantation, Hornet's Nest, Park Road, McAlpine, McDowell, Ramsey Creek, Freedom and Pineville Park in Pineville — offer excellent fishing (catfish, bream, bass and crappie). The county park fishing fee is $1 per day.

Fitness

The YMCA and YWCA offer extensive exercise programs, including stroke clinics and special activities for cardiac patients. Central Piedmont Community College holds fitness classes in a number of locations around the city and you'll also find classes at Queens College. The Jewish Community Center has exercise classes for all age groups, including a cardiac rehabilitation program.

Flying

Several schools on the outskirts of the city will teach you the basics of how to fly an airplane as well as provide the proper training for a private, instrument, commercial or instructor license. To get a private airline pilot's license, you must have at least 40 hours of instruction and be 17 years of age (you can start training and even do your solo at age 16).

Football

Even the pee wee set starts training early for football and the NFL Panthers have made the sport even more popular. Many neighborhood athletic associations have programs. Late starters can get good experience through the Charlotte/Mecklenburg junior and senior high schools or through private school programs. Call Landis Wade at 343-2000 for information about the Pop Warner League, sanctioned by the NFL.

Gymnastics

The city has several gymnastic schools. Clemmer's in Pineville, 583-9998, is the oldest, having been in business since 1935. Others are Gym Dandies, 948-7797, and Charlotte Gymnastics International, 596-1991. A number of dance studios also teach gymnastics. The YWCA on Park Road and the Harris YMCA also offer instruction and the Parks and Recreation Department has classes, gym meets and competitions.

Ice Hockey

The Charlotte Youth Hockey League is open to boys and girls ages 4 through 18. Players may opt for the House League (at-home games only) or for the Travel League, which plays opposing teams in the Southern Hockey League and the Mid-Atlantic League. There is a fee charged to play for the season and the fee includes ice time and a jersey. Players must provide their own equipment. The season runs from early to mid-September through late March with a 15 to 20 game schedule. The Travel League involves additional expenses. For information, contact the Charlotte Amateur Hockey Association at 519-0303. For adult hockey team information, contact the Ice Capades Chalet at Eastland Mall, 568-0772. The Ice House in Pineville also offers ice hockey instruction. Call 889-9000 for information.

Horseback Riding

Latta Equestrian Center is located in historic Latta Plantation Park, 5225 Sample Road, Huntersville, 875-0808. First built by the County Park and Recreation Department as a horse show facility, Latta Equestrian Center has 194 stalls, 2 show rings, 2 practice rings and 10 miles of scenic trails, all available to the public for shows or use with privately owned horses.

Horses are available at the center for guided trail rides and for group or private lessons. Latta Equestrian Center offers pig pickin's and hay rides for private parties, along with horse shows, Hunter Paces and other activities that are open to the public. Check the Yellow Pages for places to board your horse or take horseback riding lessons.

Jogging, Running, Walking

Charlotte's mild climate makes it ideal for jogging, running, walking — even skipping — out of doors most of the year. You'll find trails and tracks in city and county parks as well as at public junior and senior high schools. Many of the commercial health clubs and Y's have indoor tracks that become quite appealing during 20-degree or 100-degree days. Local runners train yearlong for *The Charlotte Observer* Marathon, a spring event that attracts participants from all over the United States. The 1995 running included an Olympic pretrial to qualify runners for the 1996 Olympic games in Atlanta. You can buy a T-shirt or sweatshirt at the shop on the first floor of the Knight Publishing Building on South Tryon Street, whether you're a marathon runner or just a spectator.

FYI

Unless otherwise noted, the area code for all phone numbers in this chapter is 704.

In late November, the annual SouthPark Turkey Trot takes place. A Thanksgiving Day tradition, this 8K road race benefits local charities. Call the Hyatt Charlotte at SouthPark, 554-1234, extension 2002, for more details. Most public schools and many private ones offer the sport of track to students. McAlpine Creek Park offers a 2-mile bike-jogging path and a 5K Cross Country running course.

Karate/Martial Arts

There are many schools in the Charlotte area that teach karate, martial arts and self defense. Instruction is also available at some of the YMCAs. Unless you already know the specific sort of instruction you want, check at several of the studios and ask questions before you sign up. Many studios will let you observe a class.

Performing Arts

If you want to get in on the act — whether it's a dance act, theater production or concert — the city abounds with opportunities. Spirit Square has the longest list of offerings for children and adults and will be happy to put you on its mailing list to receive a class schedule each quarter. Just call 372-9664. Community

Photo by Robert Thomason

Fall soccer programs are very popular.

School of the Arts, 377-4187, offers a variety of musical instruction, plus classes in drama, dance and art.

The Children's Theatre, 376-5745, teaches drama, puppetry and related courses to children. Stagestruck adults can find opportunities for acting at local theaters such as Theatre Charlotte, 376-3777, CPCC Theatre, 330-2722, and Charlotte Repertory Theatre, 375-4796.

The Mecklenburg County Park and Recreation Department and the YWCA are other options for classes. (See our Arts chapter for more on performing arts opportunities.)

Polo

Located off Tom Short Road, southeast of Charlotte, is a unique opportunity for a day of family-oriented fun and festivities. The Charlotte Polo Club takes to the field against teams throughout the Carolinas for some "divot-stomping" excitement. The 9-week spring season runs from May through June with the 10-week fall season running from September through November. Two matches are played each Sunday with the gates to Cato Farms opening at noon, allowing fans to picnic and tailgate before the 3 PM main event. The polo matches have proven to be a favored pastime for Charlotteans in the spring and fall with each match attracting several thousand fans. Call 846-1010 for more information.

Skating

Charlotte's ice rink is the Ice Capades Chalet located in Eastland Mall. Instruction is available — just call 568-0772. Roller skating rinks in the area include Grand Central, 536-0800, on Central Avenue; Tradewinds, 523-6455, on Old Pineville Road; and Roll-a-Round, 568-5700, on E. Harris Boulevard.

Skydiving

Charlotte Skydivers perform aerial tricks at the airport in Chester, South Carolina. Member John Ainsworth performs with the Prism Skydiving Team, national champions. For details on this daring sport, call Skydive Carolina at (803) 581-5867.

Photo by Robert Thomason

Sailing at one of the many lakes in the area has become a favorite local pastime.

Soccer

A number of athletic associations offer soccer programs. One of the top three is sponsored by the Harris YMCA with approximately 1,100 participants. Groups such as Charlotte Junior Soccer, North Mecklenburg Youth Soccer and the American Youth Soccer Organization (AYSO) also sponsor programs of similar size. Programs are also available through the Mecklenburg County Park and Recreation Department and the YMCAs. The city offers organized league play for youths ages 7 to 18. The fall program is played outdoors and is geared to recreational teams in the 7 to 15 age group. The winter program is played indoors for recreational and selected teams in the 7 through 18 age group. Leagues have been organized through recreation centers and neighborhood associations. Sign-ups are usually held at participating recreation centers.

Softball

Programs are offered by neighborhood athletic associations, the Mecklenburg County Park and Recreation Department and various churches. The city offers organized league play for adult men and women through industrial and co-recreational teams. Registration for the spring/summer program is in January and February with league play occurring from mid-April through early August. Registration for the fall program is during July and August with games scheduled from early September through November. For more information, call 336-3854.

Special Populations Programs

The Mecklenburg County Park and Recreation Department offers recreational programs for all Mecklenburg citizens, but places a special emphasis on programs for the physically, mentally and emotionally challenged at the Marion Diehl Recreation Center, 527-0237. The Center, among the few of its type in the nation and the only fully accessible center and playground for the developmentally challenged in the state, has a therapeutic playground and wheelchair fitness course. The Center operates Camp Spirit during daytime in the summer.

Swimming

The Mecklenburg Aquatic Center (MAC) opened its doors to the public in 1991. Located on East Second Street in Uptown, MAC is a full-service swimming, diving and fitness center offering a wide variety of }instructional, recreational and competitive aquatic programs. Call 336-DIVE for more information.

The Mecklenburg County Park and Recreation Department operates two indoor and four outdoor public pools. Marion Diehl Center offers one of those indoor facilities. It is also worth noting that the center's swimming pool and pool room's temperature is kept several degrees warmer than at other pools in order to aid working out sore muscles.

Free swimming lessons are given at all pool sites in June. There is a citywide two-week session, co-sponsored by the American Red Cross, at Revolution Pool. The YMCAs and YWCAs have pools and swimming classes year round, including life-saving classes. The Jewish Community Center offers a full aquatic program.

The Mecklenburg Aquatic Center is outfitted with an 8-lane, 50-meter competitive pool and a state-of-the-art timing system. Diving enthusiasts have access to two 3-meter diving boards and two 1-meter boards. The facility also offers a 25-yard hydrotherapy pool, a 16-foot in-ground spa, an exercise/fitness room, sunning deck and meeting rooms, all for minimal daily or annual fees. Other public pools include Cordelia, Double Oaks and Greenville.

Tennis

Tennis took Charlotte by storm a decade ago and it's still going strong. Many of the city and county parks have excellent courts and they're free! Country clubs and private swim-tennis clubs require membership. Olde Providence Racquet Club, 366-9817, is the best known tennis club in town; another is Charlotte Tennis Club, 554-7777. Most tennis clubs, including the Y's, belong to leagues.

Volleyball

This team sport is one of the hottest activities in town, particularly with singles. You can play at several locations, including Myers Park United Methodist Church, the Jewish Community Center and St. John's Baptist Church. Mecklenburg County Park and Recreation Department offers a league based on various ability levels. Leagues are divided into high, moderate and novice levels for team competition. There are three seasonal leagues — spring, fall and winter. The winter program is for co-recreational teams only. To find out more about this }exciting activity, call the Mecklenburg County Park and Recreation Department at 336-3854.

Other Sports

Other not so well-known sporting activities exist in and around Charlotte as well. Steeplechase has joined polo as a sporting and social event. The Queen's Cup is held in April. Call 423-3400 for more information. Scuba diving and lacrosse both have clubs in the area. For information on these and other "off the beaten path" recreational opportunities, you might try either *The Charlotte Observer* sports department or your local YMCA.

Insiders' Tips

A number of athletic associations offer soccer programs. One of the top three is sponsored by the Harris YMCA with approximately 1,100 participants. Other private groups such as Charlotte Junior Soccer, North Mecklenberg Youth Soccer and the American Youth Soccer Organization (AYSO) also sponsor programs of similar size.

Charlotte golfers can find a challenge at one of 30 public golf courses, 23 private courses, three par-3 courses and 17 practice ranges.

Golf in the Carolinas

Say the word around here and eyes will glaze over. With all due respect to basketball and football, another of Charlotte's passions, golf, is the unofficial sport of the Carolinas. Golf is practically a religion in the Charlotte area and little wonder. With temperate climates and some of the best courses in the world within easy reach, golf is far more than a pastime. Upwards of 11 percent of all Carolinians play, not to mention the millions of visiting players who frequent our courses each year. All of this is big business and a big boost to the regional economy.

While not necessarily a golfing destination, Charlotte has a rich golfing history. Charlotte's first golf course was designed by renowned course architect Donald Ross in 1918. That course is none other than the Charlotte Country Club, a private course and club filled with Charlotte's elite. It continues to rank as one of the finest courses in the state and the country.

In 1972, Charlotte Country Club played host to the U.S. Amateur Championship. Prior to World War II, a tournament known as the Charlotte Open attracted many professional Tour stars to another fine course and private club, Myers Park Country Club.

The PGA Tour returned to the Queen City from 1969 through 1979 with the Kemper Open played at Quail Hollow Country Club past SouthPark. Tom Weiskopf, Raymond Floyd and Andy Bean were among the event's champions.

Carolina Golf & Country Club, a smaller private course off Wilkinson Boulevard on Donald Ross Drive, is also a Ross design.

Considerably less expensive to join than Quail Hollow Country Club, Charlotte Country Club, Myers Park Country Club and others, Carolina Golf & Country Club is a delightful and tricky course nestled in the shadow of the Uptown skyline. It has produced many a fine golfer, including Charlotte attorney David Strawn, who played on the Tour for several years.

Today, many of those same players return to Charlotte annually for the Senior PGA Tour's Home Depot Invitational. Held for years at Quail Hollow Country Club, the Tour moved the event to the Tournament Players Club at Piper Glen when that private club and course opened. Arnold Palmer, who maintains a home in the Quail Hollow area, acts as host each year. Another popular Tour, the Fieldcrest Cannon LPGA Classic, is held each September at The Peninsula Club on Lake Norman.

Charlotte has contributed to the ranks of the PGA over the years. Clayton Heafner was a PGA Tour star in the 1940s and '50s. He played on two Ryder Cup teams and twice finished second in the U.S. Open. In 1961, Charlie Sifford became the first African-American golfer to play on the PGA Tour full time. Currently on the Tour, superstar Davis Love III has more than eight PGA victories to his credit.

Golfers across the city can play on a number of courses designed with their passion in mind. Within a 30-mile radius of Uptown Charlotte, golfers of all skill levels can find a challenge at one of 30 public golf courses, 23 private courses, three par-3 courses and 17 practice ranges — with more being designed and built each year.

Over the past decade, golfing facilities have not expanded fast enough to meet the growing demand. That's now changing with new courses coming on line each year and new public courses available to challenge the scratch golfer. While tee times are still hard to come by Saturday mornings during the spring, there's a course for everyone at a cost per round for every pocketbook.

Public Golf Courses

Charlotte Golf Links
11500 Providence Rd. • 846-7990

Located in populous southeast Charlotte, this course represents the next best thing to playing the links of Scotland at a fraction of the cost. Noted architect Tom Doak designed this par-71, 6520-yard links course that opened in the spring of 1993. The tract is virtually wide open except for the high rough guarding the fairways. Try your bump-and-run shot around the pot bunkers here. This highly regarded course is as close as you'll get to playing in the British Open.

Crystal Springs Golf Club
N.C. 51, Pineville • 588-2640

Crystal Springs offers a delightful and challenging 18-hole championship course. Serviced by both a restaurant and lounge, the course, conveniently located near Pineville, is open seven days a week.

Eagle Chase Golf Club
3215 Brantley Rd., Marshville • 385-9000

A short 25-minute drive from the Charlotte area, Eagle Chase opened in late 1994 and is situated in Marshville off N.C. 205. This par-72, 6800-yard layout was built by a group of local investors who saw the need for an upscale public facility in Union County. They've got that and more with this course designed by Tom Jackson. Located 10 miles northeast of Monroe, the links are set along a rugged ridge and feature unexpected elevation changes and spectacular views.

Eastwood Golf Course
4400 The Plaza • 537-7904

Eastwood is one of Charlotte's oldest public courses and was once owned by famed

Photo Courtesy of N.C. Travel & Tourism

Professional or weekend duffer, Charlotte's courses
have something for everyone.

golfer Clayton Heafner. The layout has undergone numerous on-course improvements over the past few years. It's a short course at just 5850 yards, but many locals love it and enjoy the old-fashioned design and small, crowned greens.

Highland Creek Golf Club
7001 Highland Creek Pkwy. • 875-9000

One of Charlotte's newest and arguably best public golf courses, Highland Creek is well worth the drive into the ever-developing countryside of northeast Mecklenburg County. Its fairways and greens are maintained as well, if not better, than many private courses and the clubhouse staff makes you feel like a member. The course offers a variety of challenging holes that are balanced, fair, aesthetically pleasing and tough. It has the highest slope rating of any area public facility at 133. Not to worry. You'll vividly remember each hole of this par-72, 7008-yard course. Saving the best for last, the 18th hole is a reachable par-4 with a lake running down its entire right side.

Lakewood Golf Links
Lakewood Rd., Belmont • 825-2852

Just a short drive from the Charlotte Coliseum, Lakewood is situated in nearby Belmont. Open seven days a week, it's a nice par-71 course convenient to Charlotte but a world apart.

Larkhaven Golf Club
4801 Camp Stewart Rd. • 545-4653

This 18-hole championship course is not hard to find, off Harrisburg Road to Robinson Church then right on Camp Stewart. A par-72, 6440-yard course, Larkhaven features Bermuda fairways and a brand new clubhouse. Complete with bar and grill, the club also has a fully stocked pro shop for your convenience.

Mallard Head Golf Club
Brawley School Rd., Mooresville • 664-7031

Located north of Charlotte on Lake Norman in Mooresville, the course is easily reached via I-77 to Exit 33. It's a rolling course of 6900 yards and is known for its well-kept greens. The front nine is relatively tight with the long, downhill par-3 seventh hole playing over

water. It's a potential card wrecker. The back nine is more forgiving of wayward shots, but it ends with a tough 18th hole demanding a long and precise tee shot to a small landing area.

Regent Park Golf Club
U.S. 21 S., Fort Mill, S.C. • (803) 547-1300

This par-72 course opened in autumn 1994 near Pineville in the Fort Mill, South Carolina, area just south of Charlotte. The layout, designed by course architect Ron Garl, actually crosses over both states and three different counties. Multiple teeing grounds, generous landing areas and removed undergrowth allow all levels of golfers to compete. Well-positioned hazards and multilevel greens present a challenge.

Renaissance Park Golf Course
1525 W. Tyvola Rd. • 357-3373

The most convenient public course in Charlotte is also one of its most popular. Located on Tyvola Road, a 3-iron away from the Charlotte Coliseum, Renaissance Park may well be one of the area's most difficult courses. Tight landing areas and sloping greens characterize this par-72, 6880-yard layout, designed over an old county landfill. It offers golfers four of the area's best par-3s, ranging from 140 to 200 yards. The front nine, while aesthetically pleasing, is no match for its fairer counterpart on the back nine. Renaissance annually hosts the Mecklenburg County Amateur Championships.

Sunset Hills Golf Course
800 Radio Rd. • 399-0980

Its slogan says it all — "Maximum Golf, Minimum Cost." Sunset Hills is one of the least expensive courses in the area. While there are few challenges from tee to green on this 6400-yard course, it offers many crowned and sloped greens. It's a great place for family play.

Tega Cay Country Club
Gold Hill Rd., Tega Cay, S.C.
• (803) 548-2918

Nestled within a private community on Lake Wylie in nearby South Carolina, this public-access course offers a private club setting. Tega Cay's 6400-yard course features a wide variety of holes and is a favorite among locals.

Westport Golf Course
N.C. 16 • 483-5604

On the western side of Lake Norman, Westport presents a straightforward, challenging layout that stretches to 6800 yards. The par-4 fourth hole quickly gets your attention. At 424 yards, it's one the area's toughest. Golfers must lay up in front of a pond and then face a 200-yard approach shot to an elevated green. Westport's greens are usually in great condition and the course offers a quiet getaway from the bustle of other Charlotte facilities.

Other public courses

Birkdale Golf Club
16500 Birkdale Commons Pkwy., Huntersville • 895-8038

Buffalo Shoals National Golf Club
1000 Broken Arrow Dr., Statesville • 873-4653

Carolina Downs Country Club
294 Shiloh Rd., York, S.C. • (803) 684-5878

Charles T. Myers Golf Course
7817 Harrisburg Rd. • 536-1692

Charlotte National Golf Club
6920 Howey Bottoms Rd. • 882-8282

The Divide
6803 Stevens Mill Rd., Matthews • 882-8088

Emerald Lake Golf Club
1 Tournament Dr., Matthews • 882-7888

Fort Mill Golf Club
101 Country Club Dr., Fort Mill, S.C. • (803) 547-2044

Fox Den Country Club
170 Fox Den Circle, Statesville • 872-9990

Mooresville Municipal Golf Club
West Wilson Ave., Mooresvillle • 663-2539

Oak Hills Golf Club
4008 Oakdale Rd. • 394-2834

Olde Sycamore Golf Plantation
7504 Olde Sycamore Dr. • 573-1000

Paradise Valley (Nine Holes)
9615 N. Tryon St. • 548-8114

Photo by Tim Johnson

Beautiful homes overlook the greenways on private golf courses like the Peninsula Club on Lake Norman, designed by Rees Jones.

Pawtuckett Golf Club
1 Pawtuckett Rd. • 394-5890

Pebble Beach Par-3
Indian Trail • 821-7276

Pinetuck Golf Club
2578 Tuckaway Rd., Rock Hill, S.C.
• (803) 327-1141

Revolution Park (Nine Holes)
2661 Barringer Dr. • 342-1946

River Bend Golf Club
NC Hwy. 150, Shelby • 825-2651

Rocky River Golf Club
Concord • 455-1200

Spring Lake Country Club
1375 Spring Lake Rd., York, S.C.
• (803) 684-4898

Stonebridge Golf Club
2721 Swilcan Burn Dr., Monroe • 283-8998

The Tradition
3800 Prosperity Church Rd. • 549-9400

Photo by Robert Thomason

Some courses, such as Providence Country Club, are the centerpieces of residential developments.

Private Club Courses

The Charlotte regional area is also blessed with a spectacular array of private golf clubs. Unfortunately, many golfers aren't members. So if you want to play the course, call the club and ask about their guest policy. If you're a member of another private club, ask your professional to call about reciprocal agreements. If you get the chance, play some of the venerable courses like Charlotte Country Club, Quail Hollow Country Club, Carmel Country Club, Myers Park Country Club and Carolina Golf & Country Club. In addition, notable clubs such as Raintree, Cedarwood, Pine Lake, Pine Island, Pawtuckett, Cramer Mountain, River Hills and others are nearby.

Some of the newer private courses have been built within the last five to seven years as centerpieces of residential developments. Providence Country Club in Southeast Charlotte and the Tournament Players Club at Piper Glen, which was designed by Arnold Palmer, are two examples. The Peninsula Club on Lake Norman was designed by Rees Jones, and Raymond Floyd served as a consultant on the tough River Run Golf & Country Club in nearby Davidson.

Carolina Courses

Because Charlotte's smack in the middle of the Carolinas, area golfers have access to some of the best golfing facilities in the world. By car, it's two hours to the mountains, three hours to Myrtle Beach, two hours to Pinehurst and Southern Pines and four hours to Hilton Head Island.

Try your hand at Tanglewood Park, (336) 778-6320. One hour away, just outside Winston-Salem, the 11,200-acre park and its 18-hole championship course make for a great daytrip. It's not often that a golfer gets to tee it up at the site of a Senior PGA Tour event and former host of the 1974 PGA Championship. Obviously, the course is extremely demanding, with several long par-4s and 110 bunkers. With water on only three holes and little undergrowth, the average golfer can scrap it around with great enjoyment. Tanglewood's companion, the Reynolds Park Golf Course, (910) 650-7660, is no slouch either. Many regulars consider its tight, tree-lined back nine the park's toughest.

The Appalachian Mountains of North Carolina offer golfers the challenge of dramatic elevation changes and wildlife-filled forests along with the pleasures of scenic beauty and cool temperatures. Patrons of Springdale Country Club, (800) 553-3027, can take advantage of all these aspects. Thirty minutes southwest of Asheville, Springdale actually has a split personality. The front nine of this family-owned resort is wooded and mountainous, while the back nine is open and flat.

Fifteen minutes north of Asheville, Reems Creek Golf Club, (828) 645-4393, features a rare treat of immaculately kept bentgrass tees, fairways and greens. It's very much a target golf course with lay-up and blind shots the norm. Large, tiered greens add to the challenge.

Golfers can let loose a little more on Reems' sister course, Mount Mitchell Golf Club, (828) 675-5454. Nestled at the base of the highest peak east of the Rockies, the course is actually relatively flat and features bentgrass from tee to green. The natural hazards of streams and forests have been wonderfully incorporated into the course to form another major distraction — breathtaking scenery. Beware especially of the picturesque 10th and 14th holes.

In the northwest corner of the state, Jefferson Landing, (336) 246-5555, opened in 1991 along the world's second-oldest river, remarkably called "The New River." Former U.S. Open and PGA champion Larry Nelson designed this 7111-yard layout. Its gently rolling, open terrain would allow golfers a greater margin for error if it weren't for the creeks and ponds, which are in play on 15 holes.

Just a two-hour drive or a 20-minute flight from Charlotte is perhaps the mecca of golf enthusiasts all over the world — Pinehurst Resort and Country Club, (910) 295-3186. Pinehurst, which celebrated its Centennial in 1995, pulled out all the stops. Established in 1895 by Boston soda fountain magnate James Walker Tufts, Pinehurst's first course was finished in 1898. In 1900, Scottish-born architect Donald Ross redesigned Pinehurst No. 1 and created the famed Nos. 2, 3 and 4, which to this day stand as monuments to his ingenuity.

Guests at the resort can choose from one of seven courses, but Pinehurst No. 2 is the grandaddy of them all. Its crowned greens are characterized by humps, bumps and greenside swales. For professional golfers like Ben Hogan, Jack Nicklaus and Paul Azinger, No. 2 has been the charm. Another name will be added to that distinguished list of winners in 1999 when the U.S. Open returns to Pinehurst.

Moore County, North Carolina, where Pinehurst is located, is home to more than 34 golf courses. Just west of Pinehurst, Foxfire Resort and Country Club, (910) 295-5555, has two courses, East and West. Both were designed by Gene Hamm. Although the East is longer and carries a more difficult rating, the West is favored by locals because of its variety of holes and rustic feel. You can't go wrong with either one.

The Sandhills of the state are full of other top-notch courses. South of Aberdeen, Legacy Golf Links, (800) 344-8825, is a newer public layout designed by Jack Nicklaus II. The label "challenging, yet enjoyable" fits this course perfectly. Picturesque par-3s, reachable par-5s and testing par-4s naturally flow over former pasture land. Legacy is one of the most fun courses to play in the Carolinas.

If you prefer golfing on the coast, plan to visit Sea Trail Resort & Golf Links, (800) 624-6601, a golf haven if there ever was one. With three different but challenging championship courses, this 2,000-acre resort is environmentally designed to preserve the marshes and wetlands.

Across the border is Myrtle Beach, South Carolina, home of the famous Grand Strand. Here golfers have 100 courses from which to choose. Certainly at the top of the list is The Dunes Golf and Beach Club, (803) 449-5914, the site of the Senior Tour Championship. Although semiprivate, the course grants guest privileges to several area hotels. Test the par-5 13th hole, a sharp dogleg right around water. It's not reachable, but the hole's name "Waterloo" reveals past failures to heed similar warnings.

In North Myrtle Beach, Bay Tree Golf Plantation, (800) 845-6191, stands as a tried and true favorite. With three 18-hole courses created by George Fazzio and Russell Breeden, the complex has a design for every golfer: the rolling Gold Course, site of the 1977 LPGA Championship; the 7044-yard Green Course, nicknamed "The Green Monster"; and the diverse Silver Course.

A newer course in the Cherry Grove area, Tidewater Golf Club & Plantation, (803) 249-3829, has garnered tremendous praise for its playability and straightforward test of golfing skills. Ten holes run along the waterway and all of them feature fast, sloping bentgrass greens.

Moving down the coast to the South Carolina lowcountry, Wild Dunes, (800) 845-8880, was one of the original island developments and its Tom Fazzio designed Links Course has withstood both newer courses and Hurricane Hugo. Seaside golf simply doesn't get any better than this, especially when the 17th and 18th are true links holes that run parallel to the ocean.

On the other side of Charleston, Kiawah Island, (800) 654-2924, offers four top-drawer courses. The most famous is the Ocean Course, designed by Pete Dye, and host to the memorable 1991 Ryder Cup Matches.

Photo Courtesy of Sea Trail Resort & Golf Links

Sea Trail Resort & Golf Links is environmentally designed to preserve the marshes and wetlands.

Set hard by the Atlantic, if the wind blows the course becomes the most difficult you'll ever play. Try making par on the 205-yard 17th hole or just getting it over the water!

If you don't tire of playing world-famous courses, then continue down to Hilton Head and Harbour Town Golf Links, (803) 363-4485. When it opened in 1969, the course's small greens, railroad tie-supported bunkers and tight fairways were considered quite radical. Today, professionals rave about the course at the MCI Heritage Classic held here each spring.

Glen Rice of the Charlotte Hornets drives against Shawn Kemp
during an exciting moment at The Hive.

Spectator Sports

Charlotte reigns as the Queen City of professional sports in the Carolinas. Ever since Charlotte was awarded an NBA franchise, the Charlotte Hornets, and an NFL team, the Carolina Panthers, pride for the Queen City's sports has been shown by the fan's intensity as they play stadium and armchair point guard and quarterback.

Area baseball and hockey fans won't be disappointed either, as Charlotte offers the AAA Knights and the East Coast Hockey League's Checkers the home field advantage. At the Charlotte Motor Speedway, the annual Coca-Cola 600 is the second largest single sporting event in the world.

Amid Charlotte's rapidly growing sports scene, ACC basketball still remains a dominant sports thrill. With teams like the University of North Carolina Tarheels, Duke, N.C. State, Wake Forest and Clemson just a short drive away, some of the nation's most competitive college basketball is right on our doorstep. Although Charlotte isn't home to an ACC school, March Madness reaches a fever pitch here, especially when the 24,000-seat Charlotte Coliseum hosts the ACC championship.

For college-level athletics in the Charlotte area, Johnson C. Smith and UNC Charlotte have become highly touted programs in their own right. UNC Charlotte took its team to the Men's NCAA Tournament in 1997 and 1998, and the school looks forward to continued exciting competition in Conference USA.

During the summer of 1997, the Amateur Athletic Union Junior Olympic Games were held in Charlotte, bringing more than 30,000 athletes, coaches and family members to the area. UNC Charlotte, Independence Arena, Ovens Auditorium, the IceHouse in Pineville, five area high schools and several other venues hosted events. The 12-day event was one of the largest convention-sized sporting events in North Carolina.

In this chapter you'll find information for the spectator — from professional and collegiate sports teams to the most popular sporting events in the area. For recreational activities and participant sports, see our chapter on Parks and Recreation.

Baseball

Charlotte Knights
Knights Stadium • (704) 36-HOMER
Ft. Mill, S.C. • (803) 548-8050

Charlotte's AAA Knights are affiliated with the Major League Florida Marlins. The affiliation with the Marlins began in 1995 and continues through 1998. From 1988 until 1992, the Knights were the AA affiliate of the Chicago Cubs. In 1992, Charlotte was awarded AAA distinction and became affiliated with The Cleveland Indians in 1993. During its inaugural season, the Knights brought Charlotte an International League Championship and enjoyed similar success in 1994. Although 1995 and 1996 did not produce memorable seasons, 1997's turnaround in which the team finished in second place in the International League West showed significant promise. The Knights

Knights Stadium is the site for AAA baseball.

were recently purchased by Don Beaver, who also owns four other AAA baseball teams.

Games are played at Knights Stadium, a 10,000-seat stadium with an infrastructure suitable for Major League expansion should Charlotte be awarded a team. The state-of-the-art stadium has full concession facilities, including The Home Plate Cafe restaurant. Knight's Stadium is located in Fort Mill, S.C., on I-77 S. and Gold Hill Road at Exit 88, just one mile south of Carowinds Boulevard and a short 15-minute drive from Uptown. The season runs from early April until September, with the Knights at home for 72 games. Game times are scheduled Monday through Saturday at 7:00 PM and Sundays at 2:00 PM. Call the Knights for game schedules and ticket information.

Basketball

Charlotte Hornets
Hive Drive • 357-0489
Ticketmaster • 522-6500

Through owner George Shinn's efforts, Charlotte was awarded an NBA team on April 22, 1987. Although many doubted the community's ability to give up their ACC loyalty and support a professional team, fan support has never waned.

Like all expansion teams, the Hornets struggled through their early years, winning 20, 19 and 26 games in their first three seasons. In 1991-92, new head coach Allan Bristow and NBA first overall draft pick Larry Johnson propelled Charlotte to a 31-51 record. With the addition of Alonzo Mourning in the 1992 NBA Draft, the Hornets improved to 44-33 in 1992-93 and advanced to the NBA Playoffs for the first time. In a thrilling postseason, Charlotte upset Boston in the first round before falling to New York in the second.

Due to injuries to Johnson and Mourning, Charlotte ended the 1993-94 season with a 41-41 record, but with the team healthy again a year later, the 1994-95 squad posted a then-franchise record 50-32 mark and once more advanced to post-season play.

The 1995-96 season began a period of change for the Hornets. Bob Bass was hired as the team's new Vice President of Basketball Operations and began to build a team that would earn him NBA Executive of the Year honors in 1997. With the franchise unable to come to contract terms with Mourning, Bass dealt the center to Miami in a trade that brought Glen Rice and Matt Geiger to the Queen City. Charlotte finished the 1995-96 campaign with a 41-41 record.

The transition continued in the summer of 1996. Hall-of-Famer Dave Cowens was hired as the franchise's fourth head coach and brought with him a defensive philosophy that would spawn the cry of "Hornets Hardball." Anthony Mason and Vlade Divac were added in trades with the Knicks and Lakers to enforce the new Hardball mentality. With these additions, the All-Star play of Rice and original Hornets Muggsy Bogues (the NBA's shortest player at 5'3") and Dell Curry, Charlotte won a club record of 54 games in 1996-97 and advanced to the NBA Playoffs for the third time.

Free agent point guard David Wesley was acquired in the summer of 1997. The Hornets finished the 1997-98 regular season with a 51-31 record, averaging 96.6 points per game. For the fourth time, the Hornets advanced to the playoffs, but were eliminated by the Chicago Bulls in the second round. The future promises excitement and optimism with more fans than ever cheering the Hornets on.

Charlotte Sting
3808 Oak Lake Blvd., Ste. 400 • 357-0252
Ticket Information 424-WNBA
Ticketmaster • 522-6500

The Charlotte Sting is one of the 10 new franchises in the Women's National Basketball Association that began play in the

• **Two Distinct Menus**
• **Exciting Atmosphere**
• **80 TVs and 16 Satellites**

Open Daily
From 11 AM to 2 AM
Monday through Saturday
10 AM to 2AM Sunday
4109 Southstream Blvd.
Charlotte, NC
423-0001

summer of 1997. The Sting began its inaugural season on June 21, 1997, and finished as one of the league's top teams with a 15-13 overall record. The Sting was one of four teams that advanced to postseason WNBA play before losing in the semifinal game to the eventual WNBA champion Houston Comets.

The Sting was almost unstoppable in its home confines of the Charlotte Coliseum with a league-best 12-2 record at home. On August 16, 1997, the Sting set a record by attracting 18,937 fans for a home game victory over the Houston Comets.

The Sting is led by Charlotte-native Andrea Stinson, two-time Olympian Vicky Bullett and Asheville-product Rhonda Mapp.

Photo by Robert Thomason

Known affectionately as "The Hive," the Charlotte Coliseum is home for the NBA Hornets and the WNBA Sting.

Photo by Robert Thomason

Ericsson Stadium is the home of the NFL's Carolina Panthers.

Charlotte 3 on 3
Central YMCA, 400 E. Morehead St.
334-3663

This annual tournament allows the basketball junkie to test his or her skills against players of similar ability. Held in Uptown Charlotte every August, the tournament is open to all ages and skill levels with all proceeds going to Habitat for Humanity. Each team, made up of four players (3 at a time on the court), is categorized by age, height, basketball experience and ability, and is scheduled against similar teams in one of several divisions.

Football

Carolina Panthers
227 W. Trade St. • 358-7000

On October 26, 1993, NFL owners granted all Carolina football fans their wish by unanimously awarding them a professional football team. The Panthers became the 29th NFL team, the first expansion team in the league since 1976 and the only one to win the bid by total owner acclamation.

Owner Jerry Richardson's dream of a football team for the Carolinas grew from his own experience in the NFL. An All-American at Wofford College in Spartanburg, South Carolina, Richardson went on to play professionally as a receiver for the Baltimore Colts. With the Colts (now in Indianapolis), he was the 1959 Rookie of the Year and caught a touchdown pass from Johnny Unitas

in the team's 31-16 victory over the New York Giants in the 1959 World Championship Game.

After playing again in 1960, Richardson took his $4,694 championship bonus and purchased a Hardee's Hamburger franchise. Richardson's fast-food business escalated into one of the largest food service companies in the world. He stepped down as chairman of the empire he built to concentrate solely on his new venture, the Carolina Panthers. Richardson hired Mike McCormack in 1989 as an executive consultant to help obtain the NFL franchise and named him team president in January 1994. McCormack, an offensive lineman who became an assistant coach with Washington in the late '60s and coach of the Philadelphia Eagles in 1973 before being hired as director of the Seattle Seahawks in 1982, was inducted into the Hall of Fame in 1984. McCormack was instrumental in bringing in Bill Polian as general manager and Coach of the Year Dom Capers as head coach. After two great seasons, McCormack resigned as president in March 1997 and was replaced by Mark Richardson, the franchise owner's son and director of business operations.

General Manager Bill Polian had helped lead the Buffalo Bills to four straight Super Bowls. In Buffalo, Polian took a squad that was the butt of all NFL jokes from 1984 to 1986 and built a championship team that compiled a 58-22 record from 1988-1992, going to three Super Bowls, four AFC championship games and five AFC divisional playoffs. In polls sponsored by *The Sporting News,* Polian has been named NFL Executive of the Year four times, surpassing Bobby Beathard and George Young, who are two-time winners of this prestigious award. Polian left the Panthers to become president of the Indianapolis Colts and the Panthers replaced him with two new employees: Jack Bushofsky, director of player personnel, and Marty Humey, director of football administration.

While deciding on a head coach, Dom Capers' name kept surfacing when candidates' names were brought up by the Panthers decision-making team. In 11 professional seasons Capers had been associated with eight playoff teams and involved with only one losing team since 1981—the 7-9 New Orleans Saints. His abilities as a head coach emerged when he joined the Pittsburgh Steelers in 1992. His defense led the NFL in take-aways and fumble recoveries and was tied for the league lead with 21 touchdowns allowed. In 1993, the Steeler defense ranked first in the AFC in defending against the run and a total of 37 forced fumbles led all teams as well. Capers' 1994 defense was second overall best in the league. His three seasons with the Panthers have led to records of 7-9 (1995), 12-4 (1996) and 7-9 (1997).

The Panthers played at Clemson University's Death Valley their first season. The 72,500-seat Ericsson Stadium was well worth the wait. Nestled on a 33-acre site in Uptown Charlotte, the open-air natural grass facility was financed through a public-private venture that included the sale of Permanent Seat Licenses. PSLs give buyers the ability to permanently control and purchase season tickets for all Panthers home games. The team's 70,000 single-game tickets for 10 preseason and regular-season home games for the 1997 season sold out in 2 hours — an average of 7,000 tickets per game.

The Carolina Panthers are a very successful new franchise. The 1996 season showed signs of continuing maturity in increasingly talented and dedicated players. Led by a tenacious defense, which topped the NFL in sacks, the Panthers achieved a 12-4 regular season record, a NFL Western Division championship and a berth in the NFL Championship playoffs against the Dallas Cowboys. Their victory resulted in a match against the Green Bay Packers in the NFC Championship Game. Although the Packers went on to win the Super Bowl, the Panthers have the distinction of being the first two-year expansion team to make the playoffs. However, the Panthers struggled throughout the 1997 season and finished with a disappointing 7-9 overall record. Capers told his team at the end of the season to "remember how it feels because we don't want to have this feeling again." Expectations were higher than team results and everyone is focusing on the promise of the 1998 season. The Panther defense will be bolstered considerably through the recent additions of former Washington Redskin defensive tackle Sean Gilbert, who signed a seven-year, $46.5-million contract, and first-round draft pick Jason Peter, a former defensive tackle for the Nebraska Cornhuskers.

Ice Hockey

Charlotte Checkers
2700 E. Independence Blvd. • 342-4423

In 1993, after a 16-year hiatus, professional hockey returned to the Queen City when it became home to the Charlotte Checkers of the East Coast Hockey League. The team is one of 25 teams in the ECHL and is associated with the Boston Bruins and the New York Rangers.

The Checkers have qualified for the ECHL playoffs in all five seasons. In 1996 the Checkers won the playoffs and captured the Jack Riley Cup in a 4-0 playoff sweep against the Jacksonville Lizard Kings. Goalie Nick Vitucci was named playoff MVP and right wing Phil Berger led all ECHL players in playoff scoring. The Checkers, who had the league's third-best regular season record in 1997, also swept their first-round series and went 13-3 in the four rounds of the Riley Cup. In 1998, the Checkers finished with a regular season record of 35-24-11 and advanced to the playoffs, falling to the Pensacola Ice Pilots in the second round. The Checkers played 36 home games in the 9,570-seat Independence Arena during the 1998 season, averaging over 6,000 fans per game.

In September of 1996, Timothy Braswell became the team's sole owner. Steve Camp, former director of the Charlotte Coliseum Authority, became president and general manager in 1998.

Racing

Charlotte Motor Speedway
Concord • 455-3200

The racing fervor that fills the Queen City during Race Week — or anytime NASCAR races are taking place — is something that must be experienced by anyone who visits Charlotte. The city is a hotbed for racing enthusiasts, as tens of thousands convene at Charlotte Motor Speedway when the big races come to town.

Located 12 miles northeast of Charlotte, the 2,010-acre Charlotte Motor Speedway hosts many racing auto shows year round, but the main attractions are its three Winston Cup events: The Winston, Coca-Cola 600 and UAW-GM 500, and the two Busch Grand Nationals: the Car Quest 300 and All Pro Bumper To Bumper 300.

If you're a racing novice and you're planning a trip to Charlotte Motor Speedway, here are several key points to keep in mind before heading to the track. Since many events are sold out in advance, get your tickets early. The best seats are higher up in the stands on the front stretch. Leave for the track very early and allow plenty of time for parking. Bring a cooler packed with refreshments, as this will save time waiting in line at the concession stands. You may also want to bring a seat cushion since many of the seats are concrete.

In May 1995 the first-annual 600 Festival came to Charlotte Motor Speedway in celebration of the NASCAR Winston Cup Series. The event is no longer a spectator sport, as area businesses and civic organizations have banded together to put on a fast-lane celebration of the color and pageantry of motor sports. The festival includes a student art contest, a miniature NASCAR race called the Real Yellow Pages/Mini 600 for Junior Achievement and street party events that culminate in an action-packed parade featuring NASCAR drivers and marching bands. Then there's the Score Board Speed Street. For this event, Tryon Street is transformed into a wonderland of live music, nightly laser and fireworks shows, interactive racing and a pit crew challenge. Famous drivers are on hand to sign autographs. Call the Festival Association at 455-6814 for more information about the 600 Festival.

The Speedway offers tours to the public Monday through Saturday from 9 AM until 4 PM and Sunday from 1 until 4 PM. Call the track office for more information.

Road Races

Charlotte Observer Marathon & Festival
Uptown Charlotte • 358-5798

In April each year, *The Charlotte Observer* hosts the Queen City's most popular running event. In addition to the 26-mile marathon, races of all skill levels are featured, such as a 10K wheelchair race, a one-mile "fun run" and a 10K fitness walk, a half marathon bicycle ride for the family and a half marathon in-line skating ride for the family. The 1996 running of the marathon featured a US Olympics pretrial run for Olympic hopefuls. In 1998, 1,094 competitors finished the marathon and 3,678 finished the 10K race.

Many Charlotte streets are blocked off for the event as participants meander through area neighborhoods.

SouthPark Turkey Trot
Hyatt Charlotte • 554-1234

On Thanksgiving Day of each year, the Hyatt Charlotte at SouthPark hosts the SouthPark Turkey Trot. It's an 8K road race that routes through the streets in the SouthPark area. All funds raised go to the Leukemia Society and UNICEF.

Photo courtesy of Charlotte Motor Speedway

NASCAR is the fastest growing spectator sport in the country. The Charlotte Motor Speedway is host to three Winston Cup events.

Dilworth Jubilee
Latta Park • 353-1246

In August of every year, Charlotteans participate in the city's oldest road race run through the Queen City's second oldest neighborhood. Starting at 8 AM to beat the muggy August heat, the 8K Dilworth Jubilee is held each summer in the beautiful historic Dilworth area near Uptown. Volunteers and supporters are welcome at this long-standing Charlotte tradition. The run is followed by a day-long neighborhood celebration and tour of historic area homes.

Soccer

Charlotte Eagles
2101 Sardis Rd. N. • 841-8644

As soccer participation grows in the surrounding area so has support of the Charlotte Eagles professional soccer team. The Eagles compete in the United System of Independent Soccer League's Division III Pro League (40 teams). The team is a dominant presence in the South Atlantic Division, advancing to the playoffs in 4 of 5 seasons, and placing second in the nation in 1996 and

1997. The season runs from mid-April until late August and the team plays other South Atlantic rivals such as the Myrtle Beach Seadawgs, Wilmington Hammerheads and the South Carolina Shamrocks. General admission for adults is $6 and $4 for children. Season tickets and group rates are also available. Attending the Eagles' games provides a fun, entertaining atmosphere for the entire family.

In addition to fielding a professional team, the Charlotte Eagles conduct summer soccer camps for children ages 5 to 14, manage a youth club and offer free clinics and school programs year round.

Swimming

Charlotte UltraSwim
Mecklenburg Aquatic Club
9850 Providence Rd. • 846-5335

The Mecklenburg Aquatic Club hosts the UltraSwim at Mecklenburg County Aquatic Center every June. This nationally recognized event attracts some of the world's best swimmers. Past and future Olympians can be seen competing at this unique event.

Off The Beaten Path

Cricket

The Charlotte Cricket Club • 358-5935
10820 Independence Point Pkwy., Matthews

In 1989, a group of British and South African ex-patriots who recently moved to the area started the Charlotte Cricket Club because they missed playing their favorite sport. Since its inception, the CCC has gained quite a following and has grabbed the attention of thousands of locals.

The game resembles baseball in many respects, but novices will find the sport difficult to follow. You'll soon learn that no other sport combines athletics with grace and aggression quite like cricket. Each year, the club organizes a team made up of Americans who have never played or seen the game before. In the spring and fall, the club puts its game of dexterity to the ultimate test as it plays local and regional teams. The season concludes with a three-day tournament.

The Charlotte Cricket Club has benefited from community support driven by local businesses. It always welcomes new sponsors and players. Those curious about playing need not have experience to join and will soon find out why cricket is the most civilized of all the outdoor sports.

Soccer's popularity continues to increase on college campuses.

Polo

Charlotte Polo Club • 846-1010
11331 Tom Short Rd.

A favored pastime for all Charlotteans, polo is a sport for horse lovers and thrill seekers alike. The sport of kings is truly the king of sports. Every spring and fall, the Charlotte Polo Club takes to the field against regional teams throughout the Carolinas. Matches are played off Tom Short Road in Southeast Charlotte on Sundays at 3 PM on the fields of Cato Farms. The gates open at 1 PM to allow for tailgating and picnicking. The spring season runs from May through June and the fall season runs from September through November. No matter what season, the matches attract thousands of Charlotteans every Sunday.

Collegiate Sports

Davidson College
Davidson, N.C.
Sports Information • 892-2815
Tickets • 892-2088

The Davidson College athletic program has traditionally provided students with opportunities for participation at various levels of interest and skill. Sports on the varsity level are fiercely competitive and draw much support on game days. At a less intense level, club sports are provided for the average student and more than 80 percent of all students participate in intramural sports.

The Davidson football team is an Independent Division I-AA team. All other varsity sports are NCAA Division I and compete in the Southern Conference. Davidson has consistently provided competitive basketball teams and men's and women's tennis teams. Other men's varsity sports include baseball, indoor/outdoor track, cross country, wrestling, golf, swimming and diving. Women's teams include field hockey, tennis, volleyball, indoor/outdoor track, cross country, soccer, lacrosse, basketball, swimming and diving. Since 1991, the women's field hockey team has won six Deep South Championships.

Photo courtesy of Davidson College

Johnson C. Smith University
100 Beatties Ford Rd.
Sports Information • 378-1209
Tickets • 378-3505

Year after year, students cheer their Golden Bulls to victory. Johnson C. Smith University is a member of the Intercollegiate Athletic Association (CIAA).

Coach William Davis fields Charlotte's only area collegiate football team, which plays at Memorial Stadium. JCSU participates in the NCAA's Division II in football, cross country, volleyball, men's and women's track, softball, tennis and golf.

Queens College
1900 Selwyn Ave. • 332-7121

Queens College participates in nine sports as an independent on the NCAA Division II level. Student athletes participate in men's and women's basketball, men's golf, men's and women's soccer, tennis, women's volleyball and women's softball. Queens College is well-known for Ovens Auditorium, one of Charlotte's most popular and versatile sports arenas. It serves as home to the Charlotte Pro-Am summer basketball league.

UNC Charlotte
9201 University City Blvd.
Sports Information • 547-4937
Tickets: • 547-4949

The University of North Carolina at Charlotte provides the most highly visible athletic department in the city with its NCAA Division I, 16-varsity-sports, athletic program. The school is a part of Conference USA.

The men's basketball team has played in several postseason tournaments, including the 1998 NCAA Tournament where it fell to UNC-Chapel Hill 83-93 in the second round. The women's basketball program has also become a popular sporting event. Since 1996, both teams have played on campus in

Photo courtesy of UNC Charlotte

Basketball at UNC continues to draw crowds and thrill fans.

the 9,105-seat Halton Arena. Melvin Watkins is the men's basketball head coach and Ed Baldwin leads the women.

In addition to basketball, the fall sports lineup features men's and women's soccer, cross country and women's volleyball. The men's soccer team is nationally renowned. In the spring, the UNC Charlotte schedule includes baseball, softball, tennis, track and golf.

In 1994 and 1995, the men's baseball team captured the regular season championship. The women's soccer team was the 1995 Conference USA champion and in 1996, the men's soccer team reached the NCAA semifinals. The men's golf team won the 1996 Conference USA championship.

INSIDERS' TIPS

Tickets for professional sports events can be hard to get. Many seats are held by dedicated season-ticket holders who will definitely attend. If you want to go to a pro sports event, plan early and buy quickly.

From Charlotte you are only a daytrip from the sand dunes of Myrtle Beach or a half-day's drive to the highest peak on the East Coast.

Daytrips and Weekend Vacations

From Charlotte you are only a daytrip from the sand dunes of Myrtle Beach or a half-day's drive to the highest peak on the East Coast. You will find that the Charlotte area is surrounded by historical sites, museums and other educational attractions.

Down The Road In The Carolinas (Daytrips & Weekend Vacations) covers daytrips in both North and South Carolina and includes over $1,000 in valuable coupons. The book may be purchased from your local bookstore or by calling (800) 777-4843. North Carolina and South Carolina provide catalogs and brochures on various regions and special events.

S.C. Beaches and Ports

Myrtle Beach

Myrtle Beach has been the beach of choice for Charlotteans for as long as anyone can remember. It's the closest, about a 3-hour drive, and offers a variety of activities for fun and excitement. Staying at the beach is affordable and the rates will reflect the season. There are a variety of accommodations available from campgrounds to luxury resorts. The Myrtle Beach Chamber of Commerce, (800) 356-3016, will be glad to send you a package of information on accommodations, attractions and restaurants.

Now known as the Grand Strand, Myrtle Beach is the place where the '60s beach dance craze the "Shag" was born. A few years back, some nostalgic souls sent the word out that a shag reunion would be held at the beach. Four to five hundred people were expected — thousands showed up and folks of all ages have been shagging up and down the Strand ever since.

At one time, the beach was pretty much a late-spring and summer activity. The pace at Myrtle Beach has changed as more shops, restaurants, entertainment centers, golf courses and the like have been built. Although the other seasons may attract sun worshippers, it has become an affordable golfer's paradise for fall and winter. For information on golf, call Myrtle Beach Golf Holiday, (800) 845-4653.

Myrtle Beach is currently emerging as a year-round entertainment capital second only to Disney World in Florida. Calvin Gilmore, the founder of The Carolina Opry music show, featuring a multitude of talented singers and musicians, started it all when he opened a theater in Surfside Beach. Since then, he's started several other shows. The Carolina Opry is located at the north junction of 17 By-Pass and Business 17 at restaurant row. Call (803) 238-8888 for information on The Carolina Opry, Legends in Concert (impersonations of stars) and Eddie Miles Theater ('50s and '60s music and Elvis impersonations). Right next door, country music legend Dolly Parton has built a music hall for her Wild West dinner show called The Dixie Stampede, (800) 433-4401. The two shows are timed so that you can watch Dolly's show and then walk a few paces and see the show at The Carolina Opry. Fantasy Harbor, located at Highway 501 at Waccamaw, is the home of The Gatlin Brothers Theatre, The All American Music Theater and the Savoy Theatre, featuring the Big Band at the Savoy starring the Jimmy Dorsey Orchestra. Call (800) 681-5209 for reservations. At this same complex is Medieval Times, which provides an exciting four-course dinner show featuring a tournament, (800) 436-4386. The Alabama Theatre at Barefoot Landing offers a Celebrity Concert Series, *Christmas in Dixie* and an *American Pride Show*. Call (800) 342-2262 for reservations. The latest addition to the Myrtle Beach music scene at Barefoot Landing is the House of Blues, (803) 272-3000.

A $250-million shopping/entertainment center called Broadway at the Beach opened in the summer of 1995 and Ripley's Aquarium, (803) 916-0888, opened in 1997. Numerous restaurants and shops are located there along with the Hard Rock Cafe. Located nearby is the famous Planet Hollywood and The Palace Theater, (800) 905-4228, providing star studded-entertainment, Broadway plays and shows like the *Radio City Christmas Spectacular*.

If you go south or north of Myrtle Beach, you can find less crowded, less touristy conditions. North Myrtle Beach is a favorite for families and golfers. Barefoot Landing was the original waterfront entertainment center. Not much has changed at Murrells Inlet or Pawley's Island (known for its hand-made hammocks) except for the increase in places to shop.

Be sure to see Brookgreen Gardens, which is built around an old rice plantation and contains more than 500 massive sculptures, making it the largest figure sculpture garden in the world. To learn more about this area, pick up a copy of *The Insiders' Guide to Myrtle Beach*.

Photo Courtesy of S.C. Tourism

Only three hours away, Myrtle Beach offers beautiful beaches and exciting year-round entertainment.

Photo Courtesy of S.C. Tourism

Georgetown's waterfront is lined with quaint shops and restaurants.

Georgetown

The rice capital of the United States in the 1800s, Georgetown attracts a large number of visitors who appreciate its historic buildings and sites, bed and breakfast inns and charming waterfront lined with quaint shops and restaurants. Georgetown bills itself as "the real South" and there are over 40 sites you can visit in the historic district. Some of the more popular sites are The Rice Museum, the Kaminski House (a seafarer's house dating to 1760), the Man-Doyle House (a rice planter's townhouse dating to 1775), the Prince George Winyah Episcopal Church (erected in 1747) and two rice plantations located south of town (Hampton Plantation State Park and the Hopsewee Plantation). Call The Georgetown County Chamber of Commerce and Information Center, (800) 777-7705, for more details.

Charleston

Although only 3 1/2 to 4 hours away from Charlotte, Charleston should be enjoyed over at least a weekend. Since its founding in 1670, this aristocratic colonial port city has been steeped in history. As a city, it has withstood fires, earthquakes, pirates, a Civil War and hurricanes, yet it still retains its charm and beauty.

The city boasts over 73 pre-Revolutionary buildings, 136 from the late 18th century and more than 600 structures built prior to the 1840s. The historic structures, cobblestone streets, antique shops, boutiques, quaint bed and breakfasts and world-class restaurants make Charleston a "must see" destination for any newcomer. Some of the many historic homes open to the public for tours include the Aiken-Rhett House, Edmondston-Alston House, Nathaniel Russell House, Heyward-Washington House and the Joseph Manigault House. There are so many historic churches in Charleston that the city is often called The Holy City. Be sure to visit Patriots Point Naval and Maritime Museum and Battery Park and White Point Gardens where you'll have a lovely view of the harbor and distant Fort Sumter. Charles Towne Landing is the site of the first permanent English settlement in South Carolina and offers tram ride guided tours of the original 1670 fortification as well as beautiful English gardens. If you loved *Gone With The Wind,* try to see some of the beautiful plantations located close by: Boone Hall, Drayton Hall and the adjoining Magnolia Plantation and Gardens and Middleton Place. Call the Charleston Visitors Reception and Transportation Center, (803) 853-8000, for tour information or stop by the Center at the corner of Meeting and

Photo Courtesy of S.C. Tourism

Charleston is an aristocratic port city steeped in history.

Ann streets. To learn more about this area, pick up a copy of *The Insiders' Guide to Charleston, SC.*

Hilton Head Island

One of the most popular resort areas in eastern America, Hilton Head has come a long way since its discoverer William Hilton advertised for settlers in 17th-century London papers. Not connected to the mainland until 1956, the island boomed when the bridge was built and now features 12 miles of broad beaches, championship tennis and golf. Another major reason for coming to Hilton Head is shopping with choices spanning outlet stores to specialty shops. Accommodations range from oceanfront camping to world-class resorts. Call the Hilton Head Chamber of Commerce for more information, (803) 785-3673.

N.C. Beaches and Ports

When people in Charlotte talk about the beach, they usually are talking about Myrtle Beach, but North Carolina also has some of the finest beaches on the East Coast. The areas known as the Crystal Coast, the Cape Fear Coast or Wrightsville Beach at Wilmington and the Outer Banks are beautiful

and definitely worth a visit, but will take more than a weekend to explore. The port cities of Wilmington, Morehead City, Beaufort and New Bern offer a unique blend of history and modern-day commerce.

The Southern Coast

Some of the more popular Southern beaches of North Carolina include Wrightsville, Carolina, Kure, Holden, Ocean Isle and Sunset. Though intimidating to early European explorers who named the area Cape Fear, today's traveler will enjoy the rugged beauty of the coast, its waters and the gracious hospitality of its people. From Charlotte, Wilmington is a 4-hour drive down U.S. 74. To learn more about this area, pick up a copy of *The Insiders' Guide to Wilmington, NC.*

Wilmington

Wilmington, the state's largest port city, is on the Cape Fear River and is really worth more than a daytrip. This historical city is now becoming well known for its growing film industry.

Wilmington is the permanent home of the *USS North Carolina*, a 35,000-ton battleship memorial to the men and women who served in World War II. In town, Wilmington has a tour of historic homes and Chandler's Wharf, which shows the city as it was in the 1800s.

The restored Cotton Exchange building is home to a variety of unique shops and restaurants near the Hilton Hotel.

Fort Fisher is located at Kure Beach, site of one of the country's largest land-sea battles in 1865 and houses a museum of items from Confederate blockade runners. The North Carolina Aquarium is less than 2 miles away. Here you can view live marine life and participate in special aquatic programs. Kids will also enjoy the amusement park atmosphere of Carolina Beach, a short drive down U.S. 421 South.

Orton Plantation near Wilmington, (910) 371-6851, is one of North Carolina's best-known Southern plantations and rivals those of Virginia. It was an 18th-century rice plantation and the gardens are now open to the public. The best time to visit is in the spring when the plantation's dazzling azaleas are in full bloom.

Wrightsville Beach

Wrightsville Beach, just over the bridge from Wilmington, is on the barrier islands, which protect the state's Atlantic coast. This is an upscale community with miles of beautiful sandy beaches perfect for long walks, swimming, surf fishing or most any water sport you may enjoy.

The Crystal Coast

The name "Crystal Coast" describes the area around Beaufort, Morehead City and the beaches of Bogue Banks. Visitors can choose among the historic preservation area of Beaufort, Morehead City's famous seafood boardwalk, golf courses and shopping or any of the public beaches. From Charlotte, the Crystal Coast is a 5-hour drive. To learn more about this area, pick up a copy of The Insiders' Guide to North Carolina's Central Coast.

Beaufort

This quaint seaport has a wide boardwalk along the waterfront and narrow streets lined with white frame houses. It has become a favorite dockage for seagoing yachts. Many of

the town's beautiful historic homes have been restored and are nestled between grocery stores and gift shops.

Bogue Banks

Bogue Banks (Atlantic Beach, Pine Knoll Shores, Salter Path, Emerald Isle) is one of 23 barrier islands off the North Carolina coast. Unlike most of the outer banks, the 27-mile-long Bogue Banks runs from east to west. The Atlantic Ocean drums its southern shore while Bogue Sound laps its beaches to the north. This unusual orientation leads to one of the island's unique features: the sun both rises and sets over the ocean.

Atlantic Beach is the most highly developed of the Bogue Banks beaches. Its surf is mild, the beach is very wide and the sun-warmed shallow water is the most enjoyable of the state's beaches.

The North Carolina Aquarium at Pine Knoll Shores is one of the three nationally accredited aquariums on the North Carolina coast. It is open daily from 9 AM until 5 PM.

Salter Path is a residential community making the transition to a tourist community. West of Salter Path is Emerald Isle, which was incorporated as a resort town in the mid-50s and has been attracting North Carolina's sun lovers ever since. Emerald Isle features houses for rent — beachfront, soundside, modern, rustic, casual, elegant and in every price range. The annual Beach Music Festival is a popular event held in mid-May and features top beach music groups. Nearby is the Crystal Coast Amphitheatre where Worthy is the Lamb, an outdoor drama based on the Passion of Christ, is performed.

Fort Macon State Park

More people visit Fort Macon than any other state park. Fort Macon was built between 1828 and 1835, then restored in 1936. Fort Macon stood guard over Beaufort inlet during the Civil War and World War II. You can fish from the rock jetties, swim at the public beach or enjoy your lunch at the picnic areas.

The Tryon Palace in New Bern was North Carolina's first State Capitol.

Morehead City

Morehead City ("Morehead" to everyone at the coast) is an easy town to like. Fill the town with internationally renowned sport fishing fleets and scuba diving charters that explore the "Graveyard of the Atlantic" and even then you only have half the story.

The Morehead Waterfront is devoted to commercial fishing, sport fishing, preparing fish and eating fish. Unlike most coastal waterfronts, the Morehead Wharf is not devoted entirely to tourism. Shipping and fishing-related commercial activities keep the area bustling.

In addition, the waterfront offers scuba diving charters (Olympus Dive Shop is world famous), sport fishing charters, boat rentals, sailboat excursions, party boat tours, day trips to Cape Lookout and seafood sold fresh off the boats.

New Bern

This historic little town of lacy crape myrtle trees is a 4-hour drive from Charlotte. New Bern is located at the confluence of the Neuse and Trent rivers. Most of the waterfront activity buzzes around Union Point Park, where these two rivers meet. It was New Bern's linkage to Pamlico Sound and the Atlantic Ocean that made this an ideal port. The town was founded in 1710 and named for Baron Christopher DeGraffenried's home of Bern, Switzerland. It became the first colonial capital of North Carolina.

When Royal Governor William Tryon began building his residence/government capitol offices, they took on the appearance of a palace more than a modest government home with offices. The original palace burned in 1798, but it was completely rebuilt and restored to its former splendor. The restoration includes the Tryon Palace, the John Wright Stanly House, the Dixon-Stevenson House that was occupied by Union troops during the Civil War and the new Academy Museum.

In the spring, the Royal English Gardens are abloom with tulips. During the summer costumed guided tours bring history alive. Actors portray Governor Tryon, his wife and their servants talking about the everyday happenings in the 1700s. By early December, the palace is decorated much as it was during the holidays in 1770 for the Tryon Palace Christmas Celebration, a must-see holiday event.

Outer Banks

The Outer Banks are a long day's drive from Charlotte and would be difficult to really enjoy in just a weekend. These barrier islands are marked with the names of American history and still include the longest stretch of undeveloped beach in the country. The Southern Banks include Ocracoke, a quaint village only reachable by ferry; Hatteras, home of the fabled Cape Hatteras Lighthouse; Bodie, home of the Bodie Island Lighthouse; and Roanoke Island, where history is reenacted in the outdoor drama, *The Lost Colony.* Before show time, visitors can stroll through the authentic Elizabethan Gardens. Other worthwhile tours include a visit to Fort Raleigh, site of the first English settlement;

FYI

Eastern North Carolina area code 919 became 252 on March 22, 1998. Areas include New Bern, Rocky Mount, Greenville, Elizabeth City and the Outer Banks.

the Elizabeth II, a 16th-century English ship; and The North Carolina Aquarium.

The Northern Banks include Nags Head, Kitty Hawk, Kill Devil Hills, Duck, Corolla and Southern Shores. Of course, this is the area famous throughout the world as the birthplace of aviation. The Wright Brothers Memorial is located on Kill Devil Hills. The Outer Banks have changed dramatically over the past 20 years with miles of open beach becoming populated with resorts, restaurants and strip malls. Even still, the Outer Banks remain a haven for anyone wanting to enjoy the beautiful beaches, fishing, windsurfing or even golf. To learn more about North Carolina's Outer Banks, pick up a copy of *The Insiders' Guide To North Carolina's Outer Banks* or call the Dare County Tourist Bureau, (800) 446-6262.

Photo Courtesy of N.C. Travel & Tourism. Photo by William Russ

The Cape Hatteras Lighthouse is one of the most famous landmarks on the North Carolina coast.

The Piedmont

The region located between the coastal areas and the mountains is known as The Piedmont and includes the Charlotte area. In order to make it easier to understand, we have subdivided the Piedmont further into Central Piedmont, the Triad and the Triangle areas.

Central Piedmont

Bentonville Battleground

Located in Newton Grove, off U.S. 95, a 3 1/2-hour drive from Charlotte, this historic site is popular with American history buffs. The Battle of Bentonville was the last full-scale action in the Civil War, fought over 3 days, from March 19 through March 21, 1865. There were over 4,000 casualties in the armies fighting under Union Gen. William T. Sherman and Confederate Gen. Joseph E. Johnston, who surrendered on April 26th at Bennett Place near Durham.

The Harper House, where a field hospital was established, still stands and is outfitted as it might have appeared during the battle. The battleground maintains a picnic area and visitors center. Maps inside the center and a film presentation tell the history of the battle, the largest ever fought in North Carolina. On occasion, the battle's anniversary is observed by reenactments. Call Mr. John Good at (910) 594-0789 for more information.

Fayetteville

Fayetteville is home to Fort Bragg and Pope Air Force Base and boasts a variety of other attractions, such as the wonderful architecture of many buildings, several colorful festivals and outstanding regional theater. Those interested in historic architecture will want to view Fayetteville's Market House in the center of the downtown area. When Union General William T. Sherman and his men passed through Fayetteville in 1865, they destroyed the Confederate Arsenal and many other buildings but left the Market House intact, it is said, because of its beauty. For information on Fayetteville, contact the Fayetteville Area Convention and Visitors Bureau, (800) 255-8217.

N.C. Zoological Park

About 15 minutes north of Seagrove is the North Carolina Zoological Park, (800) 488-0444, in Asheboro. Like the famous San Diego Zoo in California, North Carolina's Zoological Park gives visitors the chance to observe animals while they roam in areas similar to their native habitats. This is a perfect outing for the whole family. Here you can observe more than 625 wild animals and birds amidst 10,000 exotic plants. By the year 2000, this ever-expanding facility is expected to be the largest natural habitat zoo in the world.

You won't want to miss the R.J. Reynolds Forest Aviary, the only one of its kind. A 55-foot-high glass dome houses exotic plants and birds from all over the world. Walking through the aviary is like exploring a tropical forest, complete with all the sights and sounds. The newest sections in the zoo are the Sonora Desert Habitat and the North American Region, which has everything from polar bears to alligators.

The zoo is located off of N.C. 220, south of Asheboro. The zoo is open daily, except Christmas Day, from 9 AM to 5 PM from April to October and 9 AM to 4 PM from November through March. Admission is charged.

Pottery Museums

North of Uwharrie National Forest and just about 2 hours from Charlotte, you'll find pottery being made from native clays, just as it was in the 1700s. In fact, some of the local potters belong to the same families that were shaping this native clay two centuries ago. Stop first at the Seagrove Potters Museum, (336) 873-7887, in Seagrove along N.C. 220. Here you'll see samples of the area's world-famous pottery from its earliest days to the present. At the museum, which is open free to the public Monday through Saturday, 10 AM to 4 PM, you can also pick up a map to the shops of some 75 local potters. Our personal favorites are Phil Morgan's Pottery, Jugtown and Westmoore Pottery.

North Carolina Zoological Park

See more than 1,000 animals representing North America and Africa in one of the World's largest Natural Habitat Zoos.

Open daily 9am-5pm April through October
9am-4pm November through March

4401 Zoo Parkway
Asheboro, NC 27203
1-800-488-0444
Fax (910) 879-2891

An Accredited Institution of the
American Zoo and Aquarium Association

Raven Rock State Park

About an hour north of Fayetteville is Raven Rock State Park, (910) 893-4888. Raven Rock is a 2,731-acre state park that makes a pleasant picnic outing. Located on the Cape Fear River, it's about a 2 1/2-hour drive from Charlotte and has hiking trails that aren't too taxing. The rocks along the river are huge and in winter giant icicles 15 to 20 feet in length hang from them. Take along water or something to drink because there's no fountain or facilities once you get down to the river.

Snow Camp

About an hour northeast of Asheboro off N.C. 49, is Snow Camp, (336) 376-6948. The name derives from Pennsylvania hunters who camped here and cut trees level with the two to three feet of snow blanketing the camp. When they returned, they recognized their earlier campsite from the tall stumps! The village contains a number of historic buildings and a restaurant. Today Snow Camp is the site of two popular outdoor dramas. A cast of up to 75 presents the shows on alternate days at 8:30 PM, Wednesdays through Saturdays from late June to mid-August. The *Sword of Peace*

portrays the conflict experienced by peace-loving Quakers confronted by events of the American Revolution at Alamance and Guilford Courthouse, while the *Pathway to Freedom* is the story of how anti-slavery North Carolinians and freed African-Americans helped hundreds of escaped slaves to flee to the north prior to the Civil War. A museum is open on show days. Ticket prices for the 1997 season were $10 for adults; $8 for seniors and $5 for children under 11.

Uwharrie National Forest

Covering parts of three counties, Uwharrie National Forest, (910) 576-6391, contains over 47,000 acres of scenic landscapes, nature trails, campgrounds and picnic areas. Three rivers, the Uwharrie, Yadkin and Pee Dee cross through the forest. Town Creek Indian Mound, (910) 439-6802, is located near Mount Gilead in the Uwharrie Mountains. This state historic site commemorates the life of the Indians who inhabited the area hundreds of years ago. The reconstruction is based on archaeological excavations. Guided tours are available. Just across Badin Lake on the Pee Dee River is Morrow Mountain State Park, (704) 982-4402. The park has 4,600 acres for hiking, camping, boating and swimming.

At SciWorks, you can have your picture taken floating in space.

The Triad

The Triad refers to the cities of Greensboro, High Point and Winston-Salem.

Greensboro

The Guilford Courthouse National Military Park, (336) 288-1776, in Greensboro is the site of the Revolutionary War battle that pitted General Nathanael Greene against British General Lord Charles Cornwallis. In mid-March each year, a mock battle is staged in adjacent Tannenbaum City Park, (336) 545-5315, by Redcoats and soldiers of the Revolution in uniform. The battlefield is now a national park with a number of monuments and a visitors center. It is open daily from 8:30 AM to 5 PM and admission is free.

Plan to visit the Blandwood Mansion and Carriage House, (336) 272-5003. This 19th-century home of Governor John Motley Morehead is on the National Register of Historic Places and a National Historic Landmark.

Greensboro is also home to the Natural Science Center, (336) 288-3769. Adjacent to

Photo Courtesy of SciWorks the Guilford Battleground, this fine museum for children has reproductions of dinosaur skeletons, rock and mineral exhibits, fish and reptiles and a small petting zoo. The Science Center also has a planetarium show. The Center is open Monday through Saturday from 9 AM to 5 PM and Sunday 12:30 to 5 PM. There is an admission fee for the museum and the planetarium show.

High Point

Known for its furniture manufacturers, the Furniture Discovery Center is the only museum in the nation that shows how furniture is actually made. The High Point Museum and Historical Park features restored 18th-century buildings and the Angela Peterson Doll and Miniature Museum contains one of the South's largest doll collections.

Winston-Salem

About a 1 1/2-hour drive north of Charlotte is Winston-Salem's restored 18th-century Moravian village, Old Salem, (336) 721-7300. There are almost 100 restored buildings here; 12 are open to the public, including Winkler Bakery (where you can buy delicious Moravian sugar cake), the Salem Tavern, the Single Brothers' and Sisters' Houses and many other shops and restored homes. Special events are held at Christmas, Easter and July 4th. Old Salem is open Monday through Saturday 9 AM to 4:30 PM and on Sunday from 12:30 to 4:30 PM. Admission is charged. Adjacent to Old Salem, the Museum of Early Southern Decorative Arts (MESDA), (336) 721-7360, features 19 furnished rooms, demonstrating the varied styles and periods of Southern furnishings. It's an antique lover's dream. Admission is charged.

Reynolda House, (336) 725-5325, the former home of R.J. Reynolds of tobacco fame, is now a museum of American art. The collection features paintings by diverse artists ranging from 19th-century landscape painter Frederic Church to Thomas Eakins and Mary Cassatt. The house contains many of its original furnishings and is fascinating in its own right. Admission is charged for the house and gardens. It is open Tuesday through Saturday from 9:30 AM to 4:30 PM and from 1:30 to 4:30 PM on Sunday. Just down the road from Reynolda House is the Southeastern Center For Contemporary Art (SECCA), (336) 725-1904. SECCA is well worth a visit. It is a complex of galleries with rotating exhibits by contemporary Southern artists. It is located on the former estate of the Hanes family and many of the galleries are in the Hanes home. It is open Tuesday through Saturday 10 AM to 5 PM and Sunday 2 to 5 PM. Admission is free.

A trip to Winston-Salem wouldn't be complete without making a stop at SciWorks, (336) 767-6730. This interactive "touch me" museum offers children and adults a variety of exhibits and displays utilizing nature, science and technology. Be sure to view the African exhibit and the Carolina Piedmont Wildlife exhibit. Before scheduling a trip, call first for planetarium show times. The 50-foot tilted dome has a Spitz star machine that produces eye-boggling laser effects. The museum also has a room for toddlers and preschool children to play. Open Monday through Saturday from 10 AM to 5 PM and Sunday 1 to 5 PM. Admission is charged.

Southwest of Winston-Salem is Tanglewood Park, (336) 778-6300, located in Clemmons. Tanglewood's hardwood forest was so tangled with gnarled overgrowth back in the 1900s that it looked like a mythical place from Hawthorne's *Tanglewood Tales*. The idyllic lake, now called Mallard Lake, completed this fantasy setting for Margaret Griffith, who gave the park its name. In the early '50s, Tanglewood was left to the people of Forsyth County to use as a park. Tanglewood's brambling undergrowth has been cut back to provide for horseback riding trails, a swimming pool, tennis courts, a fenced area for deer, a steeplechase course, nature trails, a rose garden, a lake filled with canoes and paddleboats and campgrounds. A championship golf course and driving ranges also run along the forest.

The park hosts a variety of events from a Spring Steeplechase to the Festival of Lights display during the holidays. Camping is available or you may stay at the historic Manor House Bed and Breakfast Inn. Tanglewood Park is open year round from dawn to dusk. A small admission fee is charged. There are additional fees charged for golf, tennis and horseback riding.

Photo Courtesy of N.C. Travel & Tourism

The Governor's Mansion in Raleigh is a classic example of Queen Anne Cottage-Style Victorian architecture.

The Triangle

The Triangle refers to the area that includes Cary and Raleigh, Durham and Chapel Hill. Historical sites, major universities, museums and government buildings make the Triangle well worth the visit. To learn more about this area, pick up a copy of *The Insiders' Guide to The Triangle*.

Cary and Raleigh

Cary is known as a place where visitors come to shop. There's even an annual craft festival, Lazy Daze in late August, where the entire downtown area is blocked off and thousands of visitors arrive for a shopping frenzy.

Raleigh is the state's capital and offers a variety of interesting sites and events. Before coming to Raleigh, you may want to contact the Raleigh Convention & Visitors Bureau, 225 Hillsborough Street, Raleigh 27603 or call (919) 834-5900. When you arrive, be sure to visit the Capital Area Visitors Center, 301 N. Blount Street, (919) 733-3456, to get area information. Then take a walking tour of the

Governor's Mansion, 200 N. Blount Street, (919) 733-3871. The mansion is a classic example of Queen Anne Cottage-Style Victorian architecture, also known as the gingerbread style. The 40,000-square-foot building was completed in 1891, using mostly native materials, and is filled with antiques. Governor Jim Hunt and his family live in the mansion. Tours take about 30 minutes and are open to the public in the fall and spring. The State Legislative Building on Jones Street, (919) 733-7928, is the only state building in the country devoted exclusively to the legislative branch. Watch history in the making as House Representatives and State Senators discuss and debate law. The desks and chairs in the building were built by Raleigh cabinetmaker William Thompson in 1840 and are in mint condition today. Free tours are given daily. The N.C. State Capitol, (919) 733-3456, built in 1840, is one of the best preserved examples of Greek Revival architecture in the country. The Capitol is still in use. Tours may be scheduled.

The N.C. Museum of History, 5 Edenton Street, (919) 715-0200, opened in 1994 and

Photo Courtesy N.C. Travel & Tourism

The State Fair in Raleigh is a not-to-be-missed event for many North Carolinians.

contains four grand display areas for North Carolina historical collections. Across the plaza is the N.C. Museum of Natural Sciences, (919) 733-7450. This museum is in the process of building a new 200,000-square-foot building to be completed in 1999. This popular place for school-aged children is home to thousands of preserved and living creatures.

Historic Oakwood and the Mordecai Historic Park, (919) 834-4844, site of President Andrew Johnson's birthplace, are close by. Thirty years before there was a Raleigh, Colonel Joel Lane settled here. The Joel Lane House, (919) 833-3431, at Hargett and St. Mary's streets is listed in the National Register of Historic Places and is the oldest house in Raleigh.

City Market is also located close to downtown, adjacent to Moore Square, (919) 828-4555. The circa 1914 buildings, originally a farmers market and the cobblestone streets are home to a variety of shops, restaurants and art galleries. The State Farmers Market is located off I-40 10 minutes south of downtown. North Carolina State University is located off Hillsborough Street. The N.C. State Fairgrounds at Hillsborough Street and Blue Ridge Road, (919) 733-2145, is the site for the State Fair which lasts 10 days, starting on the third Friday of October. The fair highlights agriculture and features top name entertainment, rides, food, horticulture, crafts and fireworks. Close by, the N.C. Museum of Art is located at 2110 Blue Ridge Road, (919) 839-6262. This premier art museum has become one of North Carolina's treasure houses for the visual arts. Its 181,000 square feet displays permanent collections in American, ancient and European art. The European paintings by Italian, Dutch and Flemish artists are considered the museum's finest.

Durham and Chapel Hill

One of the more notable historical sites in Durham is Bennett Place, (919) 383-4345. In April 1865, two battle-fatigued adversaries — Generals Joseph E. Johnston and William T. Sherman — met on the farm of James and Nancy Bennett to work out a peaceful settlement to the Battle of Bentonville fought near Newton Grove. Johnston surrendered, resulting in the largest troop surrender of the Civil War and ending the fighting in the Carolinas, Georgia and Florida. The present buildings were reconstructed in the 1960s from Civil War sketches and early photographs. While in Durham, be sure to also visit the Duke Homestead and Tobacco Museum, (919) 477-5498; N.C. Museum of Life and Science, 433 Murray Avenue, (919) 220-5429; and the Sarah Duke Memorial Gardens at Duke University.

Chapel Hill is the home of the University of North Carolina. The N.C. Botanical Garden is also a part of UNC, located on 330 acres off U.S. 15-501, (919) 962-0522. As the largest natural botanical garden in the southeast, the Botanical Garden provides native plants arranged by habitat and more than 2 miles of trails through the woods. Although established for research and conservation of plants native to the southeastern U.S., the garden is open to the public. A trip to Chapel Hill would not be complete without a visit to the Morehead Planetarium at 250 E. Franklin Street, (919) 962-1236.

Mountains

Just 1 1/2 hours west of Charlotte you begin an ascent into the third distinct region of North Carolina: the Mountains. This region itself is divided into three areas: Northern Mountains, Central Mountains and Southern Mountains. Each area demands at least a weekend to explore. For further reading on this area, pick up a copy of The Insiders' Guide To North Carolina's Mountains.

Asheville

Called the "Land of the Sky," this mountain city where wealthy vacationers once came for relief from the summer heat is still drawing visitors. The centerpiece of the downtown historic district is Pack Place Education, Arts and Science Center. This bustling complex contains four museums, a performing arts theatre, courtyards, permanent exhibitions, a gift shop, restaurant and lobby galleries. Tickets

Photo Courtesy N.C. Travel & Tourism

Biltmore Estate is one of the most popular daytrips from Charlotte.

are required for admission to theater events and to each of the four museums: the Asheville Art Museum, The Colburn Gem and Mineral Museum, The Health Adventure and the YMI Cultural Center. You may buy a one-day pass that is good for all four or you can buy single tickets. No admission charge is required for visitors to enter Pack Place and view the historic exhibit "Here is the Square," visit the Craft Gallery that spotlights regional crafts or shop in the Museum Gift Store. The fourth Friday of each month is "Free Day," when you may visit all of the museums with no charge for admission. Call (828) 257-4500 for further ticket information and hours.

A landmark in itself, Pack Place also serves as the logical starting point for a number of walking tours of downtown Asheville featuring buildings of architectural and historic significance, including the home of Thomas Wolfe. A popular retreat into the past, this is the Dixieland Boarding House readers will remember from Wolfe's novel *Look Homeward, Angel*. For more information, call the Asheville Area Convention and Visitors Bureau at (800) 257-1300.

Biltmore Estate and Winery

One of the best daytrip excursions is to the Biltmore Estate, Gardens and Winery, which is still the largest private residence in the United States. Between 1888 and 1890, George Washington Vanderbilt, grandson of the railroad promoter Cornelius Vanderbilt, purchased a total of 125,000 acres of land for the estate he planned to build. The architectural style was designed by Richard Morris Hunt to resemble a chateau in France's Loire Valley and it rivals the grandest palaces abroad. The castle-like house contains 255 rooms, which took 1,000 artisans five years to build for the six residents and their guests (not including the 100 servants). You can tour the main house with its beautiful antique furnishings, priceless paintings and ceiling frescoes that are kept in excellent condition. The servant's quarters, where even the butler had his own servant, are also interesting.

A favorite time is the Christmas season when the house is resplendent with thousands of poinsettias and Christmas trees trimmed with many original ornaments. Musical concerts fill the magnificent halls. The estate is open from 9 AM to 5 PM year round except Thanksgiving, Christmas Day and New Year's. For more information, call (828) 255-1700 or (800) 543-2961.

Another enjoyable — as well as tasty — tour is that of the estate's winery, which was converted from an old dairy barn. The winery started producing wine in 1978 and now has an annual production rate of almost 75,000 cases. The tour offers a video presentation and interactive displays explaining the wine-making process. The Tasting Room offers samples of more than 20 varieties available for purchase.

The open-air restaurant, aptly named Deerpark (you may see herds of deer roaming the land), serves an assortment of entrees. Afterward, stop at Biltmore Village where the original construction worker's houses have been converted into shops and restaurants.

FYI

Western Carolina area code 704 became 828 on June 1, 1998.

Blowing Rock

Blowing Rock is a resort town with its main street lined with pyramid-shaped planters, spilling over with pink and white begonias. Since the days when the rambling 100-year-old Green Park Inn was built over the center of the Continental Divide, the town has taken on an aristocratic appeal.

Window shopping on Main Street is a favorite pursuit with lots of antiques and Oriental rug shops. The park on Main Street is a gathering place for tennis, people-watching and craft shows.

You may enjoy horseback riding along the trails of Moses Cone Estate on the Blue Ridge Parkway. The adventurous will enjoy canoeing and white-water rafting through Class 3 to Class 5 rapids down the Nolichucky.

Children in North Carolina grow up on

Photo Courtesy N.C. Travel & Tourism

Tweetsie Railroad features a 3-mile adventurous train ride on an original mountain train, complete with Indian attacks and settler rescues.

trips to Tweetsie Railroad on U.S. 321/221 near Blowing Rock. The drawing card is a 3-mile adventurous train ride on an original mountain train, complete with Indian attacks and settler rescues. The attraction has amusement rides, live entertainment, crafts, shops and picnic tables. It's open daily from May through October and on weekends in November. Contact the Blowing Rock Chamber of Commerce at (800) 295-7851 for more information.

Blue Ridge Parkway and Mount Mitchell

The scenic Blue Ridge Parkway meanders uninterrupted for 500 miles through three states. Although begun in the early 1900s, construction was halted during WWI. As a public works project during the Depression, the parkway was opened in 1935, but it took many years to complete it. The last link was the Linn Cove Viaduct over Grandfather Mountain. It is considered to be one of America's most scenic parkways. The frequent overlooks afford breathtaking panoramas of high peaks, waterfalls and lakes tucked into verdant valleys. Spring is alive with color as mountain laurel and red rhododendron bloom in awesome abundance and fall brings its own spectacular display in a blaze of color with crimson, rust and gold leaves.

An interesting side trip on N.C. 90 in Edgemont is Coffey's General Store. Built in the early 1900s, the store was moved twice from its original location on the other side of the creek. In 1916, floodwaters changed the creek's course and the owners moved the store. In 1940, floodwaters actually moved the store. You can see the buckled floor and find out more about the area when you visit this "old-time" general store — if it is open.

An excellent daytrip is to Mount Mitchell State Park at Milepost 355. Mount Mitchell is the highest peak east of the Mississippi River and you can hike through the park's many nature trails. To camp here, call (828) 675-4611 to reserve one of the nine campsites. At Milepost 331, visit the North Carolina Mineral Museum with over 300 varieties of minerals on display. In Little Switzerland at Milepost 334, you'll find the North Carolina Mining Museum at Emerald Village. The museum offers an underground tour of the mine and panning the flume for gems. The Mitchell County Chamber of Commerce at (828) 765-9483 can provide you with more information.

Photo Courtesy of *Horn in the West*

Daniel Boone is an important figure in the outdoor drama, *Horn In The West.*

Boone

In the heart of Boone lies the beautiful campus of Appalachian State University. Boone is also home to the Appalachian Cultural Museum where the evolving lifestyle of mountain people is displayed with artifacts and information on the abundant variety of rare and unusual herbs and plants.

During the summer (mid-June to mid-August), make reservations for Kermit Hunter's outdoor drama *Horn In The West*, now in its fourth decade of performances. The musical drama highlights the life of early families in this region, particularly those "Regulators" who fled into the mountains to escape British tyranny.

Photo by Tim Johnson

Coffey's General Store in Edgemont was built in the early 1900s.

Daniel Boone is not the hero of the drama, but is an important figure. The show runs nightly, except Monday, and starts at 8:30 PM. Bring bug spray. For reservations call (828) 264-2120. On the grounds of the complex, you'll find Hickory Ridge Homestead, which is an interesting tour of five representative home sites of the 1800s and the 8-acre Daniel Boone Native Gardens.

Brevard

Surrounded by the Pisgah National Forest, Brevard offers a variety of activities from rugged outdoor adventures to communing quietly with nature or delving into the magical mountain lore through music, drama or local crafts.

You can spend the day locating a few of the 250 waterfalls in Transylvania County and Brevard. The best way to see them is to take the scenic 79-mile drive that loops through the Pisgah National Forest. You may also hike along the designated trails or explore on horseback.

Check out the annual summer Brevard Music Festival that features many well-known musicians. It's held at the Brevard Music Center. If you're a bluegrass fan, go to Silvermont on East Main Street for original mountain music and bluegrass. Drive back down U.S. 64 to Flat Rock and take in a play at the Flat Rock Playhouse, the state theater of

North Carolina. Flat Rock is also the site of Connemara, the home of poet laureate Carl Sandburg.

Throughout the mountains you'll find handmade quilts, mountain furniture and toys. Insiders like the Curb Market (Farmers Market) in downtown Hendersonville on Tuesday and Saturday mornings. You'll find handmade articles, jellies, fresh vegetables and fruit and the like. Call the Brevard Chamber of Commerce, (800) 648-4523.

Cashiers

Beautiful Cashiers, high in the Blue Ridge Mountains, is a resort town famous for its many waterfalls, including the beautiful Rainbow Falls, which plunges some 200 feet and Whitewater Falls, which at 411 feet is the longest waterfall in the Eastern United States. For more information, contact the Cashiers Chamber of Commerce at (828) 743-5191.

Cherokee

The history of the Cherokee Indian Nation and the 58,000-acre reservation can be explored by a stop at the Cherokee Historical Association. Across the street on Darma Road is the Museum of the Cherokee Indian. This is a

Rock Mountain, in Cashiers, is reflected in Hampton Lake.

modern museum displaying artifacts over 10,000 years old with explanatory audio/visual programs that chronicle the events of the Cherokee.

The not-to-be-missed Oconaluftee Indian Village is a reproduction of how the Eastern Band of the Cherokees lived 200 years ago. The Qualla Arts and Crafts Mutual in the village is a shop that looks more like a museum. This shop of artisans' works is responsible for keeping alive the authentic arts and crafts of the Cherokee. It is also the only place that you'll find these distinct crafts.

No trip to Cherokee would be complete without attending *Unto These Hills* at the Mountainside Theatre. The outdoor drama unfolds the tragic story of how the proud Cherokees were driven west on the "Trail of Tears" from their Smoky Mountain homeland.

Cherokee is also the home of Harrah's Cherokee Casino, which opened on the Cherokee Indian Reservation in late 1997. It is the only legal gambling casino south of Atlantic City and east of the Mississippi. The casino only serves soft drinks and has 1,800 video games offering poker, blackjack, slots and craps with a maximum payoff of $25,000.

Before leaving the area, drive north half a mile on U.S. 441 to the entrance of the Great Smoky Mountains National Park. Just inside is Pioneer Homestead, a series of 15 buildings needed by settlers to survive in the mountain wilderness. Additional information on this area can be obtained from Smoky Mountain Host of N.C. at (800) 432-4678.

Chimney Rock, Lake Lure

The town of Chimney Rock, with a river running beside it, is a favorite of tourists. At Chimney Rock Park, (800-277-9611), you can climb the mountain or ride up a 26-story elevator inside the mountain. You'll be at the top of the chimney-shaped rock with a panoramic view that is worth the trip by itself. This is where the spectacular scenery was shot for the movie, *The Last of the Mohicans*. Below is Hickory Nut Gorge, which includes the French Broad River and Lake Lure, a tranquil lake that is ideal for swimming, fishing and boating. The annual Hickory Nut Gorge Dogwood Festival is held each April. Pack a picnic lunch to enjoy at one of the park's many picnic areas. For more information, contact Henderson County Travel and Tourism at (800) 828-4244.

Grandfather Mountain

This famed 6,000-foot mountain can be seen for miles around and looks like a giant sleeping grandfather. It is considered North Carolina's top scenic attraction. You'll want to visit the natural habitats for native black bear, white-tailed deer, cougar and bald and golden eagles. Stop in at the nature museum that offers state-of-the-art displays along with entertaining movies on native wildlife (especially the film on the red-tailed hawk). For those brave enough to cross it, the Mile High Swinging Bridge, which connects Linville's Peak with the visitors center, rewards you with a spectacular view.

The museum's restaurant is a great place for lunch. You can also picnic on the mountain. Grandfather Mountain is open year round, weather permitting. Call (800) 468-7325 for information.

An exciting Grandfather Mountain experience is the annual Highland Games, the second weekend in July. You don't have to be Scottish to enjoy the bagpipes, dancing, caber-toss and watching Border Collies return lost sheep to the flock, as well as other games of skill. Another popular yearly event that comes the fourth Sunday in June is Singing on the Mountain.

Linville Falls, Linville Caverns, Old Hampton Store

At Linville Falls and Gorge, there are three hiking trail options, from easy to rugged, depending on your energy and time. The gorge is the deepest slash in the earth's crust east of the Grand Canyon. The river tumbles into the gorge to form a 90-foot fall of water. To reach the falls, you'll walk through a 1/2-mile tunnel of towering trees so dense that spatters of sunlight are rare. Waterfalls, some dramatic, others serene, draw visitors to watch their grand displays. This is not a picnic area, but restrooms are available and the park is open year round, depending on the weather.

There may be undiscovered caves all through the mountains. Linville Caverns, like others, was discovered accidentally in 1822, when curious fishermen followed trout

Grandfather Mountain is framed by flowering trees in the spring.

Photo Courtesy N.C. Travel & Tourism

disappearing into the side of a mountain. Trout in this 20-million-year-old limestone cave are blind due to the lack of a light source. The cavern, on three levels, is an interesting and enjoyable half-hour experience. It's open year round, but check times, (828) 756-4171.

The Old Hampton Store, (828) 733-5213, sits just outside the town of Linville. This neat 1921 general store, restaurant and grist-mill offers a wide assortment of notions that you need and some that you probably don't — such as horse hoof medication. Churns and washtubs hang from the ceiling and the back screened door is perpetually in motion. Out back, the stone gristmill grinds cornmeal and grits nearly every afternoon. These products are sold along with apple butter, local jams and old fashioned tin cookware.

Best of all is lunch. The store serves the leanest and most delicious barbecue around and its root beer is excellent. Top this off with a slice of terrific carrot cake.

Maggie Valley

Maggie Valley is the center for clogging, the mountain dance that evolved from Scottish and Irish jigs. Check out the Stompin' Ground. If you like the Old West, visit Ghost Town in the Sky, a frontier village theme park with gun fights, western shows and exciting rides. See a first-rate zoo in town called Soco Gardens Zoo with guided tours and a petting

zoo. Call the Haywood County Tourism Development Authority at (800) 334-9036 for more information.

Ski Country

During the winter, North Carolina provides some of the best snow skiing in the south. Each year thousands of Charlotte skiers listen to weather reports, watch the sky and wax skis in hope of bringing on the winter's first snow. That's when you'll see packed cars bearing ski racks heading for one of our many downhill ski resorts.

Appalachian Ski Mountain, home of the French-Swiss Ski College outside Boone, has one of the best teaching schools for beginners. It has eight slopes with a peak elevation of 4,000 feet. Ski Beech, north of Banner Elk, has 14 slopes and a peak elevation of 5,505 feet, making it the highest in the East with a vertical drop of 830 feet. The resort has a charming Swiss Village-type appearance with an outdoor ice skating rink encircled with shops and restaurants. Sugar Mountain Ski Resort, south of Banner Elk on N.C. 184, boasts 18 slopes, peak elevation of 5,300 feet with a vertical drop of 1,200 feet and needless to say, fairyland views. Ski Hawksnest is sometimes less crowded and has seven slopes, a peak of 4,819 feet and a vertical drop of 619 feet, plus night skiing.

Linville Falls offers a variety of trails for the beginner to the advanced.

Sugar Mountain is one of many popular ski resorts in North Carolina.

All of these resorts have chair lifts, rope tows, lockers and restaurants. Beech and Sugar even have nurseries. You can get a ski report by calling (800) 962-2322. High Country Hosts at (800) 438-7500 is a good source of mountain area information.

You can ski cross-country at Moses Cone Park on the parkway just outside Blowing Rock and at other gated-off areas by calling the Ranger's office at (828) 295-7591.

S.C. Olde English District

Many of the Palmetto state's undiscovered treasures lie hidden in the Olde English District, a seven-county area due south of Charlotte that includes Chester, Chesterfield, Fairfield, Kershaw, Lancaster, Union and York.

The Olde English District offers a variety of accommodations — from luxury hotels and motels to bed and breakfast inns. The Wade-Beckham House in Lancaster (dating to the 1800s) offers three guest rooms. Cheraw has two bed and breakfast inns in the historic district — 505 Market Street and 501 Kershaw Street. Cabins are also available at Cheraw State Park. Camden has several options, including the Greenleaf Inn. The Inn at Merridun in Union is a destination in itself, offering dinner by reservation and a four-course breakfast. Built in 1855, it has five bedrooms, each with a private bath. A good place to hang your hat in Rock Hill is the Book and the Spindle across from Winthrop University. Camping is offered at Paramount's Carowinds and in a number of the state parks.

Camden

Steeplechase fans know this town well. It's the scene of the Carolina Cup Race in the spring and the Colonial Cup in the Fall. Horses aside,

Camden is an interesting place to visit any time of the year. The Camden Historic District, which is on the National Register of Historic Places, covers 3 square miles and features many beautiful historical homes and estates dating to the 18th and 19th centuries. Many of the buildings are open to the public and others can be visited during home and garden tours during the year.

The Fine Arts Center of Kershaw County holds exhibits and special performances featuring nationally renowned artists throughout the year. A permanent gallery features the work of equine artist Carroll K. Bassett. Researchers enjoy the collections at Camden Archives and Museum. A restored 18th-century grain mill and a general store are on Boykin Mill Pond, located about 8 miles south of Camden on S.C. 261.

Cheraw

Picturesque Cheraw, located on U.S. 1 in the northeastern corner of the Olde English District, is home to The Cheraw Lyceum Museum. Housed in a building dating to 1825, the museum is a treasure trove of history — with exhibits ranging from the Cheraw Indians to the days of English settlement (which occurred about 1740) to 1938, when the last steamer made its voyage up the Pee Dee River. Artifacts from sunken ships, some dating from Revolutionary and Civil War times, can also be seen in the law office of Miller S. Ingram Jr. on Market Street.

A must-see in Cheraw is Old St. David's Church, the last Anglican church to be established under King George III in 1772. Buried within its shadows are the town's most prominent citizens, including a steamboat captain or two. General Sherman's troops found Cheraw to be "a pleasant town and an old one with southern aristocratic bearing" and left it intact. In 1880, Cheraw was the setting for the last legal duel in South Carolina between Col. E.B.C. Cash and Col. William M. Shannon.

Chester

South on U.S. 321 is Chester, a lovely historic district with three Revolutionary War battlefields and a state park centered around the old Landsford Canal, built in 1832. Another park

ideal for fishing and picnicking is Chester State Park, 2 miles west of town on S.C. 72. East of Chester on the same highway, you'll find Cruse Vineyards and Winery, which offers free wine tastings on Friday and Saturday afternoons.

Chesterfield

Located on S.C. 102, Chesterfield serves as the county seat of Chesterfield County. Tour brochures are available at the Hospice Building on Main Street. Chesterfield claims to be the site of the first secession meeting in South Carolina (November 19, 1860), but it also boasts a courthouse designed by Robert Mills and several historic homes. The John Craig House, built in 1798, is where Sherman spent one night while passing through the state.

Fort Mill

Paramount's Carowinds' attractions and shows centered around famous films are also commemorated in granite on the North Carolina-South Carolina state line, which runs through the middle of the park.

Lancaster

Lancaster is known for its Robert Mills Courthouse (built in 1828) and the Andrew Jackson Birthplace Site, now a state park on U.S. 521. A small museum is housed in the Visitors Center, and a one-room schoolhouse, similar to one that was here in the mid-1700s, has been reconstructed. The Lancaster County Council of the Arts holds an annual spring festival here. Also in Lancaster County, near Taxahaw, is the Flat Creek Heritage Preserve and Forty-Acre Rock, a 1,325-acre natural preserve of rare and endangered plants, including the pool sprite, which grows in water reserves trapped on the huge rock surface. The preserve is open during daylight hours only.

Rock Hill

The "Gateway to the City" and the "Civitas" sculptures, which incorporate pillars from the old Masonic Temple in Charlotte, can be seen in Rock Hill. Also worth your time is Glencairn Gardens, where the Come-See-Me festival is

The Inn at Merridun is a beautiful example of the architectural details you'll find on buildings throughout South Carolina's Olde English District.

staged each spring. At the Museum of York County, you can see Catawba Indian pottery, illustrations by Vernon Grant (who originated Kellogg's Snap, Crackle and Pop), the Settlemyre Planetarium and the Stans African Hall.

South of Rock Hill off U.S. 321 is Historic Brattonsville, a restored village of 18th- and 19th-century structures. The Revolutionary battle that occurred here in 1780 — the Battle of Huck's Defeat — was the first defeat of the British in South Carolina after the fall of Charleston.

Union

South on S.C. 49, the Federal-style home of Secession Governor William Henry Gist is located at Rose Hill Plantation State Park. Built between 1828 and 1832, it once overlooked thousands of acres of cotton.

Winnsboro

Off I-77 in Fairfield County and south of Chester off U.S. 321, in Fairfield County,

Winnsboro has a Robert Mills courthouse (built in 1823) and the Ebenezer Associate Reformed Presbyterian Church dating to 1788. Winnsboro is best known for its town clock, which has run continuously since 1833. The Fairfield County Museum is outstanding and genealogy buffs delight in its collections. At the *News & Herald Tavern*, housed in the old newspaper office, you can catch up on all the local happenings and enjoy some of the best food in the Olde English District.

York

Northwest of Rock Hill on S.C. 5 is York. Often called the "Charleston of the Upcountry," it has historic structures dating to 1700s. The Yorkville Historical Society has developed a walking tour of the area. Their brochure is available at the McCelvey Center, a center for arts and history, on E. Jefferson at College.

N▮ighborhoods

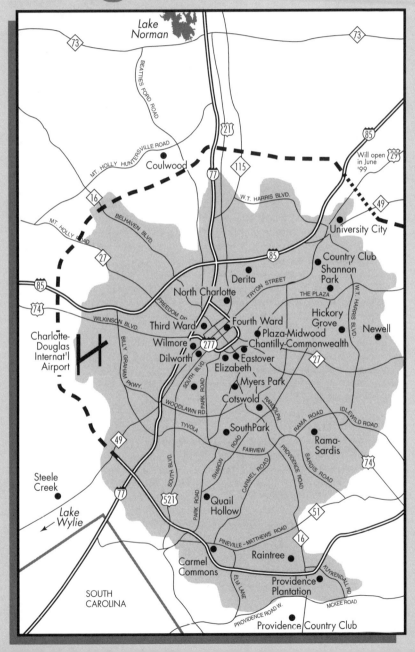

Real Estate & Neighborhoods

Charlotte offers a wide variety of housing options for every age and life-style, from historic Fourth Ward in busy Uptown to quiet homes in the country.

The Charlotte Chamber of Commerce, 330 South Tryon Street, Charlotte, NC 28232, 378-1300, provides information on the city to residents and potential residents.

The Charlotte Observer's Real Estate section should be your first stop for up-to-the-minute market offerings. For the resale housing market, there are two publications that can be of assistance: *Homes & Land* (366-8799) and *The Real Estate Book* (845-5800). Below are several local publications that can be helpful if you are buying a home.

The New Home Finder
528 E. Blvd. • 373-0051, (800) 277-5679

Published bimonthly, this guide offers detailed information about new single-family homes, condominiums and townhomes. It provides a brief overview of each area and a reader service card to request more information.

First Impressions Newcomer's Guide
5200 Park Rd., Ste. 104 • 522-6001

An information-packed annual magazine highlighting the real estate market, it provides basic details on public services, education, health care, retirement and recreation.

The Greater Charlotte New Home Guide
1515 Mockingbird La., Ste. 112 • 527-2022

Published quarterly, this full-color magazine provides information on new home communities based on geographical area. Timely articles, mortgage information and a reader service card to request additional information are provided.

Buyers' Agents

The use of buyers' agents is gaining popularity throughout the nation. These agents represent the buyer in the negotiation and purchase of homes and other real estate. Some real estate companies now provide buyer representation exclusively while other traditional listing companies offer both buyer and seller services. Buyers' agents are licensed in the full spectrum of real estate transactions and provide Multiple Listing Services as all Realtors do.

Home Inspectors

Before you buy a home, you will want to be certain everything is in top condition. A qualified home inspector can give you peace of mind. Most of these companies provide full structural and mechanical inspections. Many offer specialized services such as testing for radon, lead, carbon monoxide and gas leaks. The American Society of Home Inspectors is a national certification organization. If a firm displays the ASHI symbol, you can be assured its home inspectors are qualified.

Realtors

There are thousands of licensed real estate agents in the Charlotte area and membership in the Multiple Listing Service allows Realtors to access information on homes located throughout the area. The companies listed below provide a sampling, but they are not the only ones to consider. For a complete list, check the Yellow Pages.

Helen Adams Realty
2301 Randolph Road • 375-8598

This company, with 22 agents, specializes in exclusive listings in the Myers Park, Eastover and Southeast areas of Charlotte and in many new developments in the Charlotte area. It is a member of the MLS and International Relocation Services.

The Allen Tate Company
Relocation Center • 6632 Fairview Rd.
• 364-6400, (800) 277-6901
Carmel • 7824 Pineville-Matthews Rd.
• 541-6200
East Charlotte • 7212 Albemarle Rd.
• 563-6000
Lake Norman • N.C. 73, Jetton Rd.
• 896-8283
Matthews • 165 S. Trade St.
• 847-6400
University City • 145 W. W.T. Harris Blvd.
• 547-8900

Charlotte's largest locally owned independent real estate company was founded in 1957 by Allen Tate and currently has 563 agents in 12 local offices. The company's Relocation Center is extensive, offering a personalized newcomer kit, a video presentation, homefinding tours and special information for families with children. A referral service and mortgage financing are also available.

Bissell-Hayes Realtors
4515 Sharon Rd. • 364-4515

Founded in 1964 by Charlotte natives Betty Hayes and Smoky Bissell, this realty company with 55 agents is still locally owned and operated. The firm offers relocation and referral services. The company is very active in community agencies and arts organizations.

Century 21
These are independently owned affiliates:
4401 E. Independence Blvd. • 568-5134
8401 University Exec. Park Dr. • 547-0210
Coulwood Shopping Ctr. • 399-4848
10801 Johnston Rd. • 541-6306
Cornelius-Lake Norman • 892-6556

Coldwell Banker
Flouhouse Realtors
Relocation Center • (800) 325-0986
Corporate Offices • 542-4200
7907 Providence Rd. • 541-6100
6548 Carmel Rd. • 541-5111
1811 Sardis Rd. N. • 845-2900
6633 Fairview Rd. • 364-3300
1001 W.T. Harris Blvd. • 547-8490

Serving North and South Carolina, Coldwell Banker also offers a nationwide relocation service.

Cottingham-Chalk & Associates, Inc.
6846 Morrison Blvd. • 364-1700

This community-spirited company has 71 experienced sales professionals. Established in 1983, the company's expertise is evident by its affiliation with RELO, the world leader in relocation. The company has been heavily involved in assisting transferring families whose firms have relocated to Charlotte. It also offers mortgage financing.

Dickens-Mitchener & Associates
6010 Fairview Road, Ste. 118 • 554-7800

Founded in 1991 and one of the largest real estate agencies in the Charlotte area, the firm's 42 agents specialize in customer service, assuring a smooth transition.

Finding the right home should be a moving experience.

A home is more than a construction of wood or brick. It's held together with dreams and memories. It's the place where family comes together. So if you're relocating, call us. We'll make sure that your new home and neighborhood are just as fulfilling as the ones you left behind.

Prudential
Carolinas Realty
4529 Sharon Road 366-5545

First Charlotte Properties, Inc.
Relocation Services, 1361 E. Morehead St.
• 377-9000

First Charlotte Properties, active in the Charlotte market since 1978, prides itself on sound business principles and practices, a history of solid growth and deep community involvement. The firm has 29 agents and its comprehensive Relocation Department is dedicated to providing first-class service to its customers and clients.

First Properties of Tega Cay
2222 Tega Cay Dr., Tega Cay, S.C.
• 335-8601 (Charlotte Number)

Established in 1980, First Properties of Tega Cay has 12 agents. It offers a relocation and referral service.

Lake Norman Realty
Relocation Dept., I-77 & N.C. 73,
Cornelius • 892-9673
Mooresville • 663-3655

Lake Norman Realty was founded in 1978

and with 32 agents has grown to meet the exciting new development needs of the area. Relocation and referral services are also offered.

Lake Properties Ltd.
Relocation, N.C. Hwy. 73, Cornelius
• 892-5518, (800) 232-6447

Established in 1984 by experienced real estate professional Mary Ann Drag, Lake Properties serves Lake Norman, north Mecklenburg and south Iredell County properties with 40 agents.

The Prudential Carolinas Realty Inc.
Relocation Service Center • 366-5545
7301 Carmel Executive Park • 542-1100
2034-A Randolph Rd. • 334-6677
8320 University Executive Pk. Dr. • 548-8700
4529 Sharon Rd. • 364-1580

This firm is the largest independently owned and operated real estate company in North Carolina. The company offers in-house mortgage services.

RE/MAX
6842 Morrison Blvd. • 362-5570
7800 Providence Rd. • 543-6680
7421 Carmel Exec. Pk. • 542-4242

Each office in this nationwide realty firm is independently owned.

Wanda Smith & Associates
Relocation • (800) 755-3261
423 S. Sharon Amity Rd. • 366-6667

Founded in 1987, the Wanda Smith agency is one of the best known names in the Charlotte real estate market. The company, with 24 agents, specializes in home resales and serves as the exclusive sales agency for many of Charlotte's top home builders.

Neighborhoods

The Multiple Listing Service divides Charlotte into nine areas, which branch out from the city limits in pie-shaped wedges. Starting to the north and running clockwise, the areas encompass Uptown.

Area One, North Mecklenburg

Extending north from the city limits between U.S. 21 and U.S. 29 to the Mecklenburg County line, this area contains the historic Fourth Ward, the northern part of University City and many new as well as established neighborhoods.

Fourth Ward

Renovated in the mid-70s, Fourth Ward is a mixture of Victorian homes and brick and frame condominiums standing side-by-side. Just a few blocks from Uptown, Fourth Ward combines the charm of small-town living with the convenience of living in the city.

University City

A planned development built near UNC Charlotte, this area contains a bustling commercial district with hotels, restaurants, movie theaters and retail shops off W.T. Harris Boulevard. University Hospital and the business complexes of University Research Park and University Executive Park are also located here.

Derita

This sprawling community is an older neighborhood that offers country living close to the city. The area is a combination of older homes mixed with new.

Some new communities in this area are Cheshunt, Davis Lake, Devonshire, Forest Pond, Fox Glen, Hayden Commons, Leacroft, Quail Ridge, Rolling Oaks and Rossmore Townhomes. The average price for homes is $148,000; however, you can find new homes for as low as $110,000. Townhome prices start in the $70,000 range.

Area Two, Northeast Mecklenburg

Bordered by U.S. 29 and Central Avenue/Albemarle Road, this area includes the southern part of University City and many older, established neighborhoods.

University City

UNC Charlotte is located in this part of University City, along with retail and office development on University City Boulevard.

Photo by Tim Johnson

The Peninsula, in Cornelius, offers elegant living on Lake Norman.

Custom Quality!
All Brick Exteriors!

*E*njoy the low-maintenance lifestyle offered when living in an all brick home by William Trotter Company, a local, family-owned builder. With over 39 years of experience building homes in the Charlotte area, Trotter Builders offers both exceptional quality and excellent prices ($190s-$260s). You can choose from 3, 4, or 5 bedroom plans in a transitional or traditional style. We offer over 16 plans to suit any need, including basement plans, two-story plans, or ranch plans. Most feature either a bonus room or recreation room for hobbies or offices. All plans have a true two-car garage. And our standard features are upgrades with many builders.

704-525-1783
www.trotterbuilders.com

Customer Service!
Outstanding Value!

Wynfield Forest
Huntersville
From the $200s
North on I-77 to Exit 23;
left on Gilead Road.
Two miles to Wynfield
on the right.

Providence West
South Charlotte
From the $190s
N.C. 51 to Elm Lane;
cross Ballantyne
Commons Parkway;
stay straight until
it becomes
Providence Road
West to Providence
West on the right.

Instead of just
reading about the
many features of
Trotter homes, we
invite you to COME
and SEE them for
yourself. One of our
knowledgeable sales
representatives will
assist you in finding
your ideal home.
Visit one of our five
decorator furnished
models today.

Oak Park
Concord
From the $180s
Take Hwy. 85 N to Exit
55 (Hwy. 73); turn
right, go .5 miles to
Oak Park on the right.

Matthews Plantation
Matthews
From the upper $180s
Hwy. 51 to Fullwood
Lane; right on Trade St.;
bear left on Pleasant
Planes Rd. to Matthews
Plantation on the left.

Muirfield
Mooresville
From the $200s
North on I-77 to
Exit 33; right on Hwy.
21; right on West
Wilson; right on
West Lawrence;
right on Norman to
Muirfield on the right.

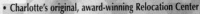

Photo by Tim Johnson

The University City area offers single family homes and townhomes.

Housing options in the University City area vary from townhomes to single family homes.

Country Club

Built in 1917, this area surrounds the Charlotte Country Club with mansions and ranches interspersed along secluded winding roads.

Hickory Grove

Intersected by Hickory Grove Road and W.T. Harris Boulevard, Hickory Grove combines apartments and shopping centers with older homes.

North Charlotte

This North Davidson Street area was originally a mill village.

Newell

On the outskirts of the city near UNC Charlotte, Newell blends rural and suburban with restored farmhouses next to new communities.

Plaza-Midwood

Located in midtown Charlotte between The Plaza and Central Avenue, this is one of Charlotte's most popular older areas. The Plaza is known for its beautiful tree-lined streets and wonderful old homes. Redevelopment along Central Avenue has spruced up the commercial district. Neighborhoods in this area offer a full-range of choices and price ranges. Bungalows and new homes line Midwood's narrow streets.

Shannon Park

Located off The Plaza between Eastway Drive and W.T. Harris Boulevard, this 1950's rolling, wooded neighborhood is home to many of its original families.

New communities in this area include Bradfield Farms, Cambridge, Winding Creek and Woodridge with homes starting at $100,000. Overall, the average price for a home is $88,000.

Area Three, East Mecklenburg

One of the busiest commercial districts in Charlotte, this section is bordered by Central

Avenue/Albemarle Road and Independence Boulevard. Homes here are conveniently located close to department stores, supermarkets, drugstores, specialty shops and a wide selection of restaurants. Along Independence Boulevard, you'll also find a large concentration of automobile showrooms, home-supply stores and membership-only warehouses.

Close to Uptown, along Independence Boulevard are Chantilly and Commonwealth. These neighborhoods offer appealing prices to first-time homeowners who may be looking for a "fixer upper."

New communities are Amber Crest, Brickfield Plantation, Drexel Glen and Southwoods with prices starting in the low $100s. The average price of a home in this area is $95,000.

Area Four, Southeast Mecklenburg

Extending from the outskirts of Uptown to the county line, Area Four is bordered by Independence Boulevard and Providence Road. This area is known for its concentration of hospitals and medical centers. Central Piedmont Community College is also headquartered here.

Cotswold

Located close to Uptown, Cotswold is a 1950's style neighborhood with a mixture of older ranches and semi-contemporary homes and newer houses and apartment complexes.

Eastover

This older neighborhood of mostly grand and expansive homes on large lots also has some upper-medium priced cottages and bungalows. Residents can choose from a variety of specialty shops and restaurants in the area or travel a few miles Uptown to enjoy the city's offerings.

Elizabeth

Subdivided into Piedmont Park, Highland Park, Oakhurst, Elizabeth Heights and Rosemont, Elizabeth is another older neighborhood with many renovated homes. The popular Elizabeth Festival, an annual neighborhood event, is held in Independence Park.

Providence Plantation

Located near Matthews, this is a close-knit community with monthly socials, barbecues and several women's clubs.

Photo by Tim Johnson

Mahogany Woods offers luxury and privacy.

Photo by Tim Johnson

Myers Park is the choice for upscale Uptown living in Charlotte.

Rama-Sardis

This is an established neighborhood with large lots and higher-priced homes. The neighborhoods of Olde Stonehaven, McClintock Woods and Medearis have active community groups.

Some of the newer communities in this area are Corinthian Place, Harrison Woods, Matthews Estates, Matthews Plantation, Providence Glen, Providence Manor, Sardis Plantation, Vista and Whitmore. The average price for a home in this area is $157,000; however, some new home communities start in the $120s.

Area Five, South Mecklenburg

Bordered by Providence Road to the east and Park Road to the west, Area Five is known for its elegant homes in older and newer neighborhoods. The Carolinas Medical Center, the city's largest hospital, and Park Road Shopping Center, the city's first shopping center, are located here.

Carmel Commons

This fast growing community contains a mixture of old and new comfortable, rambling neighborhoods.

Dilworth

Developed in 1891 by Edward Dilworth Latta, Charlotte's first suburb had an electric streetcar extending from the city to entice people to live there. Today East Boulevard, the main thoroughfare, is a thriving commercial district with many old homes converted into offices, restaurants and shops.

Myers Park

Although only a few minutes' drive from Uptown, Myers Park's gracefully curving streets and soaring shade trees provide a parklike setting for its expensive, classic houses. This area is home to Queen's College, Wing Haven Garden and Bird Sanctuary and Freedom Park.

Providence Country Club

Located south of the city on 600 acres of trees, lakes and open spaces, this upscale golf community is still growing. A family-oriented neighborhood, it has tennis courts, a pool and an 18-hole golf course highlighted by an elegant clubhouse. Homesites are available for custom homes.

Quail Hollow

Located between Park Road and Sharon Road, this area contains Seven Eagles, a private community. Spacious newer subdivisions and several apartment and condominium complexes offer residents a variety of housing options.

Raintree

Many of the homes in this community, established in the '70s, are contemporary in design and clustered around several country clubs and golf courses.

SouthPark

With over 30,000 workers, numerous office buildings, trendy restaurants and upscale shopping, this area has become a "mini city." Communities such as Foxcroft, Morrocroft, Mountainbrook, Olde Providence, Beverly Woods, Sharon Woods and Candlewyck are clustered around SouthPark Mall, which opened in 1971.

Some new communities in this area are Ballantyne, Chadwick, Ellington Park, Ivy Hall, Kingston Forest, Olde Colony, Orchid Hill, The Preserve at Belingrath, Royal Crest and Stallworth. The average price of a home in this area is $199,700. Although most new homes are in the same price range, there are a few that start in the $120,000 range.

Area Six, Southwest Mecklenburg

Extending to the South Carolina border, Area Six is a narrow strip of land bordered by Park Road to the east and Nations Ford Road to the west. South Boulevard, the main thoroughfare running through the center of this area, offers a variety of businesses and shopping centers, including a growing number of international retail establishments.

Among the companies located on South Boulevard are Pepsi-Cola Bottling Co. and Lance Inc., a manufacturer of crackers and snack foods.

The area's bustling South End Historic District contains a cluster of former textile mills that has been converted into shops, galleries and restaurants. One example is Atherton Mill, an old textile mill that now contains a variety of eating establishments and interior design stores.

Between Park Road and South Boulevard, you'll find city neighborhoods, older ranch and split-level homes and new developments. New subdivisions are further south, along U.S. 521. The average price for a home in this area is $107,000.

Area Seven, West Mecklenburg

Area Seven begins at Nations Ford Road and extends to the Catawba River on the west, south to the South Carolina state line and north to Wilkinson Boulevard. Charlotte/Douglas International Airport, the Charlotte Coliseum, home to the Charlotte Hornets and the Charlotte Sting, and the Charlotte Regional Farmers Market are located here. Arrowood, an industrial and business complex, and LakePoint, an office park with Microsoft Corp., AT&T, Belk Stores Services, Kemper Insurance and other large companies, are also located here.

Lake Wylie and Paramount's Carowinds are located on the North Carolina and South Carolina border. Both facilities offer a wide variety of recreational activities.

Steele Creek

Settled by the Scots-Irish in the mid-1700s, this community is one of the oldest in the Charlotte area. Lakeside cottages and starter homes help maintain its rustic charm while new developments and mansions bring Steele Creek into the 21st Century.

Wilmore

This older neighborhood with cottage-style homes from the early 1900s once contained two of Mecklenburg's largest gold mines. Community events include an annual parade and a "back-to-school" celebration.

Area Seven offers a mixture of established neighborhoods and brand-new

Photo by Tim Johnson

Many new subdivisions have sprouted in the Charlotte area over the last decade.

developments. The average price for a home is $98,000.

Area Eight, West Mecklenburg

Area Eight extends from Uptown on the east to the Catawba River on the west and with Wilkenson Boulevard as its southern boundary and Bellhaven Boulevard as its northern boundary. Ericsson Stadium, home to the Carolina Panthers, is located here.

Third Ward

This mid-1800's in-town neighborhood that borders Area Eight was redeveloped in the early 1980s. Condominiums, townhouses and renovated industrial buildings with restaurants, offices and studios attract a mixture of young and old. The United House of Prayer is a local landmark with its soaring angels and gilded decorations.

Area Eight offers inner-city neighborhoods, new developments and country living. The average price for a home is $75,000.

Area Nine, Northwest Mecklenburg

Extending west from Statesville Road to the Catawba River with Bellhaven Boulevard to the south and Lake Norman as its northern border, Area Nine is one of the hottest areas for new-home communities. Created by Duke Power Company to generate hydroelectric power, Lake Norman offers 520 miles of meandering shoreline. Several parks provide public access for swimming and boating.

Coulwood

This semi-rural area contains sprawling ranch homes on large lots. The Pine Island Country Club is located here. Area Nine provides a wide variety of housing options for people seeking single-family homes and condominiums. The average price for a house is $135,000.

In the past few years, Charlotte has experienced a building boom in apartment complexes.

Apartments and Temporary Housing

In the past few years, Charlotte has experienced a building boom in apartment complexes. So whether you prefer to live close to Uptown or in any of the surrounding areas, you'll find numerous apartment complexes offering a wide choice of amenities. For a temporary residence, furnished corporate apartments provide all the comforts of home. Most offer fully furnished rooms (including kitchen utensils and cookware) and provide a variety of services.

Apartment Publications

There are two free guides to Charlotte's apartment communities, which are available from a variety of outlets all over town.

The Apartment Finder
528 East Blvd. • 373-0051, (800) 277-5679

The Apartment Finder is published four times a year by Southeast Publishing Ventures, Inc. Although this is a free publication, you will occasionally see it for sale with a rebate coupon enclosed. The publishers also offer the Apartment Finder Map Guide, a detailed area map that features apartment community information, including detailed driving directions, with color photos. The guide is available at numerous grocery stores and outdoor boxes throughout Charlotte.

Apartment Guide-Greater Charlotte
1515 Mockingbird Ln. • 523-0900

This free monthly guide, published by Haas Publishing, presents over 200 shop-and-compare listings with maps, photos, features and prices. It is also offered free of charge at many area grocery stores, drugstores and convenience centers.

Corporate Temporary Housing

When you're moving to a new location, the first few months can be the toughest, especially if you haven't yet found a permanent home. There are several good temporary housing resources in Charlotte.

A Plus Accommodations and Relocation
• **553-7991, (888) 553-7991**

Fully furnished and accessorized one-, two- and three-bedroom corporate apartments are offered with flexible short-term leases, starting with a minimum of 30 days. Unfurnished apartments are also available. Maid service can be arranged.

ExecuStay
3301 Woodpark Blvd. • 599-1575, (800) 262-0841

For stays of 30 days or longer, ExecuStay offers fully furnished one-, two- and three-bedroom apartments, townhomes and private homes. Relocating families with young children, infants or pets can select their accommodations based on their preferences. Telephone service, basic cable and utilities are included on one monthly invoice. Maid service is available by request.

Globe Corporate Stay International
333-1161

One-, two- and three-bedroom apartments and townhomes are available for stays of at least 30 days and then on an "as-needed" basis. The apartments are fully furnished and maid service can be provided. Local phone, utilities, cable TV and washer/dryers are included in the monthly fee. All apartment complexes also offer amenities such as use of the exercise room, pool and clubhouse.

Home On the Road
(800) 487-8449

Home On the Road has furnished and unfurnished corporate apartments available for short- and long-term leases. A customized amenity package features a variety of home accessories and services. One-, two- and three-bedroom apartments are located throughout Charlotte and nationwide.

Homestead Village
710 Yorkmont Rd.   676-0083

Homestead Village is a new hotel that provides 138 rooms for extended stay lodging with affordable weekly and monthly rates. The large studio-style rooms feature king- and queen-size beds, a work station, a fully equipped kitchen and satellite TV. Guests also can make free local calls. The hotel is conveniently located off Billy Graham Parkway near the Charlotte-Douglas International Airport.

Manor House Aptel
2800 Selwyn Ave. • 377-2621

Neither an apartment nor a motel, this lodging facility in the heart of the Myers Park area, one of Charlotte's most exclusive areas, provides a homelike setting at affordable prices. Conveniently located three minutes from Uptown and SouthPark, it's ideal for people who may be relocating to

University Place offers elegant accommodations in a comfortable setting.

Charlotte, have relatives in the hospital or need a place for an extended stay without having to sign a lease or install a telephone. Amenities include free local calls and cable TV with HBO. There is an outdoor pool and laundry facilities and you'll find a grocery store, drugstore, restaurant and shops across the street. Stays longer than a week are discounted.

Oakwood Corporate Housing
(800) 888-0808

Oakwood Corporate Housing provides temporary housing throughout the greater Charlotte area and in over 400 cities nationwide for stays of one month or longer. Fully furnished apartments, condominiums and townhouses are supplied with linens, housewares, cable TV, telephone and maid service. Everything is billed on one convenient monthly invoice. This is the perfect solution for those on extended business travel, in training, relocating or between homes for one month or longer.

Queen Arms Corporate Apartments
233 S. Sharon Amity • 362-3800

Catering to corporate transferees, each one- and two-bedroom apartment is full-sized, fully furnished and includes cable TV, a private phone, dinnerware, utensils, linens and weekly maid service. With 20 locations throughout Charlotte, many have pools, exercise rooms and tennis courts. Pets are allowed. No lease is required and you may stay as long as you like.

Selwyn Avenue Apartments
3400 Selwyn Ave. • 527-3400

This 129-unit property offers month-to-month leases to corporations and 3-, 6- or 12-month leases to private individuals. A variety of amenities are optional — maid service, coffee maker and cable TV. Both furnished and unfurnished units are available. Rates vary according to amenities provided and the length of stay.

StudioPLUS
123 E. McCullough Dr. • 510-0108
5830 Westpark Dr. • 527-1960
(800) 646-8000

StudioPLUS provides queen and deluxe studios with fully equipped kitchens. Free local calls and an expanded cable television service are included in the very affordable rates. A pool, exercise facility and laundry room are located on the premises.

Suburban Lodge

Matthews	845-2001
Pineville	544-3993
Pressley/I-77	679-4112
UNC	599-2380

Suburban Lodges provide homelike amenities for extended-stay guests, including fully equipped kitchens, on-site laundry facilities and housekeeping services. Free local calls and cable TV with HBO, CNN and ESPN are also included.

GET THE BEST DIRECTORY AVAILABLE FOR NORTH CAROLINA JOB HUNTERS!

The North Carolina Employment Guide is the most up-to-date source of hard-to-find information that is needed by:

- *Job seekers who are looking for employment in North Carolina*
- *Executive Recruiters, Employment Agencies & Outplacement Firms*
- *Small businesses seeking to market their products & services to North Carolina businesses*

The North Carolina Employment Guide provides comprehensive information on more than 1,200 North Carolina employers:

- *Company name, address & phone number*
- *Business description & SIC code*
- *Personnel executive's name & title*
- *Chief Executive's name & title*
- *Cross referenced by city & industry*

The North Carolina Employment Guide provides comprehensive information on more than 350 North Carolina Recruiting Firms & Employment Agencies including:

- *Company name, address & phone number*
- *Who pays their fees*
- *Key industries in which they recruit*
- *Type of firm*
- *Name of a key contact person*
- *Salary range of positions they fill*
- *Types of positions they routinely fill*

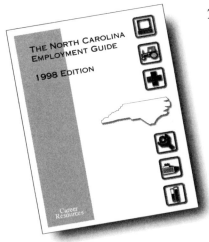

THE NORTH CAROLINA EMPLOYMENT GUIDE

1998 EDITION

Career Resources

The North Carolina Employment Guide is available in both printed form and on computer diskette. The data on diskette allows one to easily perform mass mailings by using a word processor's mail merge function.

Diskette or Book $36

To Order Call **800-777-4843**

Employment Opportunities

With an unemployment rate of under 3 percent and a labor force of almost 350,000, Charlotte offers a broad mix of employment opportunities such as retail trade, wholesale trade, finance, insurance, real estate, construction, manufacturing, transportation, agriculture and mining. This varied mix assures just about anyone from skilled labor to professional, who is looking for employment the opportunity to find it in Charlotte.

The Charlotte Chamber of Commerce takes a very active role in recruiting and maintaining employees and employers. In 1997, the Chamber helped recruit 3,700 new jobs and helped retain nine existing businesses. The Chamber is currently working with the Mecklenburg Development Corporation to develop business parks in the inner city and is also assisting the city and county governments to develop a business investment plan to retain and expand inner city jobs. Charlotte's diversity in employment opportunities draws over 100,000 commuters from 10 surrounding counties, contributing to seven years of strong growth in the Charlotte area.

Temporary Placement

One of the best ways to explore career options is with the help of temporary or permanent staffing agencies. For the newcomer, a temporary position has the advantage of providing an opportunity to become more familiar with the area and with employment options before settling on a permanent position. In addition to placement, many of these agencies also offer training and some even offer skill and personality testing to determine the best working situation for each individual.

EMPLOYMENT AGENCIES

Company	Type	Phone
AA Personnel Plus	Manufacturing, Hotel & Convention	704-377-0382
AAA Employment	Sales, Administrative, Technical	704-567-0002
Accountant Executives	Accountants, Controllers, Data Entry	704-376-0006
Accountemps	Finance, Credit & Collections	704-339-0550
Accurate Staffing	General	704-554-9675
AccuStaff, Inc.	Light Industrial, Clerical, Technical	704-375-0069
Adecco	Administrative, Legal, Secretarial	704-552-6414
Advance Personnel	Legal Sec., General Office, Industrial	704-364-7886
Ameripro Search	Technical, Finance, Sales	704-896-8991
Amicus Staffing	Attorneys, Paralegals, Legal Secretaries	704-529-5590
Arant Personnel Service	Sales, Management Training	704-588-8300
Bennett-Hall	Data Entry, Secretarial, Warehouse	704-365-8802
Career Staffing	Office Support, Administrative	704-525-8400
Carolina Employment	Accounting, Technical, Food Industry	704-372-4701
Corestaff	Clerical, Light Industrial	704-588-2281
Corporate Staffing	Technical, Clerical	704-366-1800
Creative Staffing	Secretarial, Accounting, Warehouse	704-529-0111
Dixie Staffing Services	Industrial	704-525-9311
Don Richard Assoc.	Tax Professionals, CPAs, Auditors	704-377-6447
Eden Staffing	Administrative, Customer Service	704-334-3336
First in Temporaries, Inc.	Customer Service, Marketing, Clerical	704-553-1500
Firstpro	General Office, Collections, Data Entry	704-527-2770
ForceOne	Construction, Warehouse, Industrial	704-370-6131
Fox-Morris Associates	Engineering, Banking, Human Resources	704-522-8244
Fortune Personnel	Engineering, R&D, Marketing	704-889-1100
Griffin Staffing	Administrative, Banking, Technical	704-364-3699
Guaranteed Personnel	Accounting, Secretarial, Management	704-568-7750
Interim Personnel	Secretarial, Healthcare, Technical	704-529-1534
Kelly Services	Office, Light Industrial, Technical	704-510-0900
Labor Finders	Construction, Industrial, Manufacturing	704-372-6116
Labor Ready	Temporary Construction, Landscaping, Janitorial	704-376-5440
Labor World	Industrial	704-335-0530
MAI/Executive	Banking, Investment, Healthcare	704-521-9595
Management Advisors	Financial	704-521-9595
Manpower	Office, Light Industrial, Technical	704-522-9288
McCollum & Associates	Information Specialists	704-543-6198
Mega Force	Technical, Outsourcing/Management	704-841-2077
Morgan Resources	Professional, Office, Light Industrial	704-527-5919
Norrell Financial	Financial, Accounting, Tax Specialists	704-643-2921
Office Team	Administrative, Receptionists, Clerical	704-339-0103
Olsten Professionals	Accounting, Technical, Legal Support	704-358-1990
The Perkins Group	General	704-543-1111
Personnel Unlimited	General Labor, Clerical, Administrative	704-532-2599
Phillips Staffing	Industrial, Technical, Clerical, Secretarial	803-329-9998
Quality Personnel	Clerical, Accounting, Electronics	704-332-2527
Quantum Resources	Information Technology, Engineering	704-643-0230
Remedy Intelligent Staffing	Clerical, Accounting, Light Industrial	704-521-9818
Robert Half International	Financial	704-339-0550
Sanford Rose Associates	General	704-336-0730
Staff Consultants	Clerical, Industrial, Leasing	704-532-1414

MAJOR CHARLOTTE EMPLOYERS

Company	Product/Service	# of Employees	Phone
First Union Corporation*	Banking	14,000	704-374-6161
Carolinas HealthCare System*	Health Care	11,738	704-355-2000
Charlotte-Mecklenburg Schools*	Education	9,984	704-379-7000
NationsBank*	Banking	9,708	704-386-5000
Ruddick Corporation●	Holding Co.	9,000	704-372-5404
Duke Power Company*	Utility Services	7,959	704-594-0887
US Airways	Airline and Aviation	7,000	704-359-3000
Food Lion	Groceries	6,733	704-633-8250
Fieldcrest Cannon	Manufacturing	6,200	704-939-2000
Presbyterian Healthcare System*	Health Care	5,642	704-384-4000
State of North Carolina	State Government	5,336	
Wal-Mart Stores/Sam's	Retail	4,700	704-541-7292
City of Charlotte*	City Government	4,625	704-336-2241
Mecklenburg County*	County Government	4,506	704-336-2472
Springs Industries, Inc.	Textile Manufacturing	4,500	803-547-1500
Freightliner Corp.	Truck Manufacturing	4,476	503-735-8000
United States Government	Federal Government	4,338	
Trevira	Manufacturer	4,000	704-554-2000
IBM Corporation	Computers and Software	4,000	704-594-4600
Pharr Yarns, Inc.	Yarn Manufacturing	3,051	704-824-3551
Harris-Teeter, Inc.*	Groceries	3,008	704-845-3100
United States Postal Service	Mail Delivery	2,889	704-393-4444
FlagStar Companies, Inc.	Food Service	2,653	864-597-8000
Bi-Lo Food Stores	Groceries	2,634	864-234-1600
NorthEast Medical Center	Health Care	2,600	704-783-1275
Gaston Health Care	Health Care	2,525	704-834-2000
Phillip Morris, U.S.A.	Cigarette Manufacturer	2,483	704-788-5000
BellSouth Corp.	Telecommunications	2,300	704-417-9386
Belk*	Retail	2,300	704-377-4251
Winn-Dixie Charlotte	Groceries	2,200	704-587-4000
Eckerd Corp.	Drugstores	2,097	813-399-6000
Carolina Mills, Inc.	Textile Manufacturer	2,000	704-428-9911
Celanese●	Acetate Fibers	2,000	704-554-2000
Continental General Tire, Inc.*	Manufacturing	1,940	704-588-1600
UNC at Charlotte*	Education	1,803	704-547-2000
Central Piedmont Comm. College*	Education	1,740	704-330-2722
Lance, Inc.*	Food	1,559	704-554-1421
Royal Insurance*	Insurance	1,478	704-522-2000
The Charlotte Observer	Newspaper	1,300	704-358-5000
McCopco Operations (McDonald's)*	Food Service	1,242	704-522-0797
United Parcel Service	Package Delivery	1,238	800-742-5877
Family Dollar Stores*	Retail	1,201	704-847-6961
Wachovia Bank Of North Carolina	Banking	1,130	704-378-5111
Allstate Insurance Company	Insurance	1,100	704-547-8300
The Delmar Company	Photo Finishing	954	704-845-2002
Bigger Brothers, Inc.	Food Distribution	911	704-394-7121
Pizza Hut	Food Service	851	704-849-8010
Yellow Freight System	Freight Delivery	850	704-597-1831
Coca-Cola Bottling Consolidated*	Beverage Distributor	840	704-551-4400

* Denotes Headquartered in Charlotte

COME
ON
HOME!

Banking
and Commerce

When it comes to banking, Charlotte means business. What was once a cotton-growing town and a one-time gold mining capital is now a financial force within the United States with $319 billion in bank resources, second only to New York City.

Two of the top 25 banks are headquartered here — NationsBank and First Union National Bank — with scores of others aggressively nipping at their heels. More than 17 banks, 78 commercial finance and factoring firms, 64 leasing corporations, 139 mortgage companies and 12 savings and loans operate in the Charlotte area. Add to that a branch of the Federal Reserve Bank of Richmond and you have quite a diverse mix.

NationsBank, led by the fiery Hugh McColl, is headquartered in the NationsBank Corporate Center. The $66.6 billion merger of NationsBank and BankAmerica in April 1998 created the country's largest bank based on deposits as well as the first coast-to-coast bank in the United States. NationsBank currently has an estimated 100,000 employees, including 9,700 in Charlotte.

First Union National Bank completed its merger with First Fidelity in 1995, making it the sixth-largest bank in the nation. At the close of this merger, First Union had more than 45,000 employees and assets surpassing $124 billion. With offices in 13 states and the District of Columbia, First Union is well situated to expand its already impressive customer base, which now totals 10.5 million. First Union continues to be led by the vision and experience of its chairman, Ed Crutchfield.

Wachovia Bank & Trust, headquartered in nearby Winston-Salem, is a force throughout the region and stands as one of the most profitable banks in the country. Although medium-sized financial institutions such as Winston-Salem-based BB&T, Raleigh-based First Citizens, Durham-based Central Carolina Bank, Rocky Mount-based Centura Bank and Birmingham-based SouthTrust are not headquartered in Charlotte, they all have a substantial banking presence in the Charlotte community. Smaller private banks include Home Federal Savings, Bank of Mecklenburg and Park Meridian.

Charlotte's banks provide a wealth of services to commercial and retail customers and are leaders in the nation in the development of new and innovative ways to provide better services. The advent of interstate banking and more liberal nationwide banking laws mean that Charlotte's banks are poised for a financial invasion of other states. None of this would ever have been possible without North Carolina's aggressive and proactive banking laws and the motivation of Charlotte's banking leadership.

Competition between the banks doesn't stop at assets, portfolio size or stock value. With more than 200 banking offices all over the city, Charlotte boasts one of the highest ratios of branch banks per citizen in the nation. Anywhere in the city, you are always less than 2 1/2 miles away from a branch.

Uptown bank construction began in 1954 when First Union built what is now called the First Union Bank Building on Tryon Street. It was the first new structure Uptown had seen

NationsBank supports the Charlotte arts community, as evidenced by Ben Long's famous frescoes in the NationsBank Corporate Center lobby.

in 25 years. NCNB (now NationsBank) followed suit in 1961 when it built what is now the BB&T Center diagonally across the street from First Union's tower. In 1971, First Union, bursting at the seams and in need of additional space, started construction on a 32-story building, now known as Two First Union Plaza. Not to be outdone, NationsBank countered with a 40-story building in 1974. The building, hailed as a post-modern architectural masterpiece, was strategically positioned at the corner of Trade and Tryon streets — Charlotte's historic Square. The NCNB building, as it was then called, stood as the tallest structure in the city and its surrounding region until 1987, when First Union completed construction of its 42-story headquarters on College Street. First Union then held the bragging rights to the tallest building between Atlanta and Philadelphia.

In 1992, NCNB responded with its 60-story headquarters on Tryon Street, a tower that was christened the NationsBank Corporate Center, in honor of the bank's new corporate name. The building, designed by world-renowned architect Caesar Pelli, now dominates Charlotte's skyline and can be seen from all points of entry into the city. It includes well over one million square feet of office space.

Banks throughout the Queen City deserve much credit for contributing to Charlotte's impressive standard of living and quality of life. The dominance of the banking and financial industry in Charlotte heavily influences the local economy and the sociological makeup of the city. The conservative nature of the area's banks has contributed to the fact that Charlotte is a conservative but forward thinking and "can do" cosmopolitan center.

As outstanding corporate citizens, the banks have a long history of giving money and time to a variety of projects and causes, benefiting the region and its citizens in profound ways. This culture of giving has been accepted by businesses operating in the area. Relocating companies are encouraged to contribute and get involved in the community.

Charlotte banks have fueled the phenomenal growth of Uptown, SouthPark and other areas throughout the region. The presence of these large corporations creates the need for a full-spectrum of support services. That, in turn, attracts other large business. The result — banks and their related businesses are a major source of employment in the region.

The next few years will be quite interesting for the banking industry in general. As many banks dive into uncharted interstate territory, acquiring other banks as they grow, it appears that the big banks will get even larger, leaving opportunities for small and mid-sized niche banks.

While most Charlotteans think of the city's economy as being typified by the office-oriented jobs generated by the banking industry and the numerous regional operations headquartered here, the industrial sector is surprisingly large and growing.

As the fifth-largest urban region in the nation, Charlotte has also emerged as a major national distribution and transportation center. It ranks sixth as a major distribution center and sixth in total wholesale sales with the highest per capita sales in the nation.

Many national and international companies have subsidiary headquarters in Charlotte. In the past 10 years, more than $3.5 billion has been invested in new facilities by 6,045 new firms. Charlotte is home to 385 of the Fortune 500 Companies, including 188 of the largest industrial companies and 197 of the largest service companies in the nation.

While manufacturing remains an integral part of the economy with more than 3,849 producers employing more than 330,000 workers, trade is emerging as the sector that creates more industrial jobs. Distributors appreciate Charlotte's quick and easy access through interstate highways, railroad lines, international cargo flights from Charlotte/Douglas International Airport and the ports of Charleston, South Carolina, and Morehead City and Wilmington in North Carolina.

International companies have a strong presence in Charlotte with over 340 foreign-owned companies maintaining Charlotte facilities. This figure represents one-half of all foreign companies that operate facilities in North Carolina.

The excellent quality of life, an environment that is friendly to business and a strong labor force of highly skilled workers make Charlotte very appealing to relocating companies.

BANK RELOCATION SERVICES

Local Relocation or Main Branch	Telephone Numbers
BB&T, 200 S. College St., 28202	704-954-1074
Central Carolina Bank, 101 S. Kings Dr., 28204	704-347-6050
Centura Bank , 1701 East Third St., 28209	704-331-1740
First Citizens, 128 S.Tryon St., 28202	704-338-4000
First Union National Bank, 1525 West W.T. Harris Blvd., 28288	800-473-3568
Home Federal Savings and Loan, 139 S.Tryon St., 28202	704-373-0400
NationsBank, 100 N. Tryon St., 28255	704-335-6262
SouthTrust Bank, 112 S. Tryon St., 28202	800-635-2099
Wachovia, 400 S. Tryon St., 28202	704-378-5063

Ready for a new kind of business call?

One call is all it takes to bring your company into the 21st century... with the latest in PictureTel video conferencing, integrated voice mail systems, business telephone systems, and voice/data network solutions.

ATCOM
Business Telephone Systems
One Simple Solution.

www.atcombts.com

Raleigh
(919) 832-1345

Greensboro
(336) 665-9294

Winston-Salem
(336) 721-1207

Durham
(919) 544-5751

Greenville
(252) 830-9260

Charlotte
(704) 357-7900

Government, Utilities and Services

The citizens of Charlotte/Mecklenburg pride themselves on their interactive government structure and there are plenty of opportunities for almost everyone to be involved in some aspect of local government. Since Charlotteans take their government very seriously, citizen involvement is held in high esteem, both publicly and privately. Open debates and discussions of governmental issues have led to the creation of a community consensus that enables everyone to move forward on a given problem. There is concern, however, that as Charlotte's population becomes larger and more diverse, its ability to reach a consensus will diminish.

Several years ago, Charlotte adopted a new mission statement: "Public Service Is Our Business." As part of this mission statement, employees identified core values important in serving their community: quality and excellence, accountability, productivity, teamwork, openness and personal development. Loyalty to the community, as a whole, is a deeply ingrained tradition and will hopefully continue as Charlotte faces continued growth.

Mecklenburg County Government has developed the following vision statement: "An organization that cares and is perceived as caring about all those it serves as well as those it employs and that promotes an environment which nurtures and encourages innovation and creativity in pursuit of excellence; a governmental unit that is a professionally recognized leader with a trusting and enthusiastic partnership of elected officials, staff leaders, employees and the community."

City-County Government

Charlotte/Mecklenburg is served by the city-county form of government. Generally, the city provides urban services, such as water, sewer, trash disposal and recycling, while the county provides human services such as health, education, welfare, mental health and the environment. The other towns in Mecklenburg County, Pineville, Mint Hill, Davidson, Huntersville and Cornelius, each have their own town governments. Both Charlotte and the county use a manager form of government, with the managers respectively hired by the City Council and Board of County Commissioners.

If you have a question or need information regarding city or county government, call the City-County Action Line at 336-2040. Elected officials are also accessible; you can get their numbers by calling the action line.

The City Council

The council-manager system is designed to be responsive to citizens' needs. City Council is made up of the mayor and 11 members, seven from districts and four at-large, elected every odd-numbered year in partisan elections. The mayor is also elected at this time. The mayor presides at City Council meetings and officially represents the city at special ceremonies and events. The mayor is generally responsible for the execution of local laws. The Mayor Pro Tempore, elected by a City Council vote, assumes all duties, powers and obligations of the office in the mayor's absence.

Together, the mayor and City Council are responsible for establishing the general policies under which the city operates. Their duties include: appointing the city manager, city attorney, city clerk and members of various boards and commissions; enacting ordinances, resolutions and orders; reviewing the annual budget and approving the financing of all city operations; and authorizing contracts on behalf of the city.

The City Council holds three meetings each month on Mondays in the meeting chamber of the Charlotte/Mecklenburg Government Center at 600 East Fourth Street. The meetings on the second and fourth Mondays are general business sessions that begin at 6:30 PM. On the third Monday at 6 PM, the meeting deals only with matters related to zoning. The general business sessions are broadcast live on Cable Channel 16, as is a calendar of meetings for all city boards and commissions. Contact the Office of the City Clerk (336-2247) for information about the City Council agenda or to speak at a City Council meeting.

In the council-manager form of government, the city manager administers the policy decisions made by the City Council. The manager is responsible for assuring that all city departments provide services to citizens in an efficient and cost-effective manner; assuring that city laws are faithfully executed; attending City Council meetings; reporting to City Council on the affairs and financial condition of the City; and appointing all department heads except those appointed by City Council.

The County Commission

The nine-member Board of County Commissioners, elected in partisan elections held in even-numbered years, consists of six members elected from single-member districts and three at-large members. The chair and vice-chair are elected by the members; the chair is usually the top vote-getter of the majority party.

The Board holds three meetings each month on Tuesdays in the meeting chamber of the Charlotte/Mecklenburg Government Center. The meetings on the first and third Tuesdays are general business sessions that begin at 6 PM. On the second Tuesday, the Board holds a zoning meeting. The Board also holds a luncheon meeting on the Thursday preceding the first Tuesday of each month. The Board's meetings are broadcast live on the government access channel and rebroadcast during the week in which the meeting was held. For information on the Commission's meeting agenda or to speak at a Commission meeting, contact the Clerk to the Board at 336-2559.

The Board's main responsibilities are appointing the county manager and adopting the annual county budget, setting the county property tax rate and assessing and establishing priorities on community needs. The Board also makes appointments to citizen advisory boards. The county manager is the chief administrative officer of Mecklenburg County and is responsible for implementing county policies, coordinating the work of all county agencies, representing the county in dealings with other governmental agencies and recommending the annual budget to the Commission.

State Representatives

During even-numbered years the county elects representatives to the General Assembly and, with Cabarrus County, four state senators. All of these are elected within districts.

School Board

School board elections are held in odd-numbered years and are nonpartisan. Of the nine members, six are elected from the same districts as the County Commissioners and three are elected at-large. The four-year terms are staggered.

Registering To Vote

To participate in the political process you must, of course, be registered to vote. For questions regarding registering, call the Board of Elections at 336-2133. If you have been a resident for 30 days, you are eligible to register to vote in the appropriate elections. You can register at the Board of Elections at 741 Kenilworth Avenue, Suite 202; at any branch of the Public Library; at the town halls of Cornelius, Matthews and Pineville; or at the Department of Motor Vehicles Drivers License Offices.

Getting Involved

Community involvement is a good way to meet people and make friends. One way to get involved is by serving on citizen advisory boards. Citizens can be appointed by the mayor, City Council or County Commission to about 100 city, county and joint commissions and boards, some standing, some ad hoc, including the Planning Commission, Airport Authority, Tree Commission, Sister City Committee, Building Standards Advisory Committee, Minority Affairs Committee and Park and Recreation Commission. *Citizen Participation in Mecklenburg County* describes the major citizen advisory boards. It's available at the Mecklenburg County Public Service & Information office at 600 E. Fourth Street.

To find out what appointments are coming up and to get an application, call the City Clerk's Office at 336-2247 or the County Clerk's Office at 336-2559. *The Charlotte Observer* also runs lists of upcoming appointments and the schedule for board meetings. Please attend some meetings before you apply for a specific board to find out what serving on it entails.

Getting involved in politics is also a good way to meet people. Both major political parties use precincts as their basic organizational structure and attending the annual precinct meetings is a good way to start. Both parties have clubs for men, women, seniors, young people and others who may want to form a group. To get politically involved on the state or local level, call: Local Democratic Headquarters, 525-5843; State Democratic Headquarters, (800) 229-3367; Local Republican Headquarters, 334-9127; and State Republican Headquarters, (919) 828-6423. There are also many nonpartisan groups, such as the Black Political Caucus, the Women's Political Caucus, the League of Women Voters, Concerned Charlotteans and the North Carolina

Policy Council. Another great resource is *People, Pride, Progress – A Citizen's Guide to Government and Services*. The city puts out a similar brochure entitled *City and Government Services from A to Z*. Both of these guides are a must to learn about all the programs the city and county have to offer.

If politics in any form is not for you, many community groups are looking for volunteers. The Volunteer Connection at 301 South Brevard Street brings together eager helpers and needy groups. Call the United Way at 372-7170 and ask for the Volunteer Connection.

Utilities

Cable Television
Time Warner Cable • 377-9600

Electric
Duke Power Company • 594-9400

Gas
Piedmont Natural Gas • 525-5585
Suburban Propane • 375-1721

Telephone
BellSouth • 780-2355, 780-2800

Water and Sewer
Charlotte-Mecklenburg Utilities • 336-2211

Services

Animal Care
Animal Control/Pet Licenses • 336-3786
Emergency Veterinary Clinic • 376-9622
Spay-Neuter Clinic • 333-4130

Driver's License
• 527-2562, 392-3266, 547-5786

Recycling
General Recycling Information • 336-6087
North Mecklenburg
Mulch/Compost Facility • 875-1563
North Mecklenburg
Recycling Center • 875-3707

To Learn To Become

" Our experiential, hands-on approach to teaching students to use technology is one of Charlotte Country Day School's greatest strengths. At every grade level and in every discipline, our students learn by doing. "

To learn more about Charlotte Country Day School, call the admissions office at 704/366-1241 or write us at 1440 Carmel Road, Charlotte, NC 28226.

Schools and Child Care

The mission of the Charlotte-Mecklenburg School System is "to ensure that the Charlotte-Mecklenburg School System becomes the premier urban, integrated system in the nation in which all students acquire the knowledge, skills and values necessary to live rich and full lives as productive and enlightened members of society."

In recent years, the Charlotte-Mecklenburg School System has been honored in the Outstanding School Recognition Program sponsored by the U.S. Department of Education with Myers Park High, Carmel Junior High, First Ward Elementary and Piedmont Open Middle School receiving awards. CMS has also had 12 award-winning programs in the nine-year history of the Governor's Program of Excellence.

The CMS System is the largest in North Carolina and the 26th largest in the nation, employing 9,200 faculty, staff and support personnel and serving more than 95,500 students. At current growth rates, the number of students will increase to more than 100,000 by the year 2000.

Mecklenburg County voters have a proud tradition of supporting school construction bonds. Two new high schools have opened and six more schools are scheduled to open in the 1998-99 school year.

Board of Education

The CMS System is governed by a nine-member Board of Education elected on a county-wide basis to serve rotating four-year terms. One of their duties is to appoint the Superintendent.

The Board of Education holds regular meetings on the second and fourth Tuesdays of each month in the boardroom on the fourth floor of the Education Center. These meetings are open to the public and an agenda is available in the boardroom prior to the meeting.

Registering Your Child

You should contact the Pupil Assignment Office at the Education Center, 379-7044, to find out which school your child will attend and then visit the school to register your child. School offices remain open throughout the summer. Children entering kindergarten must be 5 years old on or before October 16 of the year in which the child is presented for enrollment. Children entering first grade must be 6 years old on or before October 16 of the year in which the child is presented for enrollment. The law permits enrollment of a child who does not meet these requirements if the child has already been attending school in another state in accordance with the laws or regulations of that state before becoming a resident of North Carolina.

To register, a new student must bring a birth certificate or other acceptable proof of age and an immunization record signed by a physician. This immunization record must include five DTP, four Oral Polio Vaccines, one Rubeola, one Rubella and one Mumps Vaccine. Health assessments are required for all new kindergarten students and include a medical history and physical examination with screening for vision and hearing.

North Carolina law requires all children from ages 7 to 16 to attend school. State law requires a minimum of 180 school days per

1998-99 MAGNET PROGRAMS

ACADEMY FOR MEDICAL SCIENCES
Garinger High

ACADEMY OF FINANCE
Garinger High

ACCELERATED LEARNING ACADEMY
First Ward Elementary

CLASSICAL STUDIES
Nations Ford Elementary

COMMUNICATION ARTS AND ACADEMIC STUDIES
Cochrane Middle
David Cox Elementary
Devonshire Elementary
Garinger High
Marie G. Davis Middle
Olde Providence Elementary

INTERNATIONAL BACCALAUREATE
Davidson IB Middle
Druid Hills Elementary
Harding University High
Independence High
J.T. Williams Middle
Marie G. Davis Middle
Myers Park High
Reid Park Elementary
Sedgefield Middle

INTERNATIONAL/GLOBAL STUDIES
Lincoln Heights Elementary

LANGUAGE IMMERSION
Bruns Avenue Elementary:
  German
Collinswood Elementary:
  Spanish
Reid Park Elementary:
  French
Sedgefield Elementary:
  Japanese
Smith Middle School:
  International

LEARNING IMMERSION AND ACADEMICALLY GIFTED
Barringer Elementary
Lincoln Heights Elementary
Villa Heights Academic

MATH, SCIENCE & TECHNOLOGY
Ashley Park Elementary
Oaklawn Elementary
Spaugh Middle
Harding University High

MONTESSORI
Amy James Elementary
Billingsville Elementary

OPEN
Irwin Avenue Elementary
Piedmont Middle
West Charlotte High

PAIDEIA
Oakhurst Elementary
Randolph Middle

TRADITIONAL/CLASSICAL
Druid Hills Elementary
Elizabeth Elementary
Myers Park Elementary
Hawthorne Middle
J. T. Williams Middle

VISUAL AND PERFORMING ARTS
Chantilly Elementary
University Park Elementary
Northwest Middle and High

WORKPLACE
Education Village
Martin Middle
Morehead Elementary
Nathaniel Alexander Elementary
Vance High

YEAR ROUND
Bruns Avenue Elementary

year for grades K through 12. Each high school offers assistance to students who are preparing for the Scholastic Aptitude Test. In addition, 10th graders take the Preliminary Scholastic Aptitude Test at no charge.

Transportation

The school system provides buses for students who live at least 1.5 miles from school or who must walk through identified hazardous areas. More than 57,000 students ride buses every day and 62,000 miles are traveled. Students in CMS undergo mandatory busing to racially integrate the schools. For more information, call 343-6715. The Education Center, including the Public Information Office, is located at 701 East Second Street near the central business district.

Magnet Schools

CMS added magnet schools to its program in the 1992-93 school year. A federally funded program, magnet schools offer all core curriculum—math, science and language arts—as well as special programs. Specialties include programs such as Montessori, learning immersion and academically gifted programs, language immersion, math, science and technology, International Baccalaureate and visual and performing arts. The open education program offers a challenging and intellectual climate that encourages students to take responsibility and the Paideia (py-day-a) program allows students to become independent thinkers and creative problem solvers.

In 1998, 18 magnet programs were offered at 40 schools. It is the philosophy of CMS that the magnet schools ensure racially balanced schools. The magnet schools also offer numerous opportunities for parents to cultivate interests and strengths in their children and provide school choices all over the county.

Students are admitted to the magnet schools through a lottery process. For six weeks each year parents may apply to any program.

Priority is given to siblings in a family that has already been admitted. Once a child is admitted to a magnet school, he or she will continue there through the terminal grade at that school.

You must live in Mecklenburg County to apply for the magnet program. All students, regardless of whether they have attended public or private schools, have equal access to apply for the magnet schools.

For more information about the magnet school program, call 343-5030.

CMS Information Center
701 E. 2nd St. • 379-7010

Information about schools, including policies, programs and services, is available to parents, students, employees, local citizens, newcomers, agencies, other school systems and communities. The center provides speakers for various programs, displays at special events and tours of the Education Center, schools and other facilities. It also operates a parent-concern telephone line. The Center is open from 8 AM to 5 PM, Monday through Friday, and maintains a 24-hour service through the use of a recording device after 5 PM. Calls are returned the next working day.

Special Programs

CMS offers a variety of special programs for students. For complete listings and more detailed information, contact the CMS Information Center, 379-7010. Below are brief descriptions of some of the options available for special needs.

A Child's Place
345 N. College St. • 343-3790

This is a transitional classroom for homeless children.

Academic Internship Program

Second semester 10th graders and 11th and 12th graders are provided the opportunity to explore areas of academic or career interests by working in the community with government and civic agencies, businesses or industries.

Public schools are a valued resource in Charlotte and Mecklenburg County, receiving support from citizens, parents and public officials.

Academically Gifted Program

This is a state-mandated program providing advanced content, higher-level thinking and developmental courses for those students who need academic challenges beyond those regularly found in the advanced classes. Students must meet CMS program eligibility requirements. Call 343-6955 for more information.

Advanced Placement Courses

College-level courses are offered in a wide variety of subjects that allow students the opportunity to immediately enroll in higher level courses when they enter college.

After School
Enrichment Program

This program provides after school supervised care for children of working parents in kindergarten through 6th grade. The program is offered at 46 sites and before-school programs are also available at many sites.

Registration fees and weekly fees are involved. There is also a summer enrichment day camp for 8 weekly sessions at several elementary schools around the county. Call 343-5567 for information.

CMS Scholars Program

The CMS Scholars Program allows students with a GPA of 4.0 at the end of the first semester of their senior year the option of a free elective in lieu of the Vocational Education requirement and four units of science, counting 9th-grade science.

CPCC Articulation Program

This is a cooperative program with Central Piedmont Community College that allows students to sign up for college-level courses.

Dial-A-Teacher
701 E. 2nd St. • 375-6000

Available Monday through Thursday 5 to 8 PM during the school year, Charlotte-Mecklenburg students can call for homework assistance in math, science, social studies and English/language. The teachers do not give answers, but they help students find their own solutions to homework problems.

Dolly Tate Teen-Age Parents Services
1817 Central Ave. • 343-5418

A cooperative effort of the Mecklenburg County Department of Social Services, Carolinas Medical Center, Mecklenburg County Health Department and Charlotte-Mecklenburg Board of Education, this organization provides education and comprehensive health services to pregnant junior and senior high girls. Child care services are provided to students to enable them to complete the academic year in which their child is born.

Dropout Prevention Program
A system-wide program designed to retain students through graduation and to provide services to alleviate conditions that cause students to drop out of school.

English as a Second Language
This program provides intensive instruction in English to students whose native tongues are another language.

Evening School
Midwood High School • 343-6011

Operating from Monday through Friday, students in grades 9 to 12 may attend to earn a high school diploma.

Junior Achievement of Charlotte
4632 Holbrook Dr. • 536-9668

Devoted to teaching children about America's economic system and its private enterprise sector, Junior Achievement of Charlotte is the 12th largest in the nation. It involves volunteers from the business community and currently provides both private and public schools with programs that range from K through 12.

Metro School
700 E. 2nd St. • 343-5450

This is a self-contained school for mentally and physically handicapped students with a community-based training program that places students in more than 20 businesses and service agencies for on-the-job training.

Minority Achievement Program
Aimed at high-achieving minorities, this program, started in 1983, seeks to increase the participation of these students in programs for the academically gifted.

North Carolina Academic Scholars Program
This is an academically challenging high school program. Contact the principal or guidance counselor at your local school for more information.

Alternative Placement Program
Management School-East (6-8) • 343-3772
Management School-West (6-8) • 343-3820
Learning Academy (9-12) • 343-3774

Students at risk of exclusion from middle school, junior high or high school classes may petition the Superintendent's office for admission to this basic maintenance program. English, math, science and social studies courses allow students to learn in a corrective environment. Credits earned count partially towards advancing or graduation.

Pursuing Excellence Achievement Knowledge in Summer (PEAKS)
PEAKS is a summer program for interested and self-motivated students in art, debate, writing, math, SAT preparation, science, French and Spanish.

Summer Program
Summer programs are offered for 6 weeks at CMS elementary, middle and high schools during June and July. Students attend mandatory and optional classes five hours a day.

Special Schools and Services

Charlotte has a number of special schools and services that fulfill the needs of a child that can't be addressed in a regular public or private school.

Alexander Children's Center
6220 Thermal Rd. • 366-8712

This nonprofit agency, founded in 1888, offers several programs for children with special needs. The Residential Treatment Center provides intensive treatment for emotionally troubled children ages 6 through 12. The Markle Group Home offers family-like living for graduates of the treatment center who continue to need a stable living environment. The Crisis Stabilization and Assessment Unit provides emergency care for children removed from their homes due to abuse and neglect. The Children Development Center is an AA-licensed day program for children ages 3 months through 5 years, some of whom have special needs. The center depends on funds from individuals, churches, businesses and foundations in the community to operate its programs. It also provides many volunteer opportunities. Church, civic and community groups meet regularly at the center.

Catholic Social Services
116 E. 1st St. • 370-6155

This organization offers many services, including individual, family, adoption, marital and substance abuse counseling and pregnancy support. Fees are based on a sliding scale.

Charlotte Speech and Hearing Center
300 S. Caldwell St. • 376-1342

Screening, evaluations, consultation, education and therapy are services available to anyone who has or may have a speech/language or hearing problem. Funded in part by United Way, this nonprofit center is accredited by the Professional Services Board of the American Speech-Language-Hearing Association. The clinical staff is licensed by the state. Some services are free; others are on a sliding-fee scale.

Child and Family Development, Inc.
309 S. Laurel Ave. • 332-4834

Staffed by professional therapists, this is a private evaluation/treatment and rehabilitation center for children. It offers clinics in neurology and psychiatry to monitor the medication needs of children who need treatment. Areas of specialty include ADHD, learning disabilities, cerebral palsy, motor handicaps, speech and language disorders and emotional/social difficulties.

Dore Academy
1727 Providence Rd. • 365-5490

Dore Academy offers instructions to bright students in grades 1 through 12 who have learning disabilities, by providing a safe, nurturing environment in which they can grow and learn.

Family Center, Inc.
1616 Cleveland Ave. • 376-7180

This center serves abused children and their families.

Fletcher School
4921 Randolph Rd. • 365-4658

This special school for learning-disabled children in grades 2 through 8 provides a structured, individualized academic program to help prepare them to return to the regular classroom environment whenever possible.

McLeod Addictive Disease Center
145 Remount Rd. • 332-9001

This community agency provides counseling and support groups for chemically dependent young people and adults and their families. Services are provided through the Treatment Center, Methadone Medical Services, Outpatient Clinic, Adolescent Outpatient Services and Treatment Alternatives to Street Crimes.

Perceptual Motor Studies
UNC-Charlotte • 547-4695

Dr. John Healey, a member of the UNC Charlotte faculty, coordinates this unique program for children up to the age of 18 who are experiencing difficulty in their perceptual motor development. Each child undergoes screening before acceptance into the program and is paired with two college students who, under the direction of the coordinator, assist the child in various activities.

Photo courtesy of Charlotte Country Day School

Schools are dedicated to excellence and spirit-building events such as the hosting of the Special Olympics by Charlotte Country Day School.

Preschool Exceptional Children's Program

700 E. Stonewall St. • 343-6960

This program serves children with identified special needs. It operates by contracting with several community service providers. The program's mission is to promote community efforts to ensure all children enter school ready to learn. The program offers free screenings and evaluations.

Preschool Program For The Hearing Impaired

North Carolina School for the Deaf
2831 N. Sharon Amity Rd. • 536-9296

This program provides preschool services for hearing-impaired preschoolers from newborns to 5 year olds in Mecklenburg and surrounding counties. Instruction is given on-site and in the home.

St. Marks, Inc.

601 N. Graham St. • 333-7107

Established in 1973, this center offers programs and services to approximately 230 Mecklenburg County residents who have severe or profound mental retardation or are at high risk for a severe disability. Preschool, special education and summer school programs for children and sheltered workshops, developmental activities programs and supported employment programs for adults are offered. In 1993, the Center began The Circle School, a child development program that allows special needs children to be mainstreamed with other children.

The Relatives

1100 East Blvd. • 377-0602

This family-oriented crisis counseling center provides emergency shelter (1 to 14 days) with round-the-clock admittance for young people ages 7 to 17. Free and confidential services include individual and family counseling, community referral, follow-up and 24-hour assistance by hotline or walk-in visit. Services are available to both parents and children.

United Cerebral Palsy Developmental Center

716 Marsh Rd. • 522-9912

A branch of United Cerebral Palsy of North Carolina, this center, housed in Myers Park Baptist Church, provides education and therapy for children ages 1 to 5 with cerebral palsy or a similar neurologically based disorder, as well as training for parents in Mecklenburg and surrounding counties. Tuition is based on a sliding-fee scale.

United Family Services

301 S. Brevard St. • 332-9034

The Big Brothers/Big Sisters Division, 377-3963, provides adult friendship and guidance to children ages 7 to 15 living in single-parent families in the Mecklenburg County area. The Community Education Division, 333-3721, offers preventive education programs on family life to parents and day care providers. Family counseling is available. Workshop fees vary and are based on a sliding scale; however, no one is turned down due to an inability to pay.

Dr. Carlton G. Watkins Center

3500 Ellington St. • 336-7100

This county agency offers a number of services, including a developmental day preschool for mildly and moderately mentally retarded children, a parent-infant training program and a developmental evaluation program to determine if an individual of any age has a disability or delayed development. Fees are based on the client's ability to pay.

Private Schools

There are many independent and special schools within Mecklenburg County. Well over 10,000 students are enrolled in these schools in pre-kindergarten through 12th grade.

Success Begins Here...

CHARLOTTE CHRISTIAN S·C·H·O·O·L

A College Preparatory Program
serving K-12th Grade
Since 1950

For information call:
Admissions Office
704-366-5657 Ext. 235

**7301 Sardis Road
Charlotte, NC 28270**

Charlotte Christian School does not discriminate on the basis of sex, race, color, religion, or national origin
in administering its educational programs and employment practices.

Anami Montessori School
2901 Archdale Dr. • 556-0042

The Anami Montessori School was founded in 1986 as a fully accredited AMI (Association Montessori Internationale) institution. Programs are offered to meet the needs of children ages 2 1/2 to 12 years.

The school places emphasis on encouragement, respect for the individual, choice and personal responsibility. Anami Montessori has dedicated, caring teachers and small classes where children often work to the sounds of classical music. The spacious facilities on Archdale Drive back up to the 120-acre Park Road Park.

Bible Baptist Christian School
2724 Margaret Wallace Rd. • 535-1694

This school enrolls students in grades K through 12 with extended before- and after-school care as well. Offering a traditional curriculum, the school is college preparatory in mission.

Cabarrus Academy
5801 Poplar Tent Rd., Concord
• 786-8171

Founded in 1969, Cabarrus Academy is an independent school serving approximately 400 students in grades K through 8 on a 65-acre campus. The 48,000-square-foot school complex includes, in addition to administrative offices and classrooms, a library, foreign language lab, computer lab, art studio and music studio. Students participate in various community programs. A member of several national educational organizations, Cabarrus Academy is accredited by the N.C. State Board of Education and the Southern Association of Colleges and Schools.

Calvary Christian School
8101 Fallsdale Dr. • 394-5566

Established in 1986 by Calvary Baptist Church in the Coulwood community, this school serves over 200 students in grades K through 12. In addition to regular classes, it offers a college preparatory program, foreign languages, music, physical education and athletics for secondary students. Before- and after-school care, as well as summer child care, is available to children in grades kindergarten through 6th grade. Calvary is a member of the Association of Christian Schools International.

Charlotte Catholic High School
7702 Pineville-Matthews Rd. • 543-1127

Coeducational and college preparatory, Charlotte Catholic began as part of St. Mary's Seminary in 1877. Five elementary schools and one Catholic middle school feed into Charlotte Catholic, which serves grades 9 through 12. Non-Catholics may attend. The student/faculty ratio is 16 to 1. A member of the North Carolina Athletic Association, the school has 26 athletic teams. Charlotte Catholic is accredited by the Southern Association of Colleges and Schools, the North Carolina State Department of Public Instruction, the North Carolina Association of Independent Schools and the Diocese of Charlotte.

Charlotte Christian School
7301 Sardis Rd. • 366-5657

Charlotte Christian is an interdenominational, independent day school. Founded in 1950, it provides college preparatory education for more than 900 students in grades K through 12. In addition to its excellent academic program, the school offers athletics with teams competing within the North Carolina Independent Schools Conference. Charlotte Christian is a member of the Association of Christian Schools International, the North Carolina Association of Independent Schools and the Southern Association of Colleges and Schools.

Charlotte Country Day School
1440 Carmel Rd. • 366-1241

Founded in 1941, Charlotte Country Day is the oldest independent school in the area. The school provides a liberal education for its 1,580 students — one that develops the intellect, body, spirit and character. The school has an outstanding arts program, encompassing music, dance, drama and the visual arts. Three divisions make up the school: Lower School (junior kindergarten through grade 4), Middle School (grades 5 through 8) and Upper School (grades 9 through 12). There is also an international baccalaureate program. Small classes, dedicated teachers and individualized instruction in all classes, including athletics, allow every child to experience success. An independent, nonsectarian, coeducational school, Charlotte Country Day welcomes students regardless of race, color, national or ethnic origin, or religion.

Charlotte Latin School
9502 Providence Rd. • 846-1100

Charlotte Latin School, founded in 1970, is a coeducational day school with 1,260 students in grades pre-kindergarten through 12. Located on 92 wooded acres, Charlotte Latin is one of Charlotte's finest in terms of academic quality and diversity. The curriculum is college preparatory and 100 percent four-year college placement is the norm. It endeavors to present its students with the challenges and opportunities necessary for the development of leadership qualities and academic excellence. In addition to its well-rounded academic program, 49 Charlotte Latin School teams annually compete in 23 different sports. The school has won 80 state championship titles in various sports in its 25-year history.

Charlotte Latin has been named an Exemplary School by the United States Department of Education and is the youngest school ever chartered by the *Cum Laude* Society. In May 1997, it received the U.S. Department of Education Blue Ribbon Award. The awards are judged on leadership, school environment, parent and community support and documented success.

Charlotte Lutheran School
1001 Queens Rd. • 376-0920
1225 E. Moorehead St. • 372-7738

Founded in 1942, Charlotte Lutheran is one of the older private schools in the city and is certified by the state. The school

You'll Want To Be A Part of Our Family.

Charlotte Latin School emphasizes the development of the whole child, from academics, to athletics, to the arts. With students in grades pre-kindergarten through twelve, our goal is to provide an environment that encourages each to reach his or her full potential.

As in all families, we support one another and through that support, we continue to ensure the very brightest of futures for our children. So come get to know us—we'd love for you to be a part of our family!

 Charlotte Latin School
9502 Providence Road, Charlotte, NC 28277
Admissions, 704/846-7206

provides preschool and extended day care programs for preschool through 5th grade.

Charlotte Montessori School
212 Boyce Rd. • 366-5994
219 East Blvd. • 332-7733

Charlotte's oldest Montessori School was chartered in 1971. The school is affiliated with The American Montessori Society and is approved by the North Carolina State Department of Public Instruction. The school offers the child a unique environment that develops self-discipline, independence and an enthusiasm for learning. Programs are available for toddlers (ages 24 through 36 months), primary and kindergarten through grade 5.

Countryside Montessori School
9100 Olmstead Dr. • 547-1091
9026 Mallard Creek Rd. • 549-4253

Chartered in 1975 and affiliated with American Montessori Society, Countryside offers preschool for children ages 2 to 5 at the Olmstead location and elementary programs for 1st through 8th grade at the Mallard Creek site. Day care is available at both locations.

Covenant Day School
800 Fullwood Ln., Matthews • 847-2385

Covenant Day School, a ministry of Christ Covenant Church, is a coeducational Christian day school for grades K through 9. The school serves over 540 students and offers academic excellence in a nurturing Christian environment. Beginning with kindergarten, the school offers a superior reading program. Instruction in French and Latin is combined with modern computer technology to provide a comprehensive academic program. Extracurricular programs include art, music, journalism, yearbook and band. A varied sports program is also offered.

Garr Memorial Christian School
7700 Wallace Rd. • 568-7700

Established in 1987, the Garr Christian School serves 75 children in grades K through 7. In addition to the regular curriculum, classes are offered in music, physical education and computers. The school continues to operate its successful Playskool program.

The Lubavitch Jewish Day School of Charlotte
6619 Sardis Rd. • 366-3984

The school's Jewish culture and environment helps the 70 students in grades K through 6 develop a sense of security in their roots and a pride in who they are. They are given a multifaceted education based on academic performance, social growth and feelings of self-worth. Classes are small enough to ensure that each student receives individual attention but large enough to develop vital friendships that enhance social skills.

Mecklenburg Area Catholic Schools
1145 Buchanan Street • 370-0405

Mecklenburg Area Catholic Schools (MACS) is a system of seven schools serving 3,200 students in grades pre-K through 12. Student test scores consistently rank higher than local and national averages and college placement is the norm for all graduates of Charlotte Catholic High School. MACS is accredited by the North Carolina Department of Public Instruction and Charlotte Catholic is fully accredited by the Southern Association of Colleges and Schools as well as the North Carolina Association of Independent Schools. In the tradition of Catholic schools, particular emphasis is placed on the development of spiritual and moral values. Students of all faiths are welcomed.

Northside Christian Academy
333 Jeremiah Blvd.
Admissions • 599-9015

Founded in 1962, the school serves 750 students, K through 12, and is one of the many ministries of Northside Baptist Church. It shares facilities with the church. The school maintains dress codes and behavior guidelines. College preparatory students must complete 24 units and special help is available. Church members and families with more than one child in the school receive a discount.

INSPIRING A PASSION
FOR LEARNING

PROVIDENCE DAY SCHOOL

5800 SARDIS ROAD CHARLOTTE, NC 28270
704-887-7041
www.providenceday.org

Omni Montessori School AMI
9536 Blakeney-Heath Rd. • 541-1326

An AMI-affiliated Montessori school, this center opened in 1985 and serves up to 100 students.

Providence Christian School
4900 Providence Rd. • 364-0824

This school provides a well-rounded curriculum for students in grades K through 6. In addition to basic courses, classes in Bible, computers, foreign languages, physical education, art, music and band are offered. Classes are small with a student/teacher ratio of 15 to 1. Extended care is available from 7 to 7:30 AM and after school until 6 PM.

Providence Day School
5800 Sardis Rd. • 364-6848

Providence Day School is the only school to be cited for excellence by both the U.S. Department of Education and the National Council of Teachers of English. The school was founded in 1970 and is located on a 35-acre campus in southeast Charlotte. It serves 1,250 students in grades K through 12 and offers a traditional college preparatory education in a safe, caring environment.

College credit is granted to 70 percent of the school's students who take Advanced Placement tests. Many students receive academic, athletic and special achievement scholarships and the school is awarded more honors each year than any other school in the regional and state Science Fairs.

Resurrection Christian School
2825 Shenandoah Ave. • 334-9898

Established in 1978 as a ministry of Resurrection Lutheran Church, this school serves students in grades K through 12. It incorporates within its Bible-anchored curriculum the functions of education, worship, evangelism and fellowship. Extracurricular activities include team sports and field trips. The school is approved by the North Carolina State Board of Education.

Tutoring Services

The Charlotte/Mecklenburg School System offers free tutoring via telephone Monday through Thursday 5 PM to 8 PM. Call 375-6000. The best way to find a private tutor is to ask your child's teacher to recommend one.

Preschool and Day Care Programs

There are literally hundreds of day care programs in Mecklenburg County, including child care centers, family child care homes and part-day nursery programs. Many churches also offer facilities and programs. Nationwide child care centers such as La Petite (with 9 locations in the area) and KinderCare are popular options. You may also want to ask a friend or neighbor about a specific care provider. Child Care Resources, Inc., 376-6697, at 700 Kenilworth Avenue, a private, non-profit organization, is a marvelous resource and a great starting point for any parent looking for child care options. Funded by the United Way, it's tied into all child care and preschool education opportunities in and around the community.

A comprehensive listing of child care centers and services is provided in the Charlotte Yellow Pages.

INSIDERS' TIPS

All child care providers must be registered with the North Carolina Division of Child Development. Call (919) 662-4499 if you want to check out a center's record.

Learning is child's play.

At La Petite, children love to learn because they learn through activities they love.

It's called the La Petite Journey® program and it helps your preschooler develop learning skills by creating, discovering, experimenting and having fun with other children.

When it comes to your child's learning, La Petite is the smart choice for you.

La Petite Academy

The Parent's Partner ®

Preschool & Child Care

Charlotte	Concord
6203 Carmel Road	3505 S. Ridge Ave.
542-6773	786-1517
8726 W.T. Harris Blvd.	Huntersville
563-0064	102 College Commerce Dr.
917 East W.T. Harris Blvd.	875-0399
548-0304	Matthews
3132 Tyvola Road	13001 Idlewild Road
553-2503	847-5814
9221 York Road	9908 Monroe Road
588-5659	847-7052

Charlotte's higher education system provides knowledge and training for vocational necessities and it emphasizes and promotes arts and culture.

Colleges and Universities

Whether you are interested in getting your undergraduate degree, your master's or simply taking a class on computer programming or music, Charlotte's colleges and universities can accommodate you. Several Ph.D. programs are also available, thanks to the growth of University of North Carolina at Charlotte. All 18 area institutions strengthen the economic, cultural and social life of the community and all are constantly updating and adding programs in relation to the current educational needs of the expanding population.

A cooperative agreement has been established that allows the individual institutions to share each others' resources, further enhancing educational opportunities. Charlotte's higher education system serves a dual role: it provides knowledge and training for vocational necessities and it emphasizes and promotes arts and culture. Several of the area's colleges and universities enjoy national visibility and recognition.

Here is an overview of the many educational opportunities that exist in the Charlotte area. If you have further questions, do not hesitate to call the schools' offices.

MBA Programs

Wake Forest University-Babcock Graduate School of Management
6805 Morrison Blvd. • 365-1717

Queens College
McColl School of Business
1900 Selwyn Ave. • 337-2313

UNC Charlotte
Belk College of Business
9201 University City Blvd. • 547-2569

Wingate University
Graduate Center
227 Matthews St., Matthews • 849-2409

Winthrop University
Oakland Ave., Rock Hill, S.C. • (803) 323-2211

Pfeiffer University at Charlotte
4701 Park Rd. • 521-9116

Four-Year Institutions

Belmont Abbey College
100 Belmont-Mt. Holly Rd., Belmont
• 825-6700, (800) 523-2355

Founded in 1876 by the Order of Saint Benedict, Belmont Abbey College provides an education rooted in the 1,500-year-old Benedictine tradition of value-based teaching.

Located just minutes from Charlotte on I-85 S., the college offers many opportunities for contemporary learning and professional development while students learn timeless values and whole-life skills. Numerous undergraduate and preprofessional programs prepare students for graduate school and a variety of careers. Belmont Abbey College also offers Post-Baccalaureate Certificate Programs.

Drawing students from 25 states and 15 foreign countries, Belmont Abbey College has a diverse population of approximately 1,000 students.

The Abbey Church on the campus of Belmont Abbey College was built in 1892.

Davidson College
Davidson, N.C. • 892-2000

Davidson College is a private, coeducational liberal arts college located 19 miles north of Charlotte. Founded by the Presbyterian Church in 1837, the college is intentionally small with an enrollment of approximately 1,600 men and women and is governed by an honor code that stresses honesty and integrity.

In 1997, *U.S. News & World Report* ranked Davidson as the 8th best liberal arts college in the nation. Admission is highly selective and students come from across the United States as well as many foreign countries. In the past decade, Davidson has had seven professors honored with silver and gold medals by the Council for the Advancement and Support of Education. Included in these honorees were one national professor of the year and three state professors of the year.

Davidson alumni are known for their community service, responsible leadership and passion for lifelong learning. Among the college's 17,000 alumni are many doctors, attorneys and ministers. Ten former or current members of the U.S. Congress and two of the last three governors of North Carolina are also Davidson alumni.

Johnson C. Smith University
100 Beatties Ford Rd. • 378-1000

Johnson C. Smith University is a premier institution of higher learning and one of the nation's oldest historically black colleges. The private, coeducational liberal arts institution

U.S. News & World Report recently ranked Davidson as the 8th best liberal arts college in the nation.

JOHNSON C. SMITH UNIVERSITY

**100 Beatties Ford Road
Charlotte, NC 28216
1-800-782-7303**

Founded in 1867 under the auspices of the Committee on Freedmen of the Presbyterian Church, USA, Johnson C. Smith University is a private, four-year liberal arts institution with a record of an innovative curriculum, outstanding faculty and quality education. JCSU offers academically progressive programs in 26 fields of study, which lead to a Bachelor of Science, Arts or Social Work degree. The University offers and takes pride in its nationally acclaimed *Centers of Excellence: Banking and Finance, Honors College, International Studies, Liberal Studies and Mathematics and Science.*

web address: www.jcsu.edu

**Dorothy Cowser Yancy, Ph. D.
President**

was founded in 1867 under the auspices of the Presbyterian Church. Its 100-acre inner-city campus houses an academic division comprised of three colleges which offer 27 areas of study leading to bachelor degrees. Admission is open to all qualified people regardless of race.

The University's Centers of Excellence include Banking and Finance, Mathematics and Science, International Studies, Liberal Studies and Honors College. Its reputation grows nationally as its accomplishments in these centers, Service Learning and the *Undergraduate Research Journal* reach larger audiences. A new dimension to its multifaceted outreach initiative is the Division of Lifelong Learning, which provides credit and noncredit courses for the nontraditional adult student.

In 1996, Johnson C. Smith was one of six U.S. colleges selected to receive the prestigious MacArthur Foundation's "genius" grant for innovative education. It has joined an elite group of universities named to the John Templeton Foundation's Honor Roll for Character Building Colleges.

Pfeiffer University at Charlotte
4701 Park Rd. • 521-9116

Pfeiffer's main campus is located in Misenheimer, but the Charlotte center college offers some special opportunities for those who attend its campus located in the SouthPark area. Upper division undergraduate courses permit students to continue their education by taking junior and senior courses in accounting, business administration, criminal justice and health care management. These evening programs are designed to suit the schedules of working adults, making it possible for a student with a two-year degree to complete their bachelor's degree by attending classes two nights a week for two years. Pfeiffer also offers master's degrees in business administration, organizational management, Christian education and a dual MBA/MHA in health administration.

Photo by Robert Thomason

Queens College offers both undergraduate and graduate coed programs.

Queens College
1900 Selwyn Ave. • 337-2200, (800) 849-0202

Queens College, located in historic Myers Park, is a private college with close ties to the Presbyterian Church. Since its founding in 1857, Queens has evolved into a diversified institution of higher education serving a variety of students. More than 1,600 degree-seeking men and women of all ages are enrolled in Queens' three colleges. The College of Arts and Sciences is a coed undergraduate program that emphasizes the traditional liberal arts. The Pauline Lewis Hayworth College is a program for working men and women who want to earn undergraduate degrees through evening or Saturday classes. The Graduate School offers mostly evening and Saturday courses leading to a master's degree in business or education and offers Charlotte's only Executive MBA program. The Hugh McColl, Jr. School of Business serves business students in all three units of the college.

Of all the elements that combine to make Queens' undergraduate program distinctive, two deserve special mention: the award-winning required core curriculum in the Liberal Arts, which emphasizes the interconnection of all knowledge and the International Experience

program, which guarantees every full-time student an opportunity for travel abroad at no extra cost. In addition, Queens offers internships, both professional and exploratory, that allow students to learn more about the world of work. Queens also provides lifelong learning opportunities through three non-degree programs.

The college enjoys unusually close ties with the Charlotte community. The Learning Society of Queens College sponsors a top-notch public speakers series and the Very International People Society promotes a global outlook. Belk Chapel at Queens is a popular place for weddings and the Charlotte Repertory Orchestra, the Charlotte Philharmonic Orchestra and the Oratorio Singers perform periodically in Dana Auditorium.

University of North Carolina at Charlotte
9201 University City Blvd. • 547-2000

In 1961, the 14-year-old Charlotte College moved from Uptown Charlotte to 270 acres of undeveloped farmland located on Highway 49, eight miles to the northeast of Uptown Charlotte. In 1964, the college was expanded to 910 acres and in 1965 renamed "The University of North Carolina at

Charlotte" and was accepted as a campus of the statewide system of universities. It is the fourth largest of the 16 institutions within the University of North Carolina system and has been listed in *Barron's Best Buys in College Education* and cited for quality and value in *U.S. News & World Report* and *Money* magazines.

Enrollment exceeds 16,000 students and includes about 2,600 graduate students. The student population includes residents from across North Carolina, the United States and many foreign countries. The student faculty ratio is 16 to 1.

UNC Charlotte is composed of six colleges — The College of Arts and Sciences and five professional colleges: Architecture, Business, Education, Engineering and Nursing. It offers programs leading to bachelor's, master's and Ph.D. degrees.

The University's first emphasis is on teaching, followed by research and public service. Its contract research amounts to more than $14 million a year. Its service outreach extends into each of the 14 counties in the surrounding metropolitan region.

The University is committed to serving its community, state and nation through a variety of outreach programs, including the Urban Institute, Cameron Center for

Wingate University offers a student to faculty ratio of 13:1.

Applied Research, Ben Craig Center (a business incubator), Center for International Studies, Office of Continuing Education and Extension, Center for Engineering Research & Industrial Development and University Research Park, the sixth largest of its kind in the nation.

UNC Charlotte visitors can tour outstanding botanical gardens, including the Van Landingham Glen, a collection of hybrid and native rhododendrons and wild flowers; the Susie Harwood Gardens with an oriental motif that features ornamental plants from around the world; and the McMillan Greenhouse, which features collections of orchids, cactuses and carnivorous plants and a simulated tropical rain forest.

The campus features modern architecture surrounded by beautifully landscaped walks and trails and includes a panoramic view of Northeast Charlotte from the 10th floor of Dalton Towers, the University's 550,000-volume regional library. It also offers an outdoor sculpture garden and several art galleries and theaters.

Wingate University Graduate Center
227 Matthews St., Matthews • 849-2132

Wingate was founded in 1896 as an independent institution. It is coeducational and

UNCC's Atkins Library holds 750,000 volumes.

offers bachelors' degrees in many majors and graduate degrees in business and education. Wingate only serves 1,400 students, offering a student to faculty ratio of 13:1. Wingate's pioneering international study/travel program has made it possible for thousands of students to travel and study abroad. Another outstanding program, the United Collegiate Assistance Network, has been recognized nationally, regionally and statewide for its student volunteer record. Although Wingate's main campus is located 45 minutes from Uptown Charlotte, Wingate's Matthews Center is located in the Depot Center on Matthews Street, directly behind the Matthews Town Hall.

Winthrop University
Oakland Ave., Rock Hill, S.C. • (803) 323-2211

Winthrop was founded in 1886 as a women's college. It became coeducational in 1974 and is now a national-caliber, comprehensive teaching university. Its 4,000

Winthrop University, a national-caliber teaching institution, is located in Rock Hill.

undergraduate and 1,000 graduate students may choose among 65 undergraduate and 44 graduate programs of study in the Arts and Sciences, Business Administration, Education and Visual and Performing Arts. The University also offers the New Start Program for undergraduate students age 25 and older, as well as nationally accredited Executive MBA and traditional MBA programs.

Two-Year Institutions

Central Piedmont Community College
1201 Elizabeth Ave. at Kings Dr. • 330-6719

In 1963, Mecklenburg College and the Central Industrial Education Center were merged to establish Central Piedmont Community College. At first, the College offered about a dozen vocational programs and some liberal arts courses to less than 2,000 students. Today CPCC offers more than 1,500 courses to almost 60,000 students annually and is the largest college in North Carolina's community college system. Currently, students enroll on the Central Campus located near Uptown Charlotte; North Campus, Huntersville; South Campus, Matthews; City View, Alleghany Street; and at more than 200 other sites around the county.

In order to meet the area's expanding demand for education and training, CPCC is developing a multi-campus system. Within a few years, five new campuses will be in operation near the new outer beltway around Charlotte. These campuses are being developed in conjunction with citizen, government and business organizations near their sites.

CPCC intends to become the national leader in workforce development and is providing research and education training models that are being used nationally. Locally CPCC provides custom-designed, job-specific training for businesses and industries in addition to a comprehensive program for small business owners. Training is offered at the CPCC Corporate Training Center at Lakepointe, at other college facilities, in plant and on-line.

Photo by Greg Finley

CPCC is the largest community college in N.C.

Students may pursue college transfer and career programs in business, health, community service and technical areas. Many take classes for personal enrichment, professional advancement or to upgrade their job skills.

An open-door institution, CPCC provides academic assessment and counseling, program advisement and financial aid and career guidance, in addition to a variety of student clubs and organizations. Adult High School and GED preparation programs are available and CPCC's Adult Basic Literacy Education (ABLE) program is a national model. CPCC has been recognized as one of the five best community colleges in the country for teaching excellence.

Gaston College
N.C. 321, Dallas • 922-6200

This community college enrolls approximately 4,000 students each quarter in curriculum programs and averages 16,000 students annually in its Corporate and Community Education programs. Students may pursue associate degrees in the arts, sciences, fine arts and applied science.

York Technical College
Rock Hill, S.C. • (803) 327-8008

Just south of Charlotte in Rock Hill, York Technical College offers technical training in business, health, computers, industrial and engineering technologies, in addition to associate degrees in the arts and sciences.

Business Colleges

American Business & Fashion Institute
1515 Mockingbird Ln. • 523-3738

Founded in 1973, this college offers training in fashion merchandising, design and travel, as well as medical and general office skills. Opportunities and benefits include small classes, internships, financial and employment assistance. Courses of study are available days or evenings and take 9 to 18 months to complete. The college, located in Southeast Charlotte near SouthPark, boasts an excellent graduation and placement rate. It is also approved for Veteran's benefits and vocational rehabilitation.

Brookstone College of Business
8307 University Executive Park Dr. • 547-8600

This business college specializes in high-tech secretarial training, computerized accounting, medical health, office technology and customer service specialist with hands-on experience. Financial aid and job placement assistance are available.

King's College
332 Lamar Ave. • 372-0266

King's College was founded in 1901, making it the oldest business college in the Carolinas. King's offers a full-time job placement service with contacts throughout the business and professional community. Courses of study include administrative assistant, accounting, computer programming, computer specialist, graphic design, legal secretary, medical-office assistant, paralegal and travel and hospitality. Some programs offer on-the-job training.

Charlotte's
hospitals offer the
latest in medical
techniques as well
as some of the
most qualified
specialists.

Healthcare

Charlotte's hospitals offer the latest in medical techniques as well as some of the most qualified specialists. With health care costs below the national average, medical services are one of the best bargains in the Charlotte area.

Medical facilities are expanding at a rapid rate throughout the city and the region, so wherever you live in the area, you probably won't have to drive too far to find the services you need. The city is nationally and internationally known as a center for cardiac care and research. Hospitals in two systems, the Carolinas HealthCare System and Presbyterian Healthcare, and others perform open-heart surgery as well as other highly specialized medical services. You will not have to leave Charlotte to find the best medical care available.

Hospitals

General Hospitals

Carolinas Medical Center
1000 Blythe Blvd. • 355-2000

Carolinas Medical Center, opened in 1940, is the flagship facility of the Carolinas HealthCare System, formerly the Hospital Authority. With 777 beds, the Medical Center is the second largest hospital in North Carolina. In addition, the Medical Center also treats a significant number of patients from South Carolina and all over the Southeastern United States.

There are seven specialized intensive care units, including the Neonatal Intensive Care Nursery. The Medical Center is the regional referral center for high-risk pregnancies. MedCenter Air serves as the area's only hospital-based air ambulance service with helicopters and fixed-wing aircraft.

A Level I Trauma Center and one of only five Academic Medical Center Teaching Hospitals in North Carolina, Carolinas Medical Center offers 11 medical and dental residency programs and serves as an off-campus teaching facility of the University of North Carolina School of Medicine.

The Carolinas Heart Institute is the major center for heart transplantation in the two Carolinas. It is the only facility in the two states where pediatric and infant transplants are being performed. More than 11,000 coronary bypass operations have been performed at the Heart Institute, where skilled specialists have pioneered laser techniques to correct heart rhythm problems. A liver and pancreas transplantation program began in 1994.

The 20,000-square-foot Blumenthal Cancer Center has been designated a Teaching Hospital Cancer Program, the second highest designation available from American College of Surgeons Commission on Cancer. The Center also has an agreement with the UNC-Lineberger Comprehensive Cancer Center to develop and strengthen clinical, educational and research collaboration between the two institutions.

The Children's Hospital opened in 1992 at Carolinas Medical Center. Also offered are the Carolinas Epilepsy Center, Carolinas Diabetes Center, the Hemby Pediatric Trauma Institute and the James G. Cannon Research Center. The area's only Multiple Sclerosis Clinic offers multidisciplinary services to patients at a single location.

The Carolinas HealthCare System also includes University Hospital, Mercy Hospital, the Charlotte Institute of Rehabilitation and Carolinas Medical Center's Behavioral

Photo by Robert Thomason

Mercy Hospital offers a full array of acute care services to Charlotte residents with 336 beds and more than 700 physicians on staff.

Health Center, all of which are listed separately in this section. Other facilities are: Urgent Care Center at the Arboretum, The Women's Center, Charlotte Continence Center, Family Practice Center, Neighborhood Health Center, Sardis Nursing Home, Huntersville Oaks Nursing Home, Brookwood Retirement Community, CMHA School of Nursing and The Dilworth Inn, a lodging facility for pre-admission patients and families of patients.

Mercy Hospital
2001 Vail Ave. • 379-5000

Mercy Hospital opened in 1906 and is under the umbrella of Carolinas HealthCare System. It offers a full array of acute care services to Charlotte residents with 336 beds and more than 700 physicians. Its Heart Center provides cardiac surgery and procedures and it offers a 29-bed rehabilitation center.

Mercy diversified geographically in 1982 by opening an urgent care center in heavily populated southeast Mecklenburg County, followed by the 97-bed Mercy Hospital South (mentioned in this section) in 1987. The Mercy Maternity Center opened adjacent to Mercy Hospital South the same year.

Mercy Medical Group operations began in 1992 as a network of primary care physicians located throughout the Charlotte Metropolitan area, including Mecklenburg and Gaston counties, North Carolina, and York County, South Carolina. Mercy operates the Mercy Rehabilitation Center, which specializes in comprehensive outpatient rehabilitation services.

Other services offered by Mercy include medical detoxification through a program called Horizons, in-home assistance through Mercy Home Care and a nursing school.

Mercy Hospital South
10628 Park Rd., N.C. 51 and Park Rd. Ext. 543-2000

Mercy Hospital South is a 97-bed general medical and surgical facility designed to serve the population of southeast Mecklenburg County with quality health care, including single-room maternity care. Mercy South's location and accessibility make it the community hospital for residents of South Mecklenburg and northern South Carolina. It is owned and operated by Carolinas HealthCare System.

If you're new to Charlotte, we'd like to check up on you.

Call our free physician referral service at **384-CARE** to find a physician for you or your family. You'll receive a free first aid kit just for calling.

Presbyterian Healthcare

NOVANT HEALTH

Shaping
the future
of Caring

Photo by Robert Thomason

The Presbyterian Hospital Matthews provides residents with a full range of modern medical services.

Presbyterian Hospital
200 Hawthorne Ln. • 384-4000

Established in 1903, Presbyterian Hospital is a 593-bed regional referral, tertiary care medical center serving Charlotte-Mecklenburg and surrounding counties. It offers a wide range of specialized diagnostic and therapeutic services.

The Center for Women's Health is an area leader in services for women. More than 5,000 babies are born annually in the Family Maternity Center. It is supported by the full-service Hemby Intensive Care Nursery and other unique services such as Nursing Mothers' Place lactation consulting service.

The 72-bed Presbyterian Hemby Children's Hospital, which opened in 1993, is dedicated to family-centered care and child-right services to assure that all children's needs are met from the time of admission until they go home. The Pediatric Intensive Care Unit is supported by full-time pediatric physicians.

The Belk Heart Center offers up-to-date care including heart catheterization and open-heart surgery. The Cancer Center, the first in North Carolina designated as a Community Hospital Comprehensive Cancer Center by the American College of Surgeons' Commission on Cancer, is home for the Harris Hospice Unit, the only such unit in the area. The Center is a North Carolina affiliate of the Duke Comprehensive Cancer Center.

The Center for Psychiatry offers programs for adults, adolescents and children, plus the Center for Mind-Body Health. The 24-hour Emergency Department operates the Chest Pain Emergency Room program. Other centers of excellence include surgery, medicine and neurosciences.

The hospital also offers a full range of in-home services, including home care and the Lifeline personal emergency response system. The School of Nursing is the largest hospital-based program in the Carolinas. Free information and physician referral services are provided by Presbyterian CareConnection, 384-4111.

Presbyterian is the flagship hospital of Presbyterian Healthcare, an integrated health care system. It has four hospitals, outpatient facilities and a growing physician hospital organization with more than 90 primary care physicians and some 200 affiliated specialists.

Presbyterian Hospital Matthews
1500 Matthews Township Pkwy., Matthews • 384-6500

Opened in August 1994, Presbyterian Hospital Matthews was designed to be both efficient and user friendly for patients, their families and visitors. Located in Matthews, the hospital offers a full range of diagnostic and treatment services, including emergency, surgery (inpatient and outpatient) and maternity. All but the most specialized kinds of surgery are performed at Presbyterian Hospital Matthews.

Features include large maternity rooms with Jacuzzi tubs, TVs, VCRs, refrigerators, balconies and a daybed for dad to spend the night. All rooms in the hospital have similar features, including a daybed. With physician approval, even the critical care rooms encourage overnight visitors.

The 24-hour Emergency Department has separate entrances for drive-in and ambulance patients. Like the central facility, the hospital's Emergency Department houses a Chest Pain ER for early diagnosis and treatment.

Meals at the hospital are delivered to each patient at the time he or she specifies. The two inpatient wings each have a family medical resource center, an outside balcony and a large family kitchen.

The hospital, which is part of Presbyterian Healthcare, serves the Matthews-Mint Hill-Pineville communities as well as other areas of southern and eastern Mecklenburg and western Union counties.

University Hospital
U.S. 29 at W. T. Harris Blvd. • 548-6000

University Hospital opened in 1985 to serve the rapidly growing northern Mecklenburg, southern Iredell and western Cabarrus counties. The 130 private rooms are configured in the "snowflake" design, with every patient just a few feet from a nurses'

station, yet isolated from much of the traffic in the traditional corridor arrangement.

Now a part of the Carolinas HealthCare System, University Hospital offers a wide range of health care services. The Sleep Center is the first in the Charlotte area to be fully accredited by the American Sleep Disorders Association. Physicians use sophisticated instrumentation to identify sleep problems and causes. Obstetric and Gynecology services offer five labor and delivery suites specifically designed to create a "home birthing" environment. There is also an eight-bed intensive coronary care unit and six-bed telemetry unit for patients with more serious medical needs requiring closer supervision.

The Emergency Department is staffed 24 hours a day and is equipped to handle minor and life-threatening emergencies. University Hospital also offers rehabilitation, diagnostic radiology and mammography services along with a Respiratory Diagnostic Center and full-service laboratory for inpatients and outpatients. Adjoining the hospital is University Medical Park, a growing home for physician groups and satellite offices.

Photo by Robert Thomason

University Hospital has a Sleep Center, which is the first in the Charlotte area to be fully accredited by the American Sleep Disorders Association.

Specialty Hospitals and Centers

Behavioral Health Center/ Amethyst
1715 Sharon Rd. W. • 554-8373

Amethyst is a 94-bed private, nonprofit facility that provides various levels of care, including outpatient, for the treatment of chemical dependency for adolescents (beginning at age 12) and adults. Amethyst also offers a wide range of family treatment services, including a program called For Kids Only designed for children ages 6 to 12 who have a parent or relative in treatment or who have been affected by chemical dependency. Other services include a Cocaine Track, Women's Track, Relapse/Relapse Prevention Program, Referral, DWI assessments, intervention, education classes and professional workshops and seminars. This facility is owned and operated by the Carolinas HeathCare System.

Behavioral Health Center/Pineville
9600 Pineville-Matthews Rd. • 541-6676

Behavioral Health Center/Pineville is a 70-bed psychiatric and chemical dependency facility owned and operated by the Carolinas HealthCare System. It offers inpatient and partial hospitalization serving the psychiatric/chemical dependency/dual diagnosis needs of adults and children, including a long-term residency unit for adolescents. Each program is housed in separate units that include semiprivate rooms. The hospital also provides a gym, swimming pool, outdoor recreation and an in-house school. It offers a free, on-site evaluation and referral service for psychiatric/chemical dependency problems, 24 hours a day, seven days a week, as well as free educational lectures and/or training for area groups.

Behavioral Health Center/ Willows at Amethyst
1715 Sharon Rd. W. • 571-6100

This Carolinas HealthCare System facility specializes in the care and treatment of children and teens troubled by emotional and psychiatric disorders and substance abuse. An Extended Treatment Inpatient Program for adolescents serves as many as 40 patients around the clock, 24 hour a day and seven days a week. Through its Partial Hospitalization program, the Center provides day treatment that includes therapy and classes. Willows at Amethyst has 80 beds, 40 for inpatients and 40 for outpatients.

Carolinas HealthCare System's Behavioral Health Center
501 Billingsley Rd. • 358-2700

The Behavioral Health Center is the psychiatric medicine and behavioral sciences campus for the Carolinas HealthCare System. It has 66 beds where inpatients receive therapy needed to help them recover from emotional and mental illnesses. Patients with emergency psychiatric needs have care available to them 24 hours a day from Emergency Services.

Children, adolescents and adults may receive extensive outpatient therapy, which includes individual and group psychotherapy, comprehensive psychological testing and mental health evaluation and referral services.

Charlotte Institute of Rehabilitation
1100 Blythe Blvd. • 355-4300

The Charlotte Institute of Rehabilitation, a 143-bed facility in the Carolinas HealthCare System, is one of the premier facilities of its kind in the country. Focusing on patients suffering from stroke, brain injury and spinal cord trauma, the Charlotte Institute of Rehabilitation helps patients return to as normal a lifestyle as possible after illness or injury. Its specialists in rehabilitative medicine tailor programs to the physical and emotional needs of individual patients. Pediatric and adolescent patients are

Photo by Robert Thomason

Carolinas Medical Center is the second largest hospital in North Carolina.

treated in a special unit with separate health care providers to meet their special needs. Rehab Advantage is a work hardening and industrial medicine satellite facility of the Institute. It is equipped with state-of-the-art equipment and overseen by physiatrists, physicians skilled in physical rehabilitation.

Charter Pines Behavioral Health System
3621 Randolph Rd.
• 365-5368, (800) 332-7463

Founded in 1985, Charter Pines is a 60-bed psychiatric hospital offering both inpatient and partial hospitalization services for adolescents and adults. Outpatient treatment for chemical dependency is available and the hospital offers a free, confidential, no obligation consultation.

Presbyterian-Orthopaedic Hospital
1901 Randolph Rd. • 375-6790

Presbyterian-Orthopaedic Hospital is a 166-bed regional specialty hospital dedicated to the diagnosis and treatment of injuries and diseases of the bones and joints. The facility offers inpatient and ambulatory surgery including total joint, major back and spine, microvascular hand, knee and shoulder surgeries. It also focuses on arthritis and provides other specialized care and procedures, such as pain management, CT diagnostics, intensive care and laboratory services. The Hospital's Pain Therapy Center of Charlotte offers programs for chronic pain rehabilitation, chronic headache, acute pain and back pain.

In addition, Presbyterian-Orthopaedic offers freestanding rehabilitative services, including a work evaluation center, a sports-medicine center, a back school, evening physical therapy sessions, pediatric physical therapy, and occupational and speech therapy. The hospital is part of Presbyterian Healthcare.

Presbyterian Specialty Hospital
1600 E. 3rd St. • 384-6000

Presbyterian Specialty Hospital is a private, 15-bed facility that specializes in outpatient and inpatient eye, ear, nose and throat surgery. The hospital, which is part of Presbyterian Healthcare, also offers oral, plastic and cosmetic surgery. Specialty Hospital is also the Charlotte home of the mobile lithotripter, operated by the Stone Institute of the Carolinas, which dissolves kidney stones without surgery and the Presbyterian Sleep Medicine Center (located in the Metroview Building).

Presbyterian Wesley Care Center
3700 Shamrock Dr. • 384-8300

Presbyterian Wesley Care Center, which is part of Presbyterian Healthcare, has served older adults in the Charlotte area since 1948. Services include: physical, speech, occupational and recreation therapies five to six times a week; treatment with intravenous therapies, tracheotomies, wound care, total parenteral nutrition and hospice care; and an Alzheimer's Disease program for those experiencing memory impairment.

The Rehab Center
2610 E. 7th St. • 375-8900, (800) 968-6738

The Rehab Center is a regional outpatient multidisciplinary comprehensive rehabilitation facility, specializing in work-related injuries. Also offered are independent medical, psychological, neuropsychological, physical therapy and vocational evaluations. The Rehab Center employs a team of specialists, including physicians, psychologists, physical therapists, a neuropsychologist and a vocational specialist. The Center offers acute treatment, along with work site analyses, work capacity evaluations, water therapy, hand therapy and work hardening.

Medical Care

Charlotte provides a variety of physicians and specialists located throughout the city, and as the city grows, so does its medical community, both in terms of services offered and in geographic locations. Doctors' offices and clinics are no longer clustered near hospitals, and they now offer satellite offices and new clinics throughout the Charlotte area. So unless you're looking for someone in a highly specialized field, you will probably be able to find a doctor you like located near your home or office.

If you are visiting or if you need medical help and haven't yet found a physician, there are numerous urgent-care centers around town that provide minor medical emergency services and walk-in health care. You don't need an appointment and most have extended hours.

As with anything else, word-of-mouth is usually a good way to find a physician. Your neighbors, friends or co-workers can give you advice on the doctor's personality, how well the staff treats you or how long you can expect to wait. Charlotte also has formal services that can refer you to physicians and other health care professionals. These referral services can be a great help if you are new to the area, since the abundance and variety of medical care available can be overwhelming.

Referral Services

Care Connection
Presbyterian Hospital • 384-4111

This service, open Monday through Friday, 9 AM to 4 PM, will give physician referrals, not only by specialty, but by geographic location and type of insurance accepted. Care Connection will even help you make an appointment. You can also call for information about the hospital's programs and your other health care needs. For maternity information, call 384-4949.

Mecklenburg County Medical Society
1112 Harding Place, Ste. 200 • 376-3688

The Society gives physician referrals for family practitioners, internists or specialists by phone, 9 AM to 1 PM, Monday through Friday. It will usually give you three names.

Tips for Every Day Living
• 336-4632

This is a service of the Mecklenburg County Area Mental Health, Developmental Disabilities and Substance Abuse Authority. TIPS features mental health-related information.

Messages on a variety of topics help you keep physically and mentally healthy, recognize early signs of illness and develop skills to cope with everyday living. For directory highlights, dial the main number, then dial 333-111; for an updated list of messages, dial 333-112.

United Way Hotline (First Call for Help)
Mecklenburg County • 377-1100
Cabarrus County • 788-1156
Union County • 289-8102

A United Way service, the hotline is open from 8 AM until 12 midnight seven days a week and is staffed by referral specialists who can answer questions or provide referrals on anything regarding human services in Mecklenburg, Cabarrus or Union counties.

Special Services

If you or your child needs special assistance for physical, emotional or mental handicaps or disabilities, Charlotte offers many resources. Here are a few:

Alexander Children's Center
6220 Thermal Rd. • 366-8712

This nonprofit agency, founded in 1888, offers several programs for children with special needs. The Residential Treatment Center provides intensive treatment for emotionally troubled children ages 6 through 12. The Markle Group Home offers family-like living for graduates of the treatment center who continue to need a stable environment in which to live. The Crisis Stabilization and Assessment Unit provides emergency care for children who have to be removed from their homes because of abuse and neglect. Therapeutic after-school care and summer camps are also offered. The Children Development Center is a AA-licensed day program for children, ages 3 months through 5 years, some of whom have special needs. The Center depends on funds from individuals, churches, businesses and foundations in the Charlotte community to operate its programs. It also provides many volunteer opportunities.

Photo Courtesy of Alexander Children's Center

Alexander Children's Center offers several programs for children with special needs.

Catholic Social Services
116 E. 1st St. • 370-6155

This organization offers many services, including individual, family, adoption, marital and substance abuse counseling and pregnancy support. Fees are based on a sliding scale.

Charlotte Speech and Hearing Center
300 S. Caldwell St. • 376-1342

Screening, evaluations, consultation, education and therapy are all a part of the total service available to the community at this nonprofit center. Funded in part by United Way, the Center is accredited by the Professional Services Board of the American Speech-Language-Hearing Association and clinical staff are licensed by the state. Help is offered to anyone who has or may have a speech, language or hearing problem. Some services are free or based on a sliding-fee scale, while fees are levied for services such as speech improvement and mobile hearing tests provided on-site to industries. (These fees help support the center's nonprofit programs.) The Center operates a satellite service in Union County.

Child and Family Development, Inc.
309 S. Laurel Ave. • 332-4834
7006 Shannon Willow Rd. • 541-9080

Child & Family Development, Inc., is a private evaluation/treatment center for children, from birth through high school. It is staffed by professional therapists — psychologists, learning disability specialists, occupational therapists, physical therapists, speech and language therapists and clinical social workers — who are committed to the growth and development of children with both development and rehabilitation needs. The Center offers clinics in neurology and psychiatry to monitor the medication needs of children who need treatment. Areas of specialty include: ADHD, learning disabilities, cerebral palsy, motor handicaps, speech and language disorders and emotional/social difficulties.

Community Health Services
1401 E. 7th St. • 375-0172

CHS is a multiservice United Way agency that offers affordable (sometimes free) health screenings and educational programs. It has five program components: Diabetes Services (in Union County), Prescription Assistance, Occupational Health, Senior Health Services and Parkinson's Disease Support Groups. The Center also offers immunizations for hepatitis B, MMR and tetanus; TB tests; pneumonia vaccine for those 65 and older; and flu vaccine in the fall for anyone, ages 18 and above.

The Family Center, Inc.
1616 Cleveland Ave. • 376-7180

The Family Center provides a variety of services to abused children and their families.

Fletcher School
4921 Randolph Rd. • 365-4658

This special school for learning-disabled children in grades 2 through 8 provides a

structured, individualized academic program that prepares them to return to the regular classroom environment whenever possible. The school has been approved by the North Carolina Department of Public Instruction and the Governor's Office of Nonpublic Instruction.

Hospice at Charlotte
1420 East Seventh Street • 375-0100

Established in 1978, Hospice at Charlotte provides health care to patients experiencing life-threatening illnesses for which there is no cure and provides support to the patient's family during the course of the illness. Staffed by approximately 125 professionals and 300 direct service volunteers, Hospice at Charlotte's Board of Directors is comprised of community volunteers who direct the policies of the organization while physicians from the community serve as Volunteer Medical Directors. Care consists of such things as medical direction, nursing services, social work services, volunteer support, in-home aides, bereavement support services, spiritual care services and art therapy.

McLeod Addictive Disease Center
145 Remount Rd. • 332-9001

This community agency provides counseling and support groups for chemically dependent young people and adults and their families. Services are rendered through the Treatment Center, Methadone Medical Services, Outpatient Clinic, Adolescent Outpatient Services and Treatment Alternatives to Street Crimes.

Mecklenburg County Center For Human Development
3500 Ellington St. • 336-7100

This county agency offers a number of services, including a developmental day preschool for mildly and moderately mentally retarded children, a parent-infant training program and a developmental evaluation program to determine whether an individual of any age has a disability or delayed development. Fees are based on the client's ability to pay.

Mecklenburg County Health Department

2845 Beatties Ford Rd.
Appointments • 336-6500
Health Promotion Program & Home Health
249 Billingsley Rd.
• 336-6028, 336-4650

The department's function is to promote good health and to prevent and control disease by providing health education; maternity, family planning and well-child clinics; home and school health services; assistance to business and industry in developing employee health and safety programs; nursing services for new mothers and their infants; environmental services; and communicable and chronic disease control.

Nevins Center, Inc.

3523 Nevins Rd. • 596-1372
3127 Kalynne St. • 393-5910

This Adult Developmental Activity Program provides vocational training, supported employment and training in a sheltered workshop for mentally retarded adults.

Perceptual Motor Studies

UNC-Charlotte • 547-4695

Dr. John Healey, a member of the UNC-Charlotte faculty, coordinates this unique program for children up to the age of 18 who are experiencing difficulty in their perceptual motor development. Each child undergoes screening before acceptance into the program and is paired with two college students who, under the direction of the coordinator, assist him/her in various activities.

Preschool Program For The Hearing Impaired

North Carolina School for the Deaf
1000 E. Morehead St. • 536-9296

This total child development program provides comprehensive speech and language

development for hearing-impaired children up to 5 years old in Mecklenburg and surrounding counties. Instruction is given on-site and in the home.

Preschool Satellite Program for Hearing Impaired

2831 N. Sharon Amity Rd. • 536-9296

The Preschool is a part of the N.C. School for the Deaf at Morganton. The facility offers a 4-hr. per day preschool, serving as many as 25 preschoolers through 6 years old. The facility, which offers home-based and center-based services, has two total communications classrooms, one which employs signing and an audio-oral classroom, which uses gestures called cued speech.

St. Marks, Inc.

601 N. Graham St. • 333-7107

This center, established in 1973, offers programs and services to approximately 230 Mecklenburg County residents who have severe or profound mental retardation or are at high risk for a severe disability. Preschool, special education and summer school programs for children and sheltered workshops, developmental activities programs and supported employment programs for adults are offered. In 1993, The Circle School was developed to assist in mainstreaming special needs children with other children.

United Cerebral Palsy Developmental Center

716 Marsh Rd. • 522-9912

A branch of United Cerebral Palsy of North Carolina, this center provides education and therapy for children ages 1 through 5 with cerebral palsy or similar disorders, as well as training for parents in Mecklenburg and surrounding counties. Tuition is based on a sliding-fee scale.

The Queen City has one daily newspaper, nine weekly newspapers, 27 radio stations, seven commercial TV stations, three PBS TV stations and various cable TV stations.

Media

Charlotte's media is first class. The Queen City has one daily newspaper, nine weekly newspapers, 27 radio stations, seven commercial TV stations, three PBS TV stations and various cable TV stations. A wide variety of information and programming is available in the Charlotte market, including Traffic Patrol reports broadcast daily on local radio and TV stations. In addition to Charlotte's local media, there is also a national news program, The NBC News Channel, produced and broadcast from Charlotte.

Daily Newspapers

The Charlotte Observer
600 S. Tryon St. • 358-5000
Founded in 1886, *The Charlotte Observer* is the oldest daily newspaper in the county. Part of the Knight-Ridder chain, its paid circulation is 325,000 on Sundays and 250,000 weekly. The paper covers the central portion of bothe Carolinas with seven regional local sections that cover neighborhoods and community events.

The Gaston Gazette
2500 E. Franklin Blvd. • 825-5158
A community-oriented newspaper currently owned by Freedom Communications, *The Gaston Gazette* is a daily publication with a circulation of about 43,000. Created as a weekly paper in 1880, it covers local, regional and national news as well as offering sections on arts, entertainment, food, travel, home and family.

Other Publications

The Business Journal
128 S. Tryon St., Ste. 2250 • 347-2340
Part of the American City Business Journals, *The Business Journal* arrived in Charlotte in 1986. Publisher Mark Ethridge's staff provides the city with the latest business news and interesting in-depth articles on a weekly basis. You'll also find regular columns by local business people on their area of expertise.

Business North Carolina
5435 Seventy Seven Center Dr. • 523-6987
This monthly magazine's regular columns give an excellent overview of the state's business trends. It also features special reports on topics such as the best cities to do business in, the top private companies and the largest employers. Circulation is 28,000.

Business Properties
528 East Blvd. • 373-0051
The latest trends in commercial real estate and current market conditions in Charlotte and the surrounding areas are covered by this quarterly magazine. With a circulation of 8,000, *Business Properties* is a must for those in the Charlotte real estate market.

Carolina Bride
1819 Lyndhurst Ave. • 334-0847
Since 1991, brides-to-be have used this quarterly publication as a resource.

Charlotte's Best Magazine
4508 E. Independence Blvd. • 537-0593
This monthly magazine offers a variety of information on entertainment, dining, night life, shopping, fashion, health and medicine and kidstuff. The annual *Best of Charlotte*

Awards issue compiles readers' responses and the editors' picks to provide a comprehensive listing of Charlotte's best. Circulation is approximately 100,000.

Charlotte Magazine
120 Greenwich Rd. • 366-5000

A colorful, upscale city magazine, this publication focuses on local business, entertainment, fine living, social gatherings, fashion and the arts. The magazine has an extensive restaurant guide and covers recent medical breakthroughs and local sporting events.

The Charlotte Post
1531 Camden Rd. • 376-0496

Covering the black community since 1918, *The Charlotte Post* is published every Thursday. It has a solid reputation in the community and reaches about 12,500 readers.

CITI
1919 South Blvd. • 372-0367

The highlights of Charlotte's good life are presented in this glossy four-color bimonthly publication. Beautiful upscale homes and gardens are featured regularly. *CITI* is distributed by Realtors to high-end home buyers and to major corporations in recruitment packages. It is also available at selected newsstands and by paid subscription.

Creative Loafing
6112 Old Pineville Rd. • 522-8334

Creative Loafing is a weekly publication with a circulation of 54,000. Available every Wednesday, it is free and distributed through boxes located throughout the area. Although primarily an entertainment newspaper, it carries on the tradition of alternative papers with a different perspective on politics, business and the arts scene. *Creative Loafing's* Personals are always a hot topic of conversation.

Fifty Plus
• (800) 367-5075

With a circulation of 183,000 in the Carolinas, *Fifty Plus* is a monthly news magazine filled with features written for a mature, upscale audience. See also the Retirement chapter for a listing of this publication as well as others specifically targeted for the senior living, assisted living and retirement communities.

First Impressions Newcomer's Guide
5200 Park Rd. • 522-6001

Published annually by Impressions Marketing Group Inc., this free publication provides the inside scoop to newcomers in the Charlotte area. Information covers the city's history, business climate, real

The Charlotte Observer is a vital and respected voice of the community.

estate, apartment living, health care, entertainment, attractions and much more. The publication is distributed through area Realtors, banks, savings and loans, apartments and major employers.

Lake Norman Magazine
147 N. Harbor Dr.
Davidson • 892-7936

A tabloid-size monthly owned by *The Charlotte Observer*, this publication covers all the action on the lake from regattas to real estate. The magazine is distributed free in the four-county area surrounding Lake Norman.

The Leader Newspaper
801 E. Trade St. • 331-4842

A user-friendly weekly tabloid with a circulation of almost 38,000, *The Leader* carries local stories by staff members as well as syndicated features. The society section is well-read by locals.

North Mecklenburg Gazette
147 E. Center Ave. • 892-8809

This weekly newspaper with a circulation of 3,000 reports on the happenings in the three North Mecklenburg towns of Davidson, Cornelius and Huntersville. The classified section runs in conjunction with additional newspapers and has a total circulation of 22,000.

The Mecklenburg Times
400 E. Trade St. • 377-6221

This court and business publication comes out on Tuesdays and Fridays. *The Mecklenburg Times* gives public information on topics such as real estate transactions, residential and commercial building permits, new corporations, foreclosure notices, bankruptcies and tax liens. It also features news stories on business and career issues.

Our Kids & Teens Magazine
1100 S. Mint St. • 344-1980

Founded in 1987, this complimentary parent- and child-oriented publication offers all sorts of information essential for parents raising children. It features articles written for and by parents as well as a calendar of events containing items of interest for all members of the family. A monthly newsprint publication, *Our Kids and Teens* has a circulation of about 45,000 and can be found in supermarkets throughout the area.

The Record
809 West John St. • 849-2188

This weekly paper, published on Wednesdays, covers all the local happenings of Matthews such as town council meetings, sports and human interest stories. The newspaper is independently owned and has a circulation of about 13,000.

Southern Lifestyles
9925 Hannon Rd. • 545-1184

Printed on newsprint, *Southern Lifestyles* is mailed once a month to subscribers. In addition to great local fare, the magazine offers upbeat editorials from Andy Rooney and Paul Harvey as well as other syndicated columns such as the Frugal Gourmet.

Trip Magazine
800 Briar Creek Rd., Ste. DD518 • 376-7800

This complimentary monthly playbill-sized magazine is found in hotels, USAirways ticket counters and other visitor spots. *Trip* offers visitors tips on dining, shopping, attractions and entertainment in the area. The maps are helpful in finding your way around Charlotte and getting to local attractions.

University City Magazine
8401 University Executive Park • 549-4366

Due to the growth in the University area, *The Charlotte Observer* started this tabloid-size monthly to report on the area's happenings. It's distributed free to University residents through local businesses. The publication features information on the area's growth as well as human interest stories.

Radio

See our chart for a brief overview of call letters, dial numbers, AM or FM frequency and a short description of the station's programming. Given the nature of the industry, however, a station's format may go from hard rock to country western overnight, so don't be surprised if the music doesn't jibe with what's printed here.

Television

WAXN-64, Ind.
910 Fairview Street, Kannapolis • 933-9529

WAXN features movies, sitcom reruns, talk shows and some science fiction programming. Weekends offer lots of kids programs including a computer show for kids and an outdoor adventure show. Founded in 1996, this station is owned by Kannapolis Television Corporation.

WBTV-3, CBS
One Julian Price Pl. • 374-3500

Started in 1949, WBTV is the oldest TV station in the Carolinas and is one of the oldest CBS affiliates in the country. A sister company, Jefferson Pilot Sports, owns the rights to ACC football and co-owns the basketball rights, so WBTV is the station to turn to for ACC coverage. WBTV is the official television station of the Dom Capers Show for the Carolina Panthers.

WCCB-18, FOX
One Television Pl. • 372-1800

WCCB features the Fox network's hit programs. Other times, the 24-hour station shows movies, off-network reruns, talk shows, kids programming and some of the Carolina Panthers regular season football games. WCCB is privately owned by local, family-held Bahakel Communications Ltd.

WCNC-NBC 6
1001 Wood Ridge Center Dr. • 329-3636

Ranked in the top five by Nielsen Ratings, this station broadcasts all regularly scheduled NBC programs including lots of news and current events-oriented programming. The station was founded in 1967 and is currently owned by A.H. Belo Corporation.

WJZY-46, UPN
3501 Performance Rd. • 398-0046

WJZY began broadcasting in Charlotte in 1987 and is one of the two channels for Charlotte Hornets basketball. The UPN network affiliate for the area, it offers lots of science fiction programming and popular comedy sitcom reruns. It also features movies and kids' programs. Capitol Broadcasting Co. Inc. owns the station.

WFVT-55, WB
3501 Performance Rd. • 398-0046

Owned by Capitol Broadcasting Co. Inc., WFVT is an independent channel affiliated with the Warner Brothers network. Mornings are chock-full of children's programming while afternoons and evenings carry a mix of children's shows, comedy sitcom reruns, movies and Charlotte Hornets basketball games.

WSOC-9, ABC
1901 N. Tryon St. • 338-9999

The WSOC-TV Eyewitness News team brings viewers live reports from all over the Carolinas as well as the nation and abroad. In addition to showing ABC's programs, Channel 9 has created "Family Focus," a project dedicated to nurturing the family setting through community activities, television specials and public service announcements.

WSOC-TV is owned by Cox Broadcasting, based in Atlanta, which also owns a number of TV and radio stations, newspapers and cable companies across the country. WSOC first signed on as channel 9 in 1957.

WTVI-42, PBS
3242 Commonwealth Ave. • 372-2442

WTVI is the only community-owned PBS station in the Carolinas. It regularly broadcasts meetings of the Mecklenburg Board of County Commissioners and the Charlotte-Mecklenburg School Board, plus it produces Final Edition, a weekly half-hour program that features a lively discussion of local events by area news and business people. The station also has a weekly business update program called "Carolina Business Review."

Two other PBS stations, WUNG-Channel 58, RTP and WNSC-Channel 30, Rock Hill also reach the Charlotte market.

CHARLOTTE RADIO STATIONS

Format	Call Letters	Request Line	Programming
Adult Standards	WNMX 106.1 FM	598-1480	Big Bands
Christian, Gospel	WGIV 1600 AM	342-2644	24-Hr. Gospel
	WGSP 1310 AM	570-9477	24 Hr. Gospel
	WHVN 1240 AM	596-1240	Spoken Word Programs
	WRCM 91.9 FM	570-9200	24 Hr. Gospel
Classical	WDAV 89.9 FM	892-8900	Classical
Country	WFMX 105.7 FM	871-9369	Crook & Chase Countdown
	WKKT 96.9 FM	570-9690	
	WSOC 103.7 FM	570-9762	NASCAR Coverage
Contemporary	WBAV 101.9 FM	800-269-1019	Adult Contemporary
	WLNK 107.9 FM	570-1079	Adult Contemporary
	WLYT 102.9 FM	570-1029	Soft Adult Contemporary
	WPEG 97.9 FM	570-9734	Urban Contemporary
Jazz	WCCJ 92.7 FM	358-0586	Adult Contemp. Jazz
Modern Rock	WEND 106.5 FM	570-1065	New Music
News/Talk	WBT 99.3 FM	570-1212	
	WBT 1110 AM	570-1110	Rush Limbaugh, Dr. Laura
Oldies	WWMG 96.1 FM	570-9696	Sunday Night at the Beach
Public Radio	WFAE 90.7 FM	549-9323	Garrison Keillor, jazz, blues
Rock	WRFX 99.7 FM	570-9739	John Boy & Billy
	WSSS 104.7 FM	570-1047	Classic Rock
	WXRC 95.7 FM	800-282-9570	Howard Stern
Sports	WFNZ 610 AM	570-9610	NBA Coverage
Top 40	WNKS 95.1 FM	570-9595	Public Affairs
			w/Francine Morris

Oldies Channel 96.1 is a favorite among Charlotte's "Baby Boomers".

Retirement

Charlotte, along with the rest of the United States, is experiencing a "boom" in the senior population and has become a popular retirement destination during the past decade. As part of the Sunbelt, Charlotte steadily attracts older citizens fleeing from rigorous winters. Parents are also following their children and retiring within visiting distance of grandchildren. Older newcomers settle in Charlotte for the same reasons as younger people: good climate, vibrant cultural life, safe neighborhoods, excellent medical care and a metropolitan airport. As the senior population has grown, so have the number and level of services provided.

There has been a substantial increase in retirement communities in Charlotte and Mecklenburg County offering residents independent living, assisted living and nursing care. These continuing care communities are ideal because the level of care adapts to the needs of the resident. Some communities will not accept a senior directly into their assisted living or nursing care programs. The senior must have entered as an independent living resident. New facilities offering only assisted living have been built to fill this need. Retirement communities offer meals, housekeeping, planned activities, transportation and other amenities.

Independent-living Communities

Many residential communities in the Charlotte area have a large number of active seniors as residents, but for those who don't want the hassle of taking care of a big house, the convenience and activities of a retirement community are attractive. Housing in an independent-living community can be a single, detached house, a condominium or an apartment.

Assisted-living Communities

Assisted-living communities offer the next level of care for seniors by providing assistance with the activities of daily living such as preparing food, giving daily medications, local transportation and housekeeping. Nursing-care communities offer full-time, around-the-clock, long-term health care. While many nursing care tenants can do many things for themselves, they need assistance, either medically or physically. Such care is for those who are too ill or impaired to be ambulatory. As one guide describes such care, it's for people "with chronic illness who are not so sick as to require hospitalization." Some retirement communities even offer care by on-site physicians and nurses with their nursing care facilities.

Home Health Services

Home health care providers often bridge the gap that allows seniors to remain at home. The range of assistance can be from a companion who assists with daily living needs to a registered nurse who administers needed medications. Care Management is a relatively new field, where a geriatric-care manager evaluates what the patient needs, develops a healthcare plan and hires the necessary personnel.

Here is a sampling of a few of Charlotte's better known retirement communities. Entry fees, if any, vary greatly between communities, ranging from $650-$3,000 a month.

Brian Center Retirement Apartments
5945 Reddman Rd. • 536-1928

Now under new ownership, the Brian Center offers independent apartment living with catered care if needed. The assisted living center is called The Lodge and nursing care is located on the premises.

Brighton Gardens by Marriott
6000 Park South Dr. • 643-1400

Recently completed, this assisted living center is intended to provide services to the growing number of seniors with Alzheimer's and related memory disorders.

Brookwood
12600 Old Statesville Rd., Huntersville • 875-7540

Affiliated with the Carolinas HealthCare System and the Huntersville Oaks Nursing Home, this assisted-living facility offers cottage living in a country setting.

Carmel Hills Retirement Community
2801 Carmel Rd. • 364-8302

This 94-unit retirement community provides one daily meal, biweekly housekeeping, linen service, security, laundry, recreation and transportation.

CarMel Place Retirement Community
5512 Carmel Rd. • 541-8012

A rental retirement community, CarMel Place offers a nice South Charlotte location with a terrific amenities package, including housekeeping services, a barber and beauty salon, 24-hour security and transportation.

Carriage Club of Charlotte
5700 Old Providence Rd. • 366-4960

Located in prestigious South Charlotte, the Carriage Club was completed in 1988 and requires no entry fee. It offers apartments and villas and a variety of amenities, including a

Full Continuum Rental Retirement Community

5700 Old Providence Rd., Charlotte, NC 28226

(704) 366-4960

pool, Jacuzzi, exercise room, washer/dryer units in all apartments, housekeeping and meals. Divided into three separate centers, the Carriage Club offers 176 independent living units, the Coach House offers 54 personalized assisted-living units and the Carriage House provides 42 skilled nursing care units.

Charlottetown Manor
600 S. Kings Dr. • 377-8000

Opened in 1992, this locally owned Uptown rental retirement community does not charge an entry fee and has surprisingly low monthly fees. Three daily meals, weekly housekeeping, transportation, linen service, security, recreation, laundry, pool and trash removal are included. Medication assistance is available for a nominal monthly fee.

Covenant Village
1351 Robinwood Rd. • 867-2319

Located in neighboring Gastonia, Covenant Village offers over 180 independent and assisted-living units. Amenities include three daily meals, linen service, a fitness center, weekly housekeeping, transportation, security, recreation and private dining rooms. A library, bank, craft center and store are located on the grounds.

Epworth Place-The Methodist Home
3420 Shamrock Dr. • 532-7000

The Methodist Home opened in 1948 and is located on a 225-acre campus in Northeastern Charlotte. There are three facilities on the campus that provide quality retirement living and top-rated health care. Epworth Place provides apartments and cottages with assisted-living service available. Asbury Care Center and Wesley Nursing Center are the nursing care facilities and residents of Epworth Place are given priority at both centers if and when needed. All the necessities of daily living are available here as well as many amenities and planned activities.

Lawyers Glen Retirement Living Ctr.
10830 Lawyers Rd. • 545-9555

Opened in early 1997, this locally owned retirement center provides independent living and assisted living units.

Merrywood

A SENIOR ADULT COMMUNITY

Stop by today to see why so many seniors are calling Merrywood "home."

3600 Park Road
Charlotte, North Carolina 28209

704-523-4949

Merrywood
3600 Park Rd. • 523-4949

This beautiful, wooded site blends well with the history and southern charm of the Park Road and Dilworth neighborhoods that surround it. Close to shopping, next-door to the YWCA and just minutes away from Uptown and hospitals, Merrywood is a 174-unit rental apartment community offering active, independent living, personal care and assisted living for senior adults.

The Pines at Davidson
400 Avinger Ln., Davidson • 896-1100

This nonprofit retirement community for independent living offers apartments and cottages as well as three levels of continuing care. Standard amenities are included and residents have access to Davidson College, allowing them to audit classes and attend a multitude of cultural events. Residents also receive membership to nearby River Run Country Club.

Plantation Estates
733 Plantation Estates, Matthews • 845-5900

If you enjoy fine dining and super recreational facilities, check out the spacious, Colonial Williamsburg-style apartment homes here. Plantation Estates offers its residents all levels of care from independent living to nursing care.

Sharon Towers
The Presbyterian Home At Charlotte
5100 Sharon Rd. • 553-1670

Located in the popular SouthPark neighborhood, Sharon Towers is one of the oldest and most established retirement communities in the area, providing apartments and cottages for independent living and long-term care facilities. It offers on-site recreational facilities, a library and a bank.

Southminster Inc.
8919 Park Rd. • 551-6800

Opened in 1987, Southminster's independent living area contains apartments and cottages equipped with emergency call systems and such options as housekeeping and maintenance. A full-service dining room, barber and beauty salon, general store, bank, wellness clinic and scheduled activities and transportation are also available. The Health Center offers three levels of care – assisted living, intermediate nursing care and skilled nursing care.

Westminster Towers
1330 India Hook Rd., Rock Hill • (803) 328-5000, (800) 345-6026

Westminster Towers is the only continuing care community in York County. This independent living community provides the added conveniences of housekeeping and prepared meals. An indoor heated swimming pool, a fitness facility and planned outings and events provide a variety of social activities.

Wilora Lake Lodge
6053 Wilora Lake Rd. • 537-8848

Developed by Crosland Properties in 1987, Wilora Lake offers 136 private apartments for independent retirement living. Catering to active seniors, it provides amenities such as housekeeping, dining, 24-hour security and transportation. Access to coordinated health care is available and a RN and two activity directors are on staff.

Wilora Lake Health Care Center
6001 Wilora Lake Rd. • 563-2922

Located on a 14-acre campus off Albemarle Road, the Wilora Lake Health Center is a 120-bed nursing center offering all levels of care, including a post-acute care unit and a specialized dementia unit with 20 beds. Open since October of 1995, Wilora Lake offers its residents a full continuum of care.

Senior Centers & Services

To satisfy this rapidly growing age group, the Charlotte area offers a variety of services and publications.

Charlotte-Mecklenburg Senior Centers Inc.
2225 Tyvola Rd. • 522-6222

The Charlotte-Mecklenburg Senior Centers Inc. provides a broad range of services and programs for all adults age 55 and older. The Centers offer services such as health screenings, education, employment, "Say Y.E.S." (an intergenerational program) and the Senior Aides Project, which teaches seniors new skills through internships.

Council on Aging
200 E. Woodlawn Rd. • 527-8807

Funded by the county and the United Way, the Council acts as a resource center, clearinghouse and advocacy group for seniors. The Council offers workshops, conferences and educational programs for and about seniors.

Fifty Plus
• (800) 367-5075

With a circulation of 183,000 in the Carolinas, *Fifty Plus* is a monthly news magazine filled with features written for a mature, upscale audience.

Long-Term Ombudsman Program
1300 Baxter St. • 372-2416

This program is made up of regional ombudsmen and volunteer advocates who work to protect the rights of those living in nursing homes, rest homes and family-care homes. They are also available to answer any questions about long-term care and provide information on the options available.

Mecklenburg County Senior Citizen Nutrition Program
301 Billingsley Rd. • 336-2400

This program offers on-site meals as well as social interaction and activities in 17 different locations. It also provides home-delivered meals and transportation services.

SENIOR SERVICES

AARP	376-2298
Adult Care and Share Center	567-2700
Carolinas' Caring Connections	566-6040
Centralina Area Agency on Aging	372-2416
Community Care Service Center	384-7460
Community Link	334-7288
Council on Aging	527-8807
CPCC Older Adult Program-Continuing Education	330-6464
Family Outreach Adult Day Care	333-2033
Friendship Trays	333-9229
Health Department	336-4700
Mecklenburg Co. Tax Administrator:	
Property tax exemption for the elderly	336-2813
Mental Health Services	358-2700
Programs for Accessible Living	537-0550
Selwyn Life Center	379-5005
Special Transportation Services	
Handicapped	336-2637
Transportation Assistance (County)	336-4547

Retired Senior Volunteer Program (RSVP)
2225 Tyvola Rd. • 522-6222

This special program is geared for placing volunteers aged 60 and over in meaningful positions in nonprofit and public organizations. Volunteer positions are available all over the county in local hospitals, the American Red Cross and libraries and museums. RSVP is unique in that it reimburses its volunteers for mileage and meals and offers liability and accident insurance.

Senior Directions
PO Box 221442 • 364-2846

This free monthly newspaper carries articles pertaining to health and fitness, money matters and other issues of interest to mature adults. The publication has a circulation of about 45,000 and can be found in most area supermarkets and many doctors' offices.

Senior Living Resource Magazine Retirement Lifestyles in NC Assisted Living News
• (800) 775-4846

Published several times a year, these handy magazines offer timely articles on almost every aspect of retired life.

Shepherd's Center of Charlotte, Inc.
PO Box 6052, Charlotte, NC 28207 • 334-4637

With offices at Myers Park Baptist Church, the Shepherd's Center is an interfaith organization sponsored by churches and synagogues and serves older persons with or without religious affiliation. It promotes the concept of able people of retirement age learning and enjoying life and assisting their peers who need help to stay in their own homes. The program has two divisions: education and home service.

The Volunteer Center
301 S. Brevard St. • 372-7170

Call The Volunteer Center to learn more about the wide variety of opportunities for seniors to become involved in the community.

Bible in hand, Billy Graham preaches the Gospel to the masses
in Ericsson Stadium during his last Charlotte crusade.

Worship

In September of 1996, Charlotte's most famous native son, the Reverend Billy Graham, came home. He preached at his fourth Charlotte Evangelistic Crusade. For four nights, Ericsson Stadium's 72,000 seats were filled. Twice, the practice fields were packed with those who could not enter and had to watch on huge screens.

In many ways, this was Charlotte at its finest. A host of corporations underwrote the huge expenses. Fifty-four denominations representing 900 churches and 25,000 volunteers ushered, counseled, prayed, sang and organized to make this an unforgettable event for the more than 336,000 people who attended. *The Charlotte Observer* generated more than 250 pages of coverage, which it has permanently posted on its homepage, creating the largest website about Billy Graham on the Internet.

Since the 1740s, the boundaries of Mecklenburg have been defined by eight separate Presbyterian churches, located near rivers for the agricultural needs of the Scots-Irish who carved Charlotte out of the wilderness. Their strong work ethic, devotion to family and faith served as the cornerstones of the budding community's value structure. It's no wonder that Charlotte's more than 650 churches have firmly positioned the city as the "buckle" in the Bible Belt.

The churches in Charlotte that have grown rapidly have been the Baptist — no surprise, and the Catholics — surprise! As Charlotte has become more diverse, so have its expressions of faith. Over 80 different denominations are listed in the current Charlotte Yellow Pages. There are too many churches to mention by name, so this Guide will limit itself to a small slice of the area's mainline, traditional congregations. For more specific information about a given church, call that church's office.

Resources

The Clergy Association of Charlotte-Mecklenburg
P.O. Box 23423, Charlotte, NC 28227
• 573-9805

This association provides assistance in locating a church.

International House
322 Hawthorne Lane • 333-8099

If you are one of the thousands of international residents living in Charlotte, this organization can provide assistance in finding people of your own faith.

Activities and Outreach Programs

The religious houses of the Queen City have responded to the challenge of shrinking resources by re-involving their congregations in providing needed funds and services. Support groups, aerobic exercise classes, scouting programs — it's all about bringing a variety of people together, often at a local worship facility. You'll find that local houses of worship regularly bring in guest speakers, conduct seminars and hold breakfasts to discuss some of the more intellectual areas of faith and the everyday challenges of living. These free sessions, held across the city, are well-attended and thoroughly enriching.

Many churches and synagogues are reaching outward to provide programs that help the entire community. "Mothers Morning Out" programs are offered throughout the city. Mornings are often difficult times to find a baby-sitter and these programs offer child care for a few hours once a week. Churches and temples across Charlotte offer this service on varying days of the week. Almost all of Charlotte's larger places of worship offer day care and a host of other programs for children, youth, young adults and seniors.

Many religious plays, concerts and activities have become traditional events. One popular annual concert is a program of contemporary and traditional Christian music held at the Charlotte Coliseum on New Year's Eve. The program begins at 7 PM and ends at midnight with the dropping of a huge balloon to mark the beginning of the New Year. Crowds of up to 24,000 attend, so make your reservations early. To purchase tickets or for more information, call 734-1648.

Baptist

First Baptist Church
301 S. Davidson St. • 375-1446

Established in 1832, First Baptist Church now occupies a 1,600-seat multitiered contemporary structure with a Casavant pipe

organ dominated by beautiful stained-glass windows. The church is led by senior pastor Dr. Charles D. Page. This large congregation also has a family life center for recreation programs, physical fitness classes and other fellowship activities.

First Baptist is known for its wide range of ministries that offer opportunities for everyone to serve, develop their talents and grow spiritually. Classes are available for every age group from preschool through senior adults. Outreach programs include the Alexander Children's Home ministry, a prison ministry, international missions and Bible studies at local fire stations. The church's production of Dickens' *Christmas Journey* is an annual favorite.

First Baptist Church's morning worship services can be seen on television. Please check your local listings for time and station.

Friendship Missionary Baptist Church
3301 Beatties Ford Rd. • 392-0392

Organized in 1890, Friendship Baptist Church embraces the vision of being "a church in the heart of the community with

First Baptist Church

Highlights
Sundays:
9:15 a.m. Bible Study
10:30 a.m. Morning Worship
6:00 p.m. Evening Worship

Wednesdays:
11:30 a.m. Business Lunch & Bible Study, FH
4:45 p.m. Supper for Everyone, FH
6:00 p.m. Preschool & Children's Programs
           Student Study Break, Loft
           TEAM Meetings
6:15 p.m. Prayer Meeting, FH
7:00 p.m. Adult Choir Rehearsal
           Orchestra Rehearsal
           First Priority Outreach

Church Office 375-1446
Pastor's Office 335-3872
Family Life Center 334-LIFE
FAX 335-3870
Deaf (TDD) 334-8914

Charles D. Page, Pastor
301 S. Davidson Street
Charlotte, NC 28202

From John Belk Freeway Exit
Caldwell or 4th Streets.
From Brookshire Freeway Exit
Davidson or Brevard Streets.

FRIENDSHIP MISSIONARY BAPTIST CHURCH
"The place where worship is a genuine experience"

Dr. Clifford A. Jones, Sr., Senior Minister

Sunday School	9:30 a.m.
Morning Worship	8 a.m. & 11 a.m.
Wed. Bible Study / Prayer Mtg.	7 p.m.
Thursday Bible Study	11:30 a.m. & 7 p.m.
Saturday Night Alive	6 p.m.

Nursery provided for all services

3301 Beatties Ford Road
392-0392

DIAL-A-PRAYER 392-0315

the community in its heart." The church is on the west side of Charlotte, 4 miles from the campus of Johnson C. Smith University.

Monday through Friday, doors open at 7 AM for its Double "A"-rated child development center and for other programs, including Scouting, the Senior Citizens Satellite Center, AIDS Ministry and Tutorial Program. Saturday evening offers a "Saturday Night Alive" service. Five worship services are offered on Sundays and children may attend youth worship services or the graded Church

Photo Courtesy of First Baptist Church

The modern spire of First Baptist Church is at home in Charlotte's skyline.

School, which includes a special class for new members. A dedicated Dial-A-Prayer line is available 24 hours a day.

Hickory Grove Baptist Church
6050 Hickory Grove Rd. • 531-4000
2350 Odell School Rd. • 547-9906

In 1955, this church began in a barn with about 25 people. Today its 9,700 members gather to worship and study on a 50-acre campus across the street from its original location and at a second campus in north Charlotte. Senior pastor Dr. Joe Brown is assisted by a large staff that ministers to the community in many outreach programs and is known for its Bible study and discipleship programs.

The church has a separate Family Life Center and sponsors many athletic programs. The music department is renowned for its annual presentations of the Passion Play and the Living Christmas Tree.

If you cannot attend one of the many Sunday services, you can catch this dynamic ministry's *Challenge for Living* on television. Check local listings for time and station.

Myers Park Baptist Church
1900 Queens Rd. • 334-7232

The members of Myers Park Baptist are among the most committed in their outreach programs of any church in Charlotte. The church supports a wide range of programs. Some of the most outstanding are the North Carolina Harvest, a group that distributes food from restaurants and caterers to needy organizations; the Shepherd's Center, an education and help ministry to the elderly (co-founded and aided by other local churches); and Room In the Inn, which provides meals to the homeless.

Northside Baptist Church
333 Jeremiah Blvd. • 596-4856

One of Charlotte's spiritual foundation stones, Northside Baptist is visible to travelers on I-85. Led since 1990 by Dr. Bradley Price, Northside is among the largest of Charlotte's churches with almost 6,500 members. It serves the community through a variety of ministries, including a childcare and preschool center, Northside Christian Academy for K-12 students, a book store, mission projects, deaf ministry,

Photo Courtesy of Northside Baptist Church

Northside Baptist Church's impressive dome dominates the large facility's area.

Northside Baptist Church
The Caring Place

333 Jeremiah Boulevard • Charlotte, NC 28262 • 704/596-4856

Dr. D. Bradley Price, Pastor

Schedule Of Services
Sunday

Sunday School 9:15AM
Morning Worship 10:30AM
Evening Worship. 7:00PM

Wednesday
Prayer Meeting 7:00PM
AWANA 6:30PM

Northside *ALIVE* • TV Channel WAXN • Sunday 9:00AM

sports and recreation, television and radio and many others.

Affiliated with Southside Baptist Fellowship, this independent, fundamental Christian church features an extensive listing of special events, such as: 911 Sunday, Graduate Recognition Sunday, Single Adult Day, Passion Play, Youth Alive Conference, Family Night (Christian alternative to Halloween) and *Spirit of Christmas.* Northside Baptist Church, "The Caring Place," makes newcomers feel welcome.

Catholic

St. Peter's Catholic Church
507 South Tryon St. • 332-2901
Fresco Information • 358-0050

The cornerstone for St. Peter's Catholic Church was laid on March 17, 1851. Charlotte had just over 1,000 citizens at that time, so the dedication of a new church was a big event, attended by people of many different faiths. The church, including land, cost $1,000 — much of it donated by non-Catholics. It was not until after 1892 that the present church was built. Subsequent Catholic churches were built in Charlotte, but St. Peter's is still considered the "Mother" church.

One of St. Peter's most exciting and enduring undertakings is the Ben Long Frescoes. The family of St. Peter's joined with the entire Catholic community in cooperation with corporate donations and arts funding to make the commissioning of this ambitious project possible. The frescoes, completed in 1989, are arranged in a triptych. The left side is "The Agony in the Garden," the center is "The Resurrection of Jesus" and the right side is "The Descent of the Spirit." The public may view the frescoes from 10 AM until 4 PM Monday through Saturday and from 1 until 4 PM on Sunday.

Episcopal

St. John's Episcopal Church
1623 Carmel Rd. • 366-3034

This 1,300-member church, with its beautiful contemporary stained-glass windows, is one of Charlotte's more progressive churches.

St. John's is known for its community outreach programs, such as Job Hunters Support Group, which instructs, networks and supports the unemployed. St. John's Arts Ministry encourages expression of the gospel through such art forms as painting, drama, mime, music and liturgical dance.

Staff Photo

Ben Long's famous frescoes grace St. Peter's Catholic Church.

Evangelical

Calvary Church
5801 Pineville-Matthews Rd. • 543-1200

Calvary Church, with a soaring contemporary pink and glass facade, is one of Charlotte's larger churches. The facility, located on 100 acres, includes a sanctuary with a seating capacity of 6,000 and one of the largest pipe organs in the world. The organ has 11,499 pipes, ranging in size from smaller than a soda straw to over 40 feet tall. Calvary presents several concerts each year, usually including a passion play at Easter and a Christmas concert.

People from all denominational backgrounds attend Calvary and participate in the diverse spiritual growth, educational and social opportunities that are available. From singles classes to senior adults, from music and drama to international missions, Calvary encourages the use of everyone's talents in Christian service. The church also has a weekday preschool, a day care and a Mothers Morning Out program.

Greek Orthodox

Holy Trinity Greek Orthodox Cathedral
600 East Blvd. • 334-4771

The first Greek Orthodox Church in Charlotte was established in 1929 on South Boulevard. The Byzantine-style cathedral was built in 1953-54 to accommodate the growing congregation. Orthodox Christians draw from a rich tradition of faith and culture. Divine Liturgy is held in English at 9 AM and in Greek at 10 AM.

Each September, in the week after Labor Day, the "Yiasou!" Greek Festival is held at Holy Trinity's Hellenic Center. Participants celebrate Greek heritage with traditional foods, dance, crafts, a 5K race and Fun Run to round out the festive doings. Inside the Hellenic Center, you can see a film on the Greek Isles and learn about the Greek Orthodox religion and Greek culture. A portion of the proceeds is given to charity.

Interdenominational

Mecklenburg Community Church
8420 University Executive Park Dr., Suite 820
• 548-9404

This interdenominational church, although affiliated with the Southern Baptist Convention, is not typically Baptist. Its message is conservative, holding firm to the eternal truth of Christianity, but is contemporary in style and methods.

The unconventional approach for the Sunday morning church service falls into three categories: Music, Drama and Multimedia Event. A live band provides contemporary music, "slice of life" dramas provoke a question-and-answer session and multimedia events utilize projectors and videos. All three services are led by volunteers.

Sonshine City, an active, contemporary approach to Sunday School for children from nursery to 5th grade, runs during the Sunday morning service. The method in teaching Bible study and relationship building focuses on 1990's music, interests and happenings. This rapidly growing church, led by Dr. James White, is embarking on a full menu of social services. Dress is casual and the atmosphere is relaxed.

Jewish

Temple Beth El
5101 Providence Rd. • 366-1948

The Reformed Congregation is affiliated with the Union of American Hebrew Congregations and has been serving the Charlotte community since 1948. The temple offers regular worship services, a religious school, bar and bas mitzvah training, plus organizations for various age groups.

Temple Israel
4901 Providence Rd. • 362-2796

Temple Israel's 700-member congregation is an integral part of Shalom Park, the nationally known campus and center of Jewish life in Charlotte. The congregation, affiliated with the United Synagogue of Conservative Judaism, celebrated its 100th anniversary in 1995 and is the oldest and one of the most vibrant Jewish institutions in the Carolinas. Hands-on, welcoming and participatory, Temple Israel is dedicated to bringing the traditional values of the Conservative movement to its role as an anchor and harbor to family and single life in Charlotte.

Lutheran

St. Mark's Lutheran Church
1001 Queens Rd. • 375-9185

St. Mark's is the oldest Lutheran church in Charlotte. Begun in 1870, it was originally located downtown and in the late 1950s the congregation moved to the suburbs on Queens Road.

The church's personal, congregational and social ministries support a variety of different programs, including Bible studies, worship, outreach, Habitat for Humanity and the Hopespring program, which helps young adults from 18 to 22 years old who have been in foster homes find jobs, education and housing. Within the church is a strong Shepherds group. Core leaders pair church members to pray for and support each other and minister to the ill or those in crisis. Outreach programs work with local and international concerns.

Methodist

Little Rock AME Zion
401 N. McDowell St. • 334-3782

This traditional African-American church is affiliated with the African Methodist Episcopal Zion denomination. The present contemporary structure replaced the original building, now utilized as the Afro-American Cultural Center, in 1981.

Myers Park United Methodist
1020 Providence Rd. • 376-8584

Myers Park Methodist Church is the church with beautiful stained-glass windows that brings cheer to passersby on Providence Road. The church was completed in 1925 and has 3,600 members. The senior pastor is Dr. Tom Stockton.

The church has extensive outreach programs, but is probably best recognized for its strong Sunday School program. Even non-members attend the variety of different adult and children's classes. Primarily divided along age lines, the classes delve into a variety of Biblical as well as human relational and contemporary issues. The church offers an open forum structure for both couples and singles groups.

The active music program works with young adults to produce yearly musical dinner theater performances with the proceeds designated for outreach programs. The Adults Plus and Best Years senior groups take frequent educational and entertainment trips to varied destinations.

FYI

Unless otherwise noted, the area code for all phone numbers in this chapter is 704.

Sharon United Methodist Church
4411 Sharon Rd. • 366-9166

With its unique ski-slope roofline, Sharon United Methodist Church has long been a distinctive landmark in southeast Charlotte. First organized in the late 1960s on what was then the outskirts of Charlotte, Sharon Methodist has retained the best of its pioneering spirit and draws a regional congregation from southern Mecklenburg County. An energetic staff sets the tone with a full complement of children's, youth, adult and music ministries.

Sunday morning worship includes an informal contemporary-style worship and a "big music" worship service. The church has remained committed to providing a variety of ministries and outreach programs and is involved in many local and international mission projects.

Moravian

Little Church on the Lane
528 Moravian Ln. • 334-1381

Little Church on the Lane dates back to 1922, when the bishop at Old Salem was persuaded to establish a church in Charlotte. Today the church is led by the Reverend Steve Wilson at Wolford Chapel, the church's original sanctuary. The quaint chapel is used regularly by anyone who desires to spend some quiet time in personal prayer or meditation.

Every Christmas Eve the traditional Moravian Love Feast is held where worshippers share in singing carols and reading Scripture. Beginning at 2 PM, four consecutive services are open to the public.

Presbyterian

The Charlotte Yellow Pages lists almost one hundred Presbyterian churches in seven different categories: American, Bible, Evangelical, Orthodox, PCA, USA and just Presbyterian. Since all Presbyterian churches are not alike, ask if it is associated with any particular group. If you're not familiar with the association's beliefs, ask for further information.

Christ Covenant
800 Fullwood Ln., Matthews • 847-3505

Depth of commitment and a variety of expressions of faith and involvement characterize this dynamic congregation. The membership studies and fellowships in smaller communities, then participates with the larger body in worship events. DAWN Bible Studies, Mothers of Preschoolers, a Sports Outreach Program, Campus Outreach, Youth Ministries, the Counseling Center and the Korean worship service are just a few of the church's ministries. Singles/Singles Again studies Biblical as well as current topics and offers fellowship through socials, weekends and mission retreats. Seniors and retirees have multiple opportunities for continuing spiritual growth and involvement. Newcomers and prospective members are invited to the Pastor's Inquirers Class. The church operates Covenant Day School for students in kindergarten through 9th grade.

Worship is at 9 and 10:30 AM Sunday mornings, concurrent with adult and children's Sunday School. Evening worship is at 6 PM with concurrent choirs and classes.

800 Fullwood Lane
Matthews, NC 28105
(704) 847-3505
Worship Times
9 & 10:30AM, 6PM
Sunday Bible School
9 & 10:30AM
Perspective Radio
Broadcast:
WHVN AM 1240/12:25 M-F

Directions: Hwy 51 to light at
Fullwood Lane. See entrance.

"Developing Disciples For God's Glory"
*In our commitment to impact our community and our world with
the Gospel of Jesus Christ, Christ Covenant offers:*

• Expository Teaching
• Small Group Emphasis
• Challenging Sunday Bible School
• Jr. & Sr. High & College Ministry
• Singles & Singles Again Ministry
• Sports Programs
• Global Outreach/Missions
• Covenant Day School (K-9th)
• Worship & Fine Arts Ministry
• Seniors' Ministry

Christ Covenant
Member Presbyterian Church in America

Covenant Presbyterian
1000 East Morehead St. • 333-9071

This imposing stone structure has had worship and music as the foundation of the church's life since its inception. The church's philosophy echoes the feeling of Martin Luther, who said that "music takes people one step beyond the spoken word." All children of the church are strongly encouraged to join the choir and when they become teenagers, they can participate in the choir's SMART trip program. The anagram stands for sports, music, art, religion and travel.

Some of Covenant's outreach programs include the Crisis Assistance Ministry, CROP Walk, Project Uplift, Taps, Relatives, Shepherd's Center and Habitat For Humanity.

First Presbyterian
200 W. Trade St. • 332-5123

This local church was organized in 1821. First Presbyterian was originally a community church where all denominations met to worship. Later, as the community grew, different faiths formed their own churches and the original church became the property of the Presbytery. The present Gothic Revival style building was built in 1857. Prominent early settlers include Mary Anna Morrison Jackson, wife of General "Stonewall" Jackson. Although it is adjacent to First Presbyterian, Settlers Cemetery is not part of the church but a community graveyard where Tom Polk rests, along with other early settlers.

Dr. William P. Wood, senior minister, leads the congregation, which continues to serve the Uptown community through current-day ministries such as the Child Development Center,

Community School of the Arts and Loaves and Fishes. The church has a Sunday 11 AM television ministry on WSOC (9).

Myers Park Presbyterian
2501 Oxford Pl. • 376-3695

Worship is this active church's core strength, manifested in caring for each other and others less fortunate. The primary outreach focuses on helping children through a variety of mentoring programs. In a one-on-one relationship, a troubled or problem child assigned to a volunteer adult can count on a relationship filled with tutoring, attending an athletic or entertainment event and problem-solving assistance. The church's gymnasium, with a full-time director, provides a bevy of recreational opportunities for parishioners and other groups in the community.

The church also has an HIV/AIDS care team, which provides help to AIDS patients. The church's many programs, including concerts and workshops, are open to the public.

Unitarian

Unitarian Church of Charlotte
234 N. Sharon Amity Rd. • 366-8623

The Unitarian Church of Charlotte is part of the Unitarian Universalist denomination, which emphasizes individual freedom of belief. The church offers a nationally developed, inclusive Sunday School for children and youth, a Sunday service, classes and lectures, study and service groups and covered dish dinners. Dr. Doug Reisner ministers to this congregation.

Index

Index of Advertisers

The Insiders' Guide to Charlotte

Please take a moment to fill out our reader survey and you will receive a coupon good for **$10 off** the purchase of your next *Insiders' Guide To The Triangle or Charlotte.* Your comments are very important. In appreciation, we will enter your name in our Grand Prize drawing. Thank you!

$500 GRAND PRIZE
IN ENTERTAINMENT AND DINING GIFT CERTIFICATES

$100 SECOND PRIZE
IN ENTERTAINMENT AND DINING GIFT CERTIFICATES

FIVE $25 THIRD PRIZES
IN ENTERTAINMENT AND DINING GIFT CERTIFICATES

UNLIMITED $10 FOURTH PRIZES
COUPON GOOD TOWARD PURCHASE OF NEXT INSIDERS' GUIDE

EVERYONE'S A WINNER!

More Information

What you think is important. Please share your ideas.

IN APPRECIATION, WE WILL SEND YOU A COUPON FOR **$10.00 OFF** A COPY OF ONE OF OUR GUIDES.

Name _____

Title _____

Company _____

Address _____

City, State, Zip _____

Phone _____ **Fax:** _____

E-mail _____

Age: ❏ Under 25 ❏ 25-35 ❏ 36-50 ❏ 51-65 ❏ Over 65

Annual Household Income: ❏ Under $25K ❏ $25 to $35K
❏ $35 to $50K ❏ $50 to $75K ❏ $75 to $100K ❏ Over $100K

Charlotte Area: ❏ Newcomer ❏ Resident ❏ Student ❏ Visitor
❏ Planning to Relocate Date move projected: _____

How did you obtain *The Insiders' Guide To Charlotte*?

Purchased: ❏ Bookstore ❏ Chamber of Commerce
❏ Publisher ❏ Other_____

Gift from: ❏ Employer ❏ Friend ❏ REALTOR® _____

Will the book be used by: ❏ Individual ❏ Family ❏ Business

How many times do you refer to your guide per month?

❏ 1–3 ❏ 4–6 ❏ 7–9 ❏ 10–15 ❏ 16 and up

Suggestions for future editions: _____

_____

Please send more information on the following:

❏ University Area ❏ Lake Norman Area ❏ Uptown Charlotte

❏ South Charlotte ❏ Independence Area ❏ West Charlotte

❏ South End/Dilworth/Myers Park ❏ Other Areas_____

❏ Accommodations ❏ Banks in the area ❏ Chamber of Commerce
❏ Child Care ❏ Private Schools ❏ Employment Services
❏ Health Care ❏ Retirement ❏ Shopping

❏ Religious Organizations _____
❏ Apartments & Temporary Housing—Mo. Rent: _____ to _____
❏ REALTOR® ❏ Builders—Price Range: _____ to _____
❏ Development amenities desired: ❏ Pool ❏ Tennis ❏ Golf Course